THE
OFFICIAL
ACT
READING GUIDE

THE
OFFICIAL
ACT
READING GUIDE

ACT

WILEY

Contents

Introduction vii

Chapter 1: An Overview of the ACT Reading Test 1
Passage Types 1
Timing and Pacing 3
Checking Your Answers 3
Scaled Scoring 3
Take a Diagnostic Practice Test 4
How to Use This Guide 4

Chapter 2: General Reading Skills 7
Skimming 7
Scanning 15
Speed Reading 16
Annotating 17

Chapter 3: Test-Taking Strategies 19
Invest Most of Your Time in Answering the Questions 20
Invest Your Time in Reading Upfront 20
Save Your Worst Passage for the End 21
Worry Less about Each Individual Answer 22
Vary Your Reading Pace According to the Passage 22
Change the Order of the Passages 22
Read Half the Passage Then Answer Half the Questions 23
Answer the "Easy" Questions First 23

Chapter 4: Question and Answer Types 27
EXCEPT and NOT Questions 27
Common Wrong Answer Types 37

Chapter 5: Skills and Reporting Categories 45

Chapter 6: Key Ideas and Details 47
Main Idea Questions 47
Strategies for Determining the Main Idea for Social Science, Humanities,
    or Natural Science Passages 48
Function of Detail Questions 52
Fact Finding 58
Inferences 67
Paraphrasing Complex Ideas 75

Compare and Contrast..76
Questions about Shifts..100

Chapter 7: Craft and Structure 105
Using Context Clues..105
Word-Meaning Questions...106
Vocabulary..118
Interpreting Figurative Language..123
The Author's Point of View...127
The Primary Purpose of the Passage 133

Chapter 8: Integration of Knowledge and Ideas 139
Arguments..141
Reasoning and Evidence 142

Chapter 9: Passage Types 143
Literary Narrative Genre Conventions...143
Social Science and Humanities Genre Conventions 157
Natural Science Genre Conventions..160
Paired Passages..166

Chapter 10: Practice Questions 177

Chapter 11: Answers and Explanations.......................................239
Answer Key...240
Explanatory Answers 242

Introduction

The ACT tests measure your understanding of what you've been taught in core high school courses. This guide will help you succeed on the ACT reading test. Reading is a skill you have been practicing throughout your academic career. You read in different ways for different purposes. For example, you read a novel for your English literature course differently than you read a history textbook, and you read a novel for pleasure differently from you read one for your English course.

The following chapters contain questions taken from actual ACT reading tests that are aimed at enhancing your understanding of the knowledge and skills needed to succeed on the exam. Each question is followed by a detailed explanation of the answer. Chapters are organized by question type and passage type, which should help you see the patterns among the questions. Using this guide will help you become familiar with the content of the ACT reading test and the procedures you'll follow when you're actually taking the test. It also provides strategies for approaching the questions and content-specific test-taking tips.

This guide will help remind you of what you have already learned about reading and will likely teach you new skills and concepts as well. We hope this guide helps you identify your strengths and improve areas of weakness so you can show all that you know on your ACT reading test.

Chapter 1:
An Overview of the ACT Reading Test

Passage Types

Passages fall into four main types: literary narrative, humanities, social science, and natural science. These passage types each have conventions for form and content. Each section is followed by 10 questions that generally follow the order of the passage. You have 8 minutes and 45 seconds for each of the four sections. The test comprises four sections, three of which contain one long prose passage. The fourth section presents two shorter passages with some questions that require you to compare and contrast them. These two texts will belong to one of the four passage types. For example, this section may contain two literary narrative excerpts on the topic of travel. Every test will have one paired passage, and it can occur anywhere in the test. The following table shows the percentage of each type of passage on the test. There are 40 questions to answer in 35 minutes.

Reading Content	Percentage of Test	Number of Questions
Literary Narrative	25	10
Humanities	25	10
Social Science	25	10
Natural Science	25	10

Literary Narrative

The literary narrative passages are excerpts from novels or short stories. Literary narrative does not include poems or scripts from plays. The excerpts typically include two to three characters. These passages focus primarily on characterization developed through the dialogue, actions, and thoughts relayed through the narrator. Though a conflict may be established at some point in the narrative, there is rarely a full story arc with a climax or resolution. Typically, a passage introduces only the characters. Most passages end with what might be considered a cliff hanger. Some insights are revealed about the dynamics between the characters but very little action takes place. Though many literary narrative passages begin at a point of change in a character's life, the characters tend to remain static without underdoing dramatic changes over the course of the passage.

Humanities and Social Science Passages

Humanities and social science passages tend to address human beings and their relationships with one another, the world around them, and their shared history. Humanities passages range from excerpts of memoirs to articles about the Indian film industry. Social science passages cover topics such as politics, architecture, and sustainability. Both humanities and social science passages tend to be structured in a traditional thesis-driven essay format with a clear thesis at the end of the introduction and topic sentences that begin each body paragraph by reviewing the content of those paragraphs and how that content supports the thesis.

Natural Science

Natural science passages tend to follow a certain structure. Typically, they begin by describing a topic of study. Usually the topic is a scientific problem that will be examined or a hypothesis that will be evaluated. The introduction and initial body paragraphs then describe the knowledge that existed prior to a certain experiment or invention. Key terms will be defined. Then the later body paragraphs summarize studies that have been completed and the views of various scientists or outcomes of experiments.

Some science passages go into great depth about experiments, and others just summarize the theories of different scientists. Other passages detail all the obstacles that made the topic difficult to study in the first place.

Once a scientist is introduced with his or her first and last name, then that person is referred to by his or her last name throughout the remainder of the passage. For example, if biologist Rachel Carson is introduced at the beginning of a passage, she will be referred to as Carson for the remainder of the passage.

The conclusion paragraph typically discusses the limitations of the current data about the topic being studied. It may also offer ideas for further studies that could be completed or it may focus on the applications of the most recent data discovered. Sometimes science passages end with a reflection on the meaning of the scientific discovery.

Timing and Pacing

Your study plan should involve reviewing the content of this guide and taking timed practice tests to determine if you are retaining and applying what you have learned. You do not need to take your first practice test under timed conditions, but, eventually, you should practice using the correct pacing. For example, each English passage should take about 9 minutes. Each reading passage should take 8 minutes and 45 seconds. Many test centers only have an analog clock. If you are not able to easily read such a clock, bringing a digital watch may help you keep track of the time. Try to practice this way as well instead of using your phone's timers to time yourself during practice tests because you won't be able to use your phone during the actual test. You should also practice taking a full test in one sitting in the morning in order to mimic the testing conditions. Additionally, you should not read sentences out loud when you take practice tests because you will not be able to do this during the actual test.

The complete ACT test is always given in the same order. A break is given after the first two tests (English and math) are completed. Therefore, you should feel a bit energized as you head into test three: reading. If you do not have time to complete a full-length practice ACT, try to take a reading test after completing about an hour-and-a-half of homework because this will mimic the amount of time you will have spent taking the ACT by the time you get to the reading test.

Checking Your Answers

If you wish to double-check your work, you can do so either at the end of each passage while the content is still fresh in your memory or after finishing the complete reading test. Mark questions that you are unsure about with a symbol such as a question mark. When checking your work, be sure to consider the context of the passage as a whole, not just the referenced lines or most relevant paragraph. If you decide to change an answer, try to consciously recognize the reason for the change by saying to yourself, "I am choosing answer B because I now realize that this question includes the word EXCEPT. Answer C is incorrect because I accidentally thought the question was asking about what Ted and Vida *have* in common instead of what they do *not* have in common." Using this process to slow down and articulate your thoughts process will help you be mindful as you double-check your answers.

Scaled Scoring

Here is a recent example of top-scaled scores:

Number Correct	Scaled Score		Number Correct	Scaled Score
40	36		32	30
38–39	35		31	29
37	34		30	28
36	33		—	27
34–35	32		29	26
33	31		28	25

Take a Diagnostic Practice Test

Before taking a diagnostic reading test, read chapter 2, which offers suggestions about how to approach the reading test, and decide which approach you will practice. If you divide your time evenly among the passages, each passage should take 8 minutes 45 seconds from start to finish. You need to determine how much of that time you should dedicate to reading each passage and how much time to devote to answering the questions. Most students should first begin by spending three to four minutes reading each passage and the remaining time answering the questions. If that approach does not work well, try to spend about five to six minutes reading and the remaining time answering the questions. If possible, try to use printed copies of tests, because this enables you to practice in the same manner in which you will take your actual test. Being able to cross out answer choices, underline, and star information can help you process the passages and questions. In the online version of the test, you will have a highlighting tool.

How to Use This Guide

This guide begins with a review of a variety of approaches that can be used to tackle the ACT reading test passages. Next comes a description of a number of reading skills you will need for success on the ACT reading test and an overview of several question types that appear across different passages. These questions are accompanied by the relevant excerpts from the passages, and some excerpts are accompanied by explanatory notes that paraphrase the content of the passage. You may wish to hold off on reading the explanatory notes until you have attempted the question, using only the content from the passage itself.

Note: Entire passages are not always reproduced. Ellipses (. . .) indicate that a paragraph has been omitted. In order to provide information about which portion of the passage has been reproduced, paragraph numbers have been included in brackets as follows. Paragraph numbers will not appear on the actual exam. Line reference numbers will be included for every fifth line of text in this guide and on the actual exam.

HUMANITIES: This passage is adapted from the essay "My Life with a Field Guide" by Diana Kappel-Smith (©2002 by Phi Beta Kappa Society).

[5]

...In the thin summer shadow of the tree, quivering, like a veil, the book was
20 revealed, and I reached for it. A FIELD GUIDE TO WILD FLOWERS—PETERSON & McKENNY, its cover said. Its backside was ruled like a measuring tape, its inside was full of drawings of flowers. By the end of that week I had my own copy. I have it still.

...

[8]

I had already figured out the business of the book's colored tabs. I turned in an authoritative way to
40 the Yellow part and began to flip through. By the time the last of my friends had disappeared up the trail, I'd arrived at a page where things looked right. Five petals? Yes. Pinnate leaves? Whatever. Buttercup? There are, amazingly, *eleven* buttercups. Who would
45 have thought? However hard I tried to make it so, my item was not one of them. Next page. Aha! this looked more like it. Bushy cinquefoil? Nope, leaves not *quiiite* right, are they? As the gnats descended, I noticed that there were six more pages ahead, each packed with
50 five-petaled yellow flowers—St. John's wort loose-strifes, puccoons.

[9]

Why I persisted in carrying it around and consulting its crowded pages at every opportunity, I have no idea. The book was stubborn; well, I was stubborn, too;
55 that was part of it.

The remainder of this guide covers the content and form of the various passage types: literary narrative, humanities, social science, and natural science. Seeing questions and passages grouped by genre should help you gain a deeper understanding of how to navigate the process of reading the different passage types. As you complete practice questions, keep track of your mistakes and reflect on the processes you used to arrive at your answers. Try to develop an awareness of the types of reading passages and questions that you have trouble with so you can budget your time appropriately to maximize your score.

2 Chapter 2: General Reading Skills

Skimming

Skimming is essentially speed reading with a low level of comprehension. Use the structured nature of the humanities, social science, and natural science passages to help you vary your reading speed. For example, the first and last sentences of each paragraph are typically the most important, and the introduction and conclusion of each passage typically give the broadest framework for the content of the passage as a whole. Therefore, you can gather a great deal of information by focusing on comprehending these parts of the passage.

You might be surprised by how much you can understand from looking only at these portions of the text. When a passage includes a list such as wheat, barley, and kale, you can breeze through these details and simply try to commit to memory the location of the list within the structure of the passage in case you are asked about this information later.

Look at these key sentences from a passage adapted from *Biomimicry: Innovation Inspired by Nature* by Janine M. Benyus (©1997 by Janine M. Benyus). Compare your understanding of the main ideas of the passage based on these sentences alone to your comprehension after reading the full passage, which has these sentences underlined for you.

SOCIAL SCIENCE: This passage is adapted from *Biomimicry: Innovation Inspired by Nature* by Janine M. Benyus (©1997 by Janine M. Benyus).

Introduction First Sentence

If anybody's growing biomass, it's us. To keep our system from collapsing on itself, industrial ecologists are attempting to build a "no-waste economy."

Introduction Last Sentence

The first examples of this no-waste economy are collections of companies clustered in an ecopark and connected in a food chain, with each firm's waste going next door to become the other firm's raw material or fuel.

Topic Sentence of the First Body Paragraph

In Denmark, the town of Kalundborg has the world's most elaborate prototype of an ecopark.

Topic Sentence of the Second Body Paragraph

Waste steam from the power company is used by Novo Nordisk to heat the fermentation tanks that produce insulin and enzymes.

Topic Sentence of the Third Body Paragraph

Meanwhile, back at the Statoil Refinery, waste gas that used to go up a smokestack is now purified.

Topic Sentence of the Fourth Body Paragraph

Although Kalundborg is a cozy co-location, industries need not be geographically close to operate in a food web as long as they are connected by a mutual desire to use waste.

Topic Sentence of the Fifth Body Paragraph

So far, we've talked about recycling within a circle of companies.

Topic Sentence of the Sixth Body Paragraph

Traditionally, manufacturers haven't had to worry about what happens to a product after it leaves their gates.

First Sentence of the Conclusion

When the onus shifts in this way, it's suddenly in the company's best interest to design a product that will either last a long time or come apart easily for recycling or reuse.

Last Sentence of the Conclusion

Today's bags, which have nine thin layers made of seven different materials, will no doubt be replaced by one material that can preserve freshness and can easily be remade into a new bag.

Synthesis of the Main Idea Based on the Previous Information

Companies are beginning to take responsibility for using materials in a sustainable way that considers the life cycle of the materials used to produce goods.

SOCIAL SCIENCE: *Biomimicry: Innovation Inspired by Nature* by Janine M. Benyus (©1997 by Janine M. Benyus).

If anybody's growing biomass, it's us. To keep our system from collapsing on itself, industrial ecologists are attempting to build a "no-waste economy." Instead of a linear production system, which binges on virgin
5 raw materials and spews out unusable waste, they envision a web of closed loops in which a minimum of raw materials comes in the door, and very little waste escapes. The first examples of this no-waste economy are collections of companies clustered in an eco-park
10 and connected in a food chain, with each firm's waste going next door to become the other firm's raw material or fuel.

In Denmark, the town of Kalundborg has the world's most elaborate prototype of an eco-park. Four
15 companies are co-located, and all of them are linked, dependent on one another for resources or energy. The Asnaesverket Power Company pipes some of its waste steam to power the engines of two companies: the Statoil Refinery and Novo Nordisk (a pharmaceutical
20 plant). Another pipeline delivers the remaining waste steam to heat thirty-five hundred homes in the town, eliminating the need for oil furnaces. The power plant also delivers its cooling water, now toasty warm, to fifty-seven ponds' worth of fish. The fish revel in the
25 warm water, and the fish farm produces 150 tons of sea trout and turbot each year.

Waste steam from the power company is used by Novo Nordisk to heat the fermentation tanks that produce insulin and enzymes. This process in turn creates
30 700,000 tons of nitrogen-rich slurry a year, which used to be dumped into the fjord. Now, Novo bequeaths it free to nearby farmers—a pipeline delivers the fertilizer to the growing plants, which are in turn harvested to feed the bacteria in the fermentation tanks.

35 Meanwhile, back at the Statoil Refinery, waste gas that used to go up a smokestack is now purified. Some is used internally as fuel, some is piped to the power company, and the rest goes to Gyproc, the wallboard market next door. The sulfur squeezed from the gas
40 during purification is loaded onto trucks and sent to Kemira, a company that produces sulfuric acid. The power company also squeezes sulfur from its emissions, but converts most of it to calcium sulfate (industrial gypsum), which it sells to Gyproc for wallboard.

45 Although Kalundborg is a cozy co-location, industries need not be geographically close to operate in a food web as long as they are connected by a mutual desire to use waste. Already, some companies are designing their processes so that any waste that falls on
50 the production-room floor is valuable and can be used by someone else. In this game of "designed offal," a process with lots of waste, as long as it's "wanted waste," may be better than one with a small amount of waste that must be landfilled or burned. As author
55 Daniel Chiras says, more companies are recognizing that "technologies that produce by-products society cannot absorb are essentially failed technologies."

So far, we've talked about recycling within a circle of companies. But what happens when a product
60 leaves the manufacturer and passes to the consumer and finally to the trash can? Right now, a product visits one of two fates at the end of its useful life. It can be buried in a landfill or incinerated, or it can be recaptured through recycling or reuse.

65 Traditionally, manufacturers haven't had to worry about what happens to a product after it leaves their gates. But that is starting to change, thanks to laws now in the wings in Europe (and headed for the United States) that will require companies to take back their
70 durable goods such as refrigerators, washers, and cars at the end of their useful lives. In Germany, the take-back laws start with the initial sale. Companies must take back all their packaging or hire middlemen to do the recycling. Take-back laws mean that manufacturers
75 who have been saying, "This product can be recycled," must now say, "We recycle our products and packaging."

When the onus shifts in this way, it's suddenly in the company's best interest to design a product that will
80 either last a long time or come apart easily for recycling or reuse. Refrigerators and cars will be assembled using easy-open snaps instead of glued-together joints, and for recyclability, each part will be made of one material instead of twenty. Even simple things, like the snack
85 bags for potato chips, will be streamlined. Today's bags, which have nine thin layers made of seven different materials, will no doubt be replaced by one material that can preserve freshness and can easily be remade into a new bag.

The next question is an EXCEPT question, which asks you to find an answer choice that is not supported by the passage. It is being included here because it asks about the previous passage. Answering this question should also give you further practice with skimming and scanning for information.

91. According to the passage, waste emissions from the Asnaesverket Power Company are used to help produce all of the following EXCEPT:

   A. insulin.

   B. heating oil.

   C. plant fertilizer.

   D. industrial gypsum.

Scan for: waste emissions, insulin, heating oil, fertilizer, gypsum

The best answer is B because the passage doesn't mention waste emissions from the Asnaesverket Power Company being used to help produce heating oil. The other three answer choices are supported by the passage.

The best answer is NOT:

   A because lines 27–29 state, "Waste steam from the power company is used by Novo Nordisk to heat the fermentation tanks that produce insulin and enzymes."

   C because the process described in lines 27–29 "creates 700,000 tons of nitrogen-rich slurry a year" (lines 29–30), which Novo Nordisk gives to farmers for use as plant fertilizer.

   D because lines 41–44 state, "The power company also squeezes sulfur from its emissions, but converts most of it to calcium sulfate (industrial gypsum), which it sells to Gyproc for wallboard."

Scanning for the Conclusion or Main Idea

Often questions ask about the main idea of a passage. This information can sometimes be found in the introduction or conclusion. Taking note of the following transition words can help you identify times when a passage is drawing a conclusion, establishing a cause and effect relationship, or emphasizing a point. Sentences that synthesize information or draw conclusions can be especially helpful when it comes to determining the main idea of a passage.

Cause and Effect	Emphasis	Conclusion
accordingly	clearly	in conclusion
as a result	especially	in summary
as such	in fact	in total
because	in particular	all things considered
consequently	indeed	
ergo	however	
for	nevertheless	
hence	notably	
thus	regardless	
therefore	still	
since	though	
so		

Transitions That Signal Repetition

Some transition words essentially indicate that information will be repeated. Writers often repeat ideas for emphasis or elaboration. For example, a writer complaining about the lack of vegetarian options at a college dining hall might write the following.

Example 1

My dining hall rarely offers meatless entrées; **in fact**, last week, each entrée contained beef or poultry.

Notice that the second sentence is essentially making the same point as the first sentence does. The second sentence is simply more specific. The phrase "in fact" signals that the second sentence will reiterate the first sentence, usually in more specific terms. Sometimes the sentence that follows "in fact" will reiterate the previous idea in broader or more emphatic terms. Here are several examples of the use of these kinds of transition phrases in context. When you encounter transition words that signal emphasis or repetition, you can speed through the sentences that follow, knowing that they will not be adding any information that differs substantially from the content in the sentence directly prior to the transition phrase.

Example 2

"For extended human activities on the Moon or Mars, you must have self-sustaining biological systems, systems that are regenerative," Dixon says. **In other words**, green plants. "They give you oxygen, consume your carbon dioxide, and recycle your water."

Example 3

As we move from small to large animals, from mice to elephants or small lizards to Komodo dragons, brain size increases, but not so fast as body size. **In other words,** bodies grow faster than brains, and large animals have low ratios of brain weight to body weight. **In fact,** brains grow only about two-thirds as fast as bodies. Since we have no reason to believe that large animals are consistently stupider than their smaller relatives, we must conclude that large animals require relatively less brain to do as well as smaller animals.

Example 4

One of the things that I prided myself on was my ability to conceal my thoughts. **For example,** Rochelle had no idea that I had never even heard of field hockey or intramural sports. I had just looked her in the face and made myself a mirror, frowning when she frowned, raising my eyebrows just seconds after she'd raised hers.

Topic Sentences

The topic sentences should give you a general framework of the content of the full passage. Topic sentences are typically the first sentence of each body paragraph. They give an overview of the paragraph and how it relates to the thesis. Below you will find several topic sentences from a real ACT reading test passage. After reading the topic sentence, predict what the paragraph will be about and compare your prediction to the content of the actual paragraph. You should always read the introduction and conclusion more carefully because these sections of a passage always highlight the main idea of the passage. Therefore, the introduction has been reproduced first.

NATURAL SCIENCE: This passage is adapted from the article "Living Off the Land" by Lee Billings (©2009 by Seed Media Group LLC).

Introduction

To survive in space, astronauts need food, water, and air, all sent from the Earth at a very high price—each pound of material lofted into space costs upward of $10,000. To maximize these precious resources, a spacecraft's "physicochemical" life-support system recycles water through purifying membranes and uses electrochemical processes to replenish air with oxygen and scrub it of carbon dioxide.

Body Paragraph 1 Topic Sentence

These practices work reasonably well for the International Space Station, only some 300 kilometers above the Earth's surface, or even for the three-day trip to the Moon.

Predict what the paragraph will be about. Then compare your ideas to the following actual paragraph.

Complete Paragraph 1

These practices work reasonably well for the International Space Station, only some 300 kilometers above the Earth's surface, or even for the three-day trip to the Moon. But for extended space voyages or long-term bases on other worlds, even if all the air and water is efficiently recycled and purified, bringing along enough food can prove problematic.

Body Paragraph 2 Topic Sentence

"Food is what limits the equation in terms of long-term human space exploration," says Mike Dixon, an environmental scientist at the University of Guelph in Ontario, Canada.

Predict what the paragraph will be about. Then compare your ideas to the actual following paragraph.

Complete Paragraph 2

"Food is what limits the equation in terms of long-term human space exploration," says Mike Dixon, an environmental scientist at the University of Guelph in Ontario, Canada. For a lunar base with dozens of people, supplying food from Earth is feasible, Dixon says, but still prohibitive because "you'll spend all your payload mass just supplying dinners for lunar explorers."

Body Paragraph 3 Topic Sentence

Dixon and other researchers think the solution to the food problem is for astronauts to grow their own.

Predict what the paragraph will be about. Then compare your ideas to the actual following paragraph.

Complete Paragraph 3

Dixon and other researchers think the solution to the food problem is for astronauts to grow their own. His Controlled Environment Systems Research Facility at Guelph is considered the world's best for investigating plant growth in unearthly low-pressure atmospheric conditions.

Body Paragraph 4 Topic Sentence

"For extended human activities on the Moon or Mars, you must have self-sustaining biological systems, systems that are regenerative," Dixon says.

Predict what the paragraph will be about. Then compare your ideas to the actual following paragraph.

Complete Paragraph 4

"For extended human activities on the Moon or Mars, you must have self-sustaining biological systems, systems that are regenerative," Dixon says. In other words, green plants. "They give you oxygen, consume your carbon dioxide, and recycle your water. And you can eat them. As life-support machines, they have no equal." The problem is, plants require "life-support systems" of their own.

Body Paragraph 5 Topic Sentence

"The infrastructure and power required to support plant-based regenerative life support is actually quite large," says Sherwin Gormly, an environmental engineer at NASA.

Predict what the paragraph will be about. Then compare your ideas to the actual following paragraph.

Complete Paragraph 5

"The infrastructure and power required to support plant-based regenerative life support is actually quite large," says Sherwin Gormly, an environmental engineer at NASA. "When you examine how much material you'd need to launch to establish the system and keep it going, it's hard to justify," he says.

Body Paragraph 6 Topic Sentence

To make matters worse, one crop alone can't be a self-sufficient life-support system.

Predict what the paragraph will be about. Then compare your ideas to the actual following paragraph.

(continued)

(continued)

Complete Paragraph 6

To make matters worse, one crop alone can't be a self-sufficient life-support system—an entire artificial ecology must be constructed and maintained for long periods of time, complete with all its delicate biochemical checks and balances. This is a task so daunting we've never quite achieved it even down here on Earth, though not for lack of trying. Space agencies around the world have mounted numerous hermetically sealed ecological experiments over the years, attempting to sustain human life without relying on our planet's natural ecosystem services. None have been unqualified successes—outside inputs inevitably are needed.

Body Paragraph 7 Topic Sentence

As of 2009, the best hope for advanced life-support systems is probably the European Space Agency's Micro-Ecological Life Support System Alternative (MELiSSA) project

Predict what the paragraph will be about. Then compare your ideas to the actual following paragraph.

Complete Paragraph 7

As of 2009, the best hope for advanced life-support systems is probably the European Space Agency's Micro-Ecological Life Support System Alternative (MELiSSA) project. In development for almost two decades, MELiSSA is seeking to "close the loop" between the production and consumption of metabolic nutrients by recycling and reusing solid and liquid organic waste with 100 percent efficiency. That is, the MELiSSA team hopes to create a self-sustaining system that turns waste material into vegetables, potable water, and fresh air.

Body Paragraph 8 Topic Sentence

The project uses a mix of high-tech physicochemical and biological approaches spread across five compartments, which, according to MELiSSA's top coordinator, Christophe Lasseur, are modeled on the ecosystem of a lake.

Note: This paragraph was only one sentence so it is not possible to predict what the remainder of the paragraph would say.

Body Paragraph 9 Topic Sentence

A lake bottom covered with anaerobic sludge inspired MELiSSA's first compartment, where bacteria feed on solid waste and release nutrients.

Predict what the paragraph will be about. Then compare your ideas to the actual following paragraph.

Complete Paragraph 9

A lake bottom covered with anaerobic sludge inspired MELiSSA's first compartment, where bacteria feed on solid waste and release nutrients. Just above the lake bottom, light filters in but the water is still low in oxygen. Red algae thrives here, breaking down carbon compounds. This portion of the lake is similar to compartment two. Compartment three is akin to the shallows near the lake's surface, where oxygen is plentiful and nitrifying bacteria convert the ammonia in urine to ammonium, a potent fertilizer. Compartment four is like the surface of the lake, where carbon dioxide, sunlight, and nutrients are plentiful and photosynthetic organisms clean the water and produce oxygen and food. The crew is the final step of the process: They live in compartment five, consuming the oxygen, water, and food to create waste that enters the cycle anew.

Conclusion

Off-planet, "green" lifestyles aren't just fashionable, they're required. Any eventual residents of a lunar base or Martian habitat will almost certainly be vegetarians, and thrift will be crucial for survival.

Navigating Lists

The following is an example of the kind of list of information you can speed through as you read. Simply note to yourself that this paragraph gives several examples of the way the narrator uses a field guide to identify flowers. Then return to this portion of the text if specific questions are asked about this content. Paragraph numbers have been indicated in brackets in this passage, but these brackets are not provided in the real test. They have been provided here in order to help orient you within the context of the passage as a whole. Ellipses (. . .) indicate that paragraphs have been omitted.

HUMANITIES: This passage is adapted from the essay "My Life with a Field Guide" by Diana Kappel-Smith (©2002 by Phi Beta Kappa Society).

[5]

...In the thin summer shadow of the tree, quivering, like a veil, the book was
20 revealed, and I reached for it. A FIELD GUIDE TO WILD FLOWERS—PETERSON & McKENNY, its cover said. Its backside was ruled like a measuring tape, its inside was full of drawings of flowers. By the end of that week I had my own copy. I have it still.

. . .

[8]

I had already figured out the business of the book's colored tabs. I turned in an authoritative way to
40 the Yellow part and began to flip through. By the time the last of my friends had disappeared up the trail, I'd arrived at a page where things looked right. Five petals? Yes. Pinnate leaves? Whatever. Buttercup? There are, amazingly, *eleven* buttercups. Who would
45 have thought? However hard I tried to make it so, my item was not one of them. Next page. Aha! this looked more like it. Bushy cinquefoil? Nope, leaves not *quiiite* right, are they? As the gnats descended, I noticed that there were six more pages ahead, each packed with
50 five-petaled yellow flowers—St. John's wort loose-strifes, puccoons.

Explanatory Notes

Paragraph 5 of this passage introduces *A Field Guide to Wild Flowers*. The intervening paragraphs have not been included because they do not affect the meaning of the eighth paragraph, which gives a vivid account of the narrator's use of the guide. Instead of trying to think carefully about the content of the eighth paragraph, think about its purpose. Look for any words that might signal significance. None occur, so you know that the function of this paragraph is simply to capture the narrator's enthusiasm about using the field guide. You can, accordingly, read this portion of the passage at a fast pace.

Scanning

Scanning means looking for specific information as your eyes move over the text. It can be helpful to have a set purpose as you scan the text. For example, you may have a certain word, phrase, or date you are looking for. You should particularly pay attention to the topic sentences of paragraphs when scanning. Scanning can help you quickly identify the similarities and differences indicated in a passage, for example, by looking for comparative or superlative adjectives such as better, best, more, most, oldest, or smartest.

In order to help you develop your ability to scan effectively, many questions in this guide provide a recommend word to scan for. These scan words and phrases are not provided for big-picture questions such as main idea questions or for questions that provide a line reference already.

Speed Reading

Improving your reading speed is a process that takes time. Here we will review several key principles for improving your reading pace.

1.   **Stop subvocalizing.** You likely first learned to read by reading out loud. This is part of why most readers say each word to themselves as they read. This takes time, so you want to avoid doing this while taking practice tests. It is possible to break this habit with practice. Instead of saying each word, try to associate a word, such as *education,* with a visual representation of the word, such as a school building or a pencil. This will save you the time it would take to subvocalize the four-syllable word *education.*

2.   **See groups of words** instead of individual words. Individuals who successfully learn to read quickly learn how to perceive and process more than one word at a time. For example, reading this next sentence by focusing on just one word at a time would be quite time-consuming.

     "Ted had seen his mother walk out to the bridge at night."

     Try to group the words together and look at the center word and then see the words to the left and right of the word you are focusing on. This should improve your reading speed. Try to read the following clusters of words together and see if it feels a bit faster than reading each word individually.

     "Ted had seen   his mother walk out   to the bridge   at night."

3.   **Use your finger, your answer sheet, or a pencil to track the lines as you read them**. If you are taking the online version of the test, you can use the cursor to scan the lines of text. Though you are not consciously aware, most of us experience something called visual regression as we read. Our eyes backtrack to the previous words. So, when we read the following sentence without using a tracking tool, our eyes actually lead us to read something along the lines of the repetitious information as shown here.

"Ted had seen his mother walk out to the bridge at night."

Ted

Ted had

Ted had seen

Ted had seen his

Ted had seen his mother

Ted had seen his mother walk

Ted had seen his mother walk out

Ted had seen his mother walk out to

Ted had seen his mother walk out to the

Ted had seen his mother walk out to the bridge

Ted had seen his mother walk out to the bridge at

Ted had seen his mother walk out to the bridge at night.

Moving your finger, your pencil, or your cursor under the line of text you are reading will help your eyes track smoothly and efficiently while avoiding backtracking.

Annotating

You may heavily annotate books you read at your own pace for school or books you read for pleasure. On the ACT reading test, there is not time to thoroughly annotate the text, but you can take some notes as you read to help yourself create a map of the passage. If you are taking the online test, you can use the highlighting tool and scrap paper or your whiteboard to keep track of your thought process. Some students will find annotating aids their comprehension and others will find the process to be distracting. Use these annotations only if they aid your comprehension of the text. Overuse of these symbols will interfere with your ability to read the passage and answer the questions in the appropriate amount of time. For example, if you underline too much, what is the point of underlining at all? Below are several commonly used annotations.

* a star or asterisk can mark the thesis or main idea

= can be used to indicate similarities or equivalent concepts

X can mean NO or NOT

→ can be used to show cause-and-effect relationships

→ can be used at the end of a set of questions to remind yourself to go back to a question like a main idea question

+ can indicate evidence in favor of a position or positive information

– can indicate evidence against a position or negative information

? can indicate confusion or that you wish to return to a question later

! can indicate surprising or interesting information

[ ] can help identify important information

___ can help identify important information

Circling is sometimes used to highlight key nouns in the passage. It is likely not necessary to circle proper nouns that are capitalized because the capital letters should be enough to help you locate these names if needed.

Highlighting is a function available on the computer version of the ACT.

Chapter 3:
Test-Taking Strategies

Time is at a premium when you take the ACT reading test. You have 35 minutes to read four passages and answer 40 questions. Knowing how and where to spend your time can boost your score. This chapter gives you eight approaches you can use on ACT reading passages. Some approaches can be used together.

- Invest most of your time in answering the questions.

- Invest your time in reading upfront.

- Save your worst passage for the end.

- Worry less about each individual answer.

- Vary your reading pace according to the passage.

- Change the order of the passages.

- Read half the passage then answer half the questions.

- Answer the "easy" questions first.

Invest Most of Your Time in Answering the Questions

Instead of slowly and carefully reading the passage, some students read the passage with a low level of comprehension first and then devote the majority of their time to processing the questions. Students using this approach tend to read the passage in two to three minutes.

If you take this approach, studying the genre conventions should help you pull out the key information from each passage. For example, the introduction of a literary narrative passage typically establishes one to three characters. After quickly reading a literary narrative passage, you should generally know who the characters are and how they interact with one another. You should also have a sense of the structure and chronology of the passage.

Regardless of the passage type, you should strive to determine the general idea of the passage and how it is laid out so you can quickly find relevant textual evidence as needed when you turn to the questions. In later chapters, you will learn more about the key components of each passage type. This is one of the most popular approaches to the ACT reading test.

Invest Your Time in Reading Upfront

Invest your time in reading thoroughly. The average adult reading speed is 200–250 words per minute, which would be sufficient for this approach. Read the passages carefully on your first read through and attempt to retain the key points of what you have read. This could take three to six minutes, depending on your level of reading comprehension and speed.

If you find it helpful, you may wish to jot down some brief annotations in the margins. It is unlikely that you would have time to write out a paraphrase of each paragraph as some test prep companies advise. You may wish to identify key terms, dates, and people by circling, underlining, or starring the text. In the online test, you can use the highlighting tool.

If you are starting your preparation months before the test, you may wish to articulate in your mind a paraphrase of each paragraph after reading it in order to test your recall. As you get closer to the test date, you should see if you can do this more quickly without needing to consciously paraphrase each paragraph. You can gain practice with the complete passages found at the end of this guide.

With this approach, once you look at a question, it can be effective to identify a key word in a passage and then scan for that word as you look for textual evidence to support an answer choice. For most questions throughout this guide, you will find a suggested word or phrase that will help you practice this scanning method.

By investing time upfront in processing the passage, you should save yourself time when you turn to the questions. Ideally, when you read a question, you will recall the answer, or, at least, recall where in the passage this information can be found.

Remember that on the ACT reading test, most correct answers have direct textual evidence as support. It is rarely necessary to make numerous logical inferences in order to see the connection between the correct excerpt of the passage and the correct answer choice. If you cannot find clear textual evidence to support your answer choice, you may be overlooking the section of the text that has the answer.

Remember to not get bogged down if there are portions of a passage that you do not understand. Often you will find that the questions never even address the complicated portions of a passage.

Save Your Worst Passage for the End

If you consistently struggle to complete all four reading sections, your best bet may be to use more time on your three best passage types and then focus on simpler questions in the final passage.

Often students find that they struggle with one or more passage type. For example, many students find the literary narrative passage challenging because it tends to ask complicated questions that do not always rely purely on factual recall. A question in a literary narrative passage may ask what one character thinks of another character, for example, which requires abstract reasoning on your part based on the textual evidence in the passage.

Additionally, the structure of the literary narrative passage does not lend itself to many of the strategies that help students navigate the content of the other passage types quickly. Literary narrative passages do not typically have a clear thesis statement at the end of the introduction. Nor do they have clear topic sentences at the beginning of each body paragraph. Other students have difficulty with the natural science passage because it sometimes contains jargon that can make the content difficult to follow.

If you know that you are consistently baffled by a certain passage type, skip it temporarily, and leave it for the end of the ACT reading test. The passages are always in the same order (literary narrative, humanities, social science, and natural science), so you will know which passage to leave until the end. When you work through this final passage, focus on questions with line references because these questions will have clearly identified textual evidence to support your interpretation of the answer choices. Vocabulary in context questions should also be easy to answer. These questions often ask what a word or phrase "most nearly means." Make sure to read at least one sentence prior to the cited lines in order to get a sense of context.

Use the order of the questions to your advantage. The earlier questions tend to focus on the introduction of the passage, so those should be easier to find the answer to. Likewise, the later questions tend to focus on the conclusion of the passage. That should narrow the scope of text you will be examining in order to find your evidence. This approach can be quite effective because it enables you to maximize the points you will earn in the other passage types.

If you plan to use this approach, be sure to practice under timed conditions. Analyze which passage type is your weakest. Practice identifying which questions will be easier to tackle. Time yourself to see how long it takes to read the passage and how long it takes to answer the questions. Remember you do not lose points for wrong answers on the ACT, so *do not* skip any questions. If you run out of time, do your best to eliminate some answer choices. This greatly increases your chances of choosing the correct answer.

Worry Less about Each Individual Answer

Some students, particularly perfectionists, tend to spend too much time justifying each of their responses. This is why it is important to take practice tests with a variety of approaches. If you are consistently running out of time on the ACT reading test, practice answering the questions more quickly than you think you should. Time yourself. Complete one passage of the test at a time so that you can score yourself and immediately reflect on the effectiveness of your approach.

Often, when you begin this approach, your scores may temporarily decline, but with more practice, most students' scores ultimately improve. Don't give up just because your score goes down the first time you try this approach. Experiment and determine which approach is best for you. To maintain a fast pace as you are reading, do not get bogged down by vocabulary that you do not know. Often this vocabulary is never addressed in the questions, and context clues can provide you with enough information to effectively navigate around your gaps in knowledge.

Vary Your Reading Pace According to the Passage

Because literary narrative passages tend not to follow a traditional structure, they are challenging to read quickly. The other passage types should all have a traditional structure more or less with a thesis in the introductory paragraph and topic sentences at the beginning of each paragraph to clarify the connection to the thesis. Accordingly, you can pick up the pace when you read these passages, focusing on the topic sentences to get a sense of the passage as a whole. You can read the content of the body paragraphs as needed. You should also pick up your reading pace when it becomes evident that the passage is simply providing a list with elaborating detail. Lists can be returned to if a question asks directly about such a list.

Change the Order of the Passages

You do not need to read the passages in the order in which they appear. You can decide the order that is right for you based on the data you gather through taking timed practice tests. For example, many students require more time for the literary narrative and natural science passages. If getting these more time-consuming passages out of the way early on in the test alleviates stress for you, then that approach might work well. If you are consistently baffled by these passages, and they rattle your confidence, then, it may be better for you to complete these passage types after you have built confidence through completing the social science and humanities passages. Remember that the literary narrative passage is the most difficult passage type to skim because it does not have a traditional structure with a thesis and topic sentences to support the central claim.

Read Half the Passage Then Answer Half the Questions

Some students struggle to retain the content of the complete passage if they read the whole passage first and then turn to the questions. For those students, it can be effective to read half of the passage first and to then answer as many questions as they can until it becomes clear that the second half of the passage will need to be read in order to complete the remaining questions. Because the questions generally follow the order of the passage, this strategy can be quite effective.

In some cases, you will need to temporarily skip a question until you have completed the full passage. If this occurs, be sure to mark that question in some manner so you remember to return to it once you have completed the passage, such as marking it with an arrow or star.

Answer the "Easy" Questions First

Some students know that they struggle with certain types of questions. If you can determine which questions you struggle with, you may be able to temporarily skip those as you complete the questions that correspond with a passage. As you complete what you consider to be the "easier" questions, you tend to get a better understanding of the passage as a whole.

Some questions that are typically regarded as more difficult include questions using the words EXCEPT or NOT and questions asking you to draw a logical inference. Some students can be apprehensive when the question itself is wordy or incorporates complex vocabulary, such as the phrase "decentralized intellectual character" in the following question. The relevant portions of this excerpt have been identified in **bold font**. The explanatory notes found to the right of the excerpt paraphrase the content of the passage. You may wish to consult these notes after attempting the question on your own.

This strategy is likely to be effective for students who are still scoring below their target score on the reading test after experimenting with the other approaches previously described. One risk of this approach is that it can make bubbling the answer sheet in more complicated.

SOCIAL SCIENCE: This passage is adapted from *Library: An Unquiet History* by Matthew Battles (©2003 by Matthew Battles).

The development and spread of libraries throughout the Roman world was especially remarkable given
70 the **decentralized** and extra-official character of Roman
intellectual life. In the public sphere, the pursuit of
knowledge, like the pursuit of wealth or power, **was a
matter of private associations and casual relations
among people.** Unlike the Ptolemies, the Qin dynasty,
75 or the Aztec nobility, Roman emperors rarely sought
direct control over the life of the mind. As the classicist
Elizabeth Rawson has pointed out, **Rome lacked
schools and universities** (many Roman elite went to
Greece for schooling); **no formal competitions existed
80 for writers and artists,** as they had in Greece; **nor did
the state pay the salaries of engineers, physicians,
teachers, or other professionals, who depended on the
patronage of individual senators or the imperial house.**
In this light, the flourishing libraries of Rome are
85 unique: they are the nearest thing Rome had to incorporated, official cultural institutions as we know them
today.

Explanatory Notes

This paragraph contains a great deal of information, so you need to maintain your focus on what the paragraph is saying about **Rome's character.** What facts are given about what Rome did and did not have?

The notion that Roman intellectual life is "decentralized" is introduced in lines 68–71. The definition of *decentralized* primarily comes from lines 71–74, which state that, "the pursuit of knowledge, like the pursuit of wealth or power, was a matter of private associations and casual relations among people." In other words, the central government was not primarily responsible for the pursuit of power or wealth.

Notice that much of this paragraph describes how Rome differs from other cultures.

14. According to the passage, which of the following has been identified by Rawson as an illustration of Rome's decentralized intellectual character?

Paraphrase of the question: What shows Rome's decentralized intellectual character?

F. Rome's rapidly diminishing cultural life

G. Rome's subsidization of professionals' salaries

H. Rome's formal competitions for writers and artists

J. Rome's lack of schools and universities

Scan word: decentralized

The best answer is J because lines 77–78 clearly state that "Rome lacked schools and universities."

The answer is NOT:

F because the passage does not indicate a "rapidly diminishing cultural life." Instead, it emphasizes that libraries were "the nearest thing Rome had to incorporated, official cultural institutions."

G because the passage indicates in lines 80–83 that the state did not "pay the salaries of engineers, physicians, teachers, or other professionals, who depended on the patronage of individual senators or the imperial house."

H because the passage states in line 79 that in Rome "no formal competitions existed for writers and artists."

Try to track your thought process in your test booklet (but not on your answer sheet). For example, you should cross out answer choices as you eliminate them. If you are completing the test digitally, you can write out the letters of the answer choices (ABCD, for example) on scrap paper or your whiteboard and cross them out as you eliminate wrong answers.

It can be helpful if you circle the words that do not accurately reflect the passage. For example, you might circle a word such as *indignation* in an answer choice if it is not accurate. The word *indignant* is used for intense anger, so it is unlikely to be correct unless a character or historical figure is portrayed as incensed in a passage.

You can also keep track of which questions you have struggled with by writing a question mark next to those questions to help you realize that you should return to those questions. You should return to the harder questions once you have completed the easier questions for one passage before moving onto the next passage.

Chapter 4: Question and Answer Types

EXCEPT and NOT Questions

Some questions will include the words EXCEPT or NOT. Although these words are capitalized, it is still easy to overlook these words when answering a question. What can you do to help yourself accurately work through these questions?

When you first read the question, mark the words EXCEPT or NOT in some way. For example, you could star * the word or circle it. Then you may want to rewrite the question in simpler language. Paraphrasing an EXCEPT or a NOT question into simpler terms can help you process it more effectively. Reframing these questions so they start with the word *Eliminate* is particularly effective because then you can focus on identifying and eliminating answer choices. This is a far simpler task than wrapping one's mind around the question as it was originally articulated.

Rewriting the question in the margin costs time. Experiment and see if you need to take this additional step or if simply taking the time to reframe the question mentally is sufficient. If you find that rewriting the question is beneficial, strive to rewrite the question as succinctly as possible. For example, you might write "X shared" to signify that you are seeking to eliminate shared qualities.

Let's practice with the following EXCEPT question.

Original Question

1. The passage establishes that Vida and Ted have all of the following traits in common EXCEPT:

   A. a willingness to accommodate the requests each makes of the other.

   B. a response to elements of nature.

   C. a perception of others that surfaces in humor.

   D. an awareness of what delights the other.

Try to rephrase the question in simpler terms.

_____

_____

The following are two examples of how you could rephrase this question:

- What qualities do Vida and Ted **NOT** share?

- Eliminate traits that Vida and Ted do **NOT** both have.

Now let's look at the relevant excerpts from the passage to find our answer. This type of question can be difficult because the textual evidence could be found essentially anywhere in the passage. The full passage has been reproduced and key pieces of textual evidence have been identified in bold to demonstrate this.

LITERARY NARRATIVE: This passage is adapted from the short story "Golden Glass" by Alma Villanueva (©1982 by Bilingual Press).

It was his fourteenth summer. He was thinning out, becoming angular and clumsy, but the cautiousness, the old-man seriousness he'd had as a baby, kept him contained, ageless and safe. His humor, always dry
5 and to the bone since a small child, let you know he was watching everything.

He seemed always to be at the center of his own universe, so it was no surprise to his mother to hear Ted say: "I'm building a fort and sleeping out in it all
10 summer, and I won't come in for anything, not even food. Okay?"

This had been their silent communion, the steady presence of love that flowed regularly, daily—food. The presence of his mother preparing it, his great
15 **appetite and obvious enjoyment of it**—his nose smelling everything, seeing his mother more vividly than with his eyes.

He watched her now for signs of offense, alarm, and only saw interest. "Where will you put the fort?"
20 Vida asked.

She trusted him to build well and not ruin things, but of course she had to know where.

"I'll build it by the redwoods, in the cypress tree. Okay?"

25 **"Make sure you keep your nails together and don't dig into the trees.** I'll be checking. If the trees get damaged, it'll have to come down."

The cypress was right next to the redwoods, making it seem very remote. Redwoods do that—they
30 suck up sound and time and smell like another place. So he counted the footsteps, when no one was looking, from the fort to the house. He couldn't believe it was so close; it seemed so separate, alone—especially in the dark, when the only safe way of travel seemed flight
35 (invisible at best).

Ted had seen his mother walk out to the bridge at night, looking into the water, listening to it. He knew **she loved to see the moon's reflection in the water**. She'd pointed it out to him once by a river where they camped, her face full of longing. Then, she swam out into the water, at night, **as though trying to touch the moon.** He wouldn't look at her. He sat and glared at the fire and roasted another marshmallow the way he liked it: bubbly, soft and brown (maybe six if he could get away with it). Then she'd be back, chilled and bright, and he was glad she went. Maybe I like the moon too, he thought, involuntarily, as though the thought weren't his own—but it was.

He built the ground floor directly on the earth, with a cover of old plywood, then scattered remnant rugs that he'd asked Vida to get for him. He concocted a latch and a door. He brought his sleeping bag, some pillows, a transistor radio, some clothes, and moved in for the summer.

He began to build the top floor now but he had to prune some limbs out of the way. Well, that was okay as long as he was careful. So he stacked them to one side for kindling and began to brace things in place. It felt weird going up into the tree, not as safe as his small, contained place on the ground.

Vida noticed Ted had become cheerful and would stand next to her, to her left side, talking sometimes. But she realized she mustn't face him or he'd become silent and wander away. So she stood listening, in the same even breath and heart beat she kept when she spotted the wild pheasants with their long, lush tails trailing the grape arbor, picking delicately and greedily at the unpicked grapes in the early autumn light. So sharp, so perfect, so rare to see a wild thing at peace.

Ted was taking a makeup course and one in stained glass. There, he talked and acted relaxed; no one expected any more or less. The colors of the stained glass were deep and beautiful, and special—you couldn't waste this glass. The sides were sharp, the cuts were slow and meticulous with a steady pressure. The design's plan had to be absolutely followed or the beautiful glass would go to waste, and he'd curse himself.

The stained glass was finished and he decided to place it in his fort facing the back fields. In fact, it looked like the back fields—trees and the sun in a dark sky. During the day the glass sun shimmered a beautiful yellow, the blue a much better color than the sky outside: deeper, like night.

He was so used to sleeping outside now he didn't wake up during the night, just like in the house. One night, toward the end when he'd have to move back with everyone (school was starting, frost was coming and the rains), Ted woke up to see the stained glass full of light. The little sun was a golden moon and the inside glass sky and the outside sky matched.

In a few days he'd be inside, and he wouldn't mind at all.

An example of the original question paraphrased: Eliminate traits that Vida and Ted do NOT both have.

> **A.** a willingness to accommodate the requests each makes of the other.
>
> **B.** a response to elements of nature.
>
> **C.** a perception of others that surfaces in humor.
>
> **D.** an awareness of what delights the other.

The best answer is C because neither Vida nor Ted has a perception of others that surfaces in humor. The other three answer choices are supported by the passage.

The best answer is NOT:

> A because Vida and Ted share a willingness to accommodate each other's requests. When Ted asks Vida if it's OK if he builds and moves into a fort for the summer, she doesn't respond with "offense" or "alarm," but only with "interest" (lines 18–19). Vida sets the rules Ted has to follow: "Make sure you keep your nails together and don't dig into the trees" (lines

25–26). Though Ted never directly says he'll obey, the fact that he builds and is allowed to keep the fort suggests that he does.

B because Vida and Ted share a response to elements of nature. For example, the eighth paragraph (lines 28–35) illustrates Ted's response to the redwoods, while the ninth paragraph (lines 36–48) shows Ted's and Vida's responses to the moon.

D because Vida and Ted know what delights the other. They have a "silent communion" (line 12) through food, which Vida prepares knowing Ted's "great appetite and obvious enjoyment of it" (lines 14–15). Ted, for his part, knows Vida "loved to see the moon's reflection in the water" (line 38) and that she seemed to want to "touch the moon" (lines 41–42).

The following question draws on the same passage. Practice rewording the question in simpler terms.

2. Which of the following is NOT an accurate description of the passage?

    F. A story about a teenager whose summer experiences building and occupying a fort near his house have a positive effect on his relationship with his mother

    G. A glimpse at what connects a mother and a son and what separates them as the boy tests his own limits with a summer project

    H. A look at how two characters—one grown, one young—behave when each perceives the fragility of someone or something he or she holds dear

    J. A portrait of two family members whose painful disagreements force one to seek shelter outside the home until they reach an understanding

Suggested paraphrase of the question: Eliminate accurate descriptions of the passage.

The best answer is J because nothing in the passage indicates Ted and Vida have painful disagreements that force Ted to move out. When Ted asks Vida if it's OK if he builds and moves into a fort for the summer, she doesn't respond with "offense" or "alarm," but only with "interest" (lines 18–19). The passage lists the reasons why Ted moves back into the house—"school was starting, frost was coming and the rains" (lines 87–88)—but these reasons don't include reaching an understanding with Vida. The other three answer choices are supported by the passage.

The best answer is NOT:

    F because the passage shows Ted's relationship with Vida improving after he builds and occupies the fort: "Vida noticed Ted had become cheerful and would stand next to her, to her left side, talking sometimes" (lines 61–62), which leads Vida to think of him as "a wild thing at peace" (line 69).

    G because the passage shows what connects and separates Vida and Ted and how Ted tests his limits. Ted and Vida are connected by, among other things, food (see lines 12–17) and their fondness for the moon (see lines 36–48). They're separated by physical distance, when Ted moves out into the fort, and by emotional distance, since Vida "realized she mustn't face [Ted] or he'd become silent and wander away" (lines 63–64). The passage implies in many ways that Ted is testing his limits, such as by showing him asking for privacy and privileges from Vida (see, for example, lines 9–11) and working on the upper floor of the fort (see lines 55–60).

H because the passage shows how Vida and Ted behave when each sees the fragility of someone or something held dear. To observe Ted, Vida "stood listening, in the same even breath and heart beat she kept when she spotted the wild pheasants" (lines 64–66). Ted would "curse himself" if he wasted the "beautiful glass" (lines 76–77).

The next two questions ask EXCEPT questions about the following passage.

SOCIAL SCIENCE: This passage is adapted from Richard Moe's article "Mindless Madness Called Sprawl," based on a speech he gave on November 30, 1996, in Fresno, California (©1996 by Richard Moe).

At the time he gave the speech, Moe was president of the National Trust for Historic Preservation.

Drive down any highway leading into any town in the country, and what do you see? Fast-food outlets, office parks and shopping malls rising out of vast barren plains of asphalt. Residential subdivisions
5 spreading like inkblots obliterating forests and farms in their relentless march across the landscape. Cars moving sluggishly down the broad ribbons of pavement or halting in frustrated clumps at choked intersections. You see communities drowning in a destructive, soul-
10 less, ugly mess called sprawl.

Many of us have developed a frightening form of selective blindness that allows us to pass by the appalling mess without really seeing it. We've allowed our communities to be destroyed bit by bit, and most of
15 us have shrugged off this destruction as "the price of progress."

Development that destroys communities isn't progress. It's chaos. And it isn't inevitable, it's merely easy. Too many developers follow standard formulas,
20 and too many government entities have adopted laws and policies that constitute powerful incentives for sprawl.

Why is an organization like the National Trust for Historic Preservation so concerned about sprawl?
25 We're concerned because sprawl devastates older communities, leaving historic buildings and neighborhoods underused, poorly maintained or abandoned. We've learned that we can't hope to revitalize these communities without doing something to control the sprawl that
30 keeps pushing further and further out from the center.

But our concern goes beyond that, because preservation today is about more than bricks and mortar.

There's a growing body of grim evidence to support our belief that the destruction of traditional downtowns and
35 older neighborhoods—places that people care about—is corroding the very sense of community that helps bind us together as a people and as a nation.

One form of sprawl—retail development that transforms roads into strip malls—is frequently spurred
40 on by discount retailers, many of whom are now concentrating on the construction of superstores with more than 200,000 square feet of space. In many small towns, a single new superstore may have more **retail space** than the entire downtown business district. When
45 a store like that opens, the retail center of gravity shifts away from Main Street. Downtown becomes a **ghost town.**

Sprawl's other most familiar form—spread-out residential subdivisions that "leapfrog" from the urban
50 fringe into the countryside—is driven largely by the American dream of a detached home in the middle of a grassy lawn. Developers frequently claim they can build more "affordable" housing on the edge of town— but "affordable" for whom?

55 The developer's own expenses may be less, and the home buyer may find the prices attractive—but who picks up the extra costs of fire and police protection, new roads and new utility infrastructure in these outlying areas? We all do, in the form of higher taxes for
60 needless duplication of services and infrastructure that already exist in older parts of our cities and towns.

People who say that sprawl is merely the natural product of marketplace forces at work fail to recognize that the game isn't being played on a level field. Gov-
65 ernment at every level is riddled with policies that mandate or encourage sprawl.

By prohibiting mixed uses and mandating inordinate amounts of parking and unreasonable setback requirements, **most current zoning laws make it impos-
70 sible—even illegal—to create the sort of compact**

(continued)

(continued)

walkable environment that attracts us to older neighborhoods and historic communities all over the world.
These codes are a major reason why 82 percent of all
trips in the United States are taken by car. The average
75   American household now allocates more than 18 percent of its budget to transportation expenses, most of
which are auto-related. That's more than it spends for
food and three times more than it spends for health
care.

80   Our communities **should** be shaped by choice, not
by chance. **One of the most effective ways to reach this
goal is to insist on sensible land-use planning**. The way
we zone and design our communities either opens up or
forecloses alternatives to the automobile. **Municipali-
85   ties should promote downtown housing and mixed-use
zoning that reduce the distances people must travel
between home and work.** The goal **should** be an integrated system of planning decisions and regulations
that knit communities together instead of tearing them
90   apart. We **should** demand land-use planning that
exhibits a strong bias in favor of existing communities.

The key information to support the correct answer for the next question has been identified in bold in the passage.

14. In the passage, the author answers all of the following questions EXCEPT:

   F. How long has sprawl been happening in US cities?

   G. Is development synonymous with progress?

   H. What is one major reason that people in the United States use automobiles so much?

   J. What should communities do to combat sprawl?

When a questions asks about the content covered in a passage, you can always paraphrase such a question as follows:

Paraphrase of the question: Eliminate what **IS** addressed in the passage.

Then you can come up with words or phrases to scan for in order to try to determine what content has been covered in the passage. Some scan words have been suggested for each answer choice.

Scan for the following words and phrases:

   F. Scan for: years, decades, or years such as 1970

      To determine if the passage answers the question, "How long has sprawl been happening in US cities?" you should look for words that signal the passage of time.

   G. Scan for: development, progress, advancement, improvement, or betterment

      If the passage says that development is "synonymous with progress," then the passage would likely include the word *progress* or a synonym for *progress*.

H. Scan for: automobiles, cars, roads, major reason

If the passage addresses one major reason that people in the United States use automobiles so much, the passage will need to include words that relate to this topic.

J. Scan for: should, ought, solution, problem

Solutions to a problem are typically presented either in the body paragraphs after the initial introduction of the problem or in the conclusion if the bulk of the passage has been devoted to describing the problem itself. Notice that the first sentence of the conclusion includes the word *should,* which is a clue that the conclusion will give an overview of possible solutions to the problem of urban sprawl. The conclusion, in fact, includes four instances of the word *should,* which signals that an author is providing ample guidance about what ought to be done.

The best answer is F because the passage makes no mention of how long the problem of sprawl has been happening in US cities.

The best answer is NOT:

G because the author answers this question in lines 17–18: "Development that destroys communities isn't progress. It's chaos."

H because the author argues that current zoning laws, which make construction of a "walkable environment" impossible, "are a major reason why 82 percent of all trips taken in the United States are taken by car" (lines 69–74).

J because the author offers solutions to the problem of what to do to combat sprawl in the final paragraph in the passage.

The key information to support the correct answer for the next question has been boldfaced in the passage.

15. The author states that one superstore may do all of the following EXCEPT:

Paraphrase of the question: Eliminate what one superstore may do.

A. have more retail space than an entire downtown.

B. lead to serious downtown renovations.

C. make the downtown area into a ghost town.

D. shift the center of gravity away from downtown.

Scan for: retail space, renovations, ghost town, gravity

Strategy: As you identify words in the answer choices that make those answer choices wrong, underline or circle those words. In the online test, you can highlight these words. This will help you keep track of your logic as you eliminate wrong answers. In the case of this question, you would underline descriptions of what a superstore may do.

15. The author states that one superstore may do all of the following EXCEPT:

Paraphrase of the question: Eliminate what one superstore may do.

   A. have <u>more retail space</u> than an entire downtown.

   B. lead to serious downtown renovations.

   C. make the downtown area into a <u>ghost town.</u>

   D. <u>shift the center of gravity</u> away from downtown.

The best answer is B because the passage does not support the idea that the opening of a superstore leads to downtown renovations. Rather, the passage states that, after a superstore opens in a small town, "downtown becomes a ghost town" (lines 46–47).

The best answer is NOT:

   A because the author states that "in many small towns, a single new superstore may have more retail space than the entire downtown business district" (lines 42–44).

   C because the author states that, after a superstore opens in a small town, "downtown becomes a ghost town" (lines 46–47).

   D because the author states that, when a superstore opens in a small town, "the retail center of gravity shifts away from Main Street" (lines 45–46).

LITERARY NARRATIVE: This passage is adapted from the short story "Elba" by Marly Swick (©1991 by the University of Iowa). Fran is the narrator of the story.

[18]

60   "What about you?" she snorted, pointing a Jungle Orchid fingernail at me. "You're a grandmother." We shook our heads in disbelief. I sat silently, listening to my brain catch up with my history. Forty years old and I felt as if I had just shaken hands with
65 Death. I suppose it's difficult for any woman to accept that she's a grandmother, but in the normal order of things, you have ample time to adjust to the idea. You don't get a snapshot in the mail one day from a baby girl you gave up twenty-four years ago saying,
70 Congratulations, you're a grandma!"

   "It's not fair," I said. "I don't even feel like a mother."

   "Well, here's the living proof." Mother tapped her nail against the glossy picture. "She looks just like you. Only her nose is more aristocratic."

75   "I'm going to work." My knees cracked when I stood up. "You be all right here?"

   Mother nodded, scrutinizing the picture in her lap. "You going to write to her?"

   "Of course I am," I bristled. "I may be some
80 things, but I am not rude."

   "You going to invite them here? Her and the baby?" She swiveled her eyes sideways at me.

   "I haven't thought that far," I said.

   "Well, don't put it off." She slid her eyes back to
85 the television.

3. Which of the following statements does NOT describe one of Fran's reactions to the news that she is a grandmother?

    A. She wishes she had had time to prepare for the news.

    B. She looks forward to inviting Linda Rose and her son, Blake, over for a visit.

    C. She feels suddenly older now that the label of *grandmother* applies to her.

    D. She protests that this change in her life is unfair.

Paraphrase of the question: Eliminate answers that describe Fran's reaction to the news that she is a grandmother.

Scan for: grandmother

The best answer is B because Fran's reactions to learning she's a grandmother don't include looking forward to inviting Linda Rose and Blake over for a visit. When Fran's mother asks if Fran is going to invite Linda Rose and the baby, Fran replies, "I haven't thought that far" (line 85). The remainder of the passage suggests that Fran is nervous about such a visit. The other three answer choices are supported by the passage.

The best answer is NOT:

A because Fran notes that "in the normal order of things, you have ample time to adjust to the idea" of being a grandmother (lines 67–68). In Fran's case, however, she simply gets "a snapshot in the mail one day" (line 69) letting her know she's a grandmother.

C because Fran notes that upon getting the news about being a grandmother, she feels "as if I had just shaken hands with Death" (lines 65–66).

D because in lines 72–73, Fran says being a grandmother is "not fair" because she doesn't "even feel like a mother."

NATURAL SCIENCE: This passage is adapted from the article"When Research Is a Snow Job" by Sarah Boyle (©2002 by National Wildlife).

The figure is beyond comprehension: Every year, 1,000,000,000,000,000,000,000,000 (1 septillion) snowflakes fall worldwide. As the crystals fall, they encounter different atmospheric conditions that produce 5 flakes with unique attributes. The more complex those conditions are, the more elaborate the crystals.

Kenneth Libbrecht is a physicist at the California Institute of Technology. Along with the work of scientistsat the U.S. Department of Agriculture's Agricul-10 tural Research Service (ARS), his research is uncovering new information about the magical world of snow crystals—information that has practical applicationsin such diverse areas as agriculture and the production of electricity.

15 Snow crystals are individual crystals—usually in a hexagonal form—while snowflakes are collections of two or more snow crystals. Beginning as condensed water vapor, a crystal typically grows around a nucleus of dust. Its shape depends on how the six side facets—20 or faces—grow in relation to the top and bottom facets. If they grow relatively tall, the crystal appears column-like; if the side facets are short compared to the length of the bottom and top facets, the crystal looks platelike.

Currently Libbrecht is trying to crack the problem 25 of why the crystal facets' growth varies with temperature. He believes this may have something to do with the ice surface's "quasi-liquid" layer, which affects how water molecules stick to the surface.

By manipulating the temperature and humidity 30 within an incubation chamber (and by adding an electric current or various gases at times), Libbrecht creates

(continued)

(continued)

"designer" snowflakes in his lab. Such experiments are helping him determine how crystals form.

William Wergin, a retired ARS research biologist,
35 and a colleague, Eric Erbe, were using scanning electron microscopy to look at biological problems relating to agriculture. To avoid the laborious procedure that using such equipment usually entails, the two scientists decided to freeze the tissue they were working with and
40 look at it in the frozen state.

"One day it happened to be snowing," says Wergin, "and we were looking for a specimen. We imaged some snowflakes and were very surprised to see what we did." It was the first time anyone had
45 attempted to image snow crystals with scanning electron microscopy, which provides precise detail about the crystals' shape, structural features and metamorphosed conditions (crystals often change once on the ground depending on the surrounding environment).

50 Wergin called another ARS colleague, hydrologist Albert Rango, to see if the snow crystal magnifications had any applications for his research. Rango now uses Wergin's electron microscopy data, along with microwave satellite data, in the Snowmelt Runoff
55 Model to predict the amount of water available in a winter snowpack. For western states such as Colorado, Montana, Utah and Wyoming, about 75 percent of the annual water supply comes from snowmelt. Snowmelt water is critical to crop irrigation and hydroelectric
60 power, as well as recreation and domestic water supplies, fisheries management and flood control.

Before employing the scanning electron microscopy results, the forecasted amounts of snowpack water were inaccurate whenever the size and shape of the
65 snow crystals varied much from the norm. "The more we know about crystals," notes Rango, "the easier it will be to use microwave satellite data for predictions of the snow water equivalent."

Currently, forecasts using the model are about
70 90 percent accurate. A 1980 study estimated that improving the prediction by 1 percent would save $38 million in irrigation and hydropower in the western United States.

Rango is also looking ahead at climate change pre-
75 dictions. "Following the estimates that have been made about what will happen by 2100, things are definitely warming up," he says. Temperature increases will likely result in a reduction in stream flow as overall snow accumulation decreases, winter precipitation runs
80 off as rain, and water evaporates at a quicker rate. The gap between water supply and demand will magnify even more, greatly increasing water's economic value, anticipates Rango.

Not only does the crystal research help gauge
85 snowmelt, it is also useful in predicting avalanches, designing artificial snow, and, perhaps in the near future, examining air pollution. "You can put snow in a scanning electron microscope and tell which elements are present, such as sulfur and nitrogen," says Wergin.
90 "You can then see what kind of pollution is in the area and possibly track the source."

40. The passage states that research about snow crystals has helped scientists do all of the following EXCEPT:

F. extract pollutants from snow.

G. gauge snowmelt.

H. design artificial snow.

J. predict avalanches.

The best answer is F because although the passage does state that research about snow crystals has helped scientists to identify and possibly track the source of pollutants in snow (lines 90–91), the passage does not make any connection between research about snow crystals and the extraction of pollutants from snow.

The best answer is NOT:

G because one meaning of gauge is "to measure," and the term *snowmelt* refers to water generated by a melting snowpack; therefore, when the passage states that research about snow crystals has helped scientists to "predict the amount of water available in a winter snowpack" (lines 55–56), that statement means that research about snow crystals has helped scientists to gauge (measure) the probable amount of snowmelt. Lines 84–85 specifically state that "the crystal research help[s] gauge snowmelt."

H because the passage states that, in the process of conducting research about snow crystals, physicist Kenneth Libbrecht "creates 'designer' snowflakes in his lab" (lines 31–32).

J because the passage states that research about snow crystals "is also useful in predicting avalanches" (line 85).

Common Wrong Answer Types

There are some common patterns among wrong answer choices on the ACT reading test. Being aware of these patterns may help you eliminate wrong answers. In the following subsections you will find descriptions of several common types of wrong answers you will see on the reading test.

Partly Wrong Answers

Partly wrong answers are completely wrong. For example, in the next sample question, if one of the two adjectives is not accurate for the previous passage about Fran and her mother adapted from the short story "Elba" by Marly Swick, then the whole answer choice is wrong even if one of the words in the answer choice is precise and accurate. This is why it's so important to read each word carefully. Many students tend to mentally check out after reading the first few words of an answer choice.

Additionally, just because you do not know the meaning of a word does not mean that you should pick that answer choice. Many students convince themselves that they should choose an answer choice with a word that they do not know. This logic is not sound. In the following example, if the word *arrogant* accurately described Fran's mother but the word *cruel* did not, then answer choice **F** could be eliminated. The best answer is answer choice **G** because "strong-willed" and "caring" best describe Fran's mother. She has "dragon-lady nails" (lines 23–24) in defiance of her chemotherapy. She also firmly tells Fran not to put off contacting Linda Rose, who's "been waiting for twenty-five years" (line 87) for a meeting. But Fran's mother also cares deeply about Fran and tries to reassure her by saying, "You're [Linda Rose's] flesh-and-blood mother and that's enough. That's all it'll take" (lines 96–97).

LITERARY NARRATIVE: This passage is adapted from the short story "Elba" by Marly Swick (©1991 by the University of Iowa). Fran is the narrator of the story.

Mother, who wanted to keep her, always thought of her as some wild little bird, but I knew she was a homing pigeon. I knew that at some point in her flight path, sooner or later, she would make a U-turn. A sort 5 of human boomerang. So even though I had long since stopped expecting it, I was not surprised when I walked down the gravel drive to the mailbox, which I'd painted papaya yellow to attract good news, and found the flimsy envelope with the Dallas postmark. I didn't 10 know a soul in Dallas, or Texas for that matter, but the handwriting reminded me of someone's. My own.

I walked back inside the house.

(continued)

(continued)

"Still raining?" Mother asked. She was sitting in her new electric wheelchair in front of the TV, painting
15 her fingernails a neon violet.

"Just let up," I said. "Sun's poking through. You know anyone in Dallas, Mother?"

"Not so as I recall." She dabbed at her pinky with a cottonball. Mother was vain about her hands. I was
20 used to how she looked now, but I noticed people staring in the doctor's waiting room. She had lost some weight and most of her hair to chemotherapy, and I guess people were startled to see these dragon-lady nails on a woman who looked as if she should be lying
25 in satin with some flowers on her chest.

"Why do you ask?" she said.

I opened the envelope and a picture fluttered into my lap. It was a Polaroid of a sweet-faced blond holding a newborn baby in a blue blanket. Before I
30 even read the letter I knew. I knew how those Nazis feel when suddenly, after twenty or thirty uneventful years, they are arrested walking down some sunny street in Buenos Aires. It's the shock of being found after waiting so long.

35 "What's that?" Mother said.

I wheeled her around to face me and handed her the Polaroid. She studied it for a minute and then looked up, speechless for once, waiting for me to set the tone.

40 "That's her," I said. "Her name's Linda Rose Caswell."

We looked at the picture again. The blond woman was seated on a flowered couch, her wavy hair just grazing the edge of a dime-a-dozen seascape in a cheap gilt frame.

45 Mother pointed to the envelope. "What's she say?"

I unfolded the letter, a single page neatly written.

"She says she's had my name and address for some time but wanted to wait to contact me until after the birth. The baby's name is Blake and he weighs eight
50 pounds, eight ounces, and was born by cesarean. She says they are waiting and hoping to hear back from me soon."

"That's it?"

I nodded and handed her the letter. It was short
55 and businesslike, but I could see the ghosts of all the

long letters she must have written and crumpled into the wastebasket.

"I guess that makes you a great-grandmother," I said.

60 "What about you?" she snorted, pointing a Jungle Orchid fingernail at me. "You're a grandmother." We shook our heads in disbelief. I sat silently, listening to my brain catch up with my history. Forty years old and I felt as if I had just shaken hands with
65 Death. I suppose it's difficult for any woman to accept that she's a grandmother, but in the normal order of things, you have ample time to adjust to the idea. You don't get a snapshot in the mail one day from a baby girl you gave up twenty-four years ago saying,
70 Congratulations, you're a grandma!"

"It's not fair," I said. "I don't even feel like a mother."

"Well, here's the living proof." Mother tapped her nail against the glossy picture. "She looks just like you. Only her nose is more aristocratic."

75 "I'm going to work." My knees cracked when I stood up. "You be all right here?"

Mother nodded, scrutinizing the picture in her lap. "You going to write to her?"

"Of course I am," I bristled. "I may be some
80 things, but I am not rude."

"You going to invite them here? Her and the baby?" She swiveled her eyes sideways at me.

"I haven't thought that far," I said.

"Well, don't put it off." She slid her eyes back to
85 the television. "She's been waiting twenty-five years. You worried she's going to be trouble or ask for money? For all we know, she's married to a brain surgeon with his and her Cadillacs."

"She didn't mention any husband at all," I said,
90 getting drawn into it despite myself.

"Maybe you're worried she'll be disappointed in you," she said, "You know, that she's had this big fantasy for all these years that maybe you were Grace Kelly or Margaret Mead and who could live up to that?
95 No one. But you don't have to, Fran, that's the thing. You're her flesh-and-blood mother and that's enough. That's all it'll take."

1. Fran's mother can most accurately be characterized as:

    F. arrogant and cruel.

    G. strong-willed and caring.

    H. friendly but withdrawn.

    J. loving but embittered.

Answers That Echo the Passage's Wording

Answers that echo the language of the passage do not always echo the ideas of the passage. For example, answer choice **F** in response to the next question includes many key ideas from the passage. The passage describes a system in Denmark involving four companies that are co-located, "and all of them are linked, dependent on one another for resources or energy" (lines 14–15). This all lines up with answer choice **F**; however, these descriptions are not about the system referred to as "our system" in lines 1–2. That is a different system.

Note: Paragraph numbers have been indicated in brackets, but these brackets are not found in the real test. They are provided here in order to help orient you within the context of the passage as a whole. Ellipses (. . .) indicate that paragraphs have been omitted. The explanatory notes to the right of the passage provide advice about how to navigate the text. You may wish to attempt the question on your own first before referencing the explanatory notes. Explanatory notes are not provided in the actual test.

SOCIAL SCIENCE: This passage is adapted from *Biomimicry: Innovation Inspired by Nature* by Janine M. Benyus (©1997 by Janine M. Benyus).

[1]

If anybody's growing biomass, it's us. To keep our system from collapsing on itself, industrial ecologists are attempting to build a "no-waste economy." Instead of a linear production system, which binges on virgin
5 raw materials and spews out unusable waste, they envision a web of closed loops in which a minimum of raw materials comes in the door, and very little waste escapes. The first examples of this no-waste economy are collections of companies clustered in an ecopark
10 and connected in a food chain, with each firm's waste going next door to become the other firm's raw material or fuel.

[2]

In Denmark, the town of Kalundborg has the world's most elaborate prototype of an ecopark. Four
15 companies are co-located, and all of them are linked, dependent on one another for resources or energy. The Asnaesverket Power Company pipes some of its waste

Explanatory Notes

The question asks to whom the author is referring when she says, "our system." Scan for first person plural pronouns such as *us, we,* and *our.* You may also scan for country names such as *Denmark* or phrases such as "my country."

The first paragraph includes first-person plural pronouns *us* and *our.* It opens stating, "If anybody's growing biomass, it's *us*. To keep *our* system from collapsing on itself, industrial ecologists are attempting to build a 'no-waste economy.'" This paragraph goes on to explain how a "linear production system, which binges on raw materials and spews out unusable waste," is being replaced by a more sustainable process.

Paragraph 2 explains how four companies in Denmark are relying on each other for resources and energy.

(continued)

(continued)

steam to power the engines of two companies: the Statoil Refinery and Novo Nordisk (a pharmaceutical
20 plant). Another pipeline delivers the remaining waste steam to heat thirty-five hundred homes in the town, eliminating the need for oil furnaces. The power plant also delivers its cooling water, now toasty warm, to fifty-seven ponds' worth of fish. The fish revel in the
25 warm water, and the fish farm produces 150 tons of sea trout and turbot each year.

. . .

[7]

65   Traditionally, manufacturers haven't had to worry about what happens to a product after it leaves their gates. But that is starting to change, thanks to laws now in the wings in Europe (and headed for the United States) that will require companies to take back their
70 durable goods such as refrigerators, washers, and cars at the end of their useful lives. In Germany, the take-back laws start with the initial sale. Companies must take back all their packaging or hire middlemen to do the recycling. Take-back laws mean that manufacturers
75 who have been saying, "This product can be recycled," must now say, "We recycle our products and pack-age."

Paragraph 7 describes take-back laws headed for Europe and the United States, which would require companies to take responsibility for the waste created in the production and dissemination of their goods.

Note: Denmark and Germany are countries on the continent of Europe.

12. When the author says "our system" (lines 1–2), she is most likely referring to a production system in:

F. Denmark in which four companies are co-located in one small town and are linked by their dependence on energy resources.

G. the United States that produces recyclable durable goods such as refrigerators, washers and cars.

H. the United States and Europe in which products are developed with few virgin raw materials and leave little or no waste.

J. the United States and Europe that uses too many virgin raw materials and produces too much unused waste.

Scan for: our system, country

The best answer is J because "our system" (lines 1–2) is "a linear production system, which binges on virgin raw materials and spews out unusable waste" (lines 4–5). That "our system" is the system of the United States and Europe is implied in the seventh paragraph (lines 65–77) when the author mentions that environmental reform in the form of take-back laws is coming to these two regions.

The best answer is NOT:

F because while the passage does discuss four linked, co-located Denmark companies (see lines 13–25), the phrase "our system" refers to a wasteful system found in the United States and Europe.

G because the author implies that a system that produces recyclable durable goods such as refrigerators, washers, and cars is only "headed for the United States" (lines 68–69) via take-back laws yet to be passed. In any case, the phrase "our system" refers to a wasteful system found in both the United States and Europe.

H because it's the opposite of "our system," as described in the passage.

Answers That Contradict the Passage

Answers that contradict the passage are often tempting because they remind us of the ideas of the passage. Answer choice **H** in response to the previous question sounds appealing because it contains many ideas that are represented in the passage, but answer choice **H** is the direct opposite of the correct answer. Too many virgin raw materials are being used rather than few of those materials being used.

Flipped Relationship

Often a wrong answer choice flips the relationships between characters in the literary narrative passage, between authors in the paired passages, or between scholars in the social science, humanities, or natural science passages. For example, a wrong answer to the following question might emphasize the view that Prose took when the question is asking you to choose an answer that describes Curtis's assessment. That's an easy mistake to make, especially if you are reading too rapidly.

1. Compared to Prose's assessment of *The Family of Man*, Curtis's assessment can best be described as more:

    F. critical of the photographic style *The Family of Man* represents.

    G. skeptical of *The Family of Man* for being simple, popular art.

    H. favorable toward *The Family of Man* exhibition than the book form.

    J. respectful of *The Family of Man* as an important, serious work.

Agreeable Answer Choices Are Not Always Correct

Some wrong answer choices will provide an answer that is a widely accepted belief. These answers gain your mind's recognition because the thoughts are so agreeable. Still, an agreeable idea that is not directly stated in the passage should not be chosen as an answer to an ACT reading test question.

Here is a question and some examples of agreeable answer choices. Note that this is not a real ACT question. It has been designed to show several agreeable answer choices in response to one question. Just because these answer choices align with our basic principles does not mean that they are the right answer in the absence of textual evidence to support selecting the answer.

2. Which of the following best summarizes what the author would like to see happen:

    A. Everyone should be treated fairly.

    B. Rewards should be given for model behavior.

    C. Performance should be well documented so that it can be fairly evaluated.

Your Reaction in the Situation Rather Than the Character's Reaction

Particularly in the literary narrative passages, some wrong answer choices will reflect what the test makers likely expect will be a typical reaction from readers regarding a person's behavior. For example, if your parent were haggling with vendors in a marketplace, you might be embarrassed, but if the character in the story is not embarrassed, then you should not choose an answer that describes the character as reacting with embarrassment. Students often answer the following question incorrectly because they do not focus on the character's reaction to her mother. Key portions of the text that help support the correct answer have been identified in **bold**. The explanatory notes on the right of the excerpt paraphrase the content of the passage. You may wish to attempt the question yourself before consulting the explanatory notes.

LITERARY NARRATIVE: This passage is adapted from the novel *Monkey Bridge* by Lan Cao (©1997 by Lan Cao). The story is set in the late 1970s in Virginia, where the narrator and her mother have moved from Vietnam after the fall of Saigon.

      My mother knew the vendors and the shoppers by
30 name and would take me from stall to stall to expose me to her skills. They were all addicted to each other's oddities. My mother would **feign indifference** and they would inevitably call out to her. She would heed their call and they would immediately retreat into sudden
35 apathy. They knew **my mother's slick bargaining skills**, and she, in turn, knew how to navigate with grace through their extravagant prices and rehearsed huffiness. Theirs had been a mating dance, a match of wills.

      Every morning, we drifted from vendor to vendor.
40 Tables full of shampoo and toothpaste were pocketed among vegetable stands one day and jars of herbs the next. The market was randomly organized, and only the mighty and experienced like my mother could navigate its patternless paths.

45   But with a sense of neither drama nor calamity, my mother's ability to navigate and decipher simply became undone in our new life. She preferred the improvisation of haggling to the conventional certainty of discount coupons, the primordial messiness and fish-
50 mongers' stink of the open-air market to the aroma-free order of individually wrapped fillets.

Explanatory Notes

    This excerpt conveys the playful dynamic between the mother and the vendors. It describes haggling at a market in Vietnam. The mother is portrayed as a skilled bargainer. Even if you do not know what it means to *feign* indifference, you can use context clues to determine the meaning of the word. The vendors call out to the mother after she "feigns indifference." This implies that she pretends not to pay attention to the vendors. To *feign* means "to fake." The mother is pretending that she does not wish to buy certain goods. This is part of the "mating dance" between the mother and the vendors.

> Now, a mere three and a half years or so after her
> last call to the sky market, the dreadful truth was simply
> this: we were going through life in reverse, and I was
> 55 the one who would help my mother through the hard
> scrutiny of ordinary suburban life. I would have to forgo
> the luxury of adolescent experiments and temper
> tantrums, so that I could scoop my mother out of harm's
> way and give her sanctuary. Now, when we stepped into
> 60 the exterior world, I was the one who told my mother
> what was acceptable or unacceptable behavior.

2. It can reasonably be inferred that the narrator views her mother's approach to shopping at the sky market with a mixture of:

   A. anxiety and huffiness.

   B. surprise and embarrassment.

   C. impatience and amusement.

   D. respect and nostalgia.

The best answer is D because the narrator views her mother's approach to sky market shopping with respect and nostalgia. The narrator describes her mother's "slick bargaining skills" (line 35) and calls her "mighty and experienced" (line 43). It has been "three and a half years or so after her [mother's] last call to the sky market" (lines 52–53), and the narrator is fondly looking back in order to set up a contrast with "the hard scrutiny of ordinary suburban life" (lines 55–56) in the United States through which she has to guide her mother.

The best answer is NOT:

A because there's no evidence in the passage that the narrator views her mother's approach to sky market shopping with anxiety or huffiness.

B because there's no evidence in the passage that the narrator views her mother's approach to sky market shopping with surprise or embarrassment.

C because there's no evidence in the passage that the narrator views her mother's approach to sky market shopping with impatience and amusement.

Chapter 5:
Skills and Reporting Categories

The ACT reading test focuses on three reporting categories that organize the types of questions you will answer and also make up the composite score you will receive. Each reporting category has a different number of questions associated with it on the ACT reading test. You will not see a specific number represented on each test but rather a percentage given for each category. Following is a brief description of the three reporting categories and their percentages of the total reading score:

Key Ideas and Details	55%–60%
Craft and Structure	25%–30%
Integration of Knowledge and Ideas	13%–18%

A reporting category is composed of a set of skills that you are expected to have; each question is based on one or more of these skills. For instance, in the Key Ideas and Details reporting category, the skills range from identifying the main purpose of a passage to identifying the sequence of events. Craft and Structure questions might ask about a passage's use of figurative language or rhetorical strategies, such as rhetorical questions or personal anecdotes within an argumentative passage. Integration of Knowledge and Ideas questions may ask about the function of a sentence or a paragraph within the context of the passage.

These questions may also ask how the paired passages are similar to and different from one another in terms of form and content.

A percentage of questions for each category makes up the total score you receive. What matters is the percentage of each category in the test that will weight your final score. Here is a more detailed breakdown of the skills that fall under each category:

Key Ideas and Details (55%–60%)

- Read texts closely to determine central ideas and themes.

- Summarize information and ideas accurately.

- Read closely to understand relationships and draw logical inferences and conclusions including understanding sequential, comparative, and cause-effect relationships.

Craft and Structure (25%–30%)

- Determine word and phrase meanings, analyze an author's word choice rhetorically, analyze text structure, understand authorial purpose and perspective, and analyze characters' points of view.

- Interpret authorial decisions rhetorically and differentiate between various perspectives and sources of information.

Integration of Knowledge and Ideas (13%–18%)

- Understand authors' claims, differentiate between facts and opinions, and use evidence to make connections between different texts that are related by topic.

- Analyze how authors construct arguments and evaluate reasoning and evidence from various sources.

Chapter 6:
Key Ideas and Details

Questions that fall under the Key Ideas and Details reporting category make up 55%–60% of your ACT reading test score. These questions ask about the main idea of a passage and the ways each author supports his or her central idea. These questions may ask you to find facts that are used to support a main idea, or they may ask you to draw an inference based on the details provided in the passage. These questions also ask about how authors use comparison, contrast, and shifts in order to illustrate their main point.

Main Idea Questions

The primary purpose of a passage answers the question, "Why was this passage written?" The main idea answers the question, "What is this passage about?" or "What is it saying?" In humanities, social science, and natural science passages, the main idea will typically come at the end of the introductory paragraph. The topic sentences of each body paragraph also provide support for the main idea, so reviewing these can be helpful when answering a main idea question. In this way, questions about the main idea are also questions about the choices the author made in crafting the passage.

Literary narrative passages do not follow such a common structure. The main idea of this type of passage is usually evident toward the end of a passage, so do not worry if you are confused about the point of a literary narrative passage early on. Be patient. Typically, not that much actually occurs in a literary narrative passage. If there is an omniscient narrator, the narrative perspective may comment on what occurred in the passage to try to synthesize meaning, or one character may offer a snippet of dialogue that could be interpreted to signify a meaning of the passage. Literary narrative passages are primarily concerned with depicting one scene or emphasizing the qualities of the characters. Answering the other questions should help you determine the main point of a literary narrative passage.

Strategies for Determining the Main Idea for Social Science, Humanities, or Natural Science Passages

Strategy 1: Try to Find the Thesis at the End of the Introduction and/or Conclusion

A strategy for answering a main idea question is to skim the introduction for the thesis. Though it typically comes in the final sentence of the introduction, this is not always the case. The conclusion can also provide helpful information about the main idea.

Strategy 2: Reread the Topic Sentences of the Body Paragraphs to Determine the Main Idea

If you cannot determine the main idea from the introduction and conclusion alone, take a look at topic sentences of the body paragraphs. Try to develop your own main idea before looking at the answer choices. This should help you think more inductively about the information in the passage and the main idea it supports. If you look at the answer choices right away, you may try to force the information to fit.

The topic sentences of each body paragraph should connect to and support the thesis. Therefore, rereading these topic sentences should help you develop a picture of the main idea of the passage.

Strategy 3: Temporarily Skip the Main Idea Question

If you want to skip a question temporarily and return to it later, star that question and put an arrow at the end of the set of questions corresponding to that passage. That will remind you to return to the question that you temporarily skipped before moving onto the next passage.

Practice Questions

For these main idea and primary purpose questions the entire passages have been reproduced in order to mimic your experience of answering these questions when you take the actual test. This will enable you to gain practice with skimming the title, introduction, body paragraph topic sentences, and the conclusion in order to determine the main idea of each passage.

During the test, you will have time to process the passage as you answer other questions about it. Notice that a main idea question often comes first. It is wise to temporarily skip this question and return to it after you have answered the other questions because the process of answering the other questions will deepen your understanding of the passage as a whole.

SOCIAL SCIENCE: This passage is adapted from Richard Moe's article "Mindless Madness Called Sprawl," based on a speech he gave on November 30, 1996, in Fresno, California (©1996 by Richard Moe).

At the time he gave the speech, Moe was president of the National Trust for Historic Preservation.

Drive down any highway leading into any town in the country, and what do you see? Fast-food outlets, office parks and shopping malls rising out of vast barren plains of asphalt. Residential subdivisions

5 spreading like inkblots obliterating forests and farms in their relentless march across the landscape. Cars moving sluggishly down the broad ribbons of pavement or halting in frustrated clumps at choked intersections. You see communities drowning in a destructive, soul-

10 less, ugly mess called sprawl.

Many of us have developed a frightening form of selective blindness that allows us to pass by the appalling mess without really seeing it. We've allowed our communities to be destroyed bit by bit, and most of

15 us have shrugged off this destruction as "the price of progress."

Development that destroys communities isn't progress. It's chaos. And it isn't inevitable, it's merely easy. Too many developers follow standard formulas,

20 and too many government entities have adopted laws and policies that constitute powerful incentives for sprawl.

Why is an organization like the National Trust for Historic Preservation so concerned about sprawl?

25 We're concerned because sprawl devastates older communities, leaving historic buildings and neighborhoods underused, poorly maintained or abandoned. We've learned that we can't hope to revitalize these communities without doing something to control the sprawl that

30 keeps pushing further and further out from the center.

But our concern goes beyond that, because preservation today is about more than bricks and mortar. There's a growing body of grim evidence to support our belief that the destruction of traditional downtowns and

35 older neighborhoods—places that people care about—is corroding the very sense of community that helps bind us together as a people and as a nation.

One form of sprawl—retail development that transforms roads into strip malls—is frequently spurred

40 on by discount retailers, many of whom are now concentrating on the construction of superstores with more than 200,000 square feet of space. In many small towns, a single new superstore may have more retail space than the entire downtown business district. When

45 a store like that opens, the retail center of gravity shifts away from Main Street. Downtown becomes a ghost town.

Sprawl's other most familiar form—spread-out residential subdivisions that "leapfrog" from the urban

50 fringe into the countryside—is driven largely by the American dream of a detached home in the middle of a grassy lawn. Developers frequently claim they can build more "affordable" housing on the edge of town— but "affordable" for whom?

55 The developer's own expenses may be less, and the home buyer may find the prices attractive—but who picks up the extra costs of fire and police protection, new roads and new utility infrastructure in these out-lying areas? We all do, in the form of higher taxes for

60 needless duplication of services and infrastructure that already exist in older parts of our cities and towns.

People who say that sprawl is merely the natural product of marketplace forces at work fail to recognize that the game isn't being played on a level field. Gov-

65 ernment at every level is riddled with policies that mandate or encourage sprawl.

By prohibiting mixed uses and mandating inordinate amounts of parking and unreasonable setback requirements, most current zoning laws make it impos-

70 sible—even illegal—to create the sort of compact walkable environment that attracts us to older neighborhoods and historic communities all over the world. These codes are a major reason why 82 percent of all trips in the United States are taken by car. The average

75 American household now allocates more than 18 percent of its budget to transportation expenses, most of which are auto-related. That's more than it spends for food and three times more than it spends for health care.

(continued)

(continued)

80   Our communities should be shaped by choice, not
by chance. One of the most effective ways to reach this
goal is to insist on sensible land-use planning. The way
we zone and design our communities either opens up or
forecloses alternatives to the automobile. Municipali-
85 ties should promote downtown housing and mixed-use
zoning that reduce the distances people must travel
between home and work. The goal should be an integrated system of planning decisions and regulations
that knit communities together instead of tearing them
90 apart. We should demand land-use planning that
exhibits a strong bias in favor of existing communities.

11. The principal aim of the passage can best be classified as:

A. persuasive.

B. explanatory.

C. descriptive.

D. narrative.

The best answer is A because the passage as a whole presents a cohesive argument that sprawl is both unpleasant and harmful (lines 9–10, 25–27, 33–37, 44–47, 59–61, 74–79); that its destructive effects are too often ignored (lines 11–16); that characterizations of sprawl as either inevitable or desirable are flawed (lines 17–19, 52–54, 62–66); that policies currently in place encourage sprawl to continue (lines 19–22, 66–74); and that there are a set of alternative policies that, if adopted, would resist sprawl and reduce these harmful effects (lines 80–91). The overall effect of these linked propositions is to persuade the reader that a choice must be made between a proven harm and a beneficial alternative. Moreover, the language used to describe sprawl throughout the passage is consistently negative, including, for example, the initial identification of sprawl as a "destructive, soulless, ugly mess" (lines 9–10). In contrast to these descriptions, communities without sprawl are described as "places that people care about" (line 35) or characterized as representing a "compact walkable environment" (70–71). Drawing a contrast between attractive and unattractive descriptions, as this passage does, is a common tactic of persuasive rhetoric.

The best answer is NOT:

B because although the author explains what sprawl is, the main purpose of the passage is not merely to explain what sprawl is but to argue for measures that would control sprawl and "knit communities together" (line 89).

C because although the author does describe sprawl throughout the passage, these descriptions are more often colorful and emotional than they are precise and exact. For example, sprawl is initially characterized as a "destructive, soulless mess" (lines 9–10). By contrast, communities without sprawl are described as "places that people care about" (line 35) or characterized as representing a "compact walkable environment" (lines 70–71). Drawing a contrast between attractive and unattractive descriptions, as this passage does, is a common tactic of persuasive rather than descriptive rhetoric. Therefore, the principal aim of the passage is persuasive rather than descriptive.

D because the passage does not tell a story. Rather, it informs the reader of a problem and urges the reader not only to see sprawl as a problem as well but also to take measures to solve the problem.

The following question is based on the same passage about urban sprawl.

12. Among the following quotations from the passage, the one that best summarizes what the author would like to see happen is:

F. "laws and policies that constitute powerful incentives for sprawl" (lines 20–22).

G. "the destruction of traditional downtowns" (line 34).

H. "'affordable' housing on the edge of town" (line 53).

J. "an integrated system of planning decisions and regulations" (lines 87–88).

The best answer is J because after describing the effect of sprawl on communities, and criticizing policies that encourage sprawl, the author proposes the adoption of policies that discourage sprawl, such as "downtown housing and mixed-use zoning" (lines 85–86) and goes on to explain that "the goal should be an integrated system of planning decisions and regulations that knit communities together instead of tearing them apart" (lines 87–90). Therefore, in the context of the sentence in which it appears and in the context of the entire passage, the establishment of "an integrated system of planning decisions and regulations" is clearly something that the author would like to see happen.

The best answer is NOT:

F because the full sentence in question reads "Too many developers follow standard formulas, and too many government entities have adopted laws and policies that constitute powerful incentives for sprawl" (lines 19–22). The author's opposition to the laws in question is signaled within the sentence by the assertion that "too many government entities" enact them. In the context of the sentence in which it appears and in the context of the author's criticism of sprawl throughout the passage, the enactment of "laws . . . that provide powerful incentives for sprawl" is not something that the author would like to see happen.

G because "the destruction of traditional downtowns" (line 34) is presented as an end result of sprawl and as something that "is corroding the very sense of community that helps bind us together as a people and as a nation" (lines 35–37). In the context of the sentence in which it appears and in the context of the author's criticism of sprawl throughout the passage, "the destruction of traditional downtowns" is not something that the author would like to see happen.

H because the author explains that "'affordable' housing on the edge of town" (line 53) is only more affordable for developers (line 55), and that the construction of this housing, which is a familiar form of sprawl (lines 48–50), requires "higher taxes for needless duplication of services and infrastructure" (lines 59–60). In the context of the sentence in which it appears and in the context of the author's criticism of sprawl throughout the passage, construction of this housing is not something that the author would like to see happen.

Function of Detail Questions

For a question asking about the function of a paragraph or sentence, look at least three sentences prior to the cited line or paragraph to remind yourself of the context leading up to this portion of the passage. For a question that asks about the function of a paragraph, you may also wish to review the topic sentences of the previous paragraphs or to return to the thesis of the passage. Additionally, whenever a passage presents a sensory detail such as a sight, sound, smell, or texture, expect that a question will be asked about it and take time to think about the effect of the author's incorporation of that detail when you first read it.

Practice Questions

LITERARY NARRATIVE: This passage excerpt is adapted from the novel *The Fisher King* by Paule Marshall (©2000 by Paule Marshall).

[10]

Everett Payne took his time paying his respects to the tune as written, and once that was done, he hunched
50 closer to the piano, angled his head sharply to the left, completely closed the curtain of his gaze, and with his hands commanding the length and breadth of the keyboard he unleashed a dazzling pyrotechnic of chords (you could almost see their colors), polyrhythms, seem-
55 ingly unrelated harmonies, and ideas—fresh, brash, outrageous ideas. It was an outpouring of ideas and feelings informed by his own brand of lyricism and lit from time to time by flashes of the recognizable melody. He continued to acknowledge the little simple-
60 minded tune, while at the same time furiously recasting and reinventing it in an image all his own.

[11]

A collective in-suck of breath throughout the club.

[12]

Where, Hattie wondered, did he come by the daz-zling array of ideas and wealth of feeling? What was
65 the source? It had to do, she speculated, listening intently, with the way he held his head, angled to the left like that, tilted toward both heaven and earth. His right side, his right ear directed skyward, hearing up there, in the Upper Room among the stars Mahalia sang
70 about, a new kind of music: splintered, atonal, profane, and possessing a wonderful dissonance that spoke to him, to his soul-case. For him, this was the true music of the spheres, of the maelstrom up there. When at the piano, he kept his right ear tuned to it at all times, let-
75 ting it guide him, inspire him. His other ear? It remained earthbound, trained on the bedrock that for him was Bach and the blues.

2. The main purpose of the statement in line 62 is to:

    F. illustrate the high expectations the audience initially had for Everett Payne's performance.

    G. inform the reader of the audience's reaction to Everett Payne's performance.

    H. counteract the narrator's description of Everett Payne's performance.

    J. provide proof that Everett Payne was well known to the audience.

The best answer is G because the statement in question (line 62) describes the audience's physical reaction to Everett Payne's performance. This performance is described in great detail in the preceding paragraph (lines 48–61) as being impressive enough to warrant such a reaction.

The best answer is NOT:

F because the statement in question (line 62) refers to the audience's physical reaction to the improvisational passages that Payne played after he had taken his time "paying his respects to the tune as written" (lines 48–49). This indicates that the audience reaction was not based on "initial expectations" but rather on later developments in the playing of the song "Sonny Boy Blue."

H because the statement in question (line 62) supports, rather than counteracts, the narrator's description of Payne's performance.

J because there is no mention in the passage that Payne is well known by the audience.

LITERARY NARRATIVE: This passage is adapted from the novel *Monkey Bridge* by Lan Cao (©1997 by Lan Cao). The story is set in the late 1970s in Virginia, where the narrator and her mother have moved from Vietnam after the fall of Saigon.

I discovered soon after my arrival in Virginia that everything, even the simple business of shopping the American way, unsettled my mother's nerves. From the outside, it had been an ordinary building that held no
5 promises or threats. But inside, the A & P brimmed with unexpected abundance. Metal stands overflowed with giant oranges and meticulously arranged grape-fruits. Columns of canned vegetables and fruits stood among multiple shelves as people well rehearsed to the
10 demands of modern shopping meandered through florescent aisles. I remembered the sharp chilled air against my face, the way the hydraulic door made a sucking sound as it closed behind.

My mother did not appreciate the exacting orderli-
15 ness of the A & P. She could not give in to the preci-sion of previously weighed and packaged food, the bloodlessness of beef slabs in translucent wrappers, the absence of carcasses and pigs' heads. When we were in Saigon, there were only outdoor markets. "Sky mar-
20 kets," they were called, vast, prosperous expanses in the middle of the city where barrels of live crabs and yellow carps and booths of ducks and geese would be stacked side by side with cardboard stands of expensive silk fabric. It was always noisy there—a voluptuous
25 mix of animal and human sounds. The sharp acrid smell of gutters choked by the monsoon rain. The odor of horses, partially camouflaged by the scent of guavas and bananas.

My mother knew the vendors and the shoppers by
30 name and would take me from stall to stall to expose me to her skills. They were all addicted to each other's oddities. My mother would feign indifference and they would inevitably call out to her. She would heed their call and they would immediately retreat into sudden
35 apathy. They knew my mother's slick bargaining skills, and she, in turn, knew how to navigate with grace through their extravagant prices and rehearsed huffi-ness. Theirs had been a mating dance, a match of wills.

Every morning, we drifted from vendor to vendor.
40 Tables full of shampoo and toothpaste were pocketed among vegetable stands one day and jars of herbs the next. The market was randomly organized, and only the mighty and experienced like my mother could navigate its patternless paths.

45 But with a sense of neither drama nor calamity, my mother's ability to navigate and decipher simply became undone in our new life. She preferred the improvisation of haggling to the conventional certainty of discount coupons, the primordial messiness and fish-
50 mongers' stink of the open-air market to the aroma-free order of individually wrapped fillets.

Now, a mere three and a half years or so after her last call to the sky market, the dreadful truth was simply this: we were going through life in reverse, and I was
55 the one who would help my mother through the hard scrutiny of ordinary suburban life. I would have to forgo the luxury of adolescent experiments and temper tantrums, so that I could scoop my mother out of harm's way and give her sanctuary. Now, when we stepped into
60 the exterior world, I was the one who told my mother what was acceptable or unacceptable behavior.

All children of immigrant parents have experi-enced these moments. When it first occurs, when the parent first reveals the behavior of a child, is a defining
65 moment. Of course, all children eventually watch their

(continued)

(*continued*)

parents' astonishing return to the vulnerability of childhood, but for us the process begins much earlier than
expected.

"We don't have to pay the moment we decide to
70 buy the pork. We can put as much as we want in the
cart and pay only once, at the checkout counter." It
took a few moments' hesitation for my mother to succumb to the peculiarity of my explanation.

"I can take you in this aisle," a store clerk offered
75 as she unlocked a new register to accommodate the
long line of customers. She gestured us to "come over
here" with an upturned index finger, a disdainful hook

we Vietnamese use to summon dogs. My mother did
not understand the ambiguity of American hand
80 gestures. In Vietnam, we said "Come here" to humans
differently, with our palm up and all four fingers waved
in unison—the way people over here waved goodbye.

"Even the store clerks look down on us," my
mother grumbled. This was a truth I was only begin-
85 ning to realize: it was not the enormous or momentous
event, but the gradual suggestion of irrevocable and
protracted change that threw us off balance and made
us know in no uncertain terms that we would not be
returning to the familiarity of our former lives.

8. Which of the following statements best describes the way the seventh paragraph (lines 62–68) functions in the passage as a whole?

F. It provides the first indication that making the transition to another culture has been difficult for the narrator and her mother.

G. It sets up a contrast between the narrator's view of what it takes to adjust to a new culture and what she thought it would take before she left Saigon.

H. It shows the narrator making connections between the experiences she describes elsewhere in the passage and the experiences of the children of immigrants in general.

J. It divides the passage into two parts, one focused on the narrator, the other focused on children of immigrants in general.

The best answer is H because the passage's first six paragraphs (lines 1–61) describe the narrator's disconcerting experiences shopping with her mother at the A & P, which leads into the assertion in the seventh paragraph (lines 62–68) that "all children of immigrant parents have experienced these moments" (lines 62–63) when a parent acts like a child. The seventh paragraph goes on to contend that for children of immigrant parents, the parents' return to childlike vulnerability "begins much earlier than expected" (lines 67–68).

The best answer is NOT:

F because the seventh paragraph is not the first place in which the narrator indicates that adjusting to another culture has been difficult for her and her mother. For example, the passage's opening sentence (lines 1–3) says, "I discovered soon after my arrival in Virginia that everything, even the simple business of shopping the American way, unsettled my mother's nerves."

G because neither the seventh paragraph nor the rest of the passage discusses what the narrator, before leaving Saigon, thought it would take to adjust to a new culture.

J because while the seventh paragraph does discuss children of immigrant parents in general, the narrator relates details about her experiences both before and after the seventh paragraph.

SOCIAL SCIENCE: This passage is adapted from *Biomimicry: Innovation Inspired by Nature* by Janine M. Benyus (©1997 by Janine M. Benyus).

If anybody's growing biomass, it's us. To keep our system from collapsing on itself, industrial ecologists are attempting to build a "no-waste economy." Instead of a linear production system, which binges on virgin
5 raw materials and spews out unusable waste, they envision a web of closed loops in which a minimum of raw materials comes in the door, and very little waste escapes. The first examples of this no-waste economy are collections of companies clustered in an ecopark
10 and connected in a food chain, with each firm's waste going next door to become the other firm's raw material or fuel.

In Denmark, the town of Kalundborg has the world's most elaborate prototype of an ecopark. Four
15 companies are co-located, and all of them are linked, dependent on one another for resources or energy. The Asnaesverket Power Company pipes some of its waste steam to power the engines of two companies: the Statoil Refinery and Novo Nordisk (a pharmaceutical
20 plant). Another pipeline delivers the remaining waste steam to heat thirty-five hundred homes in the town, eliminating the need for oil furnaces. The power plant also delivers its cooling water, now toasty warm, to fifty-seven ponds' worth of fish. The fish revel in the
25 warm water, and the fish farm produces 150 tons of sea trout and turbot each year.

Waste steam from the power company is used by Novo Nordisk to heat the fermentation tanks that produce insulin and enzymes. This process in turn creates
30 700,000 tons of nitrogen-rich slurry a year, which used to be dumped into the fjord. Now, Novo bequeaths it free to nearby farmers—a pipeline delivers the fertilizer to the growing plants, which are in turn harvested to feed the bacteria in the fermentation tanks.

35 Meanwhile, back at the Statoil Refinery, waste gas that used to go up a smokestack is now purified. Some is used internally as fuel, some is piped to the power company, and the rest goes to Gyproc, the wallboard market next door. The sulfur squeezed from the gas
40 during purification is loaded onto trucks and sent to Kemira, a company that produces sulfuric acid. The power company also squeezes sulfur from its emissions, but converts most of it to calcium sulfate (industrial gypsum), which it sells to Gyproc for wallboard.

45 Although Kalundborg is a cozy co-location, industries need not be geographically close to operate in a food web as long as they are connected by a mutual desire to use waste. Already, some companies are designing their processes so that any waste that falls on
50 the production-room floor is valuable and can be used by someone else. In this game of "designed offal," a process with lots of waste, as long as it's "wanted waste," may be better than one with a small amount of waste that must be landfilled or burned. As author
55 Daniel Chiras says, more companies are recognizing that "technologies that produce by-products society cannot absorb are essentially failed technologies."

So far, we've talked about recycling within a circle of companies. But what happens when a product
60 leaves the manufacturer and passes to the consumer and finally to the trash can? Right now, a product visits one of two fates at the end of its useful life. It can be buried in a landfill or incinerated, or it can be recaptured through recycling or reuse.

65 Traditionally, manufacturers haven't had to worry about what happens to a product after it leaves their gates. But that is starting to change, thanks to laws now in the wings in Europe (and headed for the United States) that will require companies to take back their
70 durable goods such as refrigerators, washers, and cars at the end of their useful lives. In Germany, the take-back laws start with the initial sale. Companies must take back all their packaging or hire middlemen to do the recycling. Take-back laws mean that manufacturers
75 who have been saying, "This product can be recycled," must now say, "We recycle our products and packaging."

When the onus shifts in this way, it's suddenly in the company's best interest to design a product that will
80 either last a long time or come apart easily for recycling or reuse. Refrigerators and cars will be assembled using easy-open snaps instead of glued-together joints, and for recyclability, each part will be made of one material instead of twenty. Even simple things, like the snack
85 bags for potato chips, will be streamlined. Today's bags, which have nine thin layers made of seven different materials, will no doubt be replaced by one material that can preserve freshness and can easily be remade into a new bag.

The next two questions are based on the preceding passage.

13. The main purpose of the second, third, and fourth paragraphs (lines 13–44) is to show:

    A. how four companies depend on each other for resources and the recycling of waste.

    B. that Denmark is one of the world's leaders in developing new sources of energy.

    C. that one town's need for energy can be eliminated through recycling.

    D. that a no-waste economy saves money.

Strategy: Read at least a few lines prior to the paragraph in question to get a sense of the context of the paragraph. You may also wish to remind yourself of the main idea of the passage by looking at the introduction and conclusion briefly.

13. The main function of the sixth paragraph (lines 58–64) in relation to the passage as a whole is most likely to provide:

    F. evidence to support Daniel Chiras's statement in lines 54–57.

    G. a transition between the two main points discussed in the passage.

    H. a conclusion to the author's discussion about a no-waste economy.

    J. a summary of the author's main argument.

Strategy: Read at least a few lines prior to the paragraph in question to get a sense of the context of the paragraph. You may also wish to remind yourself of the main idea of the passage by looking at the introduction and conclusion briefly.

The best answer is A because the second, third, and fourth paragraphs (lines 13–44) are mainly a case study of an ecopark in Kalundborg, Denmark. The three paragraphs show how the four companies in the ecopark depend on each other for resources and the recycling of waste. For example, the Asnaesverket Power Company sends waste steam to the Statoil Refinery and Novo Nordisk for use as a power source (see lines 16–20), whereas Statoil sends purified waste gas to Asnaesverket and Gyproc (see lines 35–39).

The best answer is NOT:

    B because nowhere in the three paragraphs does the author indicate Denmark is one of the world's leading developers of new sources of energy or even that the sources of energy being used by the four companies in the ecopark are new.

    C because while the passage does say that waste steam from the power company is used "to heat thirty-five hundred homes in the town, eliminating the need for oil furnaces" (lines 21–22), this isn't the same as saying that the town's need for energy can be eliminated through recycling. The town still needs energy; it just gets some of its energy needs met by an unusual source.

    D because the three paragraphs aren't clear on whether a no-waste economy saves money, so saving money can't be their main focus.

The best answer is G because in the sixth paragraph (lines 58–64), the author uses phrases such as "so far" (line 58), "but what happens" (line 59), and "right now" (line 61) to signal a transition between the two main points in the passage: "recycling within a circle of companies" (lines 58–59) and the final fate of products once they leave the manufacturer.

The best answer is NOT:

F because the sixth paragraph doesn't provide any evidence to support Daniel Chiras's statement in lines 54–57; the discussion in the sixth paragraph is on products, not by-products.

H because the sixth paragraph offers no conclusion to the author's discussion about a no-waste economy; instead, the paragraph shifts gears between two points related to the idea of a no-waste economy.

J because while the sixth paragraph does provide something of a summary ("so far . . ."), the paragraph goes on to introduce the passage's second main point, which concerns the final fate of products once they leave the manufacturer.

SOCIAL SCIENCE: This passage is adapted from Richard Moe's article "Mindless Madness Called Sprawl," based on a speech he gave on November 30, 1996, in Fresno, California (©1996 by Richard Moe).

At the time he gave the speech, Moe was president of the National Trust for Historic Preservation.

By prohibiting mixed uses and mandating inordinate amounts of parking and unreasonable setback requirements, most current zoning laws make it impos-
70 sible—even illegal—to create the sort of compact walkable environment that attracts us to older neighborhoods and historic communities all over the world. These codes are a major reason why 82 percent of all trips in the United States are taken by car. The average
75 American household now allocates more than 18 percent of its budget to transportation expenses, most of which are auto-related. That's more than it spends for food and three times more than it spends for health care.

16. The statistics cited by the author in the tenth paragraph (lines 67–79) are used to illustrate the concept that:

   F. allowing mixed uses of land leads to environmental destruction.

   G. current zoning laws help create a compact, walkable environment.

   H. land-use regulations now in effect increase the overall costs of transportation.

   J. Americans spend too much of their budgets on food and health care.

The best answer is H because the statistics in question (lines 73–76) show that a significant majority of all trips taken in the United States are taken by car, and that American families spend a significant portion of their budget on transportation expenses. The author argues that these statistics regarding automobile transportation and its costs represent the effects of land use regulations that make it impossible to construct a "compact walkable environment" (lines 69–71).

The best answer is NOT:

F because the statistics in question (lines 73–76) do not support the idea that mixed-use zoning leads to environmental destruction. Rather, they show that a significant majority of all trips taken in the United States are taken by car and that American families spend a significant portion of their budget on transportation. According to the author, the dependence on automobile transportation is a result of current zoning laws "prohibiting mixed uses" (line 67). Because this dependence on automobile transportation is associated with sprawl, which is associated with environmental destruction throughout the passage, the statistics in question support the argument that it is the prohibition of mixed-use zoning, rather than mixed-use zoning itself, that creates environmental destruction (line 67).

G because the statistics in question (lines 73–76) show that a significant majority of all trips taken in the United States are taken by car, and that American families spend a significant portion of their budget on transportation expenses. The author argues that these statistics regarding automobile transportation and its costs represent the effects of land-use regulations that make it impossible to construct a "compact walkable environment" (lines 69–71).

J because the statistics in question do not support the idea that Americans spend too much of their budgets on food and health care. Rather, the passage states that "the average American household now allocates more than 18 percent of its budget to transportation expenses" and that this is "more than it spends for food and three times more than it spends for health care" (lines 74–79). This strongly suggests that Americans spend too much on transportation, rather than suggesting that they spend too much on food and health care.

Fact Finding

Some questions essentially ask you to find facts or evidence in the passage. These questions should be fairly straightforward because you just need to locate the given information, which, in most cases, will be worded exactly as the answer choices are worded.

One challenge of these types of questions is that they are not usually accompanied by line references. Finding appropriate evidence is, therefore, the hardest part of these questions. These questions assess your ability to understand how to quickly access the right point of the passage based on your knowledge of the structure and content of the passage. For example, fact-finding questions may test if you know that the definitions of key terms should come at the beginning of a passage and a synthesis of the main ideas usually comes at the end of a passage. Identifying a key term to scan for can help you quickly locate the appropriate information needed in order to answer a fact-finding question. Usually you can determine a word to scan for by identifying the main idea in the question itself.

Keep in mind that a classic wrong answer choice for this type of question directly echoes language from the passage but does not describe the noun or noun phrase being asked about in the question. For example, in the following question, the exact language of the answer choices exists within the passage but does not describe Hattie's reaction to "Everett Payne's performance." The following answer explanations indicate what the incorrect answer choices each describe.

Practice Questions

Paragraph numbers have been indicated in brackets in this passage, but these brackets are not provided in the real test. They have been provided here in order to help orient you within the context of the passage as a whole. Some paragraphs have been omitted, which is indicated by use of ellipses.

LITERARY NARRATIVE: This passage is adapted from the novel *The Fisher King* by Paule Marshall (©2000 by Paule Marshall).

[4]

20   That was his way, Hattie knew. His body moving absentmindedly through space, his head, his thoughts on something other than his surroundings, and his eyes like a curtain he occasionally drew aside a fraction of an inch to peer out at the world. A world far less inter-
25 esting than the music inside his head.

. . .

[9]

Quickly taking their cue from him, the bassist
45 reached for his bow, the drummer for his brushes, the two of them also treating the original as if it were a serious piece of music.

[10]

Everett Payne took his time paying his respects to the tune as written, and once that was done, he hunched
50 closer to the piano, angled his head sharply to the left, completely closed the curtain of his gaze, and with his hands commanding the length and breadth of the key-board he unleashed a dazzling pyrotechnic of chords (you could almost see their colors), polyrhythms, seem-
55 ingly unrelated harmonies, and ideas—fresh, brash, outrageous ideas. It was an outpouring of ideas and feelings informed by his own brand of lyricism and lit from time to time by flashes of the recognizable melody. He continued to acknowledge the little simple-
60 minded tune, while at the same time furiously recasting and reinventing it in an image all his own.

[11]

A collective in-suck of breath throughout the club.

[12]

Where, Hattie wondered, did he come by the daz-zling array of ideas and wealth of feeling? What was
65 the source? It had to do, she speculated, listening intently, with the way he held his head, angled to the left like that, tilted toward both heaven and earth. His right side, his right ear directed skyward, hearing up there, in the Upper Room among the stars Mahalia sang
70 about, a new kind of music: splintered, atonal, profane, and possessing a wonderful dissonance that spoke to him, to his soul-case. For him, this was the true music of the spheres, of the maelstrom up there. When at the piano, he kept his right ear tuned to it at all times, let-
75 ting it guide him, inspire him. His other ear? It remained earthbound, trained on the bedrock that for him was Bach and the blues.

[13]

Again and again he took them on a joyous, terrify-ing roller coaster of a ride it seemed to Hattie, and
80 when he finally deposited them on terra firma after close to twenty minutes, everyone in Putnam Royal could only sit there as if they were in church and weren't supposed to clap. Overcome. Until finally Alvin Edwards, who lived on Decatur Street and played
85 trumpet in the school band, leaped to his feet and renamed him.

10. The narrator states that to Hattie, Everett Payne's performance was:

   F. overly slow and formal.

   G. deliberate yet absentminded.

   H. like a song played in a church.

   J. a roller coaster of a ride.

Scan for: Hattie, performance

The best answer is J because the passage states that Payne's performance seemed to Hattie "a joyous, terrifying roller coaster of a ride" (lines 78–79).

The best answer is NOT:

F because although the passage states that Payne's rendition of the song began slowly and formally (lines 41–43), the passage goes on to contrast this beginning with a lengthy improvisational section described in terms that indicate that Hattie found the performance as a whole anything but formal (lines 48–61).

G because there is no indication in the passage that Hattie considers Payne's musical performance absentminded. Instead, she describes his body "moving absentmindedly through space" as he approaches the bandstand to play (lines 20–21).

H because the narrator does not describe Payne's performance of "Sonny Boy Blue" as resembling a song played in church. Rather, she describes the audience reacting to Payne's performance "as if they were in church and weren't supposed to clap" (lines 82–83).

LITERARY NARRATIVE: This passage is adapted from the novel *The Fisher King* by Paule Marshall (©2000 by Paule Marshall).

It was nearing the end of the second set, the jazz show winding down when Hattie heard Abe Kaiser at the microphone call Everett Payne's name. Heard his name and, to her surprise, saw him slowly stand up in
5 the bullpen up front. She hadn't seen him join the other local musicians, including Shades Bowen with his tenor sax, in what was called the bullpen, which was simply a dozen or so chairs grouped near the bandstand. The young locals gathered there each Sunday evening,
10 hoping for a chance to perform. Because toward the end of the final set, the custom was to invite one or two of them to sit in with the band. They sometimes even got to choose the tune they wanted to play.

This Sunday, Everett Payne, not long out of the
15 army, was the one being invited to sit in.

---

3. The passage most strongly suggests that the second set of the jazz shows at the club is:

A. the final set.

B. much longer than the first set.

C. followed by a third set on Sunday nights.

D. performed solely by the musicians in the bullpen.

Scan for: second set

The best answer is A because the passage describes the jazz show as "winding down" (lines 1–2) near the end of the second set. This implies that the second set is the final set of the show.

The best answer is NOT:

B because there is no description in the passage of the first set or of the length of either the first or the second set.

C because the narrator mentions that the show is "winding down" (lines 1–2), which suggests that there will be no third set.

D because the passage states that the jazz show is "nearing the end of the second set" (line 1) when the musicians in the "bullpen" were called up to play. If the entire second set was performed solely by musicians from the "bullpen," then they would not be "called up to play" only toward the end of that set.

Paragraph numbers have been indicated in brackets in this passage, but these brackets are not provided in the real test. They have been provided here in order to help orient you within the context of the passage as a whole. Some paragraphs have been omitted, which is indicated by use of ellipses.

NATURAL SCIENCE: This passage is adapted from the essay "Were Dinosaurs Dumb?" by Stephen Jay Gould (©1980 by Stephen Jay Gould).

[2]

Dinosaurs have been making a strong comeback of late, in this age of "I'm OK, You're OK." Most paleon-
15 tologists are now willing to view them as energetic, active, and capable animals. The Brontosaurus that wallowed in its pond a generation ago is now running on land, while pairs of males have been seen twining their necks about each other in elaborate sexual combat
20 for access to females (much like the neck wrestling of giraffes). Modern anatomical reconstructions indicate strength and agility, and many paleontologists now believe that dinosaurs were warm blooded.

. . .

[5]

55 If behavioral complexity is one consequence of mental power, then we might expect to uncover among dinosaurs some signs of social behavior that demand coordination, cohesiveness and recognition. Indeed, we do, and it cannot be accidental that these signs were
60 overlooked when dinosaurs labored under the burden of a falsely imposed obtuseness. Multiple trackways have been uncovered, with evidence for more than twenty animals traveling together in parallel movement. Did some dinosaurs live in herds? At the Davenport Ranch
65 sauropod trackway, small footprints lie in the center and larger ones at the periphery. Could it be that some dinosaurs traveled much as some advanced herbivorous mammals do today, with large adults at the borders sheltering juveniles in the center? . . .

Explanatory Notes

Recent evidence has revealed complex dinosaur behavior. The uncovered trackways that are described here are fossils of dinosaur footprints. The passage indicates that "multiple trackways have been uncovered, with evidence for more than twenty animals traveling together in parallel movement." This is described as a complex, coordinated, and intelligent behavior designed to protect juveniles.

33. What does the passage offer as evidence that dinosaurs may have exhibited complex behaviors?

  A. Modern anatomical reconstructions indicating strength and agility

  B. Fossils revealing that dinosaurs labored under severe burdens

  C. Footprints of varying sizes indicating that dinosaurs traveled with advanced herbivorous mammals

  D. Multiple trackways in which footprint size and location indicate social order

Scan for: complex behaviors

The best answer is D because the author describes "signs of social behavior that demand coordination, cohesiveness and recognition" (lines 57–58) in dinosaurs. These include "multiple trackways . . . with evidence for more than twenty animals traveling together in parallel movement" (lines 61–63), suggesting some dinosaurs may have lived in herds, and "small footprints" in a sauropod trackway that "lie in the center" with "larger ones at the periphery" (lines 65–66), suggesting adult dinosaurs may have flanked young, immature dinosaurs during travel in order to protect them.

The best answer is NOT:

  A because while the author mentions "modern anatomical reconstructions" that "indicate strength and agility" in dinosaurs (lines 21–22), he doesn't use these as evidence of complex behaviors in dinosaurs.

  B because in lines 60–61, the author is referring to old scientific misinterpretations, not to fossil evidence, when he mentions that at one time "dinosaurs labored under the burden of a falsely imposed obtuseness."

  C because the author doesn't say that dinosaurs traveled with advanced herbivorous mammals, only that some evidence suggests that some dinosaurs may have traveled "much as some advanced herbivorous mammals do today, with large adults at the borders sheltering juveniles in the center" (lines 67–69).

NATURAL SCIENCE: This passage is adapted from the essay "Were Dinosaurs Dumb?" by Stephen Jay Gould (©1980 by Stephen Jay Gould).

The remarkable thing about dinosaurs is not that they became extinct, but that they dominated the earth
75 for so long. Dinosaurs held sway for 100 million years while mammals, all the while, lived as small animals in the interstices of their world. After 70 million years on top, we mammals have an excellent track record and good prospects for the future, but we have yet to dis-
80 play the staying power of dinosaurs.

People, on this criterion, are scarcely worth mentioning—5 million years perhaps since *Australopithecus,* a mere 50,000 for our own species, *Homo sapiens.* Try the ultimate test within our system of values: Do you
85 know anyone who would wager a substantial sum even at favorable odds on the proposition that *Homo sapiens* will last longer than *Brontosaurus*?

Explanatory Notes

These paragraphs compare how long different species have existed on or "dominated the earth." They provide information about the reign of dinosaurs, mammals, *Australopithecus,* and our species: *Homo sapiens.*

39. The author states that the best illustration of dinosaurs' capability is their dominance of the earth for:

    A. 100,000 years.

    B. 5 million years.

    C. 70 million years.

    D. 100 million years.

Scan for: million years, dinosaurs

Strategy: Scan the text for the numbers given in the answer choices. Then be sure to identify what species each number is referring to. Is it a number about dinosaurs, human beings, mammals, *Australopithecus,* or *Homo sapiens*? You are looking for how long dinosaurs dominated the Earth.

The best answer is D because the author states, "Dinosaurs held sway for 100 million years" (line 75), which the author finds "remarkable" (line 73).

The best answer is NOT:

    A because dinosaurs dominated Earth for 100 million years, not just 100,000 years.

    B because dinosaurs dominated Earth for 100 million years, not just 5 million years.

    C because dinosaurs dominated Earth for 100 million years, not just 70 million years.

SOCIAL SCIENCE: This passage is adapted from Richard Moe's article "Mindless Madness Called Sprawl," based on a speech he gave on November 30, 1996, in Fresno, California (©1996 by Richard Moe).

At the time he gave the speech, Moe was president of the National Trust for Historic Preservation.

    One form of sprawl—retail development that transforms roads into strip malls—is frequently spurred 40 on by discount retailers, many of whom are now concentrating on the construction of superstores with more than 200,000 square feet of space. In many small towns, a single new superstore may have more retail space than the entire downtown business district. When 45 a store like that opens, the retail center of gravity shifts away from Main Street. Downtown becomes a ghost town.

17. One form of sprawl the author describes is retail development that:

    A. adjoins existing downtown areas.

    B. utilizes historic buildings.

    C. turns roads into strip malls.

    D. promotes a sense of community around a superstore.

Scan for: one form of sprawl

The best answer is C because the passage refers to "retail development that transforms roads into strip malls" (lines 38–39).

The best answer is NOT:

A because the author discusses the type of sprawl that develops far away from town centers (line 30), not adjacent to them.

B because the author argues that the development of sprawl leads to the neglect of historic buildings in towns (lines 26–27), not that sprawl leads to the utilization of these buildings.

D because the author argues that the construction of superstores is part of a process whereby "the retail center of gravity shifts away from Main Street" and "downtown becomes a ghost town" (lines 45–47). This strongly suggests that superstores are associated with the destruction, rather than the promotion, of a sense of community in the towns in which they are constructed.

LITERARY NARRATIVE: This passage is adapted from the short story "Golden Glass" by Alma Villanueva (©1982 by Bilingual Press).

He watched her now for signs of offense, alarm, and only saw interest. "Where will you put the fort?"
20 Vida asked.

She trusted him to build well and not ruin things, but of course she had to know where.

"I'll build it by the redwoods, in the cypress tree. Okay?"

25 "Make sure you keep your nails together and don't dig into the trees. I'll be checking. If the trees get damaged, it'll have to come down."

The cypress was right next to the redwoods, making it seem very remote. Redwoods do that—they
30 suck up sound and time and smell like another place. So he counted the footsteps, when no one was looking, from the fort to the house. He couldn't believe it was so close; it seemed so separate, alone—especially in the dark . . .

Explanatory Notes

The key to answering this question correctly is to quickly find the paragraph in which the redwoods are mentioned. In order to give you practice with scanning the passage for the keyword *redwoods* some of the context prior to the description of the redwoods has been included here.

19. According to the passage, Ted attributes which of the following characteristics to the redwoods?

   A. They make ideal supports for a fort because they are strong and tall.

   B. They create a sense of remoteness by absorbing time and sound and by smelling like another place.

   C. They lend a feeling of danger to whatever surrounds them because they themselves are endangered.

   D. They grace their surroundings with a serenity that softens disturbing emotions like fear of the dark.

Scan for: redwoods

The best answer is B because in Ted's view, redwoods "suck up sound and time and smell like another place" (line 30), making the cypress near the redwoods seem like a "very remote" location (line 29) for the fort.

The best answer is NOT:

A because the passage doesn't say that Ted will use the redwoods as supports for the fort, only that Ted will build the fort "by the redwoods, in the cypress trees" (line 23).

C because while the passage does say that the site for the fort "seemed so separate, alone—especially in the dark, when the only safe way of travel seemed flight (invisible at best)" (lines 33–35), it doesn't say that this was because redwoods are endangered.

D because as lines 33–35 show, the redwoods increased, rather than softened, disturbing emotions such as fear of the dark.

LITERARY NARRATIVE: This passage is adapted from the short story "Elba" by Marly Swick (©1991 by the University of Iowa). Fran is the narrator of the story.

I nodded and handed her the letter. It was short
55 and businesslike, but I could see the ghosts of all the long letters she must have written and crumpled into the wastebasket.

"I guess that makes you a great-grandmother," I said.

60 "What about you?" she snorted, pointing a Jungle Orchid fingernail at me. "You're a grandmother."

We shook our heads in disbelief. I sat silently, listening to my brain catch up with my history. Forty years old and I felt as if I had just shaken hands with
65 Death. I suppose it's difficult for any woman to accept that she's a grandmother, but in the normal order of things, you have ample time to adjust to the idea. You don't get a snapshot in the mail one day from a baby girl you gave up twenty-four years ago saying,
70 Congratulations, you're a grandma!"

7. Which of the following statements most accurately expresses Fran's feelings when she hands her mother the letter from Linda Rose?

A. Fran is disappointed about getting such a short letter after so many years of no news from Linda Rose.

B. Fran welcomes the good news about the birth of her grandson, Blake.

C. Fran is offended by the letter's cold, businesslike tone.

D. Fran knows how hard it must have been for Linda Rose to write the letter.

The best answer is D because in thinking about the letter she receives from Linda Rose, Fran notes, "I could see the ghosts of all the long letters she must have written and crumpled into the wastebasket" (lines 56–58), suggesting Fran sympathizes with Linda Rose.

The best answer is NOT:

A because while Fran acknowledges that the letter was "short" (line 55), she feels sympathy, not disappointment.

B because soon after handing her mother the letter from Linda Rose, Fran comments, "Forty years old and I felt as if I had just shaken hands with Death" (lines 64–66)—hardly a happy reaction.

C because while the letter was "businesslike" (line 56), Fran sympathizes with Linda Rose and doesn't feel offended.

Paragraph numbers have been indicated in brackets in this passage, but these brackets are not provided in the real test. They have been provided here in order to help orient you within the context of the passage as a whole. Some paragraphs have been omitted.

LITERARY NARRATIVE: This passage is adapted from the short story "Elba" by Marly Swick (©1991 by the University of Iowa). Fran is the narrator of the story.

[10]

40   "That's her," I said. "Her name's Linda Rose Caswell."

We looked at the picture again. The blond woman was seated on a flowered couch, her wavy hair just grazing the edge of a dime-a-dozen seascape in a cheap gilt frame.

. . .

[21]

"Well, here's the living proof." Mother tapped her nail against the glossy picture. "She looks just like you. Only her nose is more aristocratic."

75   "I'm going to work." My knees cracked when I stood up. "You be all right here?"

Mother nodded, scrutinizing the picture in her lap. "You going to write to her?"

"Of course I am," I bristled. "I may be some
80 things, but I am not rude."

"You going to invite them here? Her and the baby?" She swiveled her eyes sideways at me.

"I haven't thought that far," I said.

"Well, don't put it off." She slid her eyes back to
85 the television. "She's been waiting twenty-five years. You worried she's going to be trouble or ask for money? For all we know, she's married to a brain surgeon with his and her Cadillacs."

"She didn't mention any husband at all," I said,
90 getting drawn into it despite myself.

---

9. A reasonable conclusion Fran and her mother draw about Linda Rose from her letter and picture is that Linda Rose:

   A. lives near the coast of Texas with her husband.

   B. enjoys and collects fine paintings.

   C. bears a strong resemblance to Fran.

   D. cares little about how she or her house looks.

Scan for: Texas, paintings, resemblance, house

The best answer is C because after looking at the picture Linda Rose sends, Fran's mother says to Fran, "She looks just like you. Only her nose is more aristocratic" (lines 75–76).

The best answer is NOT:

A because when Fran's mother suggests that Linda Rose may be "married to a brain surgeon with his and her Cadillacs" (lines 89–90), Fran replies, "She didn't mention any husband at all" (line 91) in the letter.

B because the passage's only reference to a piece of art is to the "dime-a-dozen seascape in a cheap gilt frame" (lines 44–45) behind Linda Rose in the picture.

D because there's no evidence in the passage that either the letter or the picture reveals that Linda Rose cares little about how she or her house looks.

Inferences

Drawing an inference means considering the data available and developing a general observation based on those details. For example, let's say that while you are baking brownies with your five-year-old cousin, you leave the room for a few minutes, and, when you return, your cousin's face is covered with chocolate. You would infer that your cousin ate the brownie batter when you left the room. Let's practice drawing inference with a few examples.

Example 1

You see a woman running through the airport.

What would you infer?

Inference: The woman is late for her flight.

Example 2

A man boards a train and suddenly looks nervous. He dumps the contents of his backpack out onto the seat next to him. Among his belongings, he finds a small box and opens it to reveal a diamond ring.

What would you infer?

Inference: He will be proposing soon. A wave of relief washes over him when he finds the ring.

Example 3

A humanities passage states that Abraham Lincoln was known for his honesty. The passage then describes a time when Abraham Lincoln was working at a store and accidentally gave a customer less change than she was owed.

What would you infer would happen next?

Inference: Abraham Lincoln will find the woman and give her the remaining change.

ACT reading test passages often challenge readers to draw inferences based on the provided details. Inference questions require that you scan the passage for the content from which you are drawing an inference. Inference questions typically direct you to a certain line in the text and ask you to interpret it. The answers to inference questions will not always directly echo the language of the passage itself. Typically, the answer choices will paraphrase the content of the passage instead of reflecting the content word for word.

Practice Questions

Following are some examples of inference questions from real ACT reading tests.

NATURAL SCIENCE: This passage is adapted from the article "When Research Is a Snow Job" by Sarah Boyle (©2002 by National Wildlife).

"One day it happened to be snowing," says Wergin, "and we were looking for a specimen. We imaged some snowflakes and were very surprised to see what we did." It was the first time anyone had
45 attempted to image snow crystals with scanning electron microscopy, which provides precise detail about the crystals' shape, structural features and metamorphosed conditions (crystals often change once on the ground depending on the surrounding environment).

---

33. It can reasonably be inferred that the phrase *metamorphosed conditions* (lines 47–48) refers to the:

    A. temperature and humidity at which crystals form.

    B. process by which snow crystals develop from a speck of dust and water vapor.

    C. state of snow crystals after they reach the ground.

    D. major changes in environmental conditions.

Scan for: metamorphosed

The best answer is C because the phrase in question is immediately followed by a statement in parentheses explaining that "crystals often change once on the ground depending on the surrounding environment" (lines 48–49). Because *metamorphosed* means "changed," and conditions and environment have similar meanings, we can read the parenthetical statement as clarifying the fact that "metamorphosed conditions" refers to the state of snow crystals after they reach the ground.

The best answer is NOT:

    A because the passage does not establish a direct connection between the phrase "metamorphosed conditions" (lines 47–48) and the temperature and humidity at which crystals form. Rather, the phrase in question is immediately followed by a statement in parentheses explaining that "crystals often change once on the ground depending on the surrounding environment" (lines 48–49). Read in context, the parenthetical statement, which makes no mention of the temperature and humidity at which crystals form, can be understood as defining the phrase "metamorphosed conditions."

B because the passage does not establish a direct connection between the phrase "metamorphosed conditions" (lines 47–48) and the process by which snow crystals develop from a speck of dust and water vapor. Rather, the phrase in question is immediately followed by a statement in parentheses explaining that "crystals often change once on the ground depending on the surrounding environment" (lines 48–49). Read in context, the parenthetical statement, which makes no mention of the formation of snow crystals, can be understood as defining the term "metamorphosed conditions."

D because the phrase in question (lines 47–48) is immediately followed by a statement in parentheses explaining that "crystals often change once on the ground depending on the surrounding environment" (lines 48–49). This clarification indicates that the phrase "metamorphosed conditions" refers to changes in the snowflake that occur as a result of changes in the environment and not directly to changes in the environment.

LITERARY NARRATIVE: This passage is adapted from the novel *The Fisher King* by Paule Marshall (©2000 by Paule Marshall).

Everett Payne took his time paying his respects to the tune as written, and once that was done, he hunched
50 closer to the piano, angled his head sharply to the left, completely closed the curtain of his gaze, and with his hands commanding the length and breadth of the keyboard he unleashed a dazzling pyrotechnic of chords (you could almost see their colors), polyrhythms, seem-
55 ingly unrelated harmonies, and ideas—fresh, brash, outrageous ideas. It was an outpouring of ideas and feelings informed by his own brand of lyricism and lit from time to time by flashes of the recognizable melody. He continued to acknowledge the little simple-
60 minded tune, while at the same time furiously recasting and reinventing it in an image all his own.

A collective in-suck of breath throughout the club.

Where, Hattie wondered, did he come by the daz-zling array of ideas and wealth of feeling? What was
65 the source? It had to do, she speculated, listening intently, with the way he held his head, angled to the left like that, tilted toward both heaven and earth. His right side, his right ear directed skyward, hearing up there, in the Upper Room among the stars Mahalia sang
70 about, a new kind of music: splintered, atonal, profane, and possessing a wonderful dissonance that spoke to him, to his soul-case. For him, this was the true music of the spheres, of the maelstrom up there. When at the piano, he kept his right ear tuned to it at all times, let-
75 ting it guide him, inspire him. His other ear? It remained earthbound, trained on the bedrock that for him was Bach and the blues.

---

7. It can reasonably be inferred from the passage that Hattie believed Bach and the blues were the:

A. musical influences that Everett Payne tried to avoid representing when he played piano.

B. foundation of Everett Payne's inventive piano playing.

C. true music of the heavens that inspired Everett Payne's creativity as a piano player.

D. reason why Everett Payne's piano-playing abilities limited him to Tin Pan Alley tunes.

Scan for: Bach and the blues

The best answer is B because the narrator refers to Bach and the blues as being the "bedrock" on which Payne had been trained (lines 76–77).

The best answer is NOT:

A because there is nothing in the passage to suggest that Everett did anything to avoid representing Bach and the blues when he played piano.

C because the narrator describes Bach and the blues as being "earthbound" (line 76) and "the bedrock" (line 76) of Payne's musical inspiration. Moreover, the narrator contrasts these influences, which Payne hears through "his other ear" (line 75) with "the true music of the spheres" (lines 72–73), which he hears through "his right ear directed skyward" (line 68).

D because the passage does not imply that Everett is limited to "Tin Pan Alley" tunes. Rather, the passage states that Everett "recast" and "reinvented" the Tin Pan Alley tune "Sonny Boy Blue" "in an image all his own" (lines 60–61).

Paragraph numbers have been indicated in brackets in this passage, but these brackets are not provided in the real test. They have been provided here in order to help orient you within the context of the passage as a whole. Some paragraphs have been omitted.

LITERARY NARRATIVE: This passage is adapted from the short story "Elba" by Marly Swick (©1991 by the University of Iowa). Fran is the narrator of the story.

[1]

Mother, who wanted to keep her, always thought of her as some wild little bird, but I knew she was a homing pigeon.

…

[10]

40   "That's her," I said. "Her name's Linda Rose Caswell."

[11]

We looked at the picture again. The blond woman was seated on a flowered couch, her wavy hair just grazing the edge of a dime-a-dozen seascape in a cheap gilt frame.

[12]

45   Mother pointed to the envelope. "What's she say?"

[13]

I unfolded the letter, a single page neatly written.

[14]

"She says she's had my name and address for some time but wanted to wait to contact me until after the birth. The baby's name is Blake and he weighs eight
50   pounds, eight ounces, and was born by cesarean. She says they are waiting and hoping to hear back from me soon."

[15]

"That's it?"

[16]

I nodded and handed her the letter. It was short
55   and businesslike, but I could see the ghosts of all the long letters she must have written and crumpled into the wastebasket.

[17]

"I guess that makes you a great-grandmother," I said.

[18]

60   "What about you?" she snorted, pointing a Jungle Orchid fingernail at me. "You're a grandmother." We shook our heads in disbelief. I sat silently, listening to my brain catch up with my history. Forty years old and I felt as if I had just shaken hands with
65   Death. I suppose it's difficult for any woman to accept that she's a grandmother, but in the normal order of things, you have ample time to adjust to the idea. You don't get a snapshot in the mail one day from a baby girl you gave up twenty-four years ago saying,
70   Congratulations, you're a grandma!"

[19]

"It's not fair," I said. "I don't even feel like a mother."

[20]

"Well, here's the living proof." Mother tapped her nail against the glossy picture. "She looks just like you. Only her nose is more aristocratic."

8. It can logically be inferred from the passage that the reason it has been a long time since Fran and Linda Rose have seen each other is because:

F. Linda Rose left home to get married.

G. arguments between Fran and Linda Rose drove Linda Rose away.

H. Linda Rose chose to live with her father.

J. as a child Linda Rose was adopted by another family

Scan for: Linda Rose

The best answer is J because details in the passage suggest Fran had put Linda Rose up for adoption a quarter century ago. Fran says her mother had "wanted to keep" Linda Rose (line 1), which implies that Fran didn't. More directly, Fran notes upon receiving the letter and photograph from Linda Rose that a person doesn't usually "get a snapshot in the mail one day from a baby girl you gave up twenty-four years ago saying, 'Congratulations, you're a grandma!'" (lines 69–71).

The best answer is NOT:

F because there's no evidence in the passage that the reason it's been such a long time since Fran and Linda Rose have seen each other is that Linda Rose left home to get married.

G because there's no evidence in the passage that the reason it's been such a long time since Fran and Linda Rose have seen each other is that arguments between the two drove Linda Rose away.

H because there's no evidence in the passage that the reason it's been such a long time since Fran and Linda Rose have seen each other is that Linda Rose chose to live with her father.

NATURAL SCIENCE: This passage is adapted from the essay "Were Dinosaurs Dumb?" by Stephen Jay Gould (©1980 by Stephen Jay Gould).

Dinosaurs have been making a strong comeback of late, in this age of "I'm OK, You're OK." Most paleon-
15 tologists are now willing to view them as energetic, active, and capable animals. The *Brontosaurus* that wallowed in its pond a generation ago is now running on land, while pairs of males have been seen twining their necks about each other in elaborate sexual combat
20 for access to females (much like the neck wrestling of giraffes). Modern anatomical reconstructions indicate strength and agility, and many paleontologists now believe that dinosaurs were warm blooded . . . .

The idea of warm-blooded dinosaurs has captured
25 the public imagination and received a torrent of press coverage.

Explanatory Notes

This passage explains how the perception of dinosaurs such as the *Brontosaurus* has changed recently. Notice that several words that signal change are used including the following: *now, ago,* and *modern.*

31. In the context of the passage as a whole, it is most reasonable to infer that the phrase "the *Brontosaurus* that wallowed in its pond a generation ago is now running on land" (lines 16–18) means that:

A. the *Brontosaurus* evolved from living in the water to living on land.

B. scientists' understanding of the *Brontosaurus*'s lifestyle has changed within the last generation.

C. standard illustrations of dinosaurs still inaccurately depict their lifestyles.

D. the *Brontosaurus* eventually learned to hold up its own weight on land.

The best answer is B because lines 16–18 are introduced by the author's claim that "most paleontologists are now willing to view [dinosaurs] as energetic, active, and capable animals" (lines 14–16) despite earlier theories that dinosaurs were stupid, slow, and clumsy. It's reasonable, then, that what follows in lines 16–18 is a description of scientists' changing understanding of *Brontosaurus* lifestyle.

The best answer is NOT:

A because the words *a generation ago* and *now* in lines 16–18 indicate that the author is describing the present and recent past, not the time when *Brontosaurus* lived.

C because there's no evidence in the passage that the author believes standard illustrations of dinosaurs still inaccurately depict their lifestyles. "The standard illustration" of *Brontosaurus* mentioned in line 10 refers to an outdated image based on earlier scientific beliefs. Lines 16–22 (especially the reference to "modern anatomical reconstructions") suggest that illustrations have changed along with scientists' beliefs about dinosaurs.

D because the words *a generation ago* and *now* in lines 16–18 indicate that the author is describing the present and recent past, not the time when *Brontosaurus* lived.

LITERARY NARRATIVE: This passage is adapted from the novel *Monkey Bridge* by Lan Cao (©1997 by Lan Cao). The story is set in the late 1970s in Virginia, where the narrator and her mother have moved from Vietnam after the fall of Saigon.

[3]

My mother knew the vendors and the shoppers by
30 name and would take me from stall to stall to expose
me to her skills. They were all addicted to each other's
oddities. My mother would feign indifference and they
would inevitably call out to her. She would heed their
call and they would immediately retreat into sudden
35 apathy. They knew my mother's slick bargaining skills,
and she, in turn, knew how to navigate with grace
through their extravagant prices and rehearsed huffiness. Theirs had been a mating dance, a match of wills.

[4]

Every morning, we drifted from vendor to vendor.
40 Tables full of shampoo and toothpaste were pocketed
among vegetable stands one day and jars of herbs the
next. The market was randomly organized, and only the
mighty and experienced like my mother could navigate
its patternless paths.

45   But with a sense of neither drama nor calamity,
my mother's ability to navigate and decipher simply
became undone in our new life. She preferred the
improvisation of haggling to the conventional certainty
of discount coupons, the primordial messiness and fish-
50 mongers' stink of the open-air market to the aroma-free
order of individually wrapped fillets.

2. It can reasonably be inferred from the passage as a whole that the narrator views her mother's bargaining skills as ones that were developed:

    F. to a degree that was exceptional even in Saigon but that have no apparent outlet in the United States.

    G. to a degree that is commonplace in the competitive sky markets but that is exceptional in the United States.

    H. to a lesser degree than those of most sky market shoppers in Saigon but to a degree that seems exceptional in the United States.

    J. solidly and irrevocably over years of shopping in Saigon, putting her at an advantage in the challenging circumstances of her adopted home.

Scan for: bargaining, mother

The best answer is F because in Saigon, vendors recognized the "slick bargaining skills" (line 35) of the narrator's mother, who could "navigate with grace through their extravagant prices and rehearsed huffiness" (lines 36–38) and who was "mighty and experienced" (line 43). The narrator says, however, that "my mother's ability to navigate and decipher simply became undone in our new life" (lines 46–47) in the United States.

The best answer is NOT:

    G because the mother's skills were not commonplace in the Saigon sky markets, nor were her skills exceptional in the United States.

    H because the mother's skills were not below average in the Saigon sky markets, nor were her skills exceptional in the United States.

    J because the mother's skills didn't give her an advantage in the United States, her adopted home; in fact, they were of no use there.

The following question draws on the same passage.

3. It can reasonably be inferred from the passage that when shopping at the sky market the narrator's mother viewed which of the following as something disagreeable to overcome?

    A. The primordial messiness

    B. The extravagant prices

    C. The odors of animals

    D. The other shoppers

Scan for: sky market

The best answer is B because the narrator says that in dealing with the Saigon sky market vendors, her mother "knew how to navigate with grace through their extravagant prices and rehearsed huffiness" (lines 36–38).

The best answer is NOT:

A because the narrator says that her mother preferred "the primordial messiness and fishmongers' stink of the open-air market to the aroma-free order of individually wrapped fillets" (lines 49–51) found at the A & P.

C because the narrator says that her mother preferred "the primordial messiness and fishmongers' stink of the open-air market to the aroma-free order of individually wrapped fillets" (lines 49–51) found at the A & P.

D because while the narrator's mother "knew . . . the shoppers by name" (lines 29–30), there's no evidence in the passage that she found her fellow sky market shoppers to be something disagreeable to overcome.

NATURAL SCIENCE: This passage is adapted from *An Anthropologist on Mars* by Oliver Sacks (©1995 by Oliver Sacks). Johann Wolfgang von Goethe was an eighteenth-century German poet and philosopher; Hermann von Helmholtz was a nineteenth-century scientist and philosopher.

. . .

30   Helmholtz's great contemporary, James Clerk Maxwell, had also been fascinated by the mystery of color vision from his student days. He formalized the notions of primary colors and color mixing by the invention of a color top (the colors of which fused,
35   when it was spun, to yield a sensation of grey), and a graphic representation with three axes, a color triangle, which showed how any color could be created by different mixtures of the three primary colors. These prepared the way for his most spectacular demonstration,
40   the demonstration in 1861 that color photography was possible, despite the fact that photographic emulsions were themselves black and white. He did this by photographing a colored bow three times, through red, green, and violet filters. Having obtained three "color-
45   separation" images, as he called them, he now brought these together by superimposing them upon a screen, projecting each image through its corresponding filter (the image taken through the red filter was projected with red light, and so on). Suddenly, the bow burst
50   forth in full color. Clerk Maxwell wondered if this was how colors were perceived in the brain, by the addition of color-separation images or their neural correlates [what functions in the brain as a color-separation image], as in his magic-lantern demonstrations.
55   Clerk Maxwell himself was acutely aware of the drawback of this additive process: color photography had no way of "discounting the illuminant," and its colors changed helplessly with changing wavelengths of light.

---

32. It can be inferred that in Clerk Maxwell's 1861 demonstration a color image would not have been produced from black-and-white film emulsions without the use of color:

F. filters.

G. triangles.

H. tops.

J. slides.

Scan for: color, emulsion

The best answer is F because Clerk Maxwell showed how color photography was possible despite black-and-white emulsions "by photographing a colored bow three times, through red, green, and violet filters" (lines 42–44), then superimposing the "three 'color-separation' images" (lines 44–45) on a screen, "projecting each image through its corresponding filter" (line 47), which allowed the bow to "burst forth in full color" (lines 49–50).

The best answer is NOT:

G because the passage doesn't indicate that Clerk Maxwell's color triangle—"a graphic representation with three axes" that "showed how any color could be created by different mixtures of the three primary colors" (lines 35–38)—had any role in his 1861 demonstration.

H because the passage doesn't indicate that Clerk Maxwell's color top—which helped formalize "the notions of primary colors and color mixing" (lines 32–33)—had any role in his 1861 demonstration.

J because the passage doesn't mention color slides as being part of Clerk Maxwell's 1861 demonstration. Clerk Maxwell used "three 'color-separation' images" and three color filters, but these aren't the same as color slides.

Paraphrasing Complex Ideas

Some questions will ask you to essentially paraphrase a dense portion of a passage. Fortunately, these questions often direct you to the exact lines that need to be paraphrased.

Strategy: If you are finding it difficult to understand a dense sentence, consider ignoring or crossing out parts of the sentence. Try to focus on the subjects and verbs. Cut out modifiers such as adjectives, adverbs, prepositional phrases, and relative clauses. Relative clauses begin with relative pronouns such as *who, whose, where, when, which,* and *that.* These modifiers can distract you from the most basic meaning of a sentence.

Original

The widely held tenet of democratic faith that elected officials, as opposed to bureaucrats or the judiciary are popularly selected and democratically responsive is largely a myth which gives a useful legitimacy to a system. In fact, however, far from democratic control, the two most important forces in political life are indifference and its direct byproduct, inertia.

Edits

The ~~widely held~~ tenet ~~of democratic faith~~ that elected officials, ~~as opposed to bureaucrats or the judiciary~~ are popularly selected and democratically responsive is largely a myth ~~which gives a useful legitimacy to a system. In fact, however, far from democratic control,~~ the two most important forces in political life are indifference and ~~its direct byproduct,~~ inertia.

Simplified Version

The tenet that elected officials are popularly selected and democratically responsive is largely a myth. The two most important forces in political life are indifference and inertia.

Paraphrase

Elected official are not chosen by the people, and they do not care about voters. Apathy and laziness are the most important forces in politics.

Compare and Contrast

Some questions on the ACT reading test assess your ability to read closely to understand relationships and draw logical inferences and conclusions including understanding sequential, comparative, and cause-effect relationships. Frequently the ACT reading test questions ask about similarities and differences among the nouns described in a passage. Those nouns may be people, place, things, or concepts.

Similarities

The following words signal similarities.

Elaboration

additionally	essentially	in other words	such as
also	first	in conclusion	moreover
as well as	furthermore	in summary	
as illustrated by	for example	in essence	
as shown by	for instance	second	

Comparison

likewise	share	linked	regular
in the same way	both	tied	consistent
similarly	connected	joined	

SOCIAL SCIENCE: *Biomimicry: Innovation Inspired by Nature* by Janine M. Benyus (©1997 by Janine M. Benyus).

[2]

In Denmark, the town of Kalundborg has the world's most elaborate prototype of an ecopark. Four
15 companies are co-located, and all of them are linked, dependent on one another for resources or energy. The Asnaesverket Power Company pipes some of its waste steam to power the engines of two companies: the Statoil Refinery and Novo Nordisk (a pharmaceutical
20 plant). Another pipeline delivers the remaining waste steam to heat thirty-five hundred homes in the town, eliminating the need for oil furnaces. The power plant also delivers its cooling water, now toasty warm, to fifty-seven ponds' worth of fish. The fish revel in the
25 warm water, and the fish farm produces 150 tons of sea trout and turbot each year.

Explanatory Notes

The second and third paragraphs provide details about one example of an ecopark.

The fifth paragraph describes what types of industries pursue participation in a food web. Some statements in this paragraph refer to all industries that participate in a food web. Other sentences use words to signal that a subset of the industries has a certain property. For example, the passage explains that "**some** companies are designing their processes so that any waste that falls on the production-room floor is valuable and can be used by someone else." The use of the word *some* here indicates that not *all* industries involved in a food web follow this procedure and philosophy.

[3]

Waste steam from the power company is used by
Novo Nordisk to heat the fermentation tanks that produce insulin and enzymes. This process in turn creates
30 700,000 tons of nitrogen-rich slurry a year, which used
to be dumped into the fjord. Now, Novo bequeaths it
free to nearby farmers—a pipeline delivers the fertilizer
to the growing plants, which are in turn harvested to
feed the bacteria in the fermentation tanks.

...

[5]

45   Although Kalundborg is a cozy co-location, industries need not be geographically close to operate in a
food web as long as they are connected by a mutual
desire to use waste. Already, some companies are
designing their processes so that any waste that falls on
50 the production-room floor is valuable and can be used
by someone else. In this game of "designed offal," a
process with lots of waste, as long as it's "wanted
waste," may be better than one with a small amount of
waste that must be landfilled or burned. As author
55 Daniel Chiras says, more companies are recognizing
that "technologies that produce by-products society
cannot absorb are essentially failed technologies."

18. According to the passage, the common element for companies that want to be part of a food web is their mutual interest in:

F. relocating their operations to a common geographic area in Europe.

G. providing industrial waste to private homes and farming operations.

H. eliminating the need for raw materials.

J. using industrial waste as raw materials.

The best answer is J because lines 45–48 state that "industries need not be geographically close to operate in a food web as long as they are connected by a mutual desire to use waste."

The best answer is NOT:

F because, as the above quotation shows, companies need not relocate their operations to a common geographic area in Europe to be part of a food web.

G because while the Asnaesverket Power Company and Novo Nordisk do provide industrial waste to private homes and farming operations (see lines 16–34), the passage doesn't say that all companies that want to be part of a food web have to do this.

H because food webs, as described in the passage, don't eliminate the need for raw materials. Instead, one company's waste becomes another company's raw material, as when sulfur removed from Statoil Refinery's waste gas during purification is sent to Kemira for use in sulfuric acid production (see lines 35–41). Notice also that the word *eliminate* is an extreme word.

Differences

Some questions ask you about the differences between concepts, people, places, or things within the passage. As you read a passage, try to take note of differences that are established. For example, often science articles present the views of multiple scientists, some of whom agree with one another and others who disagree. The following words and phrases signal differences.

Contrast Words

alternatively	in comparison	or	though
alternately	in spite of	nevertheless	whereas
although	however	rather	while
but	on the one hand	surprisingly	yet
despite	on the other hand	still	
even though	otherwise		

Practice Questions

SOCIAL SCIENCE: This passage is adapted from Richard Moe's article "Mindless Madness Called Sprawl," based on a speech he gave on November 30, 1996, in Fresno, California (©1996 by Richard Moe).

At the time he gave the speech, Moe was president of the National Trust for Historic Preservation.

[1]

Drive down any highway leading into any town in the country, and what do you see? Fast-food outlets, office parks and shopping malls rising out of vast barren plains of asphalt. Residential subdivisions
5 spreading like inkblots obliterating forests and farms in their relentless march across the landscape. Cars moving sluggishly down the broad ribbons of pavement or halting in frustrated clumps at choked intersections. You see communities drowning in a destructive, soul-
10 less, ugly mess called sprawl.

...

[11]

80 Our communities should be shaped by choice, not by chance. One of the most effective ways to reach this goal is to insist on sensible land-use planning. The way we zone and design our communities either opens up or forecloses alternatives to the automobile. Municipali-
85 ties should promote downtown housing and mixed-use zoning that reduce the distances people must travel between home and work. The goal should be an integrated system of planning decisions and regulations that knit communities together instead of tearing them
90 apart. We should demand land-use planning that exhibits a strong bias in favor of existing communities.

13. The last paragraph differs from the first paragraph in that in the last paragraph the author:

   A. asks a question and then answers it.

   B. uses more statistics to support his arguments.

   C. incorporates more emotional language.

   D. offers solutions rather than stating a problem.

The best answer is D because in the first paragraph the author defines sprawl as a problem, and in the last paragraph, the author offers possible solutions to this problem, including "sensible land-use planning" (line 82), "mixed-use zoning" (lines 85–86), and "an integrated system of planning decisions and regulations" (lines 87–88).

The best answer is NOT:

A because the author does not ask a question at any point in the final paragraph. Rather, the author offers solutions to the problem explained throughout the passage.

B because the author mentions no specific statistics in the final paragraph.

C because the final paragraph does not incorporate more emotional language than the first. If anything, the opposite may be true. In the first paragraph, the author uses emotionally loaded language to encourage the reader to agree that the "destructive, soulless, ugly mess called sprawl" (lines 9–10) is a serious problem. By contrast, the last paragraph, while arguing that "our communities should be shaped by choice, not by chance" (lines 80–81), uses more precise and less emotional language to describe possible solutions to the problem of sprawl, such as "an integrated system of planning decisions and regulations" (lines 87–88). This less emotional language encourages the reader to agree that these solutions may be effective.

LITERARY NARRATIVE: This passage is adapted from the short story "Golden Glass" by Alma Villanueva (©1982 by Bilingual Press).

It was his fourteenth summer. He was thinning out, becoming angular and clumsy, but the cautiousness, the old-man seriousness he'd had as a baby, kept him contained, ageless and safe. His humor, always dry
5 and to the bone since a small child, let you know he was watching everything.

He seemed always to be at the center of his own universe, so it was no surprise to his mother to hear Ted say: "I'm building a fort and sleeping out in it all
10 summer, and I won't come in for anything, not even food. Okay?"

Explanatory Notes

As is often the case in a literary narrative passage, the introductory paragraph offers initial insights about one of the main characters. In this case, the first paragraph describes a fourteen-year-old boy named Ted as he matures into adulthood. This passage opens by focusing on Ted's changing physical appearance, stating "He was thinning out, becoming angular and clumsy." Ted's personality, however, is described as remaining consistent throughout his life. These enduring qualities include "his humor, always dry" and his "old-man seriousness he'd had as a baby."

5. Which of the following best describes the difference between Ted as a little boy and Ted at the time he builds and occupies the fort?

    A. By the time Ted builds the fort he has lost the lighthearted manner he had as a child and has become more of a brooder who avoids the company of others.

    B. As a teenager Ted is physically clumsier and more angular than he was as a child, but he retains the humor, cautiousness, and seriousness that distinguished him at an early age.

    C. As a child Ted was constantly observing others for indications of how he should behave, but as a teenager he looks more to nature for guidance.

    D. As a child Ted was outgoing in a way that appealed to adults, but as a teenager he was introspective in a way that alarmed them.

The best answer is B because the passage describes the teenage Ted as "thinning out, becoming angular and clumsy" and retaining "the cautiousness, the old-man seriousness he'd had as a baby" (lines 1–3) as well as his sense of humor, "always dry and to the bone since a small child" (lines 4–5).

The best answer is NOT:

A because Ted had always been cautious and serious, not lighthearted, and because Ted "had become cheerful" (line 61) and more talkative, not brooding and isolated, since moving into the fort.

C because while the passage says Ted even as a small child "let you know he was watching everything" (lines 5–6), it doesn't say that he watched others for indications of how he should behave or that as a teenager he looked to nature for such guidance.

D because Ted was cautious and serious, not outgoing, as a child, and because no adult, including Vida, is alarmed by Ted's introspection as a teenager. When Ted watches Vida "for signs of offense, alarm," he "only saw interest" in his plan for building and moving into a fort for the summer (lines 18–19).

LITERARY NARRATIVE: This passage is adapted from the short story "Golden Glass" by Alma Villanueva (©1982 by Bilingual Press).

He built the ground floor directly on the earth,
50 with a cover of old plywood, then scattered remnant
rugs that he'd asked Vida to get for him. He concocted
a latch and a door. He brought his sleeping bag, some
pillows, a transistor radio, some clothes, and moved in
for the summer.

55   He began to build the top floor now but he had to
prune some limbs out of the way. Well, that was okay
as long as he was careful. So he stacked them to one
side for kindling and began to brace things in place. It
felt weird going up into the tree, not as safe as his
60 small, contained place on the ground.

Explanatory Notes

This passage describes a teenage boy building a fort. The next question asks you to compare how Ted views "going up into the tree" to how he views being on the ground. Notice that the passage describes "going up into the tree" as "not as safe."

10. Ted felt that in comparison to the ground floor of the fort, going up into the tree to build the top floor seemed:

F. safer because the top floor was less accessible to intruders.

G. safer because the branches provided him with a sense of privacy.

H. less safe because the place felt bigger and more exposed.

J. less safe because the top floor was made of cypress instead of redwood.

Scan words: tree, floor

The best answer is H because lines 58–60 state, "It felt weird going up into the tree, not as safe as his small, contained place on the ground."

The best answer is NOT:

F because Ted feels less, not more, safe going up into the tree to build the top floor.

G because Ted feels less, not more, safe going up into the tree to build the top floor.

J because there's no evidence in the passage that Ted built any of the fort from redwood or cypress; the only building material mentioned by name is plywood (see lines 49–51).

LITERARY NARRATIVE: This passage is adapted from the novel *Monkey Bridge* by Lan Cao (©1997 by Lan Cao). The story is set in the late 1970s in Virginia, where the narrator and her mother have moved from Vietnam after the fall of Saigon.

[6]

Now, a mere three and a half years or so after her last call to the sky market, the dreadful truth was simply this: we were going through life in reverse, and I was
55 the one who would help my mother through the hard scrutiny of ordinary suburban life. I would have to forgo the luxury of adolescent experiments and temper tantrums, so that I could scoop my mother out of harm's way and give her sanctuary. Now, when we stepped into
60 the exterior world, I was the one who told my mother what was acceptable or unacceptable behavior.

[7]

All children of immigrant parents have experienced these moments. When it first occurs, when the parent first reveals the behavior of a child, is a defining
65 moment. Of course, all children eventually watch their parents' astonishing return to the vulnerability of childhood, but for us the process begins much earlier than expected.

---

47. The distinction the narrator makes between children in general and the children of immigrants in particular is that:

A. children of immigrants inevitably have to watch their parents return to a state of childlike vulnerability while other children may not.

B. the inevitable shift from being the vulnerable child to protecting the vulnerable parent takes place sooner for children of immigrants than for other children.

C. children of immigrants anticipate assuming the role of protectors of their parents, while other children are taken by surprise by the inevitable responsibility.

D. children of immigrants are misunderstood by their parents to a greater degree than are other children.

The best answer is B because the narrator says, "Of course, all children eventually watch their parents' astonishing return to the vulnerability of childhood, but for us [children of immigrant parents] the process begins much earlier than expected" (lines 65–68). Having experienced this shift, the narrator took on adult responsibilities so that she "could scoop [her] mother out of harm's way and give her sanctuary" (lines 58–59) in the United States.

The best answer is NOT:

A because the narrator says that "all children," not just children of immigrants, "eventually watch their parents' astonishing return to the vulnerability of childhood."

C because the narrator contends that children of immigrants are taken by surprise when "the process" of parents reverting to childlike vulnerability "begins much earlier than expected."

D because the passage provides no evidence that children of immigrants are misunderstood by their parents to a greater degree than are other children.

NATURAL SCIENCE: This passage is adapted from the article "When Research Is a Snow Job" by Sarah Boyle (©2002 by National Wildlife).

15   Snow crystals are individual crystals—usually in a hexagonal form—while snowflakes are collections of two or more snow crystals. Beginning as condensed water vapor, a crystal typically grows around a nucleus of dust. Its shape depends on how the six side facets—
20 or faces—grow in relation to the top and bottom facets. If they grow relatively tall, the crystal appears column-like; if the side facets are short compared to the length of the bottom and top facets, the crystal looks platelike.

---

37. The passage states that snowflakes differ from snow crystals in that snowflakes:

   A. grow around a nucleus of dust.

   B. combine to form snow crystals.

   C. grow in relation to top and bottom facets.

   D. are composed of more than one crystal.

Scan for: crystals

The best answer is D because the passage states that "snowflakes are collections of two or more snow crystals" (lines 16–17).

The best answer is NOT:

A because the passage does not state that snowflakes grow around a nucleus of dust. Rather, the passage states that "snowflakes are collections of two or more snow crystals" (lines 16–17) and that a crystal "typically grows around a nucleus of dust" (lines 18–19).

B because the snowflakes do not combine to form snow crystals. Rather, according to the passage, the opposite is true: snow crystals combine to form snowflakes (lines 16–17).

C because although the passage states that the shape of a snow crystal "depends on how the six side facets—or faces—grow in relation to the top and bottom facets" (lines 19–20), there is no mention of any direct relation between top and bottom facets and the growth of snowflakes.

Relationships between Persons, Places, Things and Concepts

The following questions ask about relationships that do not perfectly fall under the categories of similarities, differences, or cause and effect.

Practice Questions

NATURAL SCIENCE: This passage is adapted from the essay "Were Dinosaurs Dumb?" by Stephen Jay Gould (©1980 by Stephen Jay Gould).

Dinosaurs have been making a strong comeback of late, in this age of "I'm OK, You're OK." Most paleon-
15 tologists are now willing to view them as energetic, active, and capable animals. The *Brontosaurus* that wallowed in its pond a generation ago is now running on land, while pairs of males have been seen twining their necks about each other in elaborate sexual combat
20 for access to females (much like the neck wrestling of giraffes). Modern anatomical reconstructions indicate strength and agility, and many paleontologists now believe that dinosaurs were warm blooded. . . .

The idea of warm-blooded dinosaurs has captured
25 the public imagination and received a torrent of press coverage. Yet another vindication of dinosaurian capa- bility has received very little attention, although I regard it as equally significant. I refer to the issue of stupidity and its correlation with size. The revisionist
30 interpretation, which I support . . . does not enshrine dinosaurs as paragons of intellect, but it does maintain that they were not small brained after all. They had the "right-sized" brains for reptiles of their body size.

Explanatory Notes

In this paragraph, Gould explains how paleontologists' views of the *Brontosaurus* have changed in recent years. These dinosaurs are now viewed as "energetic, active, and capable animals" (lines 15–16). According to the passage, "many paleontologists now believe that dinosaurs were warm blooded . . . ."

If you do not know the word *revisionist*, think about in what contexts you have heard its root word *revise*. You have likely revised an essay to improve its grammar, style, and content. This paragraph is talking about how scientists have revised their understanding of the *Brontosaurus*, using new facts to refine the accuracy of their notion of what the dinosaur was like.

35. According to the passage, what is the revisionist interpretation concerning the relationship between intelligence and physical size?

A. Dinosaurs actually had relatively large brains.

B. Dinosaurs were paragons of intellect.

C. Dinosaurs were relatively small brained.

D. Dinosaurs' brains were appropriately sized.

The best answer is D because the author claims that the revisionist interpretation of the relationship between dinosaur intelligence and physical size is that dinosaurs "had the 'right-sized' brains for reptiles of their body size" (lines 32–33).

The best answer is NOT:

A because, according to the author, the revisionist position isn't that dinosaurs had relatively large brains, but rather that they had appropriately sized brains.

B because the author states, "The revisionist interpretation, which I support, . . . does not enshrine dinosaurs as paragons of intellect" (lines 29–31).

C because the author states that revisionists claim dinosaurs "were not small brained after all" (line 32).

NATURAL SCIENCE: This passage is adapted from the essay "Were Dinosaurs Dumb?" by Stephen Jay Gould (©1980 by Stephen Jay Gould).

[5]

I don't wish to deny that the flattened, minuscule
35 head of large-bodied *Stegosaurus* houses little brain from our subjective, top-heavy perspective, but I do wish to assert that we should not expect more of the beast. First of all, large animals have relatively smaller brains than related, small animals. The correlation of
40 brain size with body size among kindred animals (all reptiles, all mammals for example) is remarkably regular. As we move from small to large animals, from mice to elephants or small lizards to Komodo dragons, brain size increases, but not so fast as body size. In
45 other words, bodies grow faster than brains, and large animals have low ratios of brain weight to body weight. In fact, brains grow only about two-thirds as fast as bodies. Since we have no reason to believe that large animals are consistently stupider than their smaller re-
50 latives, we must conclude that large animals require relatively less brain to do as well as smaller animals. If we do not recognize this relationship, we are likely to underestimate the mental power of very large animals, dinosaurs in particular. . . .

Explanatory Notes

Scanning effectively is the key to answering the next question quickly. The key words in the question are *brain, body, weight,* and *ratio.* The topic sentence of the fifth paragraph of the passage makes it clear that the paragraph will address the issue of dinosaur brain size. This sentence includes two of the key words from the question: *brain* and *body.* The topic sentence for the fifth paragraph has been reproduced here with the key words identified in bold.

"I don't wish to deny that the flattened, minuscule head of large-**bodied** Stegosaurus houses little **brain** from our subjective, top-heavy perspective, but I do wish to assert that we should not expect more of the beast."

You can also find many of the question's key words in lines 45–46: "large animals have low ratios of **brain weight to body weight**." These lines provide the most direct textual evidence to support the correct answer to the question.

37. The passage states that the ratio of brain weight to body weight in larger animals, as compared to smaller animals, is:

   A. higher.

   B. lower.

   C. the same.

   D. overestimated.

Scan words: brain, body, weight, and ratio

The best answer is B because the passage states that relative to smaller animals, "large animals have low ratios of brain weight to body weight" (lines 45–46).

The best answer is NOT:

A because lines 45–46 rule out the possibility that the ratio is higher in larger animals.

C because lines 45–46 rule out the possibility that the ratio is the same in both larger and smaller animals.

D because there's no evidence in the passage that the ratio is overestimated.

The following question draws on the same passage.

38. According to the passage, which of the following correctly states the relationship of brain size to body size?

   F. The brain grows at two-thirds the rate of body growth.

   G. At maturity, the brain weighs an average of one-third of body weight.

   H. Large animals are not consistently less intelligent than smaller animals.

   J. Brain size is independent of body size.

The best answer is F because the passage states, "In fact, brains grow only about two-thirds as fast as bodies" (lines 47–48).

The best answer is NOT:

G because even though brains grow about two-thirds as fast as bodies, this doesn't mean that at maturity, the brain weighs an average of one-third of body weight.

H because while the passage does say that "we have no reason to believe that large animals are consistently stupider than their smaller relatives" (lines 48–50), this speaks to the relationship of intelligence to body size, not brain size to body size.

J because the passage does not say that brain size is independent of body size, but instead asserts that there is a relationship.

NATURAL SCIENCE: This passage is adapted from *An Anthropologist on Mars* by Oliver Sacks (©1995 by Oliver Sacks). Johann Wolfgang von Goethe was an eighteenth-century German poet and philosopher; Hermann von Helmholtz was a nineteenth-century scientist and philosopher.

30   Helmholtz's great contemporary, James Clerk Maxwell, had also been fascinated by the mystery of color vision from his student days. He formalized the notions of primary colors and color mixing by the invention of a color top (the colors of which fused,
35   when it was spun, to yield a sensation of grey), and a graphic representation with three axes, a color triangle, which showed how any color could be created by dif-ferent mixtures of the three primary colors. These pre-pared the way for his most spectacular demonstration,
40   the demonstration in 1861 that color photography was possible, despite the fact that photographic emulsions were themselves black and white. He did this by pho-tographing a colored bow three times, through red, green, and violet filters. Having obtained three "color-
45   separation" images, as he called them, he now brought these together by superimposing them upon a screen, projecting each image through its corresponding filter (the image taken through the red filter was projected with red light, and so on). Suddenly, the bow burst
50   forth in full color.

38. According to the passage, the relationship between primary colors and other colors can be best described by which of the following statements?

F. All colors are either primary colors or can be created by a combination of primary colors.

G. The human eye perceives primary colors first, then other colors.

H. Primary colors were the first colors captured on film by the camera; other colors were captured by later, more sophisticated, equipment.

J. Primary colors emerge as a result of blending nonprimary colors along the axes of Clerk Maxwell's triangle.

The best answer is F because the passage states that "any color could be created by different mixtures of the three primary colors" (lines 37–38).

The best answer is NOT:

G because there's no evidence in the passage that the human eye perceives primary colors first and then other colors.

H because the passage doesn't provide a sequence listing the order in which colors were first captured on film.

J because it's basically the opposite of what the passage says.

Sequence Questions

Each passage type tends to include questions about the order of events. The following words and phrases may signal that the passage is delivering information about the order of events.

Order	Time Period	Frequency	Conclusions/Endings
after	ago	never	ultimately
before	as a child	rarely	lastly
begin	as an infant	always	in the end
end	at age four	sometimes	in conclusion
eventually	when he was a baby	frequently	finally
first	years ago	monthly	
finish	last year	each week	
initially	in 1970	this Thursday	
later	1900s	yearly	
last	turn of the century	annually	
meanwhile	modern	daily	
next	generation	weekly	
new	eon		
now	modern		
originally	ancient		
once	old		
prior	today		
previously			
start			
second			
soon			
third			
then			
subsequently			

Determining Sequence

Let's practice determining the order of events based on the following excerpts.

Example 1

HUMANITIES: This passage is adapted from the article "You Got Eyes: Robert Frank Imagines America" by Francine Prose (©2010 by The Harper's Magazine Foundation).

What made the loneliness and isolation that *The Americans* captured even harder for the critical and general audience to accept was the fact that **a few years before** its appearance, a hugely popular exhibition and its companion volume, *The Family of Man,* had depicted the world, America included, as one giant inclusive, warm-hearted kinship system sharing the same joys and sorrows.

(continued)

(continued)

What Happened First?

The Family of Man had depicted the world, America included, as one giant inclusive, warm-hearted kinship system sharing the same joys and sorrows.

What Happened Second?

The loneliness and isolation that *The Americans* captured was hard for the critical and general audience to accept.

Example 2

SOCIAL SCIENCE: This passage is adapted from *Library: An Unquiet History* by Matthew Battles (©2003 by Matthew Battles).

Once his rivals were safely dead, Augustus set to transforming Rome into an imperial city; later he boasted that he had found Rome brick and left it marble.

What Happened First?

Augustus's rivals were safely dead.

What Happened Second?

Augustus set to transforming Rome into an imperial city.

What Happened Third?

He boasted that he had found Rome brick and left it marble.

Sequence Questions in the Literary Narrative Passage

Though all passage types can be followed by questions about sequence, the literary narrative passage is the most likely to focus on the order of events as they unfold in the narrative. When a question asks about the chronology of the passage, it is asking about the order of events in the world of the story, not the order of events in the way the passage is written. To answer chronology questions, it is also helpful to think about how we talk about time in our everyday lives. For example, if your teacher said, "You have a test **this** Thursday," then you would know that the teacher is talking about a day in the future.

The implication is also that the teacher is speaking on a day of the week that comes before Thursday. If the teacher said this on a Tuesday, it would mean that the test would be two days later. If a teacher said, "You have a test **next** Thursday," that would mean that the test would be nine days later. It would be strange to say on a Thursday, "You have a test this Thursday." Instead, the teacher would simply say, "You have a test today." Here are examples of the types of questions that are often asked about sequence.

- Which of the following is a detail from the passage that indicates the <u>length of time</u> that Payne has been a musician?

- At the time described in the passage's opening, which is Payne's <u>most immediate</u> concern?

Practice Questions

Let's take a look at a real ACT reading test question that addresses the sequence of events.

LITERARY NARRATIVE: This passage is adapted from the novel *Monkey Bridge* by Lan Cao (©1997 by Lan Cao). The story is set in the late 1970s in Virginia, where the narrator and her mother have moved from Vietnam after the fall of Saigon.

Now, a mere three and a half years or so after her last call to the sky market, the dreadful truth was simply this: we were going through life in reverse, and I was
55 the one who would help my mother through the hard scrutiny of ordinary suburban life. I would have to forgo the luxury of adolescent experiments and temper tantrums, so that I could scoop my mother out of harm's way and give her sanctuary. Now, when we stepped into
60 the exterior world, I was the one who told my mother what was acceptable or unacceptable behavior.

All children of immigrant parents have experienced these moments. When it first occurs, when the parent first reveals the behavior of a child, is a defining
65 moment. Of course, all children eventually watch their parents' astonishing return to the vulnerability of childhood, but for us the process begins much earlier than expected.

---

41. At the time of the events of the story, the narrator is:

   A. an adult remembering how hard it was on her mother when the two of them visited the United States from Saigon.

   B. an adult planning to take her mother back to their native Saigon after an unsuccessful trip to the United States.

   C. an adolescent imagining what it had been like when her mother moved to the United States years ago.

   D. an adolescent trying to ease her mother's adjustment to life in the United States.

Scan for: adult, adolescent, Saigon

The best answer is D because the narrator indicates that "now" (line 52) she "would have to forgo the luxury of adolescent experiments and temper tantrums" (lines 56–58), which indicates that the narrator is an adolescent. She takes on adult responsibilities so that she "could scoop [her] mother out of harm's way and give her sanctuary" (lines 58–59) in the United States.

The best answer is NOT:

A because the narrator is not an adult and because she and her mother are not merely visiting the United States: it has been "three and a half years or so" (line 52) since the mother's last trip to the sky market.

B because the narrator is not an adult and because there's no indication in the passage that the narrator and her mother plan to return to Saigon.

C because rather than imagining her mother's move to the United States, the narrator relates her own and her mother's shared experiences in Vietnam and the United States.

LITERARY NARRATIVE: This passage is adapted from the novel *The Fisher King* by Paule Marshall (©2000 by Paule Marshall).

[2]

This Sunday, Everett Payne, not long out of the
15 army, was the one being invited to sit in.

[3]

Breath held, Hattie watched him separate himself from the hopefuls and approach the stand, taking his time, moving with what almost seemed a deliberate pause between each step. The crowd waiting.

…

[5]

She watched now as he slowly mounted the band-stand and conferred with the bassist and drummer, those two were all he would need. Then, without announcing the name of the tune he intended playing,
30 without in any way acknowledging the audience, he sat down at the piano and brought his hands—large hands, the fingers long and splayed and slightly arched—down on the opening bars of "Sonny Boy Blue."

[6]

"Sonny Boy Blue!" That hokey-doke tune!

Explanatory Notes

The fifth paragraph describes Everett Payne's actions in chronological order. There are no words to signal that the events are described in an order that differs from the order in which they occurred. For example, if the paragraph included a phrase like "before that," you would need to exert additional effort to determine the order of events. The order of events would be presented in a more complex manner if the passage read, "Everett mounted the stage. **Before that**, he conferred with the bassist and drummer to confirm that he was welcome onstage." Instead, in this paragraph, the words that signal the passage of time indicate that the story is unfolding as a narrative just as it actually occurred. Words such as *and* and *then* serve to emphasize the passage of time. The paragraph is written in simple past tense, which also conveys the order of events in a simple and straightforward manner.

5. According to the narrator, what did Hattie see Everett Payne do prior to playing "Sonny Boy Blue"?

   A. Move quickly from his seat to the bandstand

   B. Study the audience around him

   C. Confer with the bassist and the drummer

   D. Announce the name of the tune he was going to play

Scan words: Sonny Boy Blue

The best answer is C because the narrator describes how she watched as Payne "slowly mounted the bandstand and conferred with the bassist and drummer" (lines 26–27).

The best answer is NOT:

A because Payne did not move quickly to the bandstand. Rather, the narrator describes him as moving with "a deliberate pause between each step" (lines 18–19).

B because the narrator describes Payne as sitting down to play "without in any way acknowledging the audience" (line 30).

D because the narrator says that Payne sat down at the piano "without announcing the name of the tune he intended playing" (lines 28–29).

LITERARY NARRATIVE: This passage is adapted from the novel *The Fisher King* by Paule Marshall (©2000 by Paule Marshall).

[5]

....Then, without announcing the name of the tune he intended playing, without in any way acknowledging the audience, he sat down at the piano and brought his hands—large hands, the fingers long and splayed and slightly arched—down on the opening bars of "Sonny Boy Blue."

[6]

"Sonny Boy Blue!" That hokey-doke tune!

[7]

Around her [Hattie], the purists looked askance at each other from behind their regulation shades and slouched deeper in their chairs in open disgust.

[8]

At first, hokey though it was, he played the song straight through as written, the rather long introduction, verse, and chorus. And he did so with great care, although at a slower tempo than was called for and with a formality that lent the Tin Pan Alley tune a depth and thoughtfulness no one else would have accorded it.

[9]

Quickly taking their cue from him, the bassist reached for his bow, the drummer for his brushes, the two of them also treating the original as if it were a serious piece of music.

[10]

Everett Payne took his time paying his respects to the tune as written, and once that was done, he hunched closer to the piano, angled his head sharply to the left, completely closed the curtain of his gaze, and with his hands commanding the length and breadth of the keyboard he unleashed a dazzling pyrotechnic of chords (you could almost see their colors), polyrhythms, seemingly unrelated harmonies, and ideas—fresh, brash, outrageous ideas. It was an outpouring of ideas and feelings informed by his own brand of lyricism and lit from time to time by flashes of the recognizable melody. He continued to acknowledge the little simple-minded tune, while at the same time furiously recasting and reinventing it in an image all his own.

[11]

A collective in-suck of breath throughout the club.

[12]

Where, Hattie wondered, did he come by the dazzling array of ideas and wealth of feeling? What was the source? It had to do, she speculated, listening intently, with the way he held his head, angled to the left like that, tilted toward both heaven and earth. His right side, his right ear directed skyward, hearing up there, in the Upper Room among the stars Mahalia sang about, a new kind of music: splintered, atonal, profane, and possessing a wonderful dissonance that spoke to him, to his soul-case. For him, this was the true music of the spheres, of the maelstrom up there. When at the piano, he kept his right ear tuned to it at all times, letting it guide him, inspire him. His other ear? It remained earthbound, trained on the bedrock that for him was Bach and the blues.

8. According to the passage, when Everett Payne first played "Sonny Boy Blue" straight through, he did so:

F. more slowly than was intended by the composer.

G. after it had been suggested by Abe Kaiser.

H. against the wishes of the bassist and drummer.

J. without following the original tune.

Scan words: Sonny Boy Blue, first

The best answer is F because the passage indicates that Payne first played the song "at a slower tempo than was called for" (line 41).

The best answer is NOT:

G because there is no indication in the passage that Payne spoke with anyone other than the bassist and the drummer.

H because although the passage states that Payne conferred with the bassist and the drummer (line 27), there is no mention in the passage that either the bassist or the drummer had any reaction to what Payne said to them.

J because when Payne first played "Sonny Boy Blue," he played the song "straight through as written" (line 39). The passage also states that throughout Payne's performance, he "continued to acknowledge the little simple-minded tune" (lines 59–60).

HUMANITIES: This passage is adapted from the essay "My Life with a Field Guide" by Diana Kappel-Smith (©2002 by Phi Beta Kappa Society).

25   Over the next several years this field guide would become my closest companion, a slice of worldview, as indispensable as eyes or hands. I didn't arrive at this intimacy right away, however. This wasn't going to be an easy affair for either of us.

30   I'll give you an example of how it went. After I'd owned the Peterson's for about a week, I went on a hike with some friends up a little mountain, taking the book along. Halfway up the mountain, there by the trailside was a yellow flower, a nice opportunity to take my new 35 guide for a test drive. "Go on ahead!" I said to my hiking companions, "I'll be a minute . . ." Famous last words.

27. The author states that the Peterson's became her closest companion over a period of several:

A. days.

B. weeks.

C. months.

D. years.

Scan for: Peterson's, companion

The best answer is D because the author states that "over the next several years this field guide would become my closest companion" (lines 25–26), specifying that she measures the period in question in "*years.*"

The best answer is NOT:

A because the author states that "over the next several years this field guide would become my closest companion" (lines 25–26), specifying *years* and not days as the way in which she measures the period in question.

B because the author states that "over the next several years this field guide would become my closest companion." (lines 25–26), specifying *years* and not weeks as the way in which she measures the period in question.

C because the author states that "over the next several years this field guide would become my closest companion" (lines 25–26), specifying *years* and not months as the way in which she measures the period in question.

Sequence Questions in the Natural Science Passages

Often the natural science passages trace the evolution of an understanding of a scientific area of exploration such as the nature of the planet Mars. The passage may begin, for example, with an overview of a long-held scientific view of Mars that it was once a planet that had liquid water and a thick atmosphere capable of providing the warmth, water, and air needed to support plant life. As the passage progresses, it may become clear that recent studies about the sun's lack of intensity call that viewpoint into question. Note that natural science passages are not necessarily entirely up-to-date. They may, for example, have been written in the 1980s.

Cause and Effect

Many ACT reading test questions ask about cause-and-effect relationships established within the passages. The following words signal cause-and-effect relationships.

Cause and Effect

accordingly	for
as a result	hence
as such	outcome
because	results
cause	since
consequently	so
correlated	source
correlation	thus
ergo	therefore

Practice Questions

Let's look at some real test questions that ask about cause-and-effect relationships.

LITERARY NARRATIVE: This passage is adapted from the novel *The Fisher King* by Paule Marshall (©2000 by Paule Marshall).

[2]

This Sunday, Everett Payne, not long out of the
15 army, was the one being invited to sit in.

. . .

[5]

...Then, without announcing the name of the tune he intended playing,
30 without in any way acknowledging the audience, he sat down at the piano and brought his hands—large hands, the fingers long and splayed and slightly arched—down on the opening bars of "Sonny Boy Blue."

. . .

[9]

Quickly taking their cue from him, the bassist
45 reached for his bow, the drummer for his brushes, the two of them also treating the original as if it were a serious piece of music.

[10]

Everett Payne took his time paying his respects to the tune as written, and once that was done, he hunched
50 closer to the piano, angled his head sharply to the left, completely closed the curtain of his gaze, and with his hands commanding the length and breadth of the keyboard he unleashed a dazzling pyrotechnic of chords (you could almost see their colors), polyrhythms, seem-
55 ingly unrelated harmonies, and ideas—fresh, brash, outrageous ideas. It was an outpouring of ideas and feelings informed by his own brand of lyricism and lit from time to time by flashes of the recognizable melody. He continued to acknowledge the little simple-
60 minded tune, while at the same time furiously recasting and reinventing it in an image all his own.

. . .

[12]

Where, Hattie wondered, did he come by the daz-zling array of ideas and wealth of feeling? What was
65 the source? It had to do, she speculated, listening intently, with the way he held his head, angled to the left like that, tilted toward both heaven and earth. His right side, his right ear directed skyward, hearing up there, in the Upper Room among the stars Mahalia sang
70 about, a new kind of music: splintered, atonal, profane, and possessing a wonderful dissonance that spoke to him, to his soul-case. For him, this was the true music of the spheres, of the maelstrom up there. When at the piano, he kept his right ear tuned to it at all times, let-
75 ting it guide him, inspire him. His other ear? It remained earthbound, trained on the bedrock that for him was Bach and the blues.

9. According to the passage, Hattie speculated that the source of Everett Payne's musical ideas and feelings during "Sonny Boy Blue" was in:

    A. the way he tilted his head.

    B. the simplemindedness of the song.

    C. his ability to play with great formality.

    D. his connection with the silent audience.

Scan for: speculated, source, Sonny Boy Blue

The best answer is A because Hattie speculates that Payne's talent "had to do . . . with the way he held his head . . . tilted" (lines 65–67).

The best answer is NOT:

B because the narrator never mentions the simplemindedness of the tune as being related to Payne's musical ideas and feelings. Rather, the characterization of "Sonny Boy Blue" as a "little simpleminded tune" (lines 59–60) creates a contrast between Payne's elaborate and inventive improvisations and the simple and overly familiar song that he chooses as a vehicle for those improvisations.

C because although the narrator mentions Payne's formality in playing through the parts of "Sonny Boy Blue" the first time (lines 42–43), the narrator does not identify this formality as the source of the musical ideas and feelings showcased in Payne's improvisations.

D because the passage makes no mention of any connection Payne feels with his audience. Rather, the passage states that Payne does not even acknowledge his audience before playing (line 30).

NATURAL SCIENCE: This passage is adapted from the essay "Were Dinosaurs Dumb?" by Stephen Jay Gould (©1980 by Stephen Jay Gould).

…They had the "right-sized" brains for reptiles of their body size.

I don't wish to deny that the flattened, minuscule
35 head of large-bodied *Stegosaurus* houses little brain from our subjective, top-heavy perspective, but I do wish to assert that we should not expect more of the beast. First of all, large animals have relatively smaller brains than related, small animals. The correlation of
40 brain size with body size among kindred animals (all reptiles, all mammals for example) is remarkably regular. As we move from small to large animals, from mice to elephants or small lizards to Komodo dragons, brain size increases, but not so fast as body size. In
45 other words, bodies grow faster than brains, and large animals have low ratios of brain weight to body weight. In fact, brains grow only about two-thirds as fast as bodies. Since we have no reason to believe that large animals are consistently stupider than their smaller rel-
50 atives, we must conclude that large animals require relatively less brain to do as well as smaller animals. If we do not recognize this relationship, we are likely to underestimate the mental power of very large animals, dinosaurs in particular.. . .

55 If behavioral complexity is one consequence of mental power, then we might expect to uncover among dinosaurs some signs of social behavior that demand coordination, cohesiveness and recognition. Indeed we do, and it cannot be accidental that these signs were
60 overlooked when dinosaurs labored under the burden of a falsely imposed obtuseness. Multiple trackways have been uncovered, with evidence for more than twenty animals traveling together in parallel movement. Did some dinosaurs live in herds? At the Davenport Ranch
65 sauropod trackway, small footprints lie in the center and larger ones at the periphery. Could it be that some dinosaurs traveled much as some advanced herbivorous mammals do today, with large adults at the borders sheltering juveniles in the center? . . .

Explanatory Notes

This portion of the passage addresses the question of dinosaur intelligence. The first paragraph on the left comments on dinosaurs' brain size and contradicts the notion that dinosaur's small brains meant that they had limited intelligence. Gould argues that dinosaurs' brains were "right sized" (line 33) and that it is misguided to think that brain size should increase at the same rate as body size. Gould notes, "brain size increases, but not so fast as body size. In other words, bodies grow faster than brains," (lines 44–45). This paragraph helps you evaluate whether or not answer **H** is the correct answer to question 32 because that answer focuses on dinosaur brain size.

Lines 55–69 describe dinosaur behavior. Notice that this paragraph directly echoes the language of question 32 itself, stating, "it cannot be accidental that these signs were **overlooked** when dinosaurs labored under the burden of a falsely imposed obtuseness" (lines 60–61).

The trackways that have been discovered are fossils, which could have been found by chance or through excavation with simple tools used by paleontologists for decades.

32. The passage suggests that some fossil evidence about dinosaur behavior has been overlooked in the past because scientists:

F. had preconceived ideas about the intelligence of dinosaurs.

G. believed that mammals were not capable of social formations.

H. did not have the current data about dinosaur brain size.

J. did not have the necessary equipment to discover the social patterns of dinosaurs.

Scan for: fossil, behavior, overlooked, ignored

The best answer is F because the author indicates that "signs of social behavior that demand coordination, cohesiveness and recognition" (lines 57–58) in dinosaurs "were overlooked when dinosaurs labored under the burden of a falsely imposed obtuseness" (lines 59–61). In other words, when scientists thought dinosaurs were unintelligent, they failed to see evidence of complex social behaviors, such as "multiple trackways" (line 61) and hints that adult dinosaurs flanked young, immature dinosaurs during travel in order to protect them.

The best answer is NOT:

G because there's no evidence in the passage that scientists ever believed mammals were incapable of social formations.

H because there's no indication in the passage that the information in the fourth paragraph (lines 34–54) about brain and body sizes is new to scientists.

J because the passage doesn't say that any particular equipment was needed to identify the "multiple trackways" and the evidence that adult dinosaurs protected young, immature ones while traveling. It was mainly a matter of looking at fossilized footprints without the preconceived notion that dinosaurs were unintelligent.

LITERARY NARRATIVE: This passage is adapted from the short story "Elba" by Marly Swick (©1991 by the University of Iowa). Fran is the narrator of the story.

[27]

        "Well, don't put it off." She slid her eyes back to
85 the television. "She's been waiting twenty-five years.

You worried she's going to be trouble or ask for money? For all we know, she's married to a brain surgeon with his and her Cadillacs."

        "She didn't mention any husband at all," I said,
90 getting drawn into it despite myself.

---

10. According to the passage, the reason why Fran's mother warns Fran not to put off contacting Linda Rose is that Fran's mother:

F. wants to see her new great-grandson before she dies.

G. knows Fran tends to delay making hard decisions.

H. knows how long Linda Rose has been waiting to see Fran.

J. suspects Linda Rose is in some sort of trouble.

Scan for: put off

The best answer is H because after telling Fran not to put off contacting Linda Rose and inviting her and the baby for a visit, Fran's mother says Linda Rose has "been waiting twenty-five years" (line 87).

The best answer is NOT:

F because Fran's mother never directly expresses the desire to see her new great-grandson before she dies.

G because there's no evidence in the passage that Fran generally tends to delay making hard decisions.

J because while Fran's mother wonders aloud whether Linda Rose is "going to be trouble or ask for money" (lines 88–89), she only does this because she thinks Fran might use this as an excuse to put off contacting Linda Rose and inviting her and the baby for a visit. Fran's mother goes on to say, "For all we know, [Linda Rose is] married to a brain surgeon with his and her Cadillacs" (lines 89–90).

LITERARY NARRATIVE: This passage is adapted from the short story "Golden Glass" by Alma Villanueva (©1982 by Bilingual Press).

[2]

He seemed always to be at the center of his own universe, so it was no surprise to his mother to hear Ted say: "I'm building a fort and sleeping out in it all
10 summer, and I won't come in for anything, not even food. Okay?"

…

[9]

Ted had seen his mother walk out to the bridge at night, looking into the water, listening to it. He knew she loved to see the moon's reflection in the water. She'd pointed it out to him once by a river where they
40 camped, her face full of longing. Then, she swam out into the water, at night, as though trying to touch the moon. He wouldn't look at her. He sat and glared at the fire and roasted another marshmallow the way he liked it: bubbly, soft and brown (maybe six if he could get
45 away with it). Then she'd be back, chilled and bright, and he was glad she went. Maybe I like the moon too, he thought, involuntarily, as though the thought weren't his own—but it was.

Explanatory Notes

This paragraph conveys that Vida knows her son well and that she is therefore unsurprised when he declares his intention to build a fort to sleep in all summer.

6. The passage indicates that Vida was not surprised by Ted's decision to build a fort because she:

　　F. knew that more often than not he was inclined to take projects she had started a step farther.

　　G. sensed that it fit with his tendency to approach life as if he were self-contained.

　　H. had noticed that ever since their camping trip he had been putting more and more distance between himself and her.

　　J. had noticed that he no longer worried that his fascination with nature would interfere with his longstanding craving for the company of others.

Scan for: surprised, surprise, and fort

The best answer is G because the passage states that to Vida, Ted "seemed always to be at the center of his own universe, so it was no surprise to his mother" to hear Ted's plan to build and move into a fort for the summer (lines 7–11).

The best answer is NOT:

　　F because the passage presents the fort as Ted's project, not as something Vida started.

　　H because there's no evidence in the passage that Ted had put more and more distance between himself and Vida since the camping trip.

　　J because there's no evidence in the passage that Ted had a longstanding craving for the company of others.

NATURAL SCIENCE: This passage is adapted from the article "When Research Is a Snow Job" by Sarah Boyle (©2002 by National Wildlife).

Rango is also looking ahead at climate change pre-
75 dictions. "Following the estimates that have been made about what will happen by 2100, things are definitely warming up," he says. Temperature increases will likely result in a reduction in stream flow as overall snow accumulation decreases, winter precipitation runs
80 off as rain, and water evaporates at a quicker rate. The gap between water supply and demand will magnify even more, greatly increasing water's economic value, anticipates Rango.

Not only does the crystal research help gauge
85 snowmelt, it is also useful in predicting avalanches, designing artificial snow, and, perhaps in the near future, examining air pollution. "You can put snow in a scanning electron microscope and tell which elements are present, such as sulfur and nitrogen," says Wergin.
90 "You can then see what kind of pollution is in the area and possibly track the source."

---

35. According to Rango, one reason that water's economic value is likely to increase by the year 2100 is that:

　　A. more water will be polluted by then.

　　B. less water will be wasted due to more accurate predictions of the water supply.

　　C. the sulfur and nitrogen content in snow is likely to increase.

　　D. predicted climate changes will reduce overall snow accumulation.

Scan for: water, economic value, 2100

The best answer is D because the passage states that, because of temperature increases, less snow will fall, thus "greatly increasing water's economic value" (lines 77–82).

The best answer is NOT:

A because although the passage mentions an increased ability to track water pollution via the use of crystal research (lines 90–91), the passage makes no mention of an increase of pollution as a cause of an increase in water's value.

B because the passage makes no mention of water conservation leading to an increase in water's value.

C because although the passage mentions the ability of scanning electron microscopes to detect sulfur and nitrogen in snow (lines 87–89), the passage makes no mention of a predicted increase in sulfur and nitrogen levels in snow.

NATURAL SCIENCE: This passage is adapted from the article "When Research Is a Snow Job" by Sarah Boyle (©2002 by National Wildlife).

The figure is beyond comprehension: Every year, 1,000,000,000,000,000,000,000,000 (1 septillion) snowflakes fall worldwide. As the crystals fall, they encounter different atmospheric conditions that produce
5 flakes with unique attributes. The more complex those conditions are, the more elaborate the crystals.

36. According to the passage, snowflakes have infinite variety because:

   F. enormous numbers of snow crystals fall worldwide.

   G. falling snow crystals meet with varied atmospheric conditions.

   H. snow crystals fall at various rates, creating unique snowflakes.

   J. complexities in the atmosphere slow snow crystal development.

Scan for: infinite variety

The best answer is G because the passage states that "as the crystals fall, they encounter different atmospheric conditions that produce flakes with unique attributes" (lines 3–5).

The best answer is NOT:

F because although the passage does state that 1 septillion snowflakes fall worldwide each year (lines 1–3), the passage does not make any connection between that enormous number and the infinite variety of snowflakes. Rather, the passage states that "as the crystals fall, they encounter different atmospheric conditions that produce flakes with unique attributes" (lines 3–5).

H because the passage makes no connection between the rate at which snowflakes fall and the infinite variety of snowflakes. Rather, the passage states that "as the crystals fall, they encounter different atmospheric conditions that produce flakes with unique attributes" (lines 3–5).

J because although the passage does state that more complex atmospheric conditions produce more elaborate and therefore more varied snow crystals (lines 5–6), the passage makes no connection between those complex atmospheric conditions and the speed at which snow crystals develop, and the passage makes no connection between the speed at which snow crystals develop and the infinite variety of snowflakes.

Questions about Shifts

Whenever a passage indicates that a change has occurred, anticipate that a question will be asked about that change. The following list provides some words that may signal a shift in the text.

Words Indicating a Shift

now	usually	but	change
traditionally	normally	however	shift
typically	used to	nevertheless	transformation
suddenly	previously	regardless	alter
in the past,	before	after	today

Practice Questions

SOCIAL SCIENCE: *Biomimicry: Innovation Inspired by Nature* by Janine M. Benyus (©1997 by Janine M. Benyus).

65   Traditionally, manufacturers haven't had to worry about what happens to a product after it leaves their gates. But that is starting to change, thanks to laws now in the wings in Europe (and headed for the United States) that will require companies to take back their
70 durable goods such as refrigerators, washers, and cars at the end of their useful lives. In Germany, the take-back laws start with the initial sale. Companies must take back all their packaging or hire middlemen to do the recycling. Take-back laws mean that manufacturers
75 who have been saying, "This product can be recycled," must now say, "We recycle our products and pack-aging."

When the onus shifts in this way, it's suddenly in the company's best interest to design a product that will
80 either last a long time or come apart easily for recycling or reuse.

Explanatory Notes

The word ***traditionally*** often signals where a passage will describe how a phenomenon has changed over time. This paragraph begins with a description of how manufacturers traditionally regard their responsibility when it comes to a product "after it leaves their gates."

The use of the word ***but*** signals a shift in the way manufacturers see their role in reducing waste.

Whose responsibility has changed? The company's responsibility has changed.

Who used to be responsible for properly disposing of a broken refrigerator, for example?

22. According to the passage, take-back laws in Germany shift the responsibility for recycling from the:

    A. local government to the manufacturer.

    B. manufacturer to the local government.

    C. manufacturer to the consumer.

    D. consumer to the manufacturer.

The best answer is D because the author says the German take-back laws "start with the initial sale," meaning "companies must take back all their packaging or hire middlemen to do the recycling" (lines 72–74). This fits in with the author's general discussion in the seventh paragraph (lines 65–77) of take-back laws, which "will require companies to take back their durable goods such as refrigerators, washers, and cars at the end of their useful lives" (lines 69–71).

The best answer is NOT:

A because there's no evidence in the passage that German take-back laws shift the responsibility of recycling from the local government to the manufacturer.

B because there's no evidence in the passage that German take-back laws shift the responsibility of recycling from the manufacturer to the local government.

C because it reverses the actual relationship.

LITERARY NARRATIVE: This passage is adapted from the short story "Golden Glass" by Alma Villanueva (©1982 by Bilingual Press).

[1]

It was his fourteenth summer. He was thinning out, becoming angular and clumsy, but the cautiousness, the old-man seriousness he'd had as a baby, kept him contained, ageless and safe. His humor, always dry
5 and to the bone since a small child, let you know he was watching everything.

[2]

He seemed always to be at the center of his own universe, so it was no surprise to his mother to hear Ted say: "I'm building a fort and sleeping out in it all
10 summer, and I won't come in for anything, not even food. Okay?"

[3]

This had been their silent communion, the steady presence of love that flowed regularly, daily—food. The presence of his mother preparing it, his great
15 appetite and obvious enjoyment of it—his nose smelling everything, seeing his mother more vividly than with his eyes.

Explanatory Notes

The beginning of the passage has been reproduced to provide further context for paragraph 7. The first six paragraphs establish that Ted is a teenager who wishes to build a fort in his backyard. Ted's mother Vida respects his seriousness of purpose about this project.

He is so caught up in the project that he does not even wish to be distracted by food.

The third paragraph conveys how food connects Ted and Vida. This paragraph establishes that they have a warm and loving dynamic and that Vida accepts Ted's eccentricities.

Ted expected his mother show "signs of offense" when he said he would not break away from his project even for food. Instead, Vida shows curiosity about Ted's fort.

Paragraph 5 shows that Vida trusts Ted but that she also expects to remain informed about the fort's placement.

Paragraph 7 shows that Vida is comfortable holding her son to certain standards as he builds his fort. She warns Ted to be careful to avoid harming the trees.

(continued)

(continued)

[4]

He watched her now for signs of offense, alarm,
and only saw interest. "Where will you put the fort?"
20 Vida asked.

[5]

She trusted him to build well and not ruin things,
but of course she had to know where.

[6]

"I'll build it by the redwoods, in the cypress tree.
Okay?"

[7]

25   "Make sure you keep your nails together and don't
dig into the trees. I'll be checking. If the trees get damaged, it'll have to come down."

...

[15]

He was so used to sleeping outside now he didn't
85 wake up during the night, just like in the house. One
night, toward the end when he'd have to move back
with everyone (school was starting, frost was coming
and the rains), Ted woke up to see the stained glass full
of light. The little sun was a golden moon and the
90 inside glass sky and the outside sky matched.

[16]

In a few days he'd be inside, and he wouldn't
mind at all.

13. Which of the following best describes the way the seventh paragraph (lines 25–27) functions in the passage?

F. It reinforces the image of Vida established elsewhere in the passage as someone whose skeptical nature disheartens Ted on the brink of new projects.

G. It foreshadows events described later in the passage that lead to the dismantling of the tree house once Ted is back in school.

H. It reveals that Vida takes an interest in Ted's project to the extent that she determines ways in which he needs to carry it out to avoid problems.

J. It reveals that Vida's willingness to shift responsibility to her son for his actions is greater than his willingness to accept such responsibility.

The best answer is H because the seventh paragraph (lines 25–27) illustrates both Vida's interest in Ted's project and her concerns about it. Previously, the passage says Vida showed "interest" (line 19) in Ted's plan and that "she trusted him to build well and not ruin things" (line 21). The seventh paragraph shows Vida anticipating possible problems with the proposed fort and indicating how to avoid them: "Make sure you keep your nails together and don't dig into the trees. I'll be checking. If the trees get damaged, it'll have to come down."

The best answer is NOT:

F because there's no evidence in the passage that Vida has a skeptical nature or that Ted feels disheartened.

G because the passage never says the fort was dismantled, only that Ted would have to move back inside "in a few days" (line 91).

J because there's no evidence in the passage that Vida wants to give Ted more responsibility than Ted himself wants to take on.

Chapter 7:
Craft and Structure

Questions that fall under the reporting category of Craft and Structure make up 25%–30% of your score. These questions cover the author's word choice, purpose, and organization in a passage. They may focus on word meaning in context, figurative language, or rhetorical devices. Also, you may have to analyze how opinions, factual evidence, and characterization support an author's viewpoint.

Using Context Clues

Keep in mind that it is not essential to know every word in a passage in order to sufficiently understand the passage. Often you can use context clues to determine a word's meaning. Let's practice using context to determine the general meaning of the following words identified in bold.

1. "Around her, the purists looked **askance** at each other from behind their regulation shades and slouched deeper in their chairs in open disgust."

Fortunately, this sentence tells us that the audience displays "open disgust," which clearly indicates that the word *askance* likely has a negative connotation. Indeed, the word *askance* implies "distrust and disdain."

2.   "Alvin brought everyone up with him. Including the purists who usually refused to applaud even genius. They too stood up in **languid** praise of him."

It ends up not being important to understand the meaning of the word *languid*. The context tells us what we need to know. The purists are hard to please. They "usually refuse to applaud even genius." This means that if they are applauding, it is an indication that they think the performer is such a genius that they cannot suppress their applause.

Strategy: Consider the two opposite extreme possibilities for the meaning of an unknown word. In this scenario, for example, you could consider how *praise* could be described. Think about phrases you have heard that include the word *praise*. For example, you may have heard the phrase "enthusiastic praise" or "reluctant praise." Which seems to fit this situation? Because the purists rarely applaud, it seems unlikely that they would suddenly enthusiastically applaud Everett Payne. Therefore, it would be wise to interpret the word *languid* to be negative. Indeed, the word *languid* means "lacking energy."

3.   Payne, "unleashed a dazzling **pyrotechnic** of chords."

Everett Payne took his time paying his respects to the tune as written, and once that was done, he hunched closer to the piano, angled his head sharply to the left, completely closed the curtain of his gaze, and with his hands commanding the length and breadth of the keyboard he unleashed a dazzling **pyrotechnic** of chords (you could almost see their colors), polyrhythms, seemingly unrelated harmonies, and ideas—fresh, brash, outrageous ideas. It was an outpouring of ideas and feelings informed by his own brand of lyricism and lit from time to time by flashes of the recognizable melody. He continued to acknowledge the little simpleminded tune, while at the same time furiously recasting and reinventing it in an image all his own.

Even if you do not know all the vocabulary terms, such as *pyrotechnic* or *brash,* it is still clear that his manner of playing is striking and unusual. Payne is presenting the piece in a new and different way.

Word-Meaning Questions

Any passage type can include a question asking for the meaning of a term or phrase in context. To complete these questions, follow these steps. These questions are *not* simply asking for a synonym of the given word. Often, the wrong answers are synonyms of the given word. For example, the word *crude* has multiple meanings, as can be seen in the following sentences.

- The **crude** drawing did not provide enough information to help us locate the glacial lake.

- My grandmother thinks that the profanity on television leads today's teenagers to use too much **crude** language.

- **Crude** oil must be refined before it can be used as gasoline to fuel cars.

In the first sentence, the word *crude* means simple or rudimentary. In other words, the map does not provide enough detail in order to locate the lake. In the second sentence, the word *crude* means uncultured and vulgar. In the third sentence, the word *crude* describes the natural, unrefined state of the oil. Context helps make the meaning of the word clear.

Strategy

1. Return to the passage and read the sentence, saying the word *blank* in place of the word.

2. Then predict a word that would fit well in context. You need to look at the context in order to get this question right. You cannot just rely on your preexisting knowledge about the meaning of the word. Sometimes refreshing your memory about the content of the paragraph that the sentence is within can be helpful.

3. Look at the answer choices and determine which one is most similar to your prediction.

4. Plug that answer choice into the original sentence. If it sounds logical, choose that answer. If it does not, plug in another answer choice.

Practice Questions

NATURAL SCIENCE: This passage is adapted from the essay "Were Dinosaurs Dumb?" by Stephen Jay Gould (©1980 by Stephen Jay Gould).

The remarkable thing about dinosaurs is not that they became extinct, but that they dominated the earth
75 for so long. Dinosaurs held sway for 100 million years while mammals, all the while, lived as small animals in the interstices of their world. After 70 million years on top, we mammals have an excellent track record and good prospects for the future, but we have yet to dis-
80 play the staying power of dinosaurs.

People, on this criterion, are scarcely worth mentioning—5 million years perhaps since *Australopithecus*, a mere 50,000 for our own species, *Homo sapiens*. Try the ultimate test within our system of values: Do you
85 know anyone who would wager a substantial sum even at favorable odds on the proposition that *Homo sapiens* will last longer than *Brontosaurus*?

40. As it is used in line 82, the term *Australopithecus* most nearly means:

Strategy:

Replace the word *Australopithecus* from the original sentence with the word *blank*. Then predict a word that would fit.

Original Sentence:

People, on this criterion, are scarcely worth mentioning—5 million years perhaps since ~~Australopithecus,~~ a mere 50,000 for our own species, *Homo sapiens.*

People, on this criterion, are scarcely worth mentioning—5 million years perhaps since *blank,* a mere 50,000 for our own species, *Homo sapiens.*

F. the last of the dinosaurs, which became extinct 5 million years ago.

G. the first *Homo sapiens,* who appeared on earth 50,000 years ago.

H. an early version of humankind, but a different species.

J. a physically larger species of human with a much smaller brain.

The best answer is H because the author begins the last paragraph by stating that compared to the longevity of dinosaurs, "people … are scarcely worth mentioning" (lines 81–82) and immediately after notes that it's been only 5 million years since the emergence of *Australopithecus* and only 50,000 years since "our own species, *Homo sapiens,*" emerged (line 83). It's clear from this that Australopithecus was human (a "person"), but not a modern human (*Homo sapiens*).

The best answer is NOT:

F because *Australopithecus* wasn't a dinosaur.

G because *Australopithecus* was different from *Homo sapiens* and appeared on earth 5 million years ago.

J because there's no evidence in the passage that *Australopithecus* was a physically larger species of human or that it had a much smaller brain.

LITERARY NARRATIVE: This passage is adapted from the short story "Golden Glass" by Alma Villanueva (©1982 by Bilingual Press).

He seemed always to be at the center of his own universe, so it was no surprise to his mother to hear Ted say: "I'm building a fort and sleeping out in it all
10 summer, and I won't come in for anything, not even food. Okay?"

This had been their silent communion, the steady presence of love that flowed regularly, daily—food. The presence of his mother preparing it, his great
15 appetite and obvious enjoyment of it—his nose smelling everything, seeing his mother more vividly than with his eyes.

Explanatory Notes

This portion of the narrative further establishes the dynamic between Vida and her son Ted. Ted is so immersed in the process of building his fort that he does not even want to return to house for food.

This paragraph establishes that food has served to connect Ted and his mother.

7. As it is used in the passage, the term "silent communion" (line 12) refers to the:

   A. way that without using words Ted communicates his disappointments to Vida.

   B. promise Ted made to himself that he would not return to the house all summer, even for food.

   C. way a thought shifted in Ted's mind from feeling like someone else's to feeling like his own.

   D. exchange of warm emotions between Ted and Vida during the preparation and sharing of food.

The best answer is D because the passage describes the silent communion as "the steady presence of love that flowed regularly, daily" (lines 12–13) through food: "the presence of his mother preparing it, his great appetite and obvious enjoyment of it—his nose smelling everything, seeing his mother more vividly than with his eyes" (lines 14–17).

The best answer is NOT:

A because Ted isn't disappointed but instead pleased by the food and his mother's preparation of it.

B because while Ted does promise not to return to the house all summer, even for food (see lines 9–11), he makes this promise aloud to Vida, and in any case this promise isn't what the phrase "silent communion" refers to.

C because while Ted's thought about liking the moon does shift from seeming like someone else's to seeming like his own (see lines 46–48), this shift isn't what the phrase "silent communion" refers to.

SOCIAL SCIENCE: This passage is adapted from *Biomimicry: Innovation Inspired by Nature* by Janine M. Benyus (©1997 by Janine M. Benyus).

45   Although Kalundborg is a cozy co-location, industries need not be geographically close to operate in a food web as long as they are connected by a mutual desire to use waste. Already, some companies are designing their processes so that any waste that falls on
50 the production-room floor is valuable and can be used by someone else. In this game of "designed offal," a process with lots of waste, as long as it's "wanted waste," may be better than one with a small amount of waste that must be landfilled or burned. As author
55 Daniel Chiras says, more companies are recognizing that "technologies that produce by-products society cannot absorb are essentially failed technologies."

Explanatory Notes

Notice that the definition of "designed offal" is primarily given prior to the mention of this term. The use of the demonstrative pronoun *this* in the introductory clause, "In this game of 'designed offal'…" tells readers that the definition of "designed offal" will come in the previous sentences. From this paragraph we learn that designed offal occurs when "waste that falls on the production-room floor is valuable" (lines 49–51).

The point of emphasis in this paragraph is that companies have the power to design their processes in a sustainable way. Companies can strive to reduce the amount of waste generated in their production of goods.

19. The author uses the term "designed offal" (line 51) to indicate that:

    A. companies can design ways in which their waste products can be used.

    B. industrial ecologists have designed ways to reduce waste products.

    C. technology has not kept pace with how to dispose of waste products.

    D. companies can learn to design more efficient landfill spaces.

The best answer is A because the author says "designed offal" results when companies design their processes in such a way that "any waste that falls on the production-room floor is valuable and can be used by someone else" (lines 49–51).

The best answer is NOT:

B because "designed offal" doesn't necessarily involve reducing waste products: "in this game of 'designed offal,' a process with lots of waste, as long as it's 'wanted waste,' may be better than one with a small amount of waste that must be landfilled or burned" (lines 51–54).

C because "designed offal" is a success story, not a failure of technology to keep pace with how to dispose of waste products.

D because while the author does mention landfills (see lines 51–54 and 62–64), she never discusses the idea of making landfill spaces more efficient. Her focus is on keeping products out of landfills.

NATURAL SCIENCE: This passage is adapted from the essay "Were Dinosaurs Dumb?" by Stephen Jay Gould (©1980 by Stephen Jay Gould).

[8]

    The remarkable thing about dinosaurs is not that they became extinct, but that they dominated the earth
75 for so long. Dinosaurs held sway for 100 million years while mammals, all the while, lived as small animals in the interstices of their world. After 70 million years on top, we mammals have an excellent track record and good prospects for the future, but we have yet to dis-
80 play the staying power of dinosaurs.

[9]

    People, on this criterion, are scarcely worth mentioning—5 million years perhaps since *Australopithecus*, a mere 50,000 for our own species, *Homo sapiens*. Try the ultimate test within our system of values: Do you
85 know anyone who would wager a substantial sum even at favorable odds on the proposition that *Homo sapiens* will last longer than *Brontosaurus*?

Explanatory Notes

    This excerpt emphasizes how long dinosaurs roamed the Earth.

    The first sentence of the ninth paragraph uses the demonstrative pronoun "this" in the phrase "this criterion." A pronoun takes the place of a specific noun after it is first introduced. Therefore, you should return to the last sentence of the previous paragraph to determine what "this criterion" is. It is essentially "the staying power of dinosaurs," which means the 100 million years that they "dominated the earth." In comparison, mammals have only spent "70 million years on top."

34. In the context of the passage, what does the author mean when he states that "people … are scarcely worth mentioning" (lines 81–82)?

  F. Compared to the complex social behavior of dinosaurs, human behavior seems simple.

  G. Compared to the longevity of dinosaurs, humans have been on earth a very short time.

  H. Compared to the size of dinosaurs, humans seem incredibly small.

  J. Compared to the amount of study done on dinosaurs, study of human behavior is severely lacking.

Strategy: Look at least one line before the cited line and begin reading. On your own, without looking at the answer choices, paraphrase the idea "people … are scarcely worth mentioning," taking into consideration the context of the passage. Then look at the answer choices and determine which answer choice aligns most with your prediction. Predicting your own answer first will help you think inductively about the information.

The best answer is G because the author states that while "dinosaurs held sway for 100 million years" (line 75), people have a much shorter history: "5 million years perhaps since *Australopithecus,* a mere 50,000 for our own species, *Homo sapiens*"(lines 82–83).

The best answer is NOT:

  F because while the author does see "signs of social behavior that demand coordination, cohesiveness and recognition" in dinosaurs (lines 57–58), he nowhere suggests that human behavior seems simple in comparison to the complexity of dinosaur social behavior.

  H because while the author does call dinosaurs "very large animals" (line 53), he doesn't claim that humans seem incredibly small in comparison.

  J because nowhere in the passage does the author contend that study on human behavior is severely lacking in comparison to the amount of study done on dinosaurs.

SOCIAL SCIENCE: This passage is adapted from Richard Moe's article "Mindless Madness Called Sprawl," based on a speech he gave on November 30, 1996, in Fresno, California (©1996 by Richard Moe).

At the time he gave the speech, Moe was president of the National Trust for Historic Preservation.

Sprawl's other most familiar form—spread-out residential subdivisions that "leapfrog" from the urban 50 fringe into the countryside—is driven largely by the American dream of a detached home in the middle of a grassy lawn. Developers frequently claim they can build more "affordable" housing on the edge of town—but "affordable" for whom?

18. As it is used in line 51, the word *detached* most nearly means:

  F. objective.

  G. set apart.

  H. broken apart.

  J. taken away.

The best answer is G because the sentence is describing how residential subdivisions are driven "by the American dream of a detached home in the middle of a grassy lawn" (lines 50–52). Because a grassy lawn surrounds the home being referred to, it is reasonable to assume there is space between the home and other structures. In other words, the home is "set apart."

The best answer is NOT:

F because although the word *detached* can indicate an objective point of view, *detached* is used in this context to describe a house, which does not have a point of view.

H because the passage does not provide a clear sense of what "broken apart" would mean in the context of this sentence.

J because there is nothing in the passage to suggest that the home being referred to was "taken away" from another location.

SOCIAL SCIENCE: This passage is adapted from Richard Moe's article "Mindless Madness Called Sprawl," based on a speech he gave on November 30, 1996, in Fresno, California (©1996 by Richard Moe).

At the time he gave the speech, Moe was president of the National Trust for Historic Preservation.

55   The developer's own expenses may be less, and the home buyer may find the prices attractive—but who picks up the extra costs of fire and police protection, new roads and new utility infrastructure in these outlying areas? We all do, in the form of higher taxes for
60   needless duplication of services and infrastructure that already exist in older parts of our cities and towns.

People who say that sprawl is merely the natural product of marketplace forces at work fail to recognize that the game isn't being played on a level field. Gov-
65   ernment at every level is riddled with policies that mandate or encourage sprawl.

19. The author uses the statement "The game isn't being played on a level field" (line 64) most nearly to mean that:

    A. cities needlessly duplicate essential services.

    B. higher taxes for some people make their lives more difficult.

    C. marketplace forces are at work.

    D. governmental decisions influence marketplace forces.

The best answer is D because the statement in question is preceded by, and is intended to counter, the claim made by some people that "sprawl is merely the natural product of marketplace forces at work" (lines 62–63). Therefore, the author is arguing that people who make this claim "fail to recognize" (line 63) that those market forces are influenced by governmental decisions. The author's rhetoric here assumes that the reader will recognize "a level playing field" as a popular expression for conditions governed purely by market forces and will understand that a playing field that "isn't level" (line 64) refers to conditions in which governmental decisions do influence market forces.

The best answer is NOT:

A because the "needless duplication of services and infrastructure" (line 60) referred to in the passage is identified as a result of sprawl, whereas the phrase "the game isn't being played on a level field" (line 64) is used to identify the influence of governmental decisions on market forces, and not market forces alone, as a cause of sprawl.

B because the "higher taxes" (line 59) referred to in the passage are identified as a result of sprawl, whereas the phrase "the game isn't being played on a level field" (line 64) is used to identify the influence of governmental decisions on market forces, and not market forces alone, as a cause of sprawl.

C because the phrase "the game isn't being played on a level field" (line 64) is used to identify the influence of governmental decisions on market forces, and not market forces alone, as a cause of sprawl. The author's rhetoric here assumes that the reader will recognize "a level playing field" as a popular expression for conditions governed purely by market forces, and will understand that a playing field that "isn't level" (line 64) refers to conditions in which governmental decisions do influence market forces.

SOCIAL SCIENCE: This passage is adapted from Richard Moe's article "Mindless Madness Called Sprawl," based on a speech he gave on November 30, 1996, in Fresno, California (©1996 by Richard Moe).

At the time he gave the speech, Moe was president of the National Trust for Historic Preservation.

By prohibiting mixed uses and mandating inordinate amounts of parking and unreasonable setback requirements, most current zoning laws make it impos-
70 sible—even illegal—to create the sort of compact walkable environment that attracts us to older neighborhoods and historic communities all over the world. These codes are a major reason why 82 percent of all trips in the United States are taken by car. The average
75 American household now allocates more than 18 percent of its budget to transportation expenses, most of which are auto-related. That's more than it spends for food and three times more than it spends for health care.

Note: The answer explanations below refer to paragraphs that are not represented here. Those paragraphs are not needed in order to answer this question. This question can be answered with only the information reproduced here.

20. The phrase *mixed uses* (line 67) most likely refers to:

   F. having large parking lots around even larger stores.

   G. preserving and restoring historic neighborhoods.

   H. ensuring that automobiles cannot be driven to the various local businesses.

   J. allowing one area to contain various types of development.

The best answer is J because the passage identifies zoning laws that prohibit "mixed uses" (line 67) as a primary cause of the separation of urban commercial zones and residential subdivisions described in the three paragraphs that immediately precede the sentence in question. That separation of commercial and residential land use is contrasted, in the following sentences, with "the sort of compact walkable environment that attracts us to older neighborhoods and historic communities all over the world" (lines 70–72). Therefore, the phrase "mixed uses" can be understood as referring to zoning that allows one area to contain various types of development.

The best answer is NOT:

F because the passage identifies both large parking lots (lines 3–4) and large retail stores (lines 38–42) as being characteristic of sprawl, which is encouraged by the prohibition of "mixed uses" (line 67). Furthermore, parking lots and retail stores are both understood to be commercial uses of land, and therefore the phrase "mixed uses" is unlikely to refer to them.

G because although the passage states that the prohibition of "mixed uses" (line 67) makes it "impossible—even illegal—to create the sort of compact walkable environment that attracts us to older neighborhoods and historic communities" (lines 69–72), the phrase "mixed uses" itself is not directly associated with historic preservation in any way. Rather, "mixed uses" refers to the designation of land use as residential, commercial, or industrial under zoning laws.

H because although "mixed uses" (line 67) are understood within the context of the passage as encouraging the creation of a "walkable environment" (line 71), there is no association between the phrase "mixed uses" and the prohibition of driving or parking.

HUMANITIES: This passage is adapted from the essay "My Life with a Field Guide" by Diana Kappel-Smith (©2002 by Phi Beta Kappa Society).

[5]

Later that day, a book with a green cover lay on
15　the arm of a chair under an apple tree. It was the same volume that our guide had carried as he marched us through the woods. The book had been left there, by itself. It was a thing of power. In the thin summer shadow of the tree, quivering, like a veil, the book was
20　revealed, and I reached for it. A FIELD GUIDE TO WILD FLOWERS—PETERSON & McKENNY, its cover said. Its backside was ruled like a measuring tape, its inside was full of drawings of flowers. By the end of that week I had my own copy. I have it still.

…

[9]

Why I persisted in carrying it around and consulting its crowded pages at every opportunity, I have no idea. The book was stubborn; well, I was stubborn, too;
55　that was part of it. And I had no choice, really, not if I wanted to get in. A landscape may be handsome in the aggregate, but this book led to the particulars, and that's what I wanted. A less complete guide would have been easier to start with, but more frustrating in the
60　end. A more complete book would have been impossible for me to use. So I persisted in wrestling with the Peterson's, and thus by slow degrees the crowd of plant stuff in the world became composed of individuals. As it did, the book changed: its cover was stained by
65　water and snack food, the spine grew invitingly lax, and some of the margins sprouted cryptic annotations.

---

25. As it is used in line 56, the phrase *get in* most nearly means:

　A. arrive at a physical location.

　B. be chosen for group membership.

　C. truly understand the subject.

　D. be friendly with someone.

The best answer is C because the sentence in question reads "I had no choice, really, not if I wanted to get in" (lines 55–56), and the surrounding sentences indicate that the matter she had no choice in was the use of the field guide, which "led to the particulars" (line 57), or deepened her understanding, of the landscape. Therefore, in this context, to "get in" to a subject can be understood as meaning to fully understand that subject.

The best answer is NOT:

A because the sentence in question reads "I had no choice, really, not if I wanted to get in" (lines 55–56), and there is no indication in the surrounding lines that the matter she has no choice in is her arrival in a specific location. Rather, she wants to figuratively, and not literally, arrive at a deeper understanding of the landscape, and she has no choice but to use the field guide in order to do so (lines 55–58).

B because the sentence in question reads "I had no choice, really, not if I wanted to get in" (lines 55–56), and there is no indication in the surrounding lines or the passage as a whole that the matter she has no choice in has anything to do with membership in any group. Rather, she wants to figuratively, and not literally, "get in" to a deeper understanding of the landscape, and she has no choice but to use the field guide in order to do so (lines 55–58).

D because the sentence in question reads "I had no choice, really, not if I wanted to get in" (lines 55–56), and there is no indication in the surrounding lines or the passage as a whole that the matter she has no choice in has anything to do with being friendly with someone. Rather, she wants to figuratively, and not literally, "get in" to a deeper understanding of the landscape, and she has no choice but to use the field guide in order to do so (lines 55–58).

Note: The following question draws on a portion of the same passage excerpt as the previous question. The relevant excerpts have been reproduced here so you can easily refer to the text.

HUMANITIES: This passage is adapted from the essay "My Life with a Field Guide" by Diana Kappel-Smith (©2002 by Phi Beta Kappa Society).

[9]

Why I persisted in carrying it around and consulting its crowded pages at every opportunity, I have no idea. The book was stubborn; well, I was stubborn, too;
55 that was part of it. And I had no choice, really, not if I wanted to get in. A landscape may be handsome in the aggregate, but this book led to the particulars, and that's what I wanted. A less complete guide would have been easier to start with, but more frustrating in the
60 end. A more complete book would have been impossible for me to use. So I persisted in wrestling with the Peterson's, and thus by slow degrees the crowd of plant stuff in the world became composed of individuals. As it did, the book changed: its cover was stained by
65 water and snack food, the spine grew invitingly lax, and some of the margins sprouted cryptic annotations.

28. In the context of the passage, the author's statement in lines 56–58 most nearly means that she:

F. learned to understand landscapes by looking at their overall patterns rather than their details.

G. found that landscapes lost their appeal the more she tried to understand them logically.

H. hoped to paint attractive portraits of landscapes by paying careful attention to details.

J. sought a deeper knowledge of landscapes through learning about their individual parts.

The best answer is J because the author's statement that "a landscape may be handsome in the aggregate, but this book led to the particulars, and that's what I wanted" (lines 56–58) contrasts the surface appeal of a landscape seen at a distance with the deeper knowledge of a landscape that only comes from familiarity with the "particulars," or individual parts, and specifies that this deeper knowledge of the landscape is what she sought.

The best answer is NOT:

F because the author's statement that "a landscape may be handsome in the aggregate, but this book led to the particulars, and that's what I wanted" (lines 56–58) specifies that she was more interested in the deeper knowledge of the landscape that comes from familiarity with the "particulars," or individual parts, than she was in an understanding of a landscape that might come from looking at its overall patterns.

G because although the passage does relate the way in which the field guide helps the author break landscapes down logically into their "particulars" (line 57), or individual parts, there is no indication that this made landscapes lose their appeal. Rather, she states that this kind of understanding was "what [she] wanted" (line 58) and that the logically ordered classifications in the field guide all made "such delightful sense" (lines 79–80).

H because there is no indication in the passage that the deeper understanding of landscapes that she sought through knowledge of their "particulars" (line 57), or individual parts, was in any way related to painting portraits of those landscapes.

Note: Paragraph numbers have been indicated in brackets below, but these brackets are not in the real test. They have been provided here in order to help orient you within the context of the passage as a whole. Some paragraphs have been omitted, which is indicated by use of ellipses.

NATURAL SCIENCE: This passage is adapted from the article "When Research Is a Snow Job" by Sarah Boyle (©2002 by National Wildlife).

[2]

Kenneth Libbrecht is a physicist at the California Institute of Technology. Along with the work of scientists at the U.S. Department of Agriculture's Agricul-
10 tural Research Service (ARS), his research is uncovering new information about the magical world of snow crystals—information that has practical applications in such diverse areas as agriculture and the production of electricity.

...

[8]

50   Wergin called another ARS colleague, hydrologist Albert Rango, to see if the snow crystal magnifications had any applications for his research. Rango now uses Wergin's electron microscopy data, along with microwave satellite data, in the Snowmelt Runoff
55 Model to predict the amount of water available in a winter snowpack. For western states such as Colorado, Montana, Utah and Wyoming, about 75 percent of the annual water supply comes from snowmelt. Snowmelt water is critical to crop irrigation and hydroelectric
60 power, as well as recreation and domestic water supplies, fisheries management and flood control.

39. As it is used in line 59, the word *critical* most nearly means:

A. evaluative.

B. faultfinding.

C. vital.

D. acute.

The best answer is C because the sentence in question states that "snowmelt water is critical to crop irrigation and hydroelectric power, as well as recreation and domestic water supplies, fisheries management and flood control" (lines 58–61). In context, this is understood to mean that snowmelt water is vital, or very important, to these processes and practices.

The best answer is NOT:

A because the sentence in question states that "snowmelt water is critical to crop irrigation and hydroelectric power, as well as recreation and domestic water supplies, fisheries management and flood control" (lines 58–61). In this context critical cannot be read as meaning "evaluative" because snowmelt water cannot evaluate anything or anyone.

B because the sentence in question states that "snowmelt water is critical to crop irrigation and hydroelectric power, as well as recreation and domestic water supplies, fisheries management and flood control" (lines 58–61). In this context critical cannot be read as meaning "faultfinding" because snowmelt water cannot find fault with anything or anyone.

D because the sentence in question states that "snowmelt water is critical to crop irrigation and hydroelectric power, as well as recreation and domestic water supplies, fisheries management and flood control" (lines 58–61). In context, the adjective critical is understood to mean that snowmelt water is vital, or very important, to these processes and practices. Although it is also an adjective and can sometimes be understood to mean "vital" or "important," *acute* cannot be substituted for critical in this sentence because it would be neither grammatical nor logical to say "water is acute to crop irrigation."

NATURAL SCIENCE: This passage is adapted from the article "When Research Is a Snow Job" by Sarah Boyle (©2002 by National Wildlife).

15   Snow crystals are individual crystals—usually in a hexagonal form—while snowflakes are collections of two or more snow crystals. Beginning as condensed water vapor, a crystal typically grows around a nucleus of dust. Its shape depends on how the six side facets—
20 or faces—grow in relation to the top and bottom facets. If they grow relatively tall, the crystal appears column-like; if the side facets are short compared to the length of the bottom and top facets, the crystal looks platelike.

    Currently Libbrecht is trying to crack the problem
25 of why the crystal facets' growth varies with tempera-ture. He believes this may have something to do with the ice surface's "quasi-liquid" layer, which affects how water molecules stick to the surface.

    By manipulating the temperature and humidity
30 within an incubation chamber (and by adding an elec-tric current or various gases at times), Libbrecht creates "designer" snowflakes in his lab. Such experiments are helping him determine how crystals form.

38. The term "designer" snowflakes (line 32) refers directly to the fact that:

   F. no two snowflakes are alike.

   G. Libbrecht produces the snowflakes in his lab.

   H. snowflakes are part of the grand design of nature.

   J. Libbrecht's snowflakes exhibit special beauty.

The best answer is G because the passage specifies that the physicist Kenneth Libbrecht "creates 'designer' snowflakes in his lab" (lines 31–32).

The best answer is NOT:

F because the passage makes no connection between the term "'designer' snowflakes" (line 32) and the fact that no two snowflakes are alike. Rather, the passage specifies that the physicist Kenneth Libbrecht "creates 'designer' snowflakes in his lab" (lines 31–32).

H because the passage makes no mention of the grand design of nature. Rather, the passage specifies that the physicist Kenneth Libbrecht "creates 'designer' snowflakes in his lab" (lines 31–32).

J because although the passage does state that the physicist Kenneth Libbrecht "creates 'designer' snowflakes in his lab" (lines 31–32), the passage makes no mention of the beauty of Libbrecht's snowflakes.

Vocabulary

When the ACT reading test asks you to provide a synonym for a word in a passage, there is always a good deal of textual evidence to help you piece together the meaning of a word. Words are the building blocks of sentences, which are the building blocks of paragraphs, which are the building blocks of whole passages.

Accordingly, expanding your vocabulary should improve your reading comprehension. Having a vast vocabulary can help you process passages more quickly. Many wonderful apps can help you easily study vocabulary on your phone or tablet during your free time. It can also be helpful to keep a vocabulary journal where you write down new words as you learn them. Writing down a synonym, definition, or a sentence that properly uses a word can help you retain its meaning. Physical or digital flashcards can also help you retain the meanings of words.

Students have a tendency to eliminate or gravitate toward answer choices that include vocabulary terms they do not understand. It is not logical to simply eliminate an answer choice because it contains a word you do not know. When faced with this situation, try to use your knowledge of the vocabulary in the other answer choices to eliminate some wrong answer choices.

Once you have your answer choices narrowed down to only two options, think about the meaning of the answer choice that is written in simple vocabulary. If that answer does *not* accurately reflect the passage, then you should eliminate it and choose the answer with the vocabulary term with which you are unfamiliar.

By contrast, if the answer choice that is expressed in simpler terms *does* seem to accurately reflect the content of the passage, do not be afraid to choose that answer even though it means eliminating an answer choice that includes a vocabulary term that you do not know. For example, often students do not know the meaning of the word *embittered* in the answer choices for the practice question on page 122, and they then choose answer choice **J**, assuming that because the word *embittered* sounds sophisticated, it must be correct. That logic does not hold true.

Extreme Words

In general, you should be wary of extreme words found in answer choices because these absolute words tend to neglect the complexities of material presented in the passages.

Extreme words include the following:

never	no	certainly	undeniably	constantly
always	all	obviously	undoubtedly	continually
entirely	every	definitely	incontrovertibly	eliminating
none	proves	unquestionably	indisputably	ban
prohibit	cancel	prevent	stop	reject
cease	end	begin	initially	first

It is better to choose answers with nuanced, qualified language such as the following:

often in most cases	not necessarily	most likely	
seldom in many cases	not mutually exclusive	might	
usually in rare cases	in certain situations	frequently	
some of the time	in some cases	some	sometimes

You should be suspicious of intense emotional words that do not accurately reflect the feelings of the characters or individuals in the literary narrative, social science, and humanities passages. The practice question on page 120 includes an answer choice that contains the word *indignation* (**bolded**), which is used to describe intense anger.

Note: Paragraph numbers have been indicated in brackets in this passage, but these brackets are not provided in the real test. They have been provided here in order to help orient you within the context of the passage as a whole. Some paragraphs have been omitted, which is indicated by use of ellipses.

Practice Questions

LITERARY NARRATIVE: This passage is adapted from the short story "Golden Glass" by Alma Villanueva (©1982 by Bilingual Press).

[2]

He seemed always to be at the center of his own universe, so it was no surprise to his mother to hear Ted say: "I'm building a fort and sleeping out in it all
10 summer, and I won't come in for anything, not even food. Okay?"

...

[12]

Vida noticed Ted had become cheerful and would stand next to her, to her left side, talking sometimes. But she realized she mustn't face him or he'd become silent and wander away. So she stood listening, in the
65 same even breath and heart beat she kept when she spotted the wild pheasants with their long, lush tails trailing the grape arbor, picking delicately and greedily at the unpicked grapes in the early autumn light. So sharp, so perfect, so rare to see a wild thing at peace.

[13]

70 Ted was taking a makeup course and one in stained glass. There, he talked and acted relaxed; no one expected any more or less. The colors of the stained glass were deep and beautiful, and special—you couldn't waste this glass. The sides were sharp, the cuts
75 were slow and meticulous with a steady pressure. The design's plan had to be absolutely followed or the beautiful glass would go to waste, and he'd curse himself.

Explanatory Notes

Paragraph 12 describes how Vida observes her son Ted. The narrator explains that Vida realizes when Ted is cheerfully immersed in the process of building a fort.

Paragraph 13 describes the delicacy with which Ted treats stained glass. He knows it is precious and that it must be handled carefully in order not to waste it.

3. In both the twelfth paragraph (lines 61–69) and the thirteenth paragraph (lines 70–77) the author is portraying characters who:

   A. feel compelled to act carefully in order to avoid shattering something precious.

   B. are frustrated to the point of **indignation** that success seems always slightly out of reach.

   C. are at first excited by a project but later lose interest as others get involved.

   D. discover that a personal weakness in some situations can be a personal strength in others.

The best answer is A because in the twelfth paragraph (lines 61–69), the author says Vida avoided facing Ted and remained still to keep from disturbing "a wild thing at peace" (line 69), while in the thirteenth paragraph (lines 70–77), the author describes Ted making cuts in glass that "were slow and meticulous with a steady pressure" (line 75) and carefully following the design in order to avoid wasting the glass.

The best answer is NOT:

B because Vida is neither frustrated nor unsuccessful in the twelfth paragraph, while the thirteenth paragraph only says Ted became frustrated when he failed, not that success was always slightly out of reach for him.

C because neither the twelfth nor the thirteenth paragraph shows a character losing interest in a project as others get involved.

D because neither the twelfth nor the thirteenth paragraph shows a character discovering a personal weakness in some situations becoming a personal strength in others.

LITERARY NARRATIVE: This passage is adapted from the short story "Elba" by Marly Swick (©1991 by the University of Iowa). Fran is the narrator of the story.

Mother, who wanted to keep her, always thought of her as some wild little bird, but I knew she was a homing pigeon. I knew that at some point in her flight path, sooner or later, she would make a U-turn. A sort
5 of human boomerang. So even though I had long since stopped expecting it, I was not surprised when I walked down the gravel drive to the mailbox, which I'd painted papaya yellow to attract good news, and found the flimsy envelope with the Dallas postmark. I didn't
10 know a soul in Dallas, or Texas for that matter, but the handwriting reminded me of someone's. My own.

I walked back inside the house.

"Still raining?" Mother asked. She was sitting in her new electric wheelchair in front of the TV, painting
15 her fingernails a neon violet.

"Just let up," I said. "Sun's poking through. You know anyone in Dallas, Mother?"

"Not so as I recall." She dabbed at her pinky with a cottonball. Mother was vain about her hands. I was
20 used to how she looked now, but I noticed people staring in the doctor's waiting room. She had lost some weight and most of her hair to chemotherapy, and I guess people were startled to see these dragon-lady nails on a woman who looked as if she should be lying
25 in satin with some flowers on her chest.

"Why do you ask?" she said.

I opened the envelope and a picture fluttered into my lap. It was a Polaroid of a sweet-faced blond holding a newborn baby in a blue blanket. Before I
30 even read the letter I knew. I knew how those Nazis feel when suddenly, after twenty or thirty uneventful years, they are arrested walking down some sunny street in Buenos Aires. It's the shock of being found after waiting so long.

35 "What's that?" Mother said.

I wheeled her around to face me and handed her the Polaroid. She studied it for a minute and then looked up, speechless for once, waiting for me to set the tone.

40 "That's her," I said. "Her name's Linda Rose Caswell."

We looked at the picture again. The blond woman was seated on a flowered couch, her wavy hair just grazing the edge of a dime-a-dozen seascape in a cheap gilt frame.

45 Mother pointed to the envelope. "What's she say?"

I unfolded the letter, a single page neatly written.

"She says she's had my name and address for some time but wanted to wait to contact me until after the birth. The baby's name is Blake and he weighs eight
50 pounds, eight ounces, and was born by cesarean. She says they are waiting and hoping to hear back from me soon."

"That's it?"

I nodded and handed her the letter. It was short
55 and businesslike, but I could see the ghosts of all the long letters she must have written and crumpled into the wastebasket.

"I guess that makes you a great-grandmother," I said.

60 "What about you?" she snorted, pointing a Jungle Orchid fingernail at me. "You're a grandmother." We shook our heads in disbelief. I sat silently, listening to my brain catch up with my history. Forty years old and I felt as if I had just shaken hands with
65 Death. I suppose it's difficult for any woman to accept that she's a grandmother, but in the normal order of things, you have ample time to adjust to the idea. You don't get a snapshot in the mail one day from a baby

(continued)

(continued)

girl you gave up twenty-four years ago saying,
70 Congratulations, you're a grandma!"

"It's not fair," I said. "I don't even feel like a mother."

"Well, here's the living proof." Mother tapped her nail against the glossy picture. "She looks just like you. Only her nose is more aristocratic."

75   "I'm going to work." My knees cracked when I stood up. "You be all right here?"

Mother nodded, scrutinizing the picture in her lap. "You going to write to her?"

"Of course I am," I bristled. "I may be some
80 things, but I am not rude."

"You going to invite them here? Her and the baby?" She swiveled her eyes sideways at me.

"I haven't thought that far," I said.

"Well, don't put it off." She slid her eyes back to
85 the television. "She's been waiting twenty-five years. You worried she's going to be trouble or ask for money? For all we know, she's married to a brain surgeon with his and her Cadillacs."

"She didn't mention any husband at all," I said,
90 getting drawn into it despite myself.

"Maybe you're worried she'll be disappointed in you," she said, "You know, that she's had this big fantasy for all these years that maybe you were Grace Kelly or Margaret Mead and who could live up to that?
95 No one. But you don't have to, Fran, that's the thing. You're her flesh-and-blood mother and that's enough. That's all it'll take."

Strategy: Be suspicious of extreme words. For an extreme word to be the answer choice, the passage would need clear-cut textual evidence to support such an interpretation. For example, *upset* is not an extreme word, but *enraged* is. Also pay attention to the shades of meaning for words that have the same denotation, or literal meaning, but different connotations.

Scan for: Fran, Mother

> **2.** Fran's mother can most accurately be characterized as:
>
>   **F.** arrogant and cruel.
>
>   **G.** strong-willed and caring.
>
>   **H.** friendly but withdrawn.
>
>   **J.** loving but embittered.

The best answer is G because *strong-willed* and *caring* best describe Fran's mother. She has "dragon-lady nails" (lines 23–24) in defiance of her chemotherapy. She "snorted" (line 61) a response to Fran's about her being a great-grandmother. She also firmly tells Fran not to put off contacting Linda Rose, who's "been waiting for twenty-five years" (line 87) for a meeting. But Fran's mother also cares deeply about Fran and tries to reassure her by saying, "You're [Linda Rose's] flesh-and-blood mother and that's enough. That's all it'll take" (lines 98–99).

The best answer is NOT:

F because while Fran's mother might (with some difficulty) be described as arrogant, she isn't cruel. Although Fran's mother "snorted" a response to Fran and though she firmly tells Fran not to put off contacting Linda Rose, her love for Fran and her concern for Linda Rose's feelings also come through.

H because although Fran's mother might be described as friendly, she isn't withdrawn, as revealed by her nails, her snort, and her firm warning to Fran.

J because although Fran's mother is loving, there's no evidence in the passage that she's embittered. Being *embittered* means "to feel resentment, or intense anger" often when one feels they have been wronged.

Interpreting Figurative Language

Figurative language can appear in any passage type, not just in the literary narrative passage. Typically, questions will be asked about the purpose of instances of figurative language. Figurative language means that an idea is conveyed in an indirect manner, often through sensory details. In contrast, literal language means directly stating an idea. For example, you might say, "I checked the thermometer, and the temperature is 9°F outside." This is factually quantifying how cold it is outside.

The most common forms of figurative language are similes, metaphors, extended metaphors, hyperbole, personification, and irony.

Similes and Metaphors

You have probably learned that a simile is a comparison that uses *like* or *as*. For example, if a classmate says that "the school library is like an igloo today," you know that that person is not saying that the library is literally made of blocks of ice. Your classmate is conveying that the space is freezing.

Metaphors make a comparison without using *like* or *as*. For example, the metaphor, "Ms. Hogue is a walking thesaurus," implies that Ms. Hogue has a vast vocabulary and that she can supply a synonym for any word. Poet Emily Dickinson used metaphors frequently as when she wrote, "Hope is a thing with feathers." Here, Dickinson figuratively compares the abstract concept of hope to a bird. This implies that hope is liberating because birds are typically associated with freedom due to their ability to fly. Notice that metaphors often employ a form of the verb *to be*.

Some reading questions will ask you to identify a metaphorical comparison from the passage. For example, a question might ask, "The metaphor the author uses to describe how ill the main character feels primarily draws on what type of imagery?" Try to avoid answers that are overly literal. For example, for the previous question, if one of the answer choices had been "medical," that would not likely be a good answer because the question asks about metaphors and the literal situation is medical. If the passage said, "She turned ghost white. Her eyes were bloodshot," a correct answer might be something like "colorful." The first sentence "She turned ghost white" metaphorically compares the character's skin color to a ghost. The second sentence "Her eyes were bloodshot" implies that the character's eyes are red.

Example 1

"The letter was short and businesslike, but I could see the **ghosts of all the long letters she must have written** and crumpled into the wastebasket."

Strategy: Think about the qualities of a ghost. A ghost is a spiritual trace of a person who has passed away. What would the ghost of a letter be? This metaphor implies that several letters existed and were discarded before the final letter was completed. Notice that the word *ghost* has been used in two metaphors in this chapter but the meaning has been different based on the context.

Example 2

"One of the things that I prided myself on was my ability to conceal my thoughts. I had just looked her in the face and **made myself a mirror**, frowning when she frowned, raising my eyebrows just seconds after she'd raised hers."

Paraphrase: Fortunately, this instance of figurative language is accompanied by details that make its function quite clear. The narrator is trying to convey how she mimics someone else's facial expressions in order to hide her own thoughts.

Example 3

"That was his [Payne's] way, Hattie knew. His body moving absentmindedly through space, his head, his thoughts on something other than his surroundings, and **his eyes like a curtain he occasionally drew aside a fraction of an inch to peer out at the world.** A world far less interesting than the music inside his head. She watched now as he slowly mounted the bandstand and conferred with the bassist and drummer."

Paraphrase: Hattie knows Payne well. Here, author Paule Marshall employs a simile to underscore how mysterious Payne is, comparing his eyes to a curtain that is rarely opened: "his eyes like a curtain he occasionally drew aside." This simile also conveys how Payne is immersed in his old world and unconcerned with the outside world.

Extended Metaphor

Some fiction and nonfiction works use extended metaphors, meaning a comparison is drawn out, sometimes for the duration of the piece. This is the case in Virginia Wolfe's "Two Dinners," which, on a surface level, describes meals Wolfe had on two different college campuses: the first at a men's college and the second at a women's college. Wolfe's descriptions of the food figuratively underscore the differences between the two schools on a larger scale. The meal at the men's college is described as abundant and decadent and the meal at the women's college is described as sparse and unsatisfying. On a deeper level, this piece highlights the disparity between the resources offered at the two colleges.

Hyperbole

Hyperbole is a form of figurative language because it uses exaggeration to make a point. For example, you might say "I spent a million dollars on prom" in order to convey that the event was extremely costly.

Personification

Personification gives human qualities to inanimate objects. For example, you might say, "My computer betrayed me by crashing the night before my essay was due," or "My plants were desperate for sun." Figurative language can be found in any reading passage type, but it is the most common in the literary narrative passage. When you encounter figurative language, expect that a question will be asked about it. It can be worth taking a moment to think about the meaning of the use of figurative language in context.

Irony

Some passages contain verbal irony that can be difficult to interpret. Verbal irony means there is a discrepancy between what is being said on a surface level and what is actually being said. Verbal irony is similar to sarcasm. Sarcasm is verbal irony that is intended to mock or criticize. For example, if a friend spilled his drink at a restaurant you might say, "I can't take you anywhere." You do not actually mean that you cannot take your friend anywhere. You are just mocking your friend in a lighthearted way. The following passage excerpts contain irony and the question that follows relies on a reader's understanding of this irony.

Practice Questions

LITERARY NARRATIVE: This passage is adapted from the short story "Elba" by Marly Swick (©1991 by the University of Iowa). Fran is the narrator of the story.

65   … I suppose it's difficult for any woman to accept that she's a grandmother, but in the normal order of things, you have ample time to adjust to the idea. You don't get a snapshot in the mail one day from a baby girl you gave up twenty-four years ago saying,
70 Congratulations, you're a grandma!"

"It's not fair," I said. "I don't even feel like a mother."

"Well, here's the living proof." Mother tapped her nail against the glossy picture. "She looks just like you. Only her nose is more aristocratic."

75   "I'm going to work." My knees cracked when I stood up. "You be all right here?"

Mother nodded, scrutinizing the picture in her lap. "You going to write to her?"

"Of course I am," I bristled. "I may be some
80 things, but I am not rude."

"You going to invite them here? Her and the baby?" She swiveled her eyes sideways at me.

"I haven't thought that far," I said.

"Well, don't put it off." She slid her eyes back to
85 the television. "She's been waiting twenty-five years. You worried she's going to be trouble or ask for money? For all we know, she's married to a brain surgeon with his and her Cadillacs."

"She didn't mention any husband at all," I said,
90 getting drawn into it despite myself.

"Maybe you're worried she'll be disappointed in you," she said, "You know, that she's had this big fantasy for all these years that maybe you were Grace Kelly or Margaret Mead and who could live up to that?
95 No one. But you don't have to, Fran, that's the thing. You're her flesh-and-blood mother and that's enough. That's all it'll take."

5. The main point of the last paragraph (lines 93–97) is that Fran's mother believes:

   A. Linda Rose has few illusions about Fran.

   B. Linda Rose might cause trouble or ask for money.

   C. Fran shouldn't worry about disappointing Linda Rose.

   D. Fran shouldn't write to Linda Rose until Fran is emotionally prepared.

In the last paragraph, Fran's mother is talking to her about how she is worried that Fran's daughter Linda Rose may be disappointed when she finally meets her. Fran may suppose Linda Rose has always thought of her as someone glamorous or famous, but most likely Linda Rose has a realistic view. Fran's mother expresses this idea through verbal irony, saying that, Linda Rose has perhaps "had this big fantasy for all these years that maybe you were Grace Kelly or Margaret Mead." Fran's mother doesn't actually think that Linda Rose dreams that Fran is Grace Kelly or Margaret Mead. This is a bit difficult to understand if you do not know who Grace Kelly and Margaret Mead are. Even if you do not know that Grace Kelly was a 1950s movie star who became princess of Monaco or that Margaret Mead was a cultural anthropologist who wrote about family systems in Samoa, you do know that they are women whom it might be difficult to live up to because Fran's mother says, "who could live up to that? No one. But you don't have to."

The best answer is C because the last paragraph focuses on Fran's mother's efforts to reassure Fran. Fran's mother brings up the idea of Linda Rose having a "big fantasy" (lines 94–95) that Fran is Grace Kelly or Margaret Mead and says "no one" (line 97) could live up to that. She goes on to say, though, that as Linda Rose's "flesh-and-blood mother," Fran has "all it'll take" to have a good relationship with Linda Rose (lines 98–99).

The best answer is NOT:

A because neither Fran nor her mother has seen Linda Rose for a quarter century, so they can only guess about what Linda Rose thinks.

B because the only reference to the idea that Linda Rose might cause trouble or ask for money occurs in the twenty-seventh paragraph (lines 86–90), not in the last paragraph.

D because in the last paragraph, Fran's mother tries to reassure Fran in an effort to encourage her to invite Linda Rose and Blake for a visit in the near future.

LITERARY NARRATIVE: This passage is adapted from the short story "Elba" by Marly Swick (©1991 by the University of Iowa). Fran is the narrator of the story.

[1]

Mother, who wanted to keep her, always thought of her as some wild little bird, but I knew she was a homing pigeon. I knew that at some point in her flight path, sooner or later, she would make a U-turn. A sort
5 of human boomerang. So even though I had long since stopped expecting it, I was not surprised when I walked down the gravel drive to the mailbox, which I'd painted papaya yellow to attract good news, and found the flimsy envelope with the Dallas postmark. I didn't
10 know a soul in Dallas, or Texas for that matter, but the handwriting reminded me of someone's. My own.

Explanatory Notes

The first paragraph includes a metaphor comparing Fran's daughter Linda Rose to a homing pigeon. This kind of pigeon is trained to travel long distances to deliver messages and then to return home. The implication is that Linda Rose has a strong natural instinct to return home.

4. The main point of the first paragraph is that:

    F. Fran believed Linda Rose would someday try to contact her.

    G. Linda Rose acted like a wild bird when she was young.

    H. Fran finds the arrival of a letter from Linda Rose surprising.

    J. Linda Rose's handwriting reminds Fran of her own handwriting.

Note: Answering this question may require rereading the introductory paragraph and thinking about how it functions in the context of the passage as a whole. It is not really possible to predict words or phrases to scan for in order to determine the main idea of the introductory paragraph. Of course, the main idea will relate to the main characters: Fran and Linda Rose. However, each answer choice includes both characters' names. Thus, it is not helpful to scan the passage for their names. Instead, you need to synthesize the ideas in the paragraph to determine the main point being made.

The best answer is F because the first paragraph is built on Fran's lack of surprise that Linda Rose contacted her. Fran calls Linda Rose "a homing pigeon" (lines 2–3) and "a sort of human boomerang" (lines 4–5) whom she knew "sooner or later … would make a U-turn" back to her (line 4). The paragraph closes with Fran's suspicion, based on the familiarity of the handwriting, that the letter in the mailbox is from Linda Rose. Fran claims that although she had "long stopped expecting" such a letter, she "was not surprised" when she got it (lines 5–6).

The best answer is NOT:

    G because the first paragraph doesn't claim that Linda Rose acted like a wild bird, just that Fran's mother "always thought of her as some wild little bird" (lines 1–2). In any case, the first paragraph doesn't focus on Linda Rose's behavior as a child.

    H because the passage states that Fran "was not surprised" when she got the letter from Linda Rose.

    J because while Linda Rose's handwriting reminds Fran of her own, this isn't the main point of the paragraph. It's just a detail supporting the paragraph's main idea.

The Author's Point of View

The author's point of view is related to the main idea of a passage. Each passage type could be followed by a question asking about the author's point of view on the subject-matter presented.

Determining the author's point of view is arguably the most difficult in a literary narrative passage in which the author's attitude must be inferred based on the story's plot, theme, and characterization. The narrator's view is not necessarily the same as the author's viewpoint. For example, a male author could create a female narrator who is imprisoned in a futuristic society. The author's point of view, which is also sometimes called tone, could be determined by looking at what the story positions as right and wrong.

Natural science and social science passages often involve an author weaving in multiple viewpoints, so it can be difficult to determine the author's stance.

Humanities passages may include a memoir written from the first-person perspective, and in that case the *I* perspective is the author's point of view. Many humanities passage read just like literary narrative passages similar to the following excerpt from a humanities passage.

Example 1

HUMANITIES: This passage is adapted from the essay "My Life with a Field Guide" by Diana Kappel-Smith (©2002 by Phi Beta Kappa Society).

I was seventeen when it started. My family was on vacation, and one day we went on a nature walk led by a young man a few years older than I. Probably I wanted to get his attention—I'm sure I did—so I pointed to a flower and asked, "What's that?"

"Hmmm? Oh, just an aster," he said.

Was there a hint of a sniff as he turned away? There was! It was just an aster and I was just a total ignoramus!

Humanities, social science, and natural science passages may include the first-person singular pronouns *I, me,* and *my,* or the first-person plural pronouns *us* and *we.* Sentences that include these pronouns can provide evidence of the author's viewpoint on a topic. For example, in the following excerpt, the author makes his viewpoint clear, saying "I support" the "revisionist interpretation" that dinosaurs had " 'right-sized' brains for reptiles of their body size." Phrases and sentences that demonstrated the author's viewpoint have been identified in bold.

Example 2

NATURAL SCIENCE: This passage is adapted from the essay "Were Dinosaurs Dumb?" by Stephen Jay Gould (©1980 by Stephen Jay Gould).

The idea of warm-blooded dinosaurs has captured the public imagination and received a torrent of press coverage. Yet another vindication of dinosaurian capability has received very little attention, although I regard it as equally significant. I refer to the issue of stupidity and its correlation with size. **The revisionist interpretation, which I support** … does not enshrine dinosaurs as paragons of intellect, but **it does maintain that they were not small brained after all. They had the "right-sized" brains for reptiles of their body size.**

Some authors may choose to assert their position in a more objective tone, particularly in natural science passages, omitting the use of personal pronouns. Still, the author's viewpoint can be determined by looking at sentences that include advice about what people *should* do or what *ought* to be done.

Practice Questions

HUMANITIES: This passage is adapted from the essay "My Life with a Field Guide" by Diana Kappel-Smith (©2002 by Phi Beta Kappa Society).

[1]

I was seventeen when it started. My family was on vacation, and one day we went on a nature walk led by a young man a few years older than I. Probably I wanted to get his attention—I'm sure I did—so I
5 pointed to a flower and asked, "What's that?"

[2]

"Hmmm? Oh, just an aster," he said.

[3]

Was there a hint of a sniff as he turned away? There was! It was just an aster and I was just a total ignoramus!

[4]

10 And I remember the aster. Its rays were a brilliant purple, its core a dense coin of yellow velvet. It focused light as a crystal will. It faced the sun; it was the sun's echo.

[5]

Later that day, a book with a green cover lay on
15 the arm of a chair under an apple tree. It was the same volume that our guide had carried as he marched us through the woods. The book had been left there, by itself. It was a thing of power. In the thin summer shadow of the tree, quivering, like a veil, the book was
20 revealed, and I reached for it. A FIELD GUIDE TO WILD FLOWERS—PETERSON & McKENNY, its cover said. Its backside was ruled like a measuring

tape, its inside was full of drawings of flowers. By the end of that week I had my own copy. I have it still.

[6]

25 Over the next several years this field guide would become my closest companion, a slice of worldview, as indispensable as eyes or hands. I didn't arrive at this intimacy right away, however. This wasn't going to be an easy affair for either of us.

[7]

30 I'll give you an example of how it went. After I'd owned the Peterson's for about a week, I went on a hike with some friends up a little mountain, taking the book along. Halfway up the mountain, there by the trailside was a yellow flower, a nice opportunity to take my new
35 guide for a test drive. "Go on ahead!" I said to my hiking companions, "I'll be a minute …" Famous last words.

…

[11]

My friend Julie and I identified individual plants in our rambles, but from the particulars we began to know wholes. Bogs held one community, montane forests held another, and the plants they held in
85 common were clues to intricate dramas of climate change and continental drift. So from plant communities it followed that the grand schemes of things, when they came our way, arrived rooted in real place and personal experience: quaternary geology, biogeography,
90 evolutionary biology all lay on the road that we had begun to travel.

21. The passage is best described as being told from the point of view of someone who is:

   A. tracing her developing interest in identifying flowers and in the natural world.

   B. reexamining the event that led her to a lifelong fascination with asters.

   C. reviewing her relationships with people who have shared her interest in flowers.

   D. describing how her hobby of identifying flowers became a profitable career.

The best answer is A because the passage begins with the narrator's description of an incident in which she first became interested in identifying flowers and in the natural world (lines 1–24), and the remainder of the passage describes how this early interest developed into a larger part of her life.

The best answer is NOT:

B because although the identification of an aster is part of the incident (lines 1–24) that leads to the narrator's lifelong interest in flowers and the natural world, there is no mention in the passage of the author having a lifelong fascination for asters in particular. Rather, the incident in question leads to a lifelong fascination with identifying flowers in general.

C because although the author briefly mentions hiking with companions (lines 31–32) and identifying flowers with a friend (lines 81–82), the primary focus of the passage is on the author's individual interest in flowers and how that interest developed.

D because the author does not discuss her career in the passage.

SOCIAL SCIENCE: This passage is adapted from Joseph Ellis's biography *American Sphinx: The Character of Thomas Jefferson* (©1997 by Joseph J. Ellis).

[3]

45   This is an ingeniously double-edged explanation, for it simultaneously disavows any claims to originality and yet insists that he depended upon no specific texts or sources. The image it conjures up is that of a medium, sitting alone at the writing desk and making
50   himself into an instrument for the accumulated wisdom and "harmonizing sentiments" of the ages. It is only a short step from this image to Lincoln's vision of Jefferson as oracle or prophet, receiving the message from the gods and sending it on to us and then to the
55   ages. Given the character of the natural rights section of the Declaration, several generations of American interpreters have felt the irresistible impulse to bathe the scene in speckled light and cloudy mist, thereby implying that efforts to dispel the veil of mystery rep-
60   resent some vague combination of sacrilege and treason.

[4]

Any serious attempt to pierce through this veil must begin by recovering the specific conditions inside that room on Market and Seventh streets in June 1776.

65   Even if we take Jefferson at his word, that he did not copy sections of the Declaration from any particular books, he almost surely had with him copies of his own previous writings, to include *Summary View, Causes and Necessities* and his three drafts of the Virginia con-
70   stitution. This is not to accuse him of plagiarism, unless one wishes to argue that an author can plagiarize himself. It is to say that virtually all the ideas found in the Declaration and much of the specific language had already found expression in those earlier writings.

[5]

75   Recall the context. The Congress is being overwhelmed with military reports of imminent American defeat in New York and Canada. The full Congress is in session six days a week, and committees are meeting throughout the evenings. The obvious practical course
80   for Jefferson to take was to rework his previous drafts on the same general theme. While it seems almost sacrilegious to suggest that the creative process that produced the Declaration was a cut-and-paste job, it strains credulity and common sense to the breaking point to
85   believe that Jefferson did not have these items at his elbow and draw liberally from them when drafting the Declaration.

---

12. Details in the passage suggest that the author's personal position on the question of Jefferson's alleged plagiarism is that the:

F. idea of Jefferson copying from his own writings is only common sense.

G. notion of Jefferson copying from past writings is in fact sacrilegious.

H. concept of the Declaration as a cut-and-paste job strains credulity.

J. claim that the Declaration is related in some way to *Causes and Necessities* strains common sense.

The best answer is F because in the last paragraph, the author reminds readers of the high-pressure circumstances under which the Declaration was written and says, "The obvious practical course for Jefferson to take was to rework his previous drafts on the same general theme" (lines 79–81). He dismisses the idea that Jefferson didn't draw from his older works, saying it "strains credulity and common sense to the breaking point" (lines 83–84).

The best answer is NOT:

G because while the author asserts that "it seems almost sacrilegious to suggest that the creative process that produced the Declaration was a cut-and-paste job" (lines 81–83), in trying to recover "the specific conditions inside that room on Market and Seventh streets in June 1776" (lines 63–64), the author shows he wants to question assumptions about how Jefferson composed the Declaration.

H because the idea that the Declaration was wholly original is what, in the author's mind, "strains credulity."

J because the author believes that in writing the Declaration, Jefferson "almost surely had with him copies of his own previous writings, to include *Summary View, Causes and Necessities* and his three drafts of the Virginia constitution" (lines 67–70).

SOCIAL SCIENCE: This passage is adapted from Joseph Ellis's biography *American Sphinx: The Character of Thomas Jefferson* (©1997 by Joseph J. Ellis).

[2]

No serious student of either Jefferson or the
30 Declaration of Independence has ever claimed that he foresaw all or even most of the ideological consequences of what he wrote. But the effort to explain what was in his head has spawned almost as many interpretations as the words themselves have generated
35 political movements. Jefferson himself was accused of plagiarism by enemies or jealous friends on so many occasions throughout his career that he developed a standard reply. "Neither aiming at originality of principle or sentiment, nor yet copied from any particular
40 and previous writing," he explained, he drew his ideas from "the harmonizing sentiments of the day, whether expressed in letters, printed essays or in the elementary books of public right, as Aristotle, Cicero, Locke, Sidney, etc."

[3]

45 This is an ingeniously double-edged explanation, for it simultaneously disavows any claims to originality and yet insists that he depended upon no specific texts or sources. The image it conjures up is that of a medium, sitting alone at the writing desk and making
50 himself into an instrument for the accumulated wisdom

and "harmonizing sentiments" of the ages. It is only a short step from this image to Lincoln's vision of Jefferson as oracle or prophet, receiving the message from the gods and sending it on to us and then to the
55 ages. Given the character of the natural rights section of the Declaration, several generations of American interpreters have felt the irresistible impulse to bathe the scene in speckled light and cloudy mist, thereby implying that efforts to dispel the veil of mystery rep-
60 resent some vague combination of sacrilege and treason.

[4]

Any serious attempt to pierce through this veil must begin by recovering the specific conditions inside that room on Market and Seventh streets in June 1776.
65 Even if we take Jefferson at his word, that he did not copy sections of the Declaration from any particular books, he almost surely had with him copies of his own previous writings, to include *Summary View, Causes and Necessities* and his three drafts of the Virginia con-
70 stitution. This is not to accuse him of plagiarism, unless one wishes to argue that an author can plagiarize himself. It is to say that virtually all the ideas found in the Declaration and much of the specific language had already found expression in those earlier writings.

75 Recall the context. The Congress is being overwhelmed with military reports of imminent American defeat in New York and Canada.

16. In saying "Even if we take Jefferson at his word, that he did not copy sections of the Declaration from any particular books" (lines 65–67), the author implies that he thinks Jefferson:

    F. may not have been totally honest when he said that no parts of the Declaration were copied from any previous writing.

    G. may have in fact copied some of Abraham Lincoln's writings when drafting the Declaration.

    H. should not be believed because his character has been hidden behind a veil of mystery for so long.

    J. cannot be accused of plagiarizing parts of the Declaration because it was written so long ago.

The best answer is F because the phrase "even if" (line 65) implies that the author doubts Jefferson was being totally honest about not copying from any previous writing—an implication reinforced in lines 72–74 when the author says that "virtually all the ideas found in the Declaration and much of the specific language had already found expression in [Jefferson's] earlier writings."

The best answer is NOT:

G because Lincoln was a nineteenth-century political figure (see lines 17–28), while Jefferson wrote the Declaration in the late eighteenth century (see lines 62–64), making it impossible for Jefferson to have copied from Lincoln.

H because the phrase "even if" implies some doubt, but it isn't a clear-cut assertion that Jefferson shouldn't be believed. Furthermore, the author declines "to accuse [Jefferson] of plagiarism" (line 70).

J because while the author doesn't accuse Jefferson of plagiarism, this isn't because Jefferson wrote the Declaration so long ago but because the author thinks that at worst Jefferson "plagiarize[d] himself" (lines 71–72), something the author doubts is even truly possible.

17. Use of the phrase "characteristic eloquence" (line 19) to describe Abraham Lincoln's words indicates the author's:

    A. use of irony to describe words written by Lincoln that the author finds difficult to believe.

    B. belief that Lincoln was usually a persuasive, expressive speaker and writer.

    C. notion that Lincoln was a bit of a character because of his controversial opinions.

    D. feelings of regret that Lincoln's words are so often difficult for modern readers to understand.

The best answer is B because, as used in line 19, *characteristic* most nearly means "usually," and *eloquence* translates to "persuasive" and "expressive." That the author is being sincere in his praise for Lincoln is made clear when he says that Lincoln, like Jefferson, "also knew how to change history with words" (lines 18–19).

The best answer is NOT:

A because there's nothing ironic or negative about the author's view of Lincoln, as expressed in the passage.

C because calling Lincoln "a bit of a character" would be patronizing, which is clearly not the author's intent. In addition, Lincoln's view of Jefferson "as the original American oracle" (lines 20–21) is the standard view of "several generations of American interpreters" (lines 56–57), which means, in this case anyway, that Lincoln's opinion is not controversial.

D because there's no evidence in the passage that the author feels Lincoln's words are often difficult for modern readers to understand.

The Primary Purpose of the Passage

Some questions will simply ask about the primary purpose of the passage. and what the author's intention is in writing the piece. Does the author wish to change readers' minds, to paint a vivid picture, or to describe a situation? Here is a brief description of the different types of writing generally found on the ACT reading test.

Expository

Expository writing may also be called explanatory writing. This kind of writing will focus on relaying facts in an unbiased tone. It answers questions about who, what, where, when, and how. Your history textbooks are likely written in this style. Newspaper articles that are not opinion pieces are also written in this style. Expository articles often focus on detailing a process, such as a scientific experiment or a manufacturing operation, highlighting the sequence of events. The tone of expository writing is objective, and therefore it will *not* include emotionally loaded words such as *applaud* or *condemn*. These passages will also *not* include opinionated words such as *should, must,* or *ought*.

Instead, these articles tend to include sentences with versions of the verbs *to be* or *to have*. For example, a science article might explain the process of osmosis, stating, "Osmosis **is** a process whereby molecules move from areas of low concentration to areas of high concentration. Unlike the movement of sodium and potassium ions in the sodium-potassium pump, which requires Adenosine triphosphate (ATP), the process of osmosis **is** passive."

Scientific expository writing often includes specialized terms such as "Adenosine triphosphate." Though it can be overwhelming to encounter scientific terminology that is unfamiliar to you, keep in mind that you should be able to answer all ACT reading test questions with the information provided in the passage without needing to rely on outside knowledge.

Narrative

Narrative writing can appear in any passage type, but it is most common in the literary narrative passages, which typically include first-person or third-person narrative voice. Narrative emphasizes the particular point of view of the fictional narrator or author.

Humanities, social science, and natural science passages may include narration in the form of a personal anecdote. For example, if a scientist went on an excursion to study trap-jaw ants, he might narrate his experience, writing, "I was excited to study trap-jaw ants ever since I first read about them in a scientific journal. I traveled to South America where my team and I filmed trap-jaw ants using high-speed cameras."

Humanities passages also sometimes draw from memoirs and essays, which often employ narrative techniques to craft a story such as found the following:

> **HUMANITIES:** This passage is adapted from the essay "My Life with a Field Guide" by Diana Kappel-Smith (©2002 by Phi Beta Kappa Society).
>
> By the time the next summer came, I had fully discovered the joy of the hunt, and every new species had its trophy of data—name and place and date—to be jotted down. If I'd found a flower before, I was happy to see it again. I often addressed it with enthusiasm: *Hi there, Solidago hispida!* I discovered early on that a plant's Latin name is a name of power by which the plant can be uniquely identified among different spoken tongues, across continents, and through time. The genus name lashes it firmly to its closest kin, while its species name describes a personal attribute—*rubrum* meaning red, *officinale* meaning medicinal, *odoratus* meaning smelly, and so on. It all makes such delightful sense!

Persuasive

Persuasive writing aims to support an argument. It may contain first-person singular pronouns such as *I, me, my,* or first-person plural pronouns such as *we, us, ours,* but it also may present arguments in a more objective tone, omitting these personal pronouns. For example, an article might say, "Urban sprawl is a growing problem that must be addressed before it spirals out of control." Opinion pieces in newspapers fall under this category of writing. These passages will include opinionated words such as *should, must,* or *ought.*

Keep in mind that often in persuasive writing, the first body paragraph is dedicated to addressing and refuting the counterargument. The following words and phrases signal that an author is addressing the counterargument: *granted, admittedly, although, while, despite,* or *some argue.* If a persuasive passage's thesis was that composting is worthwhile because it reduces our reliance on landfills, the first body paragraph might acknowledge the counterargument by admitting that composting requires time and resources as follows:

- "Composting is worthwhile because it reduces our reliance on landfills. **Admittedly,** composting on a broad scale may be difficult due to limited resources."

- "**Although** compositing is worthwhile, it may be difficult to implement due to limited resources."

In the following passage, key parts of the introduction, conclusion, and the topic sentences have been identified in bold font in order to help you see the connection between the main idea and these portions of the passage.

SOCIAL SCIENCE: This passage is adapted from Library: *An Unquiet History* by Matthew Battles (©2003 by Matthew Battles).

Until the time of Julius Caesar, books in Rome were largely in private hands; and the owners of great libraries shared them only with friends and fellow elites. The notion of a public library very much like our
5 own is the invention of Caesar, who had planned one for the city just before his assassination. After Caesar's death, his supporter Asinius Pollio and the writer Varro (whose treatise on library administration, the De bibliothecis, does not survive) took up the cause, building
10 Rome's first public library in the Forum around 39 BC. Following Caesar's wishes, they built a library with two reading rooms—one for Latin books, another for Greek—decorated with statues of appropriate poets and orators. This is the pattern all subsequent Roman
15 libraries take, from the great imperial repositories of Augustus and Trajan to the more modest public libraries and to the little collections of the provincial cities. It marks a strict departure from the Greek model, with its prototype at Alexandria, which had no reading
20 rooms as such. **The bilingual nature of the Roman library expressed the Mediterranean heritage to which Rome laid claim, while the emphasis on the reader's experience gives proof of its republican origins.**

In libraries as with everything else, Augustus,
25 **Rome's first true emperor, both followed Caesar and strove to best him.** Once his rivals were safely dead, Augustus set to transforming Rome into an imperial city; later he boasted that he had found Rome brick and left it marble. Among his marble edifices was the great
30 Palatine Library, adjoining his temple of Apollo, as well as a second, later library in the nearby colonnade he built in memory of his sister, Octavia. Of this second one nothing remains. But the remnants of the Palatine Library provide a picture of imperial libraries, with its
35 two side-by-side reading rooms, with niches in the walls for the placement of armaria, or doored wooden bookcases, which housed the scrolls. Deeper alcoves provided space for statues. The Roman biographer of emperors Suetonius agrees with the Roman poet Virgil
40 that the Sibylline Books were brought to this temple, where they were installed beneath a statue of the god Apollo.

Like Augustus, subsequent emperors each included a library or two in his imperial building proj-
45 **ects.** Of these perhaps the greatest was Trajan's, whose library departed from the side-by-side floor plan of the others. His two reading rooms faced each other, communicating through screened colonnades. In the court between them stood the Column of Trajan, the monu-
50 ment for which that emperor is most famous. Though it seems incredible now, this man of war and intrigue placed the supreme memorial to his life of action in the middle of a library.

The emperors didn't only put libraries in their pri-
55 **vate palaces and temples; they also gave them to the people of Rome.** In Augustus's reign, public baths—part of the "bread and circus" largesse with which the imperial city contented the masses—included libraries among their amenities. Although these libraries fol-
60 lowed the imperial layout with opposed reading rooms for the two languages, it's likely that they contained more familiar and classical literary works and fewer arcane legal, scientific, and medical treatises than the royal collections did. Whereas the books of Alexandria
65 are reputed to have met their end in the furnaces of public baths, the public library itself seems to have originated in the bathhouse.

The development and spread of libraries through-out the Roman world was especially remarkable given
70 **the decentralized and extra-official character of Roman intellectual life.** In the public sphere, the pursuit of knowledge, like the pursuit of wealth or power, was a matter of private associations and casual relations among people. Unlike the Ptolemies, the Qin dynasty,
75 or the Aztec nobility, Roman emperors rarely sought direct control over the life of the mind. As the classicist Elizabeth Rawson has pointed out, Rome lacked schools and universities (many Roman elite went to Greece for schooling); no formal competitions existed
80 for writers and artists, as they had in Greece; nor did the state pay the salaries of engineers, physicians, teachers, or other professionals, who depended on the patronage of individual senators or the imperial house. **In this light, the flourishing libraries of Rome are**
85 **unique: they are the nearest thing Rome had to incorporated, official cultural institutions as we know them today.**

First Sentence of the Introduction

Until the time of Julius Caesar, books in Rome were largely in private hands; and the owners of great libraries shared them only with friends and fellow elites. The notion of a public library very much like our own is the invention of Caesar, who had planned one for the city just before his assassination.

Last Sentence of the Introduction

The bilingual nature of the Roman library expressed the Mediterranean heritage to which Rome laid claim, while the emphasis on the reader's experience gives proof of its republican origins.

First Sentence of the Conclusion

The development and spread of libraries throughout the Roman world was especially remarkable given the decentralized and extra-official character of Roman intellectual life.

Last Sentence of the Conclusion

In this light, the flourishing libraries of Rome are unique: they are the nearest thing Rome had to incorporated, official cultural institutions as we know them today.

Typically, the introduction and conclusion should provide enough information to help you identify the main idea. If that content is not enough, then the topic sentences of the body paragraphs should provide further clarification. The topic sentence is the first sentence of a paragraph that gives a general overview of the content that will follow. These portions of the passage have been reproduced here so you can read this information altogether to get a fuller picture of the main idea of the passage.

Topic Sentence Paragraph 1

In libraries as with everything else, Augustus, Rome's first true emperor, both followed Caesar and strove to best him.

Topic Sentence Paragraph 2

Like Augustus, subsequent emperors each included a library or two in his imperial building projects.

Topic Sentence Paragraph 3

The emperors didn't only put libraries in their private palaces and temples; they also gave them to the people of Rome.

Synthesis of the Main Ideas from the Three Paragraphs

Roman libraries were different from those in Greece, particularly in terms of their availability to the public.

Here is an example of a question that asks about the purpose of a natural science passage. The passage has been reproduced in full so you can practice reading or skimming the entire passage to determine its primary purpose.

NATURAL SCIENCE: This passage is adapted from the article "When Research Is a Snow Job" by Sarah Boyle (©2002 by National Wildlife).

The figure is beyond comprehension: Every year, 1,000,000,000,000,000,000,000,000 (1 septillion) snowflakes fall worldwide. As the crystals fall, they encounter different atmospheric conditions that produce
5 flakes with unique attributes. The more complex those conditions are, the more elaborate the crystals.

Kenneth Libbrecht is a physicist at the California Institute of Technology. Along with the work of scientists at the U.S. Department of Agriculture's Agricul-
10 tural Research Service (ARS), his research is uncovering new information about the magical world of snow crystals—information that has practical applications in such diverse areas as agriculture and the production of electricity.

15 Snow crystals are individual crystals—usually in a hexagonal form—while snowflakes are collections of two or more snow crystals. Beginning as condensed water vapor, a crystal typically grows around a nucleus of dust. Its shape depends on how the six side facets—
20 or faces—grow in relation to the top and bottom facets. If they grow relatively tall, the crystal appears column-like; if the side facets are short compared to the length of the bottom and top facets, the crystal looks platelike.

Currently Libbrecht is trying to crack the problem
25 of why the crystal facets' growth varies with temperature. He believes this may have something to do with the ice surface's "quasi-liquid" layer, which affects how water molecules stick to the surface.

By manipulating the temperature and humidity
30 within an incubation chamber (and by adding an electric current or various gases at times), Libbrecht creates "designer" snowflakes in his lab. Such experiments are helping him determine how crystals form.

William Wergin, a retired ARS research biologist,
35 and a colleague, Eric Erbe, were using scanning electron microscopy to look at biological problems relating to agriculture. To avoid the laborious procedure that using such equipment usually entails, the two scientists decided to freeze the tissue they were working with and
40 look at it in the frozen state.

"One day it happened to be snowing," says Wergin, "and we were looking for a specimen. We imaged some snowflakes and were very surprised to see what we did." It was the first time anyone had
45 attempted to image snow crystals with scanning electron microscopy, which provides precise detail about the crystals' shape, structural features and metamorphosed conditions (crystals often change once on the ground depending on the surrounding environment).

50 Wergin called another ARS colleague, hydrologist Albert Rango, to see if the snow crystal magnifications had any applications for his research. Rango now uses Wergin's electron microscopy data, along with microwave satellite data, in the Snowmelt Runoff
55 Model to predict the amount of water available in a winter snowpack. For western states such as Colorado, Montana, Utah and Wyoming, about 75 percent of the annual water supply comes from snowmelt. Snowmelt water is critical to crop irrigation and hydroelectric
60 power, as well as recreation and domestic water supplies, fisheries management and flood control.

Before employing the scanning electron microscopy results, the forecasted amounts of snowpack water were inaccurate whenever the size and shape of the
65 snow crystals varied much from the norm. "The more we know about crystals," notes Rango, "the easier it will be to use microwave satellite data for predictions of the snow water equivalent."

Currently, forecasts using the model are about
70 90 percent accurate. A 1980 study estimated that improving the prediction by 1 percent would save $38 million in irrigation and hydropower in the western United States.

Rango is also looking ahead at climate change pre-
75 dictions. "Following the estimates that have been made

(continued)

(continued)

about what will happen by 2100, things are definitely warming up," he says. Temperature increases will likely result in a reduction in stream flow as overall snow accumulation decreases, winter precipitation runs
80 off as rain, and water evaporates at a quicker rate. The gap between water supply and demand will magnify even more, greatly increasing water's economic value, anticipates Rango.

   Not only does the crystal research help gauge
85 snowmelt, it is also useful in predicting avalanches, designing artificial snow, and, perhaps in the near future, examining air pollution. "You can put snow in a scanning electron microscope and tell which elements are present, such as sulfur and nitrogen," says Wergin.
90 "You can then see what kind of pollution is in the area and possibly track the source."

31. It can reasonably be inferred from the passage that the information about the scientific study of snow is presented primarily to:

   A. emphasize the importance of communication among scientists.

   B. explain how snow crystal facets influence the snowpack in some western states.

   C. showcase the varied uses of the scanning electron microscope.

   D. demonstrate some of the practical applications of the study of snow crystals.

The best answer is D because the passage states that information gained from the study of snow crystals "has practical applications in such diverse areas as agriculture and the production of electricity" (lines 12–14). Specific details about these practical applications are presented in the final five paragraphs (lines 50–91) of the passage.

The best answer is NOT:

A because although the passage does mention the fact that scientists have communicated with each other during the course of studying snow crystals (lines 50–54), communication is secondary to the main point of the passage, which is to explain the practical applications of such a study.

B because although the passage does discuss the role of snow crystal facets in the formation of snow crystals (lines 19–23) and also discusses the winter snowpack in some Western states (lines 56–61), the passage makes no specific connection between the snow crystal facets and the snowpack and does not indicate that either one is the primary reason for presenting information about the scientific study of snow.

C because although the passage does tell the story of the first time a scanning electron microscope was used in the scientific study of snow (lines 34–49), it tells this story in the context of presenting information about the practical applications of the scientific study of snow and does not explicitly discuss the varied uses of the scanning electron microscope.

8

Chapter 8: Integration of Knowledge and Ideas

Questions that fall under the category of Integration of Knowledge and Ideas, which make up 13%–18% of your overall score, may ask you to identify the main idea of a passage or the effect of a certain detail integrated into the passage. Also, you will need to analyze the arguments of an author and the evidence used in supporting the claims. Additionally, these questions ask about how the paired passages relate to one another. Let's take a look at the following passage, its argument, and how the author uses reasoning and evidence to support his central claim.

SOCIAL SCIENCE: This passage is adapted from a book titled *How Courts Govern America* by Richard Neely (©1981 by Richard Neely).

Government is a technical undertaking, like the building of rocketships or the organizing of railroad yards. Except possibly on the local level, the issues which attract public notice usually involve raising
5   money (taxes), spending money (public works), foreign wars (preventing them or arguing for fighting easy ones), education, public morals, crime in the streets, and, most important of all, the economy. When times are bad or there is a nationwide strike or disaster,
10 interest in the economy becomes all-consuming. However, the daily toiling of countless millions of civil servants in areas such as occupational health and safety, motor vehicle regulation, or control of navigable waterways escapes public notice almost completely.

15 Furthermore, even with regard to high-visibility issues, significant communication between the electorate and public officials is extremely circumscribed. Most serious political communication is limited to forty-five seconds on the network evening news. In
20 days gone by, when the only entertainment in town on a Wednesday night was to go to the county courthouse to listen to a prominent politician give a theatrical tirade against Herbert Hoover, an eloquent speaker could pack the courthouse and have five thousand people lined up
25 to the railroad tracks listening to the booming loud-speakers.

The political orator of yesteryear has been replaced by a flickering image on the tube, unlocking the secrets of the government universe in forty-five-
30 second licks. Gone forever are Lincoln–Douglas type debates on courthouse steps. Newspapers take up the slack a little, but very little. Most of what one says to a local newspaper (maybe not *The New York Times*) gets filtered through the mind of an inexperienced
35 twenty-three-year-old journalism school graduate. Try sometime to explain the intricacies of a program budget, which basically involves solving a grand equation composed of numerous simultaneous differential functions, to a reporter whose journalism school
40 curriculum did not include advanced algebra, to say nothing of calculus.

But the electorate is as interested in the whys and wherefores of most technical, non-emotional political issues as I am in putting ships in bottles: they do not
45 particularly care. Process and personalities, the way decisions are made and by whom, the level of perquisites, extramarital sexual relations, and, in high offices, personal gossip dominate the public mind, while interest in the substance of technical decisions is
50 so minimal. Reporters focus on what sells papers or gets a high Nielsen rating; neither newspapers nor television stations intend to lose their primary value as entertainment. Since the populace at large is more than willing to delegate evaluation of the technical aspects of
55 government to somebody else, it inevitably follows that voting is a negative exercise, not a positive one. Angry voters turn the rascals out and, in the triumph of hope over experience, let new rascals in. What voters are unable to do—because they themselves do not under-
60 stand the technical questions—is tell the rascals how to do their jobs better.

Serious coverage of goings-on in government is deterred by the fact that government is so technical that even career civil servants cannot explain what is
65 happening. In 1978 I attended a seminar on federal estate and gift tax, where the Internal Revenue Service lawyers responsible for this area frankly confessed that they did not understand the Tax Reform Act of 1976. Intricate technical issues such as taxation, arms control,
70 and nuclear power are difficult to understand for professionals, to say nothing of the most diligent layman.

That anything gets done by a political body at all is to be applauded as a miracle rather than accepted as a matter of course. When we recognize that in the federal
75 government, with its millions of employees, there are but five hundred and thirty-seven elected officials, put into office to carry out the "will" of a people who for the most part know little and care less about the technical functioning of their government, the absurdity of
80 the notion of rapid democratic responsiveness becomes clear. The widely held tenet of democratic faith that elected officials, as opposed to bureaucrats or the judiciary are popularly selected and democratically responsive is largely a myth which gives a useful legiti-
85 macy to a system. In fact, however, far from democratic control, the two most important forces in political life are indifference and its direct byproduct, inertia.

Arguments

The first two questions here address the main idea of the passage. You can use strategies like scanning, which was discussed previously in this guide, to identify the main idea of the passage.

11. One of the main points that the author seeks to make in the passage is that American citizens:

   A. cannot understand government because they read too many newspapers and watch too much television.

   B. have little chance of improving government because they do not understand the important details of government.

   C. can control elected officials' technical decisions through elections, but have no control over the bureaucrats.

   D. used to have a responsive government before television cut back on news and began to concentrate on entertainment.

The best answer is B because the author argues throughout the passage, and particularly in the fourth paragraph (lines 42–61), that people's lack of understanding of important details about government keeps them from improving government. He contends that people "do not particularly care" (lines 44–45) about "the whys and wherefores of most technical, non-emotional political issues" (lines 42–44) and are "more than willing to delegate evaluation of the technical aspects of government to somebody else" (lines 53–55). For the author, this means that "angry voters turn the rascals out and, in the triumph of hope over experience, let new rascals in" (lines 56–58) but that the voters are unable to "tell the rascals how to do their jobs better" (lines 60–61) because the voters "themselves do not understand the technical questions" (lines 59–60).

The best answer is NOT:

A because the author doesn't argue that American citizens read too many newspapers or watch too much television.

C because while the author does contend that people have a certain control over elected officials through voting, he also claims that voters are unable to affect how officials do their jobs while in office because the voters "themselves do not understand the technical questions." The author also doesn't directly address whether people can control bureaucrats.

D because there's no evidence in the passage that television has cut back on news to focus on entertainment. Furthermore, the author undermines the idea that Americans ever had a truly responsive government when he repeats but dismisses "the widely held tenet of democratic faith that elected officials, as opposed to bureaucrats or the judiciary are popularly selected and democratically responsive" (lines 81–84).

20. In the passage, the argument is made that citizens are unable to tell government officials how to do their jobs better because citizens:

    F. don't vote in every election.

    G. have a tendency to elect rascals.

    H. don't read enough newspapers or see enough television.

    J. don't understand the technical details of government.

The best answer is J because the author states, "What voters are unable to do—because they themselves do not understand the technical questions—is tell the rascals how to do their jobs better" (lines 58–61).

The best answer is NOT:

F or H because the passage never argues that citizens are unable to tell government officials how to do their jobs better because citizens don't vote in every election (**F**) or read enough newspapers or see enough television (**H**).

G because while the author does suggest that citizens have a tendency to elect rascals, he doesn't say that this tendency is why citizens can't tell government officials how to do their jobs better. The real reason is that citizens don't understand the technical questions.

Reasoning and Evidence

These next question asks about the evidence that supports the broader argument expressed in the passage.

13. The author uses the description of the tax seminar in 1978 to make the point that some governmental issues are:

    A. so technical that not even career civil servants can understand them.

    B. so technical that only career civil servants can understand them.

    C. more technical than they used to be before the passage of the Tax Reform Act.

    D. too technical for anyone other than an Internal Revenue Service tax lawyer to understand.

The best answer is A because according to the author, even the "Internal Revenue Service lawyers" at the tax seminar who were experts on federal estate and gift tax laws "frankly confessed that they did not understand the Tax Reform Act of 1976" (lines 66–68). The author uses this example to make the point that "government is so technical that even career civil servants cannot explain what is happening" (lines 63–65).

The best answer is NOT:

B or D because even the civil servants couldn't understand the law.
C because the author doesn't use the example to make the broad claim that some governmental issues are more technical than they used to be before passage of the act, nor is the timing of the act relevant here.

Chapter 9: Passage Types

A genre is a type of writing that has certain conventions for content, form, and style. For example, both memoir and autobiography are genres. While memoir focuses more on the writer's memories and emotions, autobiography primarily offers a factual chronology of events. It also tends to prioritize the power of the story over the authenticity of the representation of what occurred. Understanding genre conventions should help you navigate the ACT reading passages more effectively.

Literary Narrative Genre Conventions

Narrative Voice

The narrative voice in a literary narrative passage is typically either first or third person. As you likely know, **first-person narration** means that a character is speaking directly to the reader using personal pronouns such as *I*, *me*, and *my*. This perspective is comparable to the insights you would get if a friend were relaying a story to you. A first-person narrator only has access to the words and actions of the other characters. This type of narrator does not know what other characters are thinking.

A first-person plural narrator will use pronouns such as *us* and *we*. This narrative voice is more frequently found in social science and natural science passages to refer to humanity's common understanding of a topic. See the following example of a singular first-person narrative voice.

LITERARY NARRATIVE: This passage is adapted from the novel *Monkey Bridge* by Lan Cao (©1997 by Lan Cao). The story is set in the late 1970s in Virginia, where the narrator and her mother have moved from Vietnam after the fall of Saigon.

... I remembered the sharp chilled air against my face, the way the hydraulic door made a sucking sound as it closed behind.

My mother did not appreciate the exacting orderli-
15 ness of the A & P.

Explanatory Notes

Notice that this narrative voice uses first-person pronouns, including *I and my*. She also talks about her mother using third-person pronouns later in the passage.

The narrator is stating her perception of her mother's values based on what she can observe. She does not have direct access to her mother's thoughts. She can only infer what her mother thinks based on her mother's words and actions. Still, she can observe that the mother "did not appreciate the exacting orderliness of the A & P." The passage goes on to describe how drastically the A & P market differs from the markets the narrator and her mother were accustomed to in Vietnam.

A **third-person narrative** perspective is similar to the perspective one gets from watching a film that does not include voiceovers. It is an outsider's view of the action. This narrative voice will use third-person pronouns such as *he, she, it*, and *they*. A **third-person omniscient** narrator is an all-knowing narrative voice that has access to the thoughts and feelings of all of the characters.

If the perspective ever shifts in a passage, take note of this, because a question will likely be asked about this shift. For example, a literary narrative passage may begin primarily in first person but then shift to focusing on observing others using third-person pronouns such as *he, she, it*, and *they*.

LITERARY NARRATIVE: This passage is adapted from the short story "Golden Glass" by Alma Villanueva (©1982 by Bilingual Press).

It was his fourteenth summer. He was thinning out, becoming angular and clumsy, but the cautiousness, the old-man seriousness he'd had as a baby, kept him contained, ageless and safe. His humor, always dry
5 and to the bone since a small child, let you know he was watching everything.

He seemed always to be at the center of his own universe, so it was no surprise to his mother to hear Ted say: "I'm building a fort and sleeping out in it all

Explanatory Notes

Notice that this narrative voice uses third-person pronouns such as *it, he, his mother, Vida*, and *Ted*.

The dialogue includes the first-person pronoun *I*, but this doesn't mean that the narrative voice is in first person.

The narrator has access to the characters' thoughts as shown by the following lines:

10 summer, and I won't come in for anything, not even food. Okay?"

   This had been their silent communion, the steady presence of love that flowed regularly, daily—food. The presence of his mother preparing it, his great
15 appetite and obvious enjoyment of it—his nose smelling everything, seeing his mother more vividly than with his eyes.

   He watched her now for signs of offense, alarm, and only saw interest. "Where will you put the fort?"
20 Vida asked.

   She trusted him to build well and not ruin things, but of course she had to know where.

Line 9: "it was no surprise to his mother to hear Ted say, 'I'm building a fort and sleeping out in it all summer.'"

Line 21: "She trusted him to build well and not ruin things."

The narrator has access to Vida's feelings. She trusts her son, and she is not surprised when he says he wishes to sleep in his fort all summer.

The **second-person narrative** perspective is rarely used, but it is still worth noting here. The second-person narrative perspective involves use of the pronouns *you* and *yourself* throughout a passage. The effect is that you feel that the passage is directed at you and also about you. The following is an excerpt from a passage that is predominantly written in a first-person narrative perspective but also provides a second-person narrative. This passage is adapted from the short story "Elba" by Marly Swick (©1991 by the University of Iowa):

> Normally **you** have ample time to adjust to the idea of being a grandmother. **You** don't get a snapshot in the mail one day from a baby girl **you** gave up twenty-four years ago ….

Structure

Often, literary narrative passages begin with characterization or a scene that is rich in imagery. Sometimes the main idea is clear from the outset, as is the case in the following opening sentences adapted from the novel *The Untelling* by Tayari Jones (©2005 by Tayari Jones):

> People often ask Rochelle and me how we met. In this, best friends are a lot like married couples: people want to know how this union got its start.

Clearly, this passage will elaborate on how the narrator and Rochelle first met.

Often, a literary narrative passage begins by identifying a recent change in the narrator's life, as is the case in this opening. This next excerpt is adapted from the novel *Monkey Bridge* by Lan Cao (©1997 by Lan Cao) found in a previous passage.

> I discovered soon after my arrival in Virginia that everything, even the simple business of shopping the American way, unsettled my mother's nerves.

Verb Tense

Most fiction passages will be written in past tense, describing an event that unfolded in the past. Try to develop a sense of who is talking and how long ago the events of the passage took place and over what duration.

For example, the following passage from the short story "Golden Glass" is told from a third-person omniscient narrative perspective and conveys how certain elements of Ted's personality have remained constant throughout his life. The passage reads, "He was thinning out, becoming angular and clumsy, but the cautiousness, the old-man seriousness he'd had as a baby, kept him contained, ageless and safe." Though Ted is undergoing an awkward adolescent phase, he still maintains the seriousness that has characterized him since infancy. The third-person narrator tells readers that Ted's mother has observed a consistent temperament and pattern of behavior since Ted's childhood. In the following excerpt, verbs have been identified in bold to highlight the way they establish the order of events in the passage.

LITERARY NARRATIVE: This passage is adapted from the short story "Golden Glass" by Alma Villanueva (©1982 by Bilingual Press).

It was his fourteenth summer. He was thinning out, **becoming** angular and clumsy, but the cautiousness, the old-man seriousness **he'd had** as a baby, kept him contained, ageless and safe. His humor, always dry
5   and to the bone since a small child, let you know he was watching everything.

He seemed always to be at the center of his own universe, so it was no surprise to his mother to hear Ted say: "I'm building a fort and sleeping out in it all
10 summer, and I won't come in for anything, not even food. Okay?"

This had been their silent communion, the steady presence of love that flowed regularly, daily—food. The presence of his mother preparing it, his great
15 appetite and obvious enjoyment of it—his nose smelling everything, seeing his mother more vividly than with his eyes.

He watched her now for signs of offense, alarm, and only saw interest. "Where will you put the fort?"
20 Vida asked.

Explanatory Notes

The author's use of the word *becoming* underscores how Ted is changing as he transitions into adulthood. Though his physical appearance is undergoing a transformation, his personality remains constant.

Often first-person narrators reflect on a transformative moment in their lives, such as a moment in their childhoods when they moved or experienced a mental awakening or both. If any shifts occur in the verb tense, take note of this and anticipate that a question may be asked about this shift. Words signaling time have been identified in the following passage, which has also been adapted from the novel *Monkey Bridge* by Lan Cao (©1997 by Lan Cao).

Now, a mere three and a half years or so after her last call to the sky market, the dreadful truth was simply this: **we were going through life in reverse**, and I was the one who would help my mother through the hard scrutiny of ordinary suburban life. I would have to forgo the luxury of adolescent experiments and temper tantrums, so that I could scoop my mother out of harm's way and give her sanctuary. **Now,** when we stepped into the exterior world, I was the one who told my mother what was acceptable or unacceptable behavior. All children of immigrant parents have experienced these moments. **When it first occurs**, when the parent first reveals the behavior of a child, is a defining moment. Of course, all children eventually watch their parents' astonishing return to the vulnerability of childhood, but for us the process begins much earlier than expected.

Relationships between Characters

Each literary narrative passage develops the relationship between at least two characters. Therefore, as you read, try to think about how you would describe the dynamics between the characters. Do they get along? Are they bitter enemies? Are they lifelong friends? Consider how the relationship presented changes or remains the same over the course of the passage. Look for words and phrases that indicate change like the following: *now, then, years ago, in my childhood,* or years such as 1970.

LITERARY NARRATIVE: This passage is adapted from the novel *The Fisher King* by Paule Marshall (©2000 by Paule Marshall).

[5]

…Then, without announcing the name of the tune he intended playing,
30 without in any way acknowledging the audience, he sat down at the piano and brought his hands—large hands, the fingers long and splayed and slightly arched—down on the opening bars of "Sonny Boy Blue."

[6]

"Sonny Boy Blue!" That hokey-doke tune!

[7]

35 Around her [Hattie], the purists looked askance at each other from behind their regulation shades and slouched deeper in their chairs in open disgust.

[8]

At first, hokey though it was, he played the song straight through as written, the rather long introduction,
40 verse, and chorus. And he did so with great care, although at a slower tempo than was called for and with

a formality that lent the Tin Pan Alley tune a depth and thoughtfulness no one else would have accorded it.

…

[11]

A collective in-suck of breath throughout the club.

[12]

Where, Hattie wondered, did he come by the dazzling array of ideas and wealth of feeling? What was
65 the source? It had to do, she speculated, listening intently, with the way he held his head, angled to the left like that, tilted toward both heaven and earth. His right side, his right ear directed skyward, hearing up there, in the Upper Room among the stars Mahalia sang
70 about, a new kind of music: splintered, atonal, profane, and possessing a wonderful dissonance that spoke to him, to his soul-case. For him, this was the true music of the spheres, of the maelstrom up there. When at the piano, he kept his right ear tuned to it at all times, let-
75 ting it guide him, inspire him. His other ear? It remained earthbound, trained on the bedrock that for him was Bach and the blues.

4. Which of the following details is used in the passage to indicate how the purists in the audience initially reacted to Everett Payne's choice of music?

    F. The overall silence of the audience, including the purists

    G. The description of the audience's collective in-suck of breath

    H. The posture the purists assumed in their seats

    J. The fact that the purists stood up

Scan for: initially, purists

The best answer is H because the passage states that when the purists first heard Payne's choice of music, they "slouched deeper in their chairs in open disgust" (lines 36–37).

The best answer is NOT:

    F because although the passage mentions the silence following Payne's performance (lines 81–83), there is no specific mention of the audience reacting to Payne's choice of music with silence.

    G because the audience's in-suck of breath (line 62) is in response to Payne's performance, not to his choice of music.

    J because the purists stood up at the end of Payne's performance "in languid praise" (line 88) of Payne, not as a reaction to Payne's choice of music.

LITERARY NARRATIVE: This passage is adapted from the short story "Elba" by Marly Swick (©1991 by the University of Iowa). Fran is the narrator of the story.

[1]

Mother, who wanted to keep her, always thought of her as some wild little bird, but I knew she was a homing pigeon. I knew that at some point in her flight path, sooner or later, she would make a U-turn. A sort
5 of human boomerang. So even though I had long since stopped expecting it, I was not surprised when I walked down the gravel drive to the mailbox, which I'd painted papaya yellow to attract good news, and found the flimsy envelope with the Dallas postmark. I didn't
10 know a soul in Dallas, or Texas for that matter, but the handwriting reminded me of someone's. My own.

...

I opened the envelope and a picture fluttered into my lap. It was a Polaroid of a sweet-faced blond holding a newborn baby in a blue blanket. Before I
30 even read the letter I knew. I knew how those Nazis feel when suddenly, after twenty or thirty uneventful

years, they are arrested walking down some sunny street in Buenos Aires. It's the shock of being found after waiting so long.

...

"Well, here's the living proof." Mother tapped her nail against the glossy picture. "She looks just like you. Only her nose is more aristocratic."

75 "I'm going to work." My knees cracked when I stood up. "You be all right here?"

Mother nodded, scrutinizing the picture in her lap. "You going to write to her?"

"Of course I am," I bristled. "I may be some
80 things, but I am not rude."

"You going to invite them here? Her and the baby?" She swiveled her eyes sideways at me.

"I haven't thought that far," I said.

"Well, don't put it off." She slid her eyes back to
85 the television. "She's been waiting twenty-five years.

You worried she's going to be trouble or ask for money? For all we know, she's married to a brain surgeon with his and her Cadillacs."

"She didn't mention any husband at all," I said, 90 getting drawn into it despite myself.

"Maybe you're worried she'll be disappointed in you," she said, "You know, that she's had this big

fantasy for all these years that maybe you were Grace Kelly or Margaret Mead and who could live up to that? 95 No one. But you don't have to, Fran, that's the thing. You're her flesh-and-blood mother and that's enough. That's all it'll take."

1. Fran would most likely agree with which of the following statements about her relationship with Linda Rose?

    A. Their lives are still connected despite long separations of time and distance.

    B. They have built up too much resentment toward each other to have a good relationship now.

    C. Fran's dreams of a perfect daughter will interfere with any real relationship she might have with Linda Rose.

    D. The two of them have enough in common that it won't be difficult for them to get close.

Scan for: Linda Rose and Fran

The best answer is A because Fran describes Linda Rose as "a homing pigeon" (lines 2—3) and "a sort of human boomerang" (lines 4–5) who'd "make a U-turn" (line 4) back to Fran despite a twenty-five year wait. Though Fran had "long since stopped expecting" word from Linda Rose, she was still "not surprised" when she got it (lines 5–6). Fran experienced "the shock of being found after waiting so long" (lines 33–34), which again suggests she'd been expecting to hear from Linda Rose.

The best answer is NOT:

B because the passage doesn't support the idea that Fran and Linda Rose have built up resentment toward each other.

C because the passage doesn't support the idea that Fran has dreams of a perfect daughter. It's Fran's mother who brings up—and dismisses—the idea that Linda Rose has unrealistic expectations about Fran being "Grace Kelly or Margaret Mead" (lines 95–96).

D because there's no indication in the passage that Fran and Linda Rose share much of anything beyond a biological tie, similar handwriting (see lines 9–11), and physical appearance (see lines 75–76).

LITERARY NARRATIVE: This passage is adapted from the short story "Elba" by Marly Swick (©1991 by the University of Iowa). Fran is the narrator of the story.

[4]

"Just let up," I said. "Sun's poking through. You know anyone in Dallas, Mother?"

[5]

"Not so as I recall." She dabbed at her pinky with
A cottonball. Mother was vain about her hands. I was
20 used to how she looked now, but I noticed people
staring in the doctor's waiting room. She had lost some
weight and most of her hair to chemotherapy, and I
guess people were startled to see these dragon-lady
nails on a woman who looked as if she should be lying
25 in satin with some flowers on her chest.

...

[17]

"I guess that makes you a great-grandmother," I
said.

[18]

60   "What about you?" she snorted, pointing a Jungle
Orchid fingernail at me. "You're a grandmother."

6. According to the passage, when Fran looks at her mother, Fran feels:

    F. surprised by how weak and old her mother looks.

    G. embarrassed by the gaudy colors of nail polish her mother uses.

    H. pity that so many people stare at her mother in public.

    J. accustomed to her mother's frailness and unusual fingernails.

Scan for: Mother, feels, and nails

The best answer is J because Fran says that while her mother "had lost some weight and most of her hair to chemotherapy" (lines 21–22), Fran "was used to how she looked now" (lines 19–20).

The best answer is NOT:

    F because rather than being surprised, Fran says she "was used to" her mother's appearance (lines 19– 20).

    G because there's no support in the passage for the idea that Fran is embarrassed by the nail polish colors her mother uses. Fran merely notes that her mother "was vain about her hands" (line 19) and had painted her nails "Jungle Orchid" (lines 61–62).

    H because while Fran says she's "noticed people staring" at her mother (lines 20–21), there's no evidence in the passage that Fran feels pity for her mother as a result.

Navigating Dialogue

Dialogue is one tool that writers use to develop characters and plot within a story. As you read dialogue, try to determine who is speaking. It can be helpful to label the dialogue with the first letter of the first name of the character who is speaking. Think about the surface level meaning of what is being said and the underlying, unstated meaning, which is often called the subtext.

For example, consider the following dialogue adapted from the novel *The Untelling* by Tayari Jones (©2005 by Tayari Jones).

> "I'm Rochelle Satterwhite," she said, holding out her hand. "As class president I'm going to do something about the athletic department. I turned down a volleyball scholarship to come here. And we don't even have intramurals!"
>
> I looked at her yellow-white palm for a second too long. Who knew that people could get scholarships for volleyball? When I didn't make a move for her hand, she stretched her arm a little farther and caught me in her dry, snug grip.
>
> "It's more serious than you think," she said. "Girls at white schools are playing all kinds of sports. We don't even have field hockey."
>
> "I'll vote for you, but I'm uncoordinated."

Notice that the author does not say "I said," and "Rochelle said" after each instance of dialogue. Readers are expected to know that a paragraph break signifies that a new quotation is delivered by a different character. If you have trouble keeping track of who is talking, you may want to label each line with the first letter of the first name of the person who is talking. The context here tells us that Rochelle and the narrator are exchanging ideas. Typically, there will only be two characters interacting through dialogue. If there are three or more characters, the author will include indications of who is speaking.

The subtext of the dialogue is that the first-person narrator is not aware of the various scholarship paths available to young women at her school. This is clear when she says, "Who knew that people could get scholarships for volleyball!" This implies that she is likely privileged and did not need a scholarship in order to attend her school or perhaps she received a scholarship for a different reason. Rochelle comes across as eager to become a class officer and to try to make a change in her school community. Her passion for sports is evident in her campaign goal of expanding the athletic offerings at the school. A question asking about dialogue may saying something like, "The dialogue in line 72 reveals Rochelle's …"

Setting

Literary narrative passages often include a detailed description of the setting that contributes to the development of the main characters. For example, many fiction passages include characters who have recently moved across the country or across the globe. Describing such a character's previous environment can shed light on how the new environment differs from the previous one and presents new challenges.

LITERARY NARRATIVE: This passage is adapted from the novel *Monkey Bridge* by Lan Cao (©1997 by Lan Cao). The story is set in the late 1970s in Virginia, where the narrator and her mother have moved from Vietnam after the fall of Saigon.

My mother did not appreciate the exacting orderli-
15 ness of the A & P. She could not give in to the preci-
sion of previously weighed and packaged food, the
bloodlessness of beef slabs in translucent wrappers, the
absence of carcasses and pigs' heads. When we were in
Saigon, there were only outdoor markets. "Sky mar-
20 kets," they were called, vast, prosperous expanses in
the middle of the city where barrels of live crabs and
yellow carps and booths of ducks and geese would be
stacked side by side with cardboard stands of expensive
silk fabric. It was always noisy there—a voluptuous
25 mix of animal and human sounds. The sharp acrid smell
of gutters choked by the monsoon rain. The odor of
horses, partially camouflaged by the scent of guavas
and bananas.

Explanatory Notes

This paragraph describes the A & P market in terms of how it differs from the narrator's mother's experience in a market in Vietnam. The paragraph opens by stating that the narrator's mother "did not appreciate the exacting orderliness of the A & P." The details that follow paint a picture of a Vietnam market as chaotic and overwhelming.

Character Questions

As you read a literary narrative passage, try to develop a mental image of each character. Think about whom you would cast to play each character if you were directing a film adaptation of the fiction passage. Think about if the characters remind you of anyone you know. Questions in the fiction passage tend to ask about the general qualities of the characters. For example, a passage might be followed by questions like the following:

- According to the passage, what kind of student was Rochelle?

- Based on the passage, which of the following comments would Rochelle be most likely to say?

- If a stereotype of French teachers is that they are eccentric, creative, and caring, does the characterization of Ms. Wilson reinforce or weaken that stereotype?

The following questions are authentic ACT reading test questions accompanied by relevant excerpts from the passages they ask about.

LITERARY NARRATIVE: This passage is adapted from the novel *The Fisher King* by Paule Marshall (©2000 by Paule Marshall).

It was nearing the end of the second set, the jazz show winding down when Hattie heard Abe Kaiser at the microphone call Everett Payne's name. Heard his name and, to her surprise, saw him slowly stand up in
5 the bullpen up front. She hadn't seen him join the other local musicians, including Shades Bowen with his tenor sax, in what was called the bullpen, which was simply a dozen or so chairs grouped near the bandstand. The young locals gathered there each Sunday evening,
10 hoping for a chance to perform. Because toward the end of the final set, the custom was to invite one or two of them to sit in with the band. They sometimes even got to choose the tune they wanted to play.

This Sunday, Everett Payne, not long out of the
15 army, was the one being invited to sit in.

Explanatory Notes

Abe Kaiser appears to be an announcer. He is "at the microphone."

Hattie is a woman in the audience.

Everett Payne is a musician in the crowd who is called up to the stage from the "bullpen up front."

Payne joins Shades Bowen. We know Bowen is a performer because he is described as being "with his tenor sax." Bowen is in the bullpen. This section portrays the opportunity to join the band as an honor. Hattie is filled with anticipation as Payne joins the other musicians.

1. It can reasonably be inferred from the passage that Shades Bowen:

A. did not accompany Everett Payne as he played "Sonny Boy Blue."

B. had been in the army with Everett Payne.

C. was the oldest musician in the bullpen.

D. did not usually allow the local musicians to play with the band.

Skim words: Shades Bowen

The first question in a set of questions will be answered in the first paragraph. For this particular question, you may wish to skim for *Shades Bowen*. Scanning the passage for proper nouns should be easy because they include capital letters, which should stand out.

The best answer is A because the passage identifies Shades Bowen as one of the other local musicians in the "bullpen" (lines 5–6) and goes on to state that, of those local musicians, Everett Payne "was the one being invited to sit in" (line 15) and play with the band that night. In this context, "the one" indicates that only Everett was sitting in, and no mention is made in the passage of any other musician sitting in.

The best answer is NOT:

B because although the passage indicates that Everett Payne is "not long out of the army" (lines 14–15), the passage makes no mention of Shades Bowen having been in the army as well.

C because although the passage refers to all the people in the "bullpen" as "young locals" (line 9), the passage makes no mention of Shades Bowen's age.

D because the passage states that Everett Payne joined Shades Bowen in the "bullpen" (lines 5–7) where "young locals gathered ... each Sunday evening, hoping for a chance to perform" (lines 9–10). This indicates that Shades Bowen was a local musician himself, and there is no indication in the passage that Shades Bowen had any role in deciding which other local musicians were allowed to play with the band.

LITERARY NARRATIVE: This passage is adapted from the novel *The Fisher King* by Paule Marshall (©2000 by Paule Marshall).

[5]

...Then, without announcing the name of the tune he intended playing,
30 without in any way acknowledging the audience, he sat down at the piano and brought his hands—large hands, the fingers long and splayed and slightly arched—down on the opening bars of "Sonny Boy Blue."

[6]

"Sonny Boy Blue!" That hokey-doke tune!

[7]

35 Around her [Hattie], the purists looked askance at each other from behind their regulation shades and slouched deeper in their chairs in open disgust.

...

[13]

Again and again he took them on a joyous, terrifying roller coaster of a ride it seemed to Hattie, and
80 when he finally deposited them on terra firma after close to twenty minutes, everyone in Putnam Royal could only sit there as if they were in church and weren't supposed to clap. Overcome. Until finally Alvin Edwards, who lived on Decatur Street and played
85 trumpet in the school band, leaped to his feet and renamed him.

[14]

Alvin brought everyone up with him. Including the purists who normally refused to applaud even genius. They too stood up in languid praise of him.

6. The passage initially portrays the purists most nearly as:

    F. knowledgeable and open minded.

    G. snobbish and intolerant.

    H. rational and well educated.

    J. inexperienced and uninhibited.

Scan for: purists

The best answer is G because the purists are described as reacting negatively to Payne because of his choice of song (lines 35–37), suggesting intolerance. They are also described as usually refusing "to applaud even genius" (line 88), implying snobbishness.

The best answer is NOT:

F because although the term *purist* in the context of a jazz audience suggests that they may be knowledgeable about jazz music, the purists in this audience are described as reacting negatively to Payne because of his choice of song (lines 35–37), suggesting that they are intolerant rather than open-minded.

H because the passage makes no mention of whether or not the purists are educated. Additionally, the purists are not portrayed as rational, as they usually refuse to acknowledge a praiseworthy performance (lines 87–88).

J because although the purists may be "uninhibited" in that they visibly react or do not react to performances as they please, the passage makes no mention of their "inexperience" regarding jazz. In fact, the opposite impression is created by the purists' initial disgust at the prospect of hearing a "hokey" (line 38), or old-fashioned, tune such as "Sonny Boy Blue." Moreover, the term *purist* in general denotes someone devoted to the most essential or "pure" expression of a particular idea or practice, and such devotion usually indicates a deep familiarity with the object of their devotion rather than "inexperience.

Active Reading Questions for Literary Narrative

Your English teacher may have asked you to read actively or to annotate a passage before. Though heavily annotating a text is likely too time-consuming for the ACT reading test, asking yourself questions as you read a passage should help you remain focused as you read. This should help you avoid absentmindedly looking over a passage and only later realizing that your mind has gone elsewhere as your eyes scanned the page. Good readers think about these kinds of questions as they read literary narrative.

Here are some questions to ask yourself as you read a literary narrative passage.

Characterization

Who are the characters? Circle character names, or, in the online version, highlight them. Think about similarities and differences between characters. Also think about how the characters view one another. Do the characters change over the course of the passage? Do the dynamics between characters change? Sometimes characters in the ACT reading test passages are static, meaning that they do not change, and others are dynamic and change over the course of the passage or undergo a transformative experience that serves as the starting point for the passage.

Often the characters are eccentric, which means that you cannot rely on common sense to infer how these characters will think or act. In the case of a bizarre or quirky character, you will need to rely on the textual evidence provided by the author in order to answer the questions.

Strategy: As you read, try to develop an image of each character. It may help to picture a character as a certain actor or actress or as a composite of people you have met in your life.

Dialogue

Who is speaking? What is that person's attitude toward the other person? What is the subtext? In other words, what is the implied meaning?

Strategy: Label dialogue with the first letter of the person who is speaking.

Conflict and Tension

What is the situation? Is there a conflict? Usually you don't understand the situation until the last two paragraphs of the whole passage. Know that this is normal, and don't try to force yourself to understand what is going on during your first read through of the passage. There will be time to process the information presented as you answer the questions.

Figurative Language

What does the figurative language in the passage mean? Pay attention to sensory details such as sights, smells, sounds, and textures. Star or highlight this info. Examples of figurative language include "dragon lady nails" and "ghost white."

Changes

What changes take place? Take note of changes that occur in the characters or the situation. Draw a line or use the highlighting tool in the online version to show where the shift occurs. Sometimes there are strange jumps in time. For example, a passage may include a flashback or flash forward. The verb tenses may help you realize that this is taking place. Put a box around words that signal shifts in time such as *now, initially, done, final, traditionally, change, 22 years old,* or dates such as 1970.

Superlatives

What comparisons are made? Star or highlight superlative or comparative words such as *greater, greatest, lower, lowest, more, most, earlier, earliest, later, last,* or *first.* Often questions are asked about these kinds of superlatives and comparatives.

Lists

What lists are included in the passage? Star or, in the online version, highlight lists of items. You will often find questions asked about listed items. For example, if the passage says that a family grows tomatoes, potatoes, and squash, expect to answer a question about what crops they plant.

Tone

What is the tone? Try to determine the narrative voice and its tone. For example, does the narrator mock the characters? The tone is the author's attitude toward a topic. In a literary narrative passage, the tone is established through the narrative voice, which is usually from either first- or third-person perspective.

Emotions

How do the characters feel? What do they think about each other? Take note of emotions. If the narrative perspective is third-person omniscient, as it often is, then the narrator will have access to all the characters' thoughts, words, and actions. Realize that just because the omniscient narrator knows, for example, that Kathryn is jealous of Shelly, this does not necessarily mean that Shelly is aware that Kathryn is jealous of her.

Main Idea

What is the main idea of the passage? Often, this cannot be determined until the end of the passage.

Social Science and Humanities Genre Conventions

Structure

These passages tend to follow a standard thesis-driven essay format. The conclusions of humanities and social science passages tend to contextualize the presented information within a broader framework while also reiterating the central point of the passage.

Here is an example of a conclusion taken from a social science passage. Notice how the conclusion reminds readers to think of the context of the passage's exploration of Thomas Jefferson's integrity when it came to his writing of the Declaration of Independence.

Social Science Passage Conclusion Example 1

Recall the context. The Congress is being overwhelmed with military reports of imminent American defeat in New York and Canada. The full Congress is in session six days a week, and committees are meeting throughout the evenings. The obvious practical course for Jefferson to take was to rework his previous drafts on the same general theme. While it seems almost sacrilegious to suggest that the creative process that produced the Declaration was a cut-and-paste job, it strains credulity and common sense to the breaking point to believe that Jefferson did not have these items at his elbow and draw liberally from them when drafting the Declaration.

Paraphrase of the conclusion: Thomas Jefferson likely cut and pasted together his previous writing to create the Declaration of Independence.

In social science, humanities, or natural science passages, after a person is mentioned for the first time, his or her last name is used in each subsequent reference. This is why, for example, Thomas Jefferson is referred to simply as Jefferson in the conclusion. If the first paragraph introduces a doctor named Jada Russell, she would likely be referred to as Russell throughout the remainder of the passage. Still, feminine pronouns like *she* and *her* should be used when referring to Jada Russell. For example, the passage might say, "**Jada Russell** was eighteen-years old when <u>she</u> graduated from high school."

Portrayal of a Person

Social science and humanities passages are often followed by questions that ask about the depiction of a person. The following question is common for this passage type.

SOCIAL SCIENCE: This passage is adapted from Joseph Ellis's biography *American Sphinx: The Character of Thomas Jefferson* (©1997 by Joseph J. Ellis).

The most famous section of the Declaration of Independence, which has become the most quoted statement of human rights in recorded history as well as the most eloquent justification of revolution on behalf
5 of them, went through the Continental Congress without comment and with only one very minor change. These are, in all probability, the best-known fifty-eight words in American history: "We hold these truths to be self-evident; that all men are created equal; that they
10 are endowed by their Creator with certain inherent and inalienable Rights; that among these are life, liberty and the pursuit of happiness; that to secure these rights, governments are instituted among men, deriving their just powers from the consent of the governed." This is
15 the seminal statement of the American Creed, the closest approximation to political poetry ever produced in American culture. In the nineteenth century Abraham Lincoln, who also knew how to change history with words, articulated with characteristic eloquence the
20 quasi-religious view of Thomas Jefferson as the original American oracle: "All honor to Jefferson—to the man who, in the concrete pressure of a struggle for national independence by a single people, had the coolness, forecast, and capacity to introduce into a merely
25 revolutionary document, an abstract truth, and so to embalm it there, that today and in all coming days, it shall be a rebuke and a stumbling block to the very harbingers of reappearing tyranny and oppression."

No serious student of either Jefferson or the
30 Declaration of Independence has ever claimed that he foresaw all or even most of the ideological consequences of what he wrote. But the effort to explain what was in his head has spawned almost as many interpretations as the words themselves have generated
35 political movements. Jefferson himself was accused of plagiarism by enemies or jealous friends on so many occasions throughout his career that he developed a standard reply. "Neither aiming at originality of principle or sentiment, nor yet copied from any particular
40 and previous writing," he explained, he drew his ideas from "the harmonizing sentiments of the day, whether expressed in letters, printed essays or in the elem-

entary books of public right, as Aristotle, Cicero, Locke, Sidney, etc."

45 This is an ingeniously double-edged explanation, for it simultaneously disavows any claims to originality and yet insists that he depended upon no specific texts or sources. The image it conjures up is that of a medium, sitting alone at the writing desk and making
50 himself into an instrument for the accumulated wisdom and "harmonizing sentiments" of the ages. It is only a short step from this image to Lincoln's vision of Jefferson as oracle or prophet, receiving the message from the gods and sending it on to us and then to the
55 ages. Given the character of the natural rights section of the Declaration, several generations of American interpreters have felt the irresistible impulse to bathe the scene in speckled light and cloudy mist, thereby implying that efforts to dispel the veil of mystery rep-
60 resent some vague combination of sacrilege and treason.

Any serious attempt to pierce through this veil must begin by recovering the specific conditions inside that room on Market and Seventh streets in June 1776.
65 Even if we take Jefferson at his word, that he did not copy sections of the Declaration from any particular books, he almost surely had with him copies of his own previous writings, to include *Summary View, Causes and Necessities* and his three drafts of the Virginia con-
70 stitution. This is not to accuse him of plagiarism, unless one wishes to argue that an author can plagiarize himself. It is to say that virtually all the ideas found in the Declaration and much of the specific language had already found expression in those earlier writings.

75 Recall the context. The Congress is being overwhelmed with military reports of imminent American defeat in New York and Canada. The full Congress is in session six days a week, and committees are meeting throughout the evenings. The obvious practical course
80 for Jefferson to take was to rework his previous drafts on the same general theme. While it seems almost sacrilegious to suggest that the creative process that produced the Declaration was a cut-and-paste job, it strains credulity and common sense to the breaking point to
85 believe that Jefferson did not have these items at his elbow and draw liberally from them when drafting the Declaration.

11. It can reasonably be inferred from the passage that the author believes that Jefferson was:

   A. a mysterious character whose attempts at originality were very patriotic.

   B. a brilliant yet practical man, neither plagiarizer nor prophet, writing under pressure.

   C. a politician who deserves more attention for his writing than he gets.

   D. an average man who has been represented as a quasi-religious leader by later generations.

The best answer is B because throughout the passage, the author reveals his belief that Jefferson was brilliant yet practical and writing under pressure. The author calls the natural rights section of Jefferson's Declaration "the seminal statement of the American Creed, the closest approximation to political poetry ever produced in American culture" (lines 15–17). He stresses Jefferson's practicality by mentioning that "virtually all the ideas found in the Declaration and much of the specific language had already found expression in those earlier writings" (lines 72–74) of Jefferson, but the author doesn't want to "accuse [Jefferson] of plagiarism" (line 70) for this borrowing. The author provides details highlighting the pressure under which Jefferson worked: "The Congress is being overwhelmed with military reports of imminent American defeat in New York and Canada. The full Congress is in session six days a week, and committees are meeting throughout the evenings" (lines 75–79). This led Jefferson to take "the obvious practical course" (line 79), which was to draw from his previous writings in composing the Declaration.

The best answer is NOT:

   A because the author tries to "pierce through" the "veil" (line 62) of mystery surrounding Jefferson. The author also presents a complex notion of Jefferson's originality, which isn't reflected in the idea of Jefferson merely making attempts at originality.

   C because the author contends that Jefferson has received a great deal of deserved praise for the Declaration. Everyone from Abraham Lincoln to "several generations of American interpreters" (lines 56–57) has praised Jefferson and the Declaration.

   D because the author views Jefferson as anything but ordinary and because the passage never identifies Jefferson as a quasi-religious leader.

Active Reading Questions for the Social Science and Humanities Passages

- What is the main idea?

- What supporting evidence is provided?

- Who are the different people presented in the passage?

- What are the views of or about the people presented?

- Where do people, groups of people, or theories agree? Where do they disagree and to what extent?

Natural Science Genre Conventions

Natural science passages tend to follow a simple structure of presenting a problem or hypothesis and then presenting investigations or experiments aimed at addressing the problem or evaluating the hypothesis. For example, a natural science passage may involve an experiment designed to determine the primary vector of Lyme Disease. Other natural science passages focus on observational research such as in-depth studies of the behavior of a certain species of deep-sea shrimp. As you read a science passage, these are some questions you should keep in mind. Not all questions will be relevant to every science passage.

What Is the Problem, Topic, or Hypothesis?

You should be able to identify the main topic being studied. For example, one ACT reading test natural science passage examined the behaviors of trap-jaw ants. This essential information will usually appear in the first paragraph of the passage. Sometimes it comes at the very end of the paragraph. The first few sentences of an article may function as a hook to grab your attention. For example, one article begins with the following statistic to grab the reader's attention: "Every year, 1,000,000,000,000,000,000,000,000 (1 septillion) snowflakes fall worldwide."

Then the introduction or the first body paragraph will narrow the scope of the passage to focus on the main idea. Sometimes, the main idea is not clear until as late as the third body paragraph. For example, in the article on snowflakes, the question being studied is not highlighted until the third body paragraph of the passage, which states that "currently Libbrecht is trying to crack the problem of why the crystal facets' growth varies with temperature." The previous paragraphs review definitions of key terms such as *snowflakes* and *snow crystals*. In a passage that focuses on an experiment, the hypothesis and experimental design will be the focus of the introduction and initial body paragraphs.

Let's take a look at an example of the types of problems a science passage might address.

Problem

"But for extended space voyages or long-term bases on other worlds, even if all the air and water is efficiently recycled and purified, bringing along enough food can prove problematic."

Solution

"Dixon and other researchers think the solution to the food problem is for astronauts to grow their own . . . . Space agencies around the world have mounted numerous hermetically sealed ecological experiments over the years, attempting to sustain human life without relying on our planet's natural ecosystem services. None have been unqualified successes—outside inputs inevitably are needed."

Explanation

This particular passage does not review a scientific experiment. Instead, it defines a problem: the difficulty of providing adequate nutrition in outer space. Then the passage goes on to describe the most promising scientific problem solving that has been completed thus far. Essentially, instead of sending food into outer space, astronauts are learning to cultivate their own food, using available technology to aid their efforts. Though this is not a perfect solution, it is a sign of progress when it comes to tackling the problem of feeding individuals in space.

What Hypotheses Exist? What Solutions Have People Thought Of?

The beginning of a science passage usually reviews the body of knowledge that exists about the general topic. It may also review several hypotheses or common understandings that existed when the passage was originally written or observational studies that have collected data. Taking note of the year of publication for the passage can help you contextualize the information into your broader framework of scientific knowledge. For example, an article written in 1980 may have a different outlook on genetics than an article written in 2019.

What Experiments Have Already Been Done? What Solutions to the Problem Have Been Attempted?

To what extent did previous experiments provide useful information? Words and phrases such as *before, previously,* or *in the past* highlight what was previously known about a topic. Dates such as 1980 also help illustrate how a body of knowledge about a scientific topic has shifted over time.

For example, an article about snowflakes emphasizes the new information discovered by scanning electron microscopy through the use of the word *before.* The article states, **"Before** employing the scanning electron microscopy results, the forecasted amounts of snowpack water were inaccurate." The implication is that the scanning electron technology increases the accuracy of forecasts about snowpack.

An article about the changing concept of the *Brontosaurus* emphasized how drastically the perception of the dinosaur changed, stating, "The *Brontosaurus* that wallowed in its pond a generation ago is **now** running on land."

What New Hypothesis Is Examined in This Study? What Solution Is Now Being Attempted?

Many natural science passages will explore a wide range of hypotheses that exist about a topic or a number of solutions that have been attempted to address a problem. An experiment is performed in a controlled setting. It seeks proof in the form of evidence to support or reject a hypothesis. An investigation is more open-ended, exploratory, observational, and sometimes even theoretical. It aims to collect facts. The passage about the *Brontosaurus,* for example, reviews a number of hypotheses about the dinosaur including that they were perhaps warm-blooded and perhaps more intelligent than previously supposed. For that particular passage, because dinosaurs are extinct, new experiments involving the Brontosaurus are not possible. Instead, archeological evidence is provided in order to bolster the claim that these dinosaurs may have traveled in herds, which would be a sign of intelligence. The article explains, "If behavioral complexity is one consequence of mental power, then we might expect to uncover among dinosaurs some signs of social behavior that demand coordination, cohesiveness and recognition. . . . Multiple trackways have been uncovered, with evidence for more than twenty animals traveling together in parallel movement."

What Experiment Was Designed? How Is the Solution Being Implemented?

Many natural science passages will describe experiments that have been designed or solutions that have been attempted. For example, the excerpt from the passage *An Anthropologist on Mars* by Oliver Sacks examines experiments designed to mimic the way color is perceived in the brain. It describes an experiment in which James Clerk Maxwell photographed "a colored bow three times, through red, green, and violet filters. Having obtained three 'color-separation' images, as he called them, he now brought these together by superimposing them upon a screen, projecting each image through its corresponding filter (the image taken through the red filter was projected with red light, and so on). Suddenly, the bow burst forth in full color."

What Is Controlled For? What Is Different about This Solution?

In a passage focusing on an experiment, questions will often ask about the control and the variables. The control refers to what remains the same in an experimental design. For example, if you were studying the effect of water on plant growth, you would want the plant type, soil type, and sunlight the same. In a passage proposing solutions to a problem, questions will ask you whether the evidence shows that the problem has been solved effectively.

What Is Manipulated by the Experimenter?

In an experiment studying the effect of water on plant growth, the amount of water would be the independent variable manipulated by the experimenter.

What Is the Outcome of an Experiment?

The outcome of the impact of the manipulation of the independent variable is the dependent variable. In the case of the plant experiment, the growth of the plant would be the dependent variable, or the outcome of the experiment.

To What Extent Was the Research Question Answered? To What Extent Was the Problem Solved?

The last paragraph usually talks about the limitations of the findings of the research. It does not mean that the results of the study are undermined or contradicted. It just means they have limited application. That doesn't mean that the experiment was a failure or that the scientist has a negative attitude. The ACT and all scientists believe that null data is still valuable. Null data means that a study proves that a certain variable does not have an impact.

What Are the Practical Applications of This New Knowledge?

Sometimes it is necessary to synthesize information from two sentences in order to see the practical use of the knowledge acquired through a scientific study. For example, an article on snowflake structure states that "**snowmelt water** is critical to crop irrigation and hydroelectric power, as well as recreation and domestic water supplies, fisheries management and flood control." Later lines tell readers that "currently, forecasts using the [snowmelt] model are about 90 percent accurate." These sentences show how the model that was developed based on information about snowflakes' structure can help create more accurate predictions for snowmelt, which in turn affects crops, domestic water, fisheries, and flooding. In the final paragraph of the passage on snowflakes, another practical application of the model is directly stated, as follows: "Not only does the crystal research help gauge snowmelt, it is also useful in predicting avalanches, designing artificial snow, and, perhaps in the near future, examining air pollution."

The Typical Structure of a Science Passage

Science passages generally follow a common structure. If you become familiar with the structure, you will have an easier time finding information as you answer questions on the test. Science passages use the following structure:

1. First comes the hook, the introduction of key terms, and an explanation of the current understanding of a topic and questions or problems that still exist.

2. Next comes a description of experiments or investigations designed to answer a question about the concept. Sometimes, instead, the beginning of the article just describes a problem.

3. Then comes defining the control, independent variable, and dependent variable. Sometimes the article just describes solutions to a scientific challenge. Often the article will describe technology used to study a phenomenon.

4. The end of a natural science passage typically describes the findings of the study or an attempt to solve a problem.

5. The conclusion often reviews questions that still exist.

6. The conclusion also typically reviews of the implications of the studies completed. It explains how this information can be used and the value and limits of the data collected in this experiment.

Strategies for Comprehending the Science Passage

Because science passages may present information that's unfamiliar to you, you can use the following strategies to better understand their content.

1. Simplify the ideas as you read them.

2. At the end of each paragraph, try to summarize the main idea to check for understanding.

3. Underline or circle the names of scientists so that you can return to them if asked about a particular scientist's view. Try to think about who agrees and disagrees. You may wish to keep a list of names organized according to which scientists agree with each other.

4. Pay attention to words that help you understand the chronological order. Word such as *now* and *currently,* and dates such as July 20, 1969, can help you get a sense of the order of events.

Common Natural Science Question Types

You'll likely see one or more of the following questions when you work on the science passage on the ACT reading test:

1. Describe the format of the passage.

2. What would a certain scientist believe or with whom would that scientist agree?

3. Do other scientists respect or agree with the scientist highlighted in the passage?

4. How does a device or experiment function?

NATURAL SCIENCE: This passage is adapted from the article "When Research Is a Snow Job" by Sarah Boyle (©2002 by National Wildlife).

50 Wergin called another ARS colleague, hydrologist Albert Rango, to see if the snow crystal magnifications had any applications for his research. Rango now uses Wergin's electron microscopy data, along with microwave satellite data, in the Snowmelt Runoff
55 Model to predict the amount of water available in a winter snowpack. For western states such as Colorado, Montana, Utah and Wyoming, about 75 percent of the annual water supply comes from snowmelt. Snowmelt water is critical to crop irrigation and hydroelectric
60 power, as well as recreation and domestic water supplies, fisheries management and flood control.

Before employing the scanning electron microscopy results, the forecasted amounts of snowpack water were inaccurate whenever the size and shape of the
65 snow crystals varied much from the norm. "The more we know about crystals," notes Rango, "the easier it will be to use microwave satellite data for predictions of the snow water equivalent."

Currently, forecasts using the model are about
70 90 percent accurate. A 1980 study estimated that improving the prediction by 1 percent would save $38 million in irrigation and hydropower in the western United States.

Rango is also looking ahead at climate change pre-
75 dictions. "Following the estimates that have been made about what will happen by 2100, things are definitely warming up," he says. Temperature increases will likely result in a reduction in stream flow as overall snow accumulation decreases, winter precipitation runs
80 off as rain, and water evaporates at a quicker rate. The gap between water supply and demand will magnify even more, greatly increasing water's economic value, anticipates Rango.

34. According to the passage, the addition of electron microscopy data to the Snowmelt Runoff Model allows scientists using the model to include in their predictions detailed information about:

F. microwave satellite data.

G. structural variations of snow crystals.

H. locations having the most snowfall.

J. biological problems related to agriculture.

Scan for: microscopy, Snowmelt Runoff Model

The best answer is G because the passage explains that "before employing the scanning electron microscopy results, the forecasted amounts of snowpack water were inaccurate whenever the size and shape of the snow crystals varied much from the norm" (lines 62–65). This indicates that the addition of scanning electron microscopy data allowed scientists using the model to include more detailed information about structural variations in snow crystals in their predictions, making those predictions more accurate.

The best answer is NOT:

F because the passage does not specify that the addition of scanning microscopy data allowed scientists using the Snowmelt Runoff Model to include more detailed information about microwave satellite data. Rather, the passage states that Albert Rango "now uses Wergin's electron microscopy data, along with microwave satellite data, in the Snowmelt Runoff Model to predict the amount of water available in a winter snowpack" (lines 52–56). This indicates that scanning electron microscopy data and microwave satellite data are used in conjunction with each other, not that one allows the inclusion of more detailed information about the other.

H because the passage makes no mention of electron microscopy in helping provide detailed information about locations having the highest amount of snowfall.

J because although the passage mentions that William Wergin and Eric Erbe were looking for biological problems related to agriculture (lines 34–37), there is no mention of biological problems in the discussion of the Snowmelt Runoff Model, which occupies the last five paragraphs of the passage (lines 50–91).

NATURAL SCIENCE: This passage is adapted from *An Anthropologist on Mars* by Oliver Sacks (©1995 by Oliver Sacks). Johann Wolfgang von Goethe was an eighteenth-century German poet and philosopher; Hermann von Helmholtz was a nineteenth-century scientist and philosopher.

Goethe's color theory, his *Farbenlehre* (which he regarded as the equal of his entire poetic opus), was, by and large, dismissed by all his contemporaries and has remained in a sort of limbo ever since, seen as the
5 whimsy, the pseudoscience, of a very great poet. But science itself was not entirely insensitive to the "anomalies" that Goethe considered central, and Helmholtz, indeed, gave admiring lectures on Goethe and his science, on many occasions—the last in 1892. Helmholtz
10 was very conscious of "color constancy"—the way in which the colors of objects are preserved, so that we can categorize them and always know what we are looking at, despite great fluctuations in the wavelength of the light illuminating them.

71. According to the passage, regarding Goethe's color theory, Helmholtz expressed which of the following attitudes?

   A. Disbelief

   B. Respect

   C. Amusement

   D. Skepticism

Scan for: theory, Helmholtz

The best answer is B because, according to the passage, Helmholtz had respect for Goethe's color theory: "Helmholtz . . . gave admiring lectures on Goethe and his science, on many occasions" (lines 7– 9) and he, like Goethe, was interested in the idea of "color constancy" (line 10). Helmholtz was unusual in his respect for Goethe's color theory, as it "was, by and large, dismissed by all [Goethe's] contemporaries and has remained in a sort of limbo ever since, seen as the whimsy, the pseudoscience, of a very great poet" (lines 2–5).

The best answer is NOT:

   A because the reference to Helmholtz's "admiring lectures on Goethe and his science" rules out disbelief as Helmholtz's attitude.

   C because the reference to Helmholtz's "admiring lectures on Goethe and his science" rules out amusement as Helmholtz's attitude.

   D because the reference to Helmholtz's "admiring lectures on Goethe and his science" rules out skepticism as Helmholtz's attitude.

Paired Passages

Each ACT reading test will have two short passages that address a similar topic and fall under the same passage type. This counts as one of the four sections in the reading test. The paired passage could occur in any passage type. Though it is more common for the paired passage to occur in the social science, humanities, and natural sciences passages, it can appear in the literary narrative passage also.

For example, a recent test included two fiction passages both describing individuals observing strangers on public transportation. The questions that followed then asked students to compare and contrast the two passages' form and content. Expect the questions that follow to ask how the passages are similar and how they differ from each other.

The questions may also ask you to compare the passages by asking questions, such as "Which character is **most intrigued** by the other passengers on the train?" These questions may also ask about different comparable elements of the passages in questions, such as "Which of the following statements best describes how the pianist of Passage A and the audience in Passage B view their respective performances?" The word *respective* means particular. So this essentially means "How does the narrator of Passage A view the performance in Passage A?" and "How does the audience in Passage B view the performance in Passage B?"

Past paired passages have addressed the following:

- A pair of social science passages describing

  A.   The first automobiles in San Francisco

  B.   A car produced in the 1950s that was a commercial failure

- A pair of social science passages describing

  A.   An explanation of the way plastics were viewed when they were first developed

  B.   An overview of how plastic was originally viewed as cheap but later gained popularity for its flexibility, durability, and cost

- A pair of humanities passages describing

  A.   The difference between memoir and autobiography

  B.   An examination of Ernest Hemingway's autobiographical and fictional writing

Strategies for the Paired Passage

Comparing the content between two passages isn't an everyday activity for most students. To help you ace the paired passage questions, use the following strategies.

1.   Read the first passage. Try to identify its thesis or main idea. Try to star, circle, or underline the thesis statement. The online test has a highlighting tool you can use. Often the main idea appears at the end of the introductory paragraph.

2.   Then look at the questions about that passage *and* the questions about *both* passages even though you have not yet read the second passage. This may even help you eliminate some wrong answer choices just on the basis of what you have learned from reading Passage A. The questions about both tests will come at the end of the questions, and they will be identified by a box like this one.

> Questions 28–30 ask about both passages.

3.   Read the second passage. Try to identify its thesis, or main idea, and think about how it compares to the first passage. As you read the second passage, think about where the passages agree and where they differ. If the paired passage is a literary narrative passage, think about how the form and content of the passages differ.

4.   Answer the questions about Passage B.

5.   Answer the questions about *both* Passage A and Passage B.

Practice Questions

For this section, the full paired passage and questions have been reproduced. You can complete the paired passage based on the skills you have developed as you have studied the various question types posed on the ACT reading test. At the end of the questions following the paired passage, you will find answer explanations.

HUMANITIES: Passage A is adapted from the article "You Got Eyes: Robert Frank Imagines America" by Francine Prose (©2010 by The Harper's Magazine Foundation). Passage B is adapted from a review in Winterthur Portfolio by James C. Curtis (©1996 by James C. Curtis).

Passage A by Francine Prose

[1]

The most radical aspect of the photo collection of the 1959 book *The Americans* was not what it showed but how it looked—the precise offhandedness, the controlled chaos of photographer Robert Frank's style, the
5 formal elegance exchanged for a more intense and moody aesthetic. Highly charged, frequently blurred or aslant, his pictures are full of tilted planes and off-center subjects portrayed with a directness that makes them seem not so much photographed as lunged at and
10 seized. This apparently unrefined immediacy influenced and continues to influence generations of artists who justly extol Frank's seamless melding of the documentary, the personal, and the visionary.

[2]

If Frank's style was innovative, his subject matter
15 was not entirely unfamiliar. The truths his images conveyed had been documented during the Depression by dozens of WPA photographers in work that, unlike Frank's, was welcomed and acclaimed. But by the 1950s, it was widely, if not universally, agreed that our
20 Depression-era problems had been burned away during World War II, allowing a cheerful, tolerant, chicken-in-every-pot society to rise from the ashes. What had changed most markedly was the political climate: the Cold War xenophobia and the pervasive insistence on
25 hearing, and being told, that America was a paradise populated by angels.

[3]

What made the loneliness and isolation that *The Americans* captured even harder for the critical and general audience to accept was the fact that a few years
30 before its appearance, a hugely popular exhibition and its companion volume, *The Family of Man*, had depicted the world, America included, as one giant

Explanatory Notes

Passage A begins by describing the ways in which Robert Frank's photo collection entitled *The Americans* differed from the norm at the time it was published. These photos are described as direct, radical, intense, blurred, and moody. It seems as though the subjects were "lunged at and seized." This is a departure from what we usually picture when thinking about professional photography. Often, photography is staged, polished, and clear. The authenticity of the portrayal of the subjects in the moment seems to have been Frank's primary concern. The photos are not formal.

The second paragraph explains the political and cultural climate when Frank was sharing his photography with the world. This paragraph explains how, in the 1950s, people wanted to forgot about the difficulties of the Great Depression and to emphasize the prosperity of America. Here the passage also mentions that the political climate was influenced by Cold War xenophobia. Even if you did not know that *xenophobia* means "fear of that which is different," you likely knew that the word was negative if you know the meaning of the word *phobia*.

This paragraph ends by stating that there was a "pervasive insistence on hearing, and being told, that America was a paradise populated by angels." In other words, the media and the government tried to portray America as an ideal place with ideal people.

The third paragraph explains how Frank's photography differs from that of *The Family of Man*, which depicted America as "one giant, inclusive, warmhearted kindship." *The Family of Man* photo collection was popular while *The Americans* only sold "just over a thousand copies" and then went out of print.

Passage B primarily focuses on the collection *The Family of Man*. This exhibit was popular.

inclusive, warm-hearted kinship system sharing the
same joys and sorrows. Organized by Edward Steichen,
35 and featuring several of Frank's photos, the show
encouraged its audience to see photography as a merry
postman delivering candy hearts. And now that very
same messenger was bringing terrible news. By 1959,
The Family of Man had become a beloved cultural icon
40 and a coffee-table must. *The Americans*, by contrast,
sold just over a thousand copies, and roughly a year
after publication, Grove Press let it go out of print.

Passage B by James C. Curtis

In January 1955, *The Family of Man*, a photographic exhibition of more than five hundred images,
45 opened at the Museum of Modern Art (MoMA) in New
York City. In the words of its organizer, Edward
Steichen, MoMA's curator of photography, *The Family
of Man* encompassed "the gamut of life from birth to
death with emphasis on daily relationships of man to
50 himself, to his family, to the community and to the
world we live in." The exhibition proved popular
beyond Steichen's wildest imaginings. The book version of *The Family of Man*, published shortly before the
close of the MoMA show, remains in print to this day
55 and has sold millions of copies.

In his richly textured 1995 book *Picturing an
Exhibition: "The Family of Man" and 1950s America*,
Eric Sandeen provides the first comprehensive examination of Steichen's masterwork. Sandeen challenges
60 the views of such modern critics as Roland Barthes,
who argue that *The Family of Man* is more artifice than
artifact, that in its strivings for universality it shucks
off what Barthes called "the determining weight of
History."

65   Sandeen's painstaking research uncovers the historical circumstances attending both the creation and
circulation of the exhibition. He begins by noting the
essential irony that *The Family of Man*, an exhibition
advocating peace among humankind, was born of war.
70 Sixty-two years old at the time of Pearl Harbor,
Steichen persuaded the Navy to give him a commission
and to recruit a team of photographers who soon had
permission to roam the Pacific theater of operations.
Steichen was drawn to combat but repelled by its con-
75 sequences. He hoped that his realistic combat portraits
"might make a contribution toward ending the specter
of war." As war shaped the photographer's vision, so it
conditioned the home-front audience. With a patriotic
frenzy, Americans devoured mass-circulation picture
80 magazines such as *Life* and *Look*.

Explanatory Notes (*continued*)

The second body paragraph of Passage B notes that
some critics believe the collection was "more artifice than
artifact." This means that some critics think the photos
were staged and not authentic glimpses into citizens'
everyday lives.

The third paragraph describes the origins of the photo
exhibit. It explains that Steichen, who organized the exhibit, felt drawn to capturing images of war that were realistic
and that "might make a contribution toward ending the
specter of war." In other words, through his photography,
he sought to shed light on the reality of war so that it
wasn't shrouded in mystery.

The final paragraph talks about the political agenda
that may have been at play in the creation of *The Family
of Man* photo series. This paragraph describes the general
theme of the photo series, which promoted peace and unity
across the globe.

(*continued*)

(continued)

> The rising demand for images assured that the
> camera would be an essential peacemaking tool as well.
> Sandeen provides a convincing argument that the
> themes of international unity, brotherhood, and familial
> 85 strength popularized by *The Family of Man* first found
> expression in such photographic series as "People Are
> People the World Over," which appeared regularly in
> *Ladies' Home Journal* in 1948 and 1949. Sandeen is
> quick to point out the political agendas at work in these
> 90 seemingly objective visual essays.

Questions 21–24 ask about Passage A. Questions 25–27 ask about Passage B. Questions 28–30 ask about both passages.

21. One reviewer of *The Americans* described the photographs as "flawed by meaningless blur . . . and general sloppiness." Is this view consistent with the position Prose takes in Passage A?

   A. Yes, because Prose criticizes Frank's pictures for being frequently blurry or aslant.

   B. Yes, because Prose claims Frank's photographic style was poorly received by critics.

   C. No, because Prose condemns Frank's subject matter but praises Frank's photographic style.

   D. No, because Prose offers a positive assessment of Frank's photographic style.

The best answer is D because the tone of the passage is positive toward Frank's work. Frank's collection *The Americans* is said to "continue to influence generations of artists who justly extol Frank's seamless melding of the documentary, the personal, and the visionary." The author calls Frank's work innovative (line 14). Though the passage makes it clear that the general public did not appreciate Frank's work in *The Americans*, there is no indication that the author perceived Frank's photograph in the same way.

The answer is NOT:

A because although the passage does state that Frank's photos were blurry or aslant, these qualities are not portrayed in a negative light. The author notes Frank's "precise offhandedness, the controlled chaos." This implies that Frank's photography choices were deliberate rather than random or the product of incompetence. Prose focuses on the intentionality and the effect of Frank's artistic choices. The passage also indicates that Frank "continues to influence generations of artists who justly extol Frank's seamless melding of the documentary, the personal, the visionary" (lines 11–13). Prose's choice of the word *justly* to modify the word *extol* shows that Prose herself thinks Frank's photography has value. She thinks the praise of Frank's work is justified.

B because Prose's view of Frank's work is largely positive. Though the passage states that Frank's work was not "welcomed and acclaimed' in the same way the volume *The Family of Man* was, that does not mean that the author would adopt the attitude of the general public or critics (lines 15–17).

C because the word *condemn* is too negative to describe the author's attitude toward Frank's work. The purpose of this passage is descriptive, not critical.

22. Prose indicates that compared to Frank's work in *The Americans,* the work of the WPA photographers who preceded him was:

   F. much more widely accepted.

   G. radically different in subject matter.

   H. remarkably similar in photographic style.

   J. far less serious in tone.

The best answer is F because the passage directly states "The truths his [Frank's] images conveyed had been documented during the Depression by dozens of WPA photographers in work that, unlike Frank's, was welcome and acclaimed" (lines 15–18). Clearly, the WPA photographers work was more widely accepted and praised.

The answer is NOT:

G because the passage states that Frank's subject matter "was not entirely unfamiliar. The truths his [Frank's] images conveyed had been documented during the Depression by dozens of WPA photographers in work that, unlike Frank's, was welcome and acclaimed" (lines 15–18). Frank and the WPA photographers captured images of the daily lives of Americans. The passage also states that "the most radical aspect of the photo collection of the 1959 book *The Americans* was not what it showed but how it looked—the precise offhandedness, the controlled chaos of photographer Robert Frank's style" (Lines 1–4). This emphasizes that the subject-matter of his photos was not unusual while the style was.

H because, as the passage states, "Frank's style was innovative" (Line 14). This means that it was not similar to other photographers' styles. It was new and groundbreaking.

J because Frank's photographs do not seem less serious than those of the WPA photographers. In some ways, Frank's photographs do seem serious in that the subjects are "portrayed with directness that makes them seem not so much photographed as lunged at and seized" (lines 9–10). The volume *The Family of Man* does appear to be more lighthearted in tone than Frank's *The Americans* given that *The Family of Man* depicted "the world, America included, as one giant, inclusive, warm-hearted kinship system" (lines 31–33).

23. Prose includes a discussion of *The Family of Man* mainly to provide a:

    A. shift in focus away from Frank to WPA photographers.

    B. contrast to the critical and popular reaction to *The Americans*.

    C. criticism of Frank for allowing some of his pictures to appear in *The Family of Man*.

    D. word of advice to photographers on how to appeal to an audience.

The best answer is B because the volume *The Family of Man* is incorporated as a point of contrast. It is stylistically different from Frank's work and also better received by the public. The passage directly states that "the truths his [Frank's] images conveyed had been documented during the Depression by dozens of WPA photographers in work that, unlike Frank's, was welcome and acclaimed" (lines 15–18).

The answer is NOT:

    A because Frank's work is the primary focus of the passage. It is also unclear in the passage if the WPA photographers were responsible for the volume *The Family of Man*.

    C because the article mentions that some of Frank's photographs are included in the volume *The Family of Man*, but the tone is neutral rather than critical.

    D because the primary function of the passage is descriptive rather than prescriptive. The passage is not designed to serve as advice for photographers. It does not aim to tell photographers what to do. Instead, its purpose is to describe Frank's photography and how it has been received by his public audience.

24. It can reasonably be inferred that the "messenger" referred to in line 38 is:

    F. Frank.

    G. Steichen.

    H. photography.

    J. the audience.

The best answer is H because the passage states that the show *The Family of Man* "encouraged its audience to see photography as a merry postman delivering candy hearts" (lines 36–37). In other words, the audience was encouraged to see photography as a messenger of warm and positive feelings.

The answer is NOT:

    F because Frank's photography focuses on loneliness and isolation (line 27). It would not be appropriate to describe him as a "merry postman delivering candy hearts" (line 37).

    G because Steichen is described as the organizer of the popular exhibition *The Family of Man*, but it is the photographs themselves that are described as the messengers, not Steichen.

    J because the audience is being encouraged to see photography as a messenger bringing good news. The audience is not being encouraged to view itself as the bearer of good news.

25. Passage B characterizes Steichen primarily as:

A. an idealist who saw photography as a means to promote peace.

B. a manipulator who tried to use art to advance a political agenda.

C. a pacifist who stopped working as a combat photographer after experiencing war.

D. a social critic who challenged many of the core beliefs of mainstream 1950s America.

The best answer is A because Edward Steichen organized the exhibition *The Family of Man*, which popularized idealistic themes including "international unity, brotherhood, and familial strength" (lines 84–85). *The Family of Man* advocated peace among humankind. *Idealistic* means "being guided by thoughts about how the world should be."

The answer is NOT:

B because the passage portrays Steichen in a positive light. The end of the passage addresses how political agendas were often at work in objective visual displays in magazines and museums, but the passage does not focus on Steichen's political motivations.

C because the passage does indicate that Steichen's exhibit advocated "peace among humankind" (line 69), but Steichen does not stop being a combat photographer after experiencing war. He was sixty-two years old at the time of Pearl Harbor" (line 70).

D because the passage does not address core beliefs that Steichen challenged in the 1950s. It only notes that Steichen helped create realistic combat portraits that he hoped would "end the specter of war."

26. According to Steichen, as he is presented in Passage B, the exhibition of *The Family of Man* placed emphasis on:

F. world events from the early 1950s.

G. daily human relationships.

H. recovery from World War II.

J. birth and death.

The best answer is G because Steichen describes the exhibition of *The Family of Man* as running "the gamut of life from birth to death with emphasis on daily relationships of man to himself, to his family, to the community and to the world we live in" (lines 48–51). In other words, it covered our whole life span.

The answer is NOT:

F because the focus of the book is on the everyday lives of Americans rather than on broader global issues.

H because the passage briefly touches on World War II in lines 65–80, but war is not the emphasis of the passage.

J because this answer choice is an excessively literal interpretation of the description of *The Family of Man* as running "the gamut of life from birth to death with emphasis on daily relationships of man to himself, to his family, to the community and to the world we live in" (lines 48–51). The focus of the photos is the everyday lives of Americans not just their births and deaths.

27. Passage B includes Sandeen's claim that critics such as Barthes most likely attack *The Family of Man* primarily for what they see as its:

   A. pessimism.

   B. popularity.

   C. inauthenticity.

   D. lack of artistry.

The best answer is C because Sandeen defends *The Family of Man*, challenging the idea that it is "more artifice than artifact." In other words, Sandeen does not think that *The Family of Man* is fake. He believes it provides an authentic insight into the daily lives of Americans in the 1950s.

The answer is NOT:

A because *The Family of Man* collection is portrayed as idealistic. Its themes include positive concepts like "international unity, brotherhood, and familial strength" (lines 84–85). *The Family of Man* advocated peace among humankind. Therefore, it cannot be characterized as pessimistic.

B because the passage highlights the popularity of *The Family of Man,* but does not indicate that the collection's popularity itself drew criticism.

D because Barthes does not comment on the artistry of the collection.

28. Based on information in both passages, how does the purpose behind the subject matter of *The Americans* compare to the purpose behind *The Family of Man*?

   F. Both *The Americans* and *The Family of Man* depict an idealized America, one that is close to being paradise on earth.

   G. Both *The Americans* and *The Family of Man* strive to convey the truth of living in the United States and are thus beloved cultural icons.

   H. The *Americans* stresses the loneliness and isolation of life, while *The Family of Man* stresses togetherness and unity.

   J. *The Americans* encompasses a wide range of life experiences, while *The Family of Man* focuses on war and its aftermath.

The best answer is H because *The Americans* captured the loneliness and isolation of American citizens (lines 27–28) while *The Family of Man* promoted concepts such as "international unity, brotherhood, and familial strength" (lines 84–85). *The Family of Man* was an idealistic collection while *The Americans* focused on realism.

The answer is NOT:

F because *The Americans* sought to portray America as it was rather than in an idealized form. *The Americans* captured the loneliness and isolation of American citizens (lines 27–28).

G because *The Americans* is not portrayed as "beloved." It sold "just over a thousand copies, and roughly a year after publication, Grove Press let it go out of print" (lines 41–42). This means that it was not popular.

J because *The Family of Man* documented "life from birth to death with emphasis on daily relationships of man to himself, to his family, to the community and to the world we live in" (48–51).

29. Which one of the following events do the authors of both passages portray as a significant influence on photography during the 1950s?

   A. World War II

   B. The Cold War

   C. The Great Depression

   D. The first publication of photographic essays

The best answer is A because passage A indicates that "by the 1950s, it was widely, if not universally, agreed that our Depression-era problems had been burned away during World War II, allowing a cheerful, tolerant, chicken-in-every-pot society to rise from the ashes" (lines 18–22). Passage B indicates that Edward Steichen, who organized *The Family of Man* exhibit, was sixty-two years old at the time of Pearl Harbor. He "persuaded the Navy to give him a commission" and "the war shaped the photographer's vision" (lines 71–77).

The answer is NOT:

B because the Cold War is noted but its influence on photography is not indicated. Passage A notes that during the Cold War there was a political climate of xenophobia and messaging that "America was a paradise." Photography is not mentioned in relation to the Cold War. Passage B does not mention the Cold War.

C because passage A notes that during The Great Depression, WPA photographers shot subject matter similar to Frank's work.

D because the passages do not mention the first publication of photographic essays.

30. Compared to Prose's assessment of *The Family of Man,* Curtis's assessment can best be described as more:

    F. critical of the photographic style *The Family of Man* represents.

    G. skeptical of *The Family of Man* for being simple, popular art.

    H. favorable toward *The Family of Man* exhibition than the book form.

    J. respectful of *The Family of Man* as an important, serious work.

The best answer is J because *The Family of Man* collection is portrayed in Passage B as addressing important themes including positive concepts such as "international unity, brotherhood, and familial strength" (lines 84–85). *The Family of Man* advocated peace among humankind. Passage A highlights *The Family of Man* as a point of contrast with Frank's work. Its commercial popularity and warm, lighthearted nature are emphasized. Prose, the author of Passage A, clearly values Frank's unusual style. *The Family of Man,* in contrast, "encouraged its audience to see photography as a merry postman delivering candy hearts" (lines 36–37).

The answer is NOT:

    F because passage B does not say anything negative about the photographic style of *The Family of Man.*

    G because both Prose (Passage A) and Curtis (Passage B) take a relatively neutral stance toward *The Family of Man.* Prose describes how it was publicly received and how it is substantively and stylistically different from Frank's *The Americans,* but she does not seem critical of *The Family of Man.* Curtis quotes a critic Eric Sandeen, who thinks the photos in *The Family of Man* are artificial, but that is just a viewpoint that Curtis wanted to address in his article. It is not necessarily aligned with his viewpoint.

    H There is no indication that anyone liked the exhibit more than the book.

Chapter 10: Practice Questions

This chapter contains a wide variety of sample ACT reading test questions. These are all official ACT questions so be sure to look over them in detail.

Some of these questions are ones that you have seen throughout the rest of the book, but don't skip them just because you've seen them before. The more you practice, the better off you will be on the test.

Finally, this item bank is not set up like a practice test so don't feel as though you need to go through each set of questions in sequential order or on a timed basis. Simply answer the questions to the best of your ability. Be sure to look at the answer key, which provides a detailed explanation to each question.

Passage I

LITERARY NARRATIVE: This passage is adapted from the novel *The Fisher King* by Paule Marshall (©2000 by Paule Marshall).

It was nearing the end of the second set, the jazz show winding down when Hattie heard Abe Kaiser at the microphone call Everett Payne's name. Heard his name and, to her surprise, saw him slowly stand up in
5 the bullpen up front. She hadn't seen him join the other local musicians, including Shades Bowen with his tenor sax, in what was called the bullpen, which was simply a dozen or so chairs grouped near the bandstand. The young locals gathered there each Sunday evening,
10 hoping for a chance to perform. Because toward the end of the final set, the custom was to invite one or two of them to sit in with the band. They sometimes even got to choose the tune they wanted to play.

This Sunday, Everett Payne, not long out of the
15 army, was the one being invited to sit in.

Breath held, Hattie watched him separate himself from the hopefuls and approach the stand, taking his time, moving with what almost seemed a deliberate pause between each step. The crowd waiting.

20 That was his way, Hattie knew. His body moving absentmindedly through space, his head, his thoughts on something other than his surroundings, and his eyes like a curtain he occasionally drew aside a fraction of an inch to peer out at the world. A world far less inter-
25 esting than the music inside his head.

She watched now as he slowly mounted the bandstand and conferred with the bassist and drummer, those two were all he would need. Then, without announcing the name of the tune he intended playing,
30 without in any way acknowledging the audience, he sat down at the piano and brought his hands—large hands, the fingers long and splayed and slightly arched—down on the opening bars of "Sonny Boy Blue."

"Sonny Boy Blue!" That hokey-doke tune!

35 Around her, the purists looked askance at each other from behind their regulation shades and slouched deeper in their chairs in open disgust.

At first, hokey though it was, he played the song straight through as written, the rather long introduction,
40 verse, and chorus. And he did so with great care, although at a slower tempo than was called for and with a formality that lent the Tin Pan Alley tune a depth and thoughtfulness no one else would have accorded it.

Quickly taking their cue from him, the bassist
45 reached for his bow, the drummer for his brushes, the two of them also treating the original as if it were a serious piece of music.

Everett Payne took his time paying his respects to the tune as written, and once that was done, he hunched
50 closer to the piano, angled his head sharply to the left, completely closed the curtain of his gaze, and with his hands commanding the length and breadth of the keyboard he unleashed a dazzling pyrotechnic of chords (you could almost see their colors), polyrhythms, seem-
55 ingly unrelated harmonies, and ideas—fresh, brash, outrageous ideas. It was an outpouring of ideas and feelings informed by his own brand of lyricism and lit from time to time by flashes of the recognizable melody. He continued to acknowledge the little simple-
60 minded tune, while at the same time furiously recasting and reinventing it in an image all his own.

A collective in-suck of breath throughout the club.

Where, Hattie wondered, did he come by the dazzling array of ideas and wealth of feeling? What was
65 the source? It had to do, she speculated, listening intently, with the way he held his head, angled to the left like that, tilted toward both heaven and earth. His right side, his right ear directed skyward, hearing up there, in the Upper Room among the stars Mahalia sang
70 about, a new kind of music: splintered, atonal, profane, and possessing a wonderful dissonance that spoke to him, to his soul-case. For him, this was the true music of the spheres, of the maelstrom up there. When at the piano, he kept his right ear tuned to it at all times, let-
75 ting it guide him, inspire him. His other ear? It remained earthbound, trained on the bedrock that for him was Bach and the blues.

Again and again he took them on a joyous, terrifying roller coaster of a ride it seemed to Hattie, and
80 when he finally deposited them on terra firma after close to twenty minutes, everyone in Putnam Royal

could only sit there as if they were in church and weren't supposed to clap. Overcome. Until finally Alvin Edwards, who lived on Decatur Street and played
85 trumpet in the school band, leaped to his feet and renamed him.

Alvin brought everyone up with him. Including the purists who normally refused to applaud even genius. They too stood up in languid praise of him.

1. It can reasonably be inferred from the passage that Shades Bowen:

    A. did not accompany Everett Payne as he played "Sonny Boy Blue."
    B. had been in the army with Everett Payne.
    C. was the oldest musician in the bullpen.
    D. did not usually allow the local musicians to play with the band.

2. The main purpose of the statement in line 62 is to:

    F. illustrate the high expectations the audience initially had for Everett Payne's performance.
    G. inform the reader of the audience's reaction to Everett Payne's performance.
    H. counteract the narrator's description of Everett Payne's performance.
    J. provide proof that Everett Payne was well known to the audience.

3. The passage most strongly suggests that the second set of the jazz shows at the club is:

    A. the final set.
    B. much longer than the first set.
    C. followed by a third set on Sunday nights.
    D. performed solely by the musicians in the bullpen.

4. Which of the following details is used in the passage to indicate how the purists in the audience initially reacted to Everett Payne's choice of music?

    F. The overall silence of the audience, including the purists
    G. The description of the audience's collective in-suck of breath
    H. The posture the purists assumed in their seats
    J. The fact that the purists stood up

5. According to the narrator, what did Hattie see Everett Payne do prior to playing "Sonny Boy Blue"?

    A. Move quickly from his seat to the bandstand
    B. Study the audience around him
    C. Confer with the bassist and the drummer
    D. Announce the name of the tune he was going to play

6. The passage initially portrays the purists most nearly as:

    F. knowledgeable and open minded.
    G. snobbish and intolerant.
    H. rational and well educated.
    J. inexperienced and uninhibited.

7. It can reasonably be inferred from the passage that Hattie believed Bach and the blues were the:

    A. musical influences that Everett Payne tried to avoid representing when he played piano.
    B. foundation of Everett Payne's inventive piano playing.
    C. true music of the heavens that inspired Everett Payne's creativity as a piano player.
    D. reason why Everett Payne's piano-playing abilities limited him to Tin Pan Alley tunes.

8. According to the passage, when Everett Payne first played "Sonny Boy Blue" straight through, he did so:

    F. more slowly than was intended by the composer.
    G. after it had been suggested by Abe Kaiser.
    H. against the wishes of the bassist and drummer.
    J. without following the original tune.

9. According to the passage, Hattie speculated that the source of Everett Payne's musical ideas and feelings during "Sonny Boy Blue" was in:

    A. the way he tilted his head.
    B. the simplemindedness of the song.
    C. his ability to play with great formality.
    D. his connection with the silent audience.

10. The narrator states that to Hattie, Everett Payne's performance was:

    F. overly slow and formal.
    G. deliberate yet absentminded.
    H. like a song played in a church.
    J. a roller coaster of a ride.

Passage II

SOCIAL STUDIES: This passage is adapted from Richard Moe's article "Mindless Madness Called Sprawl," based on a speech he gave on November 30, 1996, in Fresno, California (©1996 by Richard Moe).

At the time he gave the speech, Moe was president of the National Trust for Historic Preservation.

Drive down any highway leading into any town in the country, and what do you see? Fast-food outlets, office parks and shopping malls rising out of vast barren plains of asphalt. Residential subdivisions
5 spreading like inkblots obliterating forests and farms in their relentless march across the landscape. Cars moving sluggishly down the broad ribbons of pavement or halting in frustrated clumps at choked intersections. You see communities drowning in a destructive, soul-
10 less, ugly mess called sprawl.

Many of us have developed a frightening form of selective blindness that allows us to pass by the appalling mess without really seeing it. We've allowed our communities to be destroyed bit by bit, and most of
15 us have shrugged off this destruction as "the price of progress."

Development that destroys communities isn't progress. It's chaos. And it isn't inevitable, it's merely easy. Too many developers follow standard formulas,
20 and too many government entities have adopted laws and policies that constitute powerful incentives for sprawl.

Why is an organization like the National Trust for Historic Preservation so concerned about sprawl?
25 We're concerned because sprawl devastates older communities, leaving historic buildings and neighborhoods underused, poorly maintained or abandoned. We've learned that we can't hope to revitalize these communities without doing something to control the sprawl that
30 keeps pushing further and further out from the center.

But our concern goes beyond that, because preservation today is about more than bricks and mortar. There's a growing body of grim evidence to support our belief that the destruction of traditional downtowns and
35 older neighborhoods—places that people care about—is corroding the very sense of community that helps bind us together as a people and as a nation.

One form of sprawl—retail development that transforms roads into strip malls—is frequently spurred
40 on by discount retailers, many of whom are now concentrating on the construction of superstores with more than 200,000 square feet of space. In many small towns, a single new superstore may have more retail space than the entire downtown business district. When
45 a store like that opens, the retail center of gravity shifts away from Main Street. Downtown becomes a ghost town.

Sprawl's other most familiar form—spread-out residential subdivisions that "leapfrog" from the urban
50 fringe into the countryside—is driven largely by the American dream of a detached home in the middle of a grassy lawn. Developers frequently claim they can build more "affordable" housing on the edge of town—but "affordable" for whom?

55 The developer's own expenses may be less, and the home buyer may find the prices attractive—but who picks up the extra costs of fire and police protection, new roads and new utility infrastructure in these outlying areas? We all do, in the form of higher taxes for
60 needless duplication of services and infrastructure that already exist in older parts of our cities and towns.

People who say that sprawl is merely the natural product of marketplace forces at work fail to recognize that the game isn't being played on a level field. Gov-
65 ernment at every level is riddled with policies that mandate or encourage sprawl.

By prohibiting mixed uses and mandating inordinate amounts of parking and unreasonable setback requirements, most current zoning laws make it impos-
70 sible—even illegal—to create the sort of compact walkable environment that attracts us to older neighborhoods and historic communities all over the world. These codes are a major reason why 82 percent of all trips in the United States are taken by car. The average
75 American household now allocates more than 18 percent of its budget to transportation expenses, most of which are auto-related. That's more than it spends for food and three times more than it spends for health care.

80 Our communities should be shaped by choice, not by chance. One of the most effective ways to reach this goal is to insist on sensible land-use planning. The way we zone and design our communities either opens up or forecloses alternatives to the automobile. Municipali-
85 ties should promote downtown housing and mixed-use zoning that reduce the distances people must travel between home and work. The goal should be an integrated system of planning decisions and regulations that knit communities together instead of tearing them
90 apart. We should demand land-use planning that exhibits a strong bias in favor of existing communities.

11. The principal aim of the passage can best be classified as:

A. persuasive.
B. explanatory.
C. descriptive.
D. narrative.

12. Among the following quotations from the passage, the one that best summarizes what the author would like to see happen is:

   F. "laws and policies that constitute powerful incentives for sprawl" (lines 20–22).
   G. "the destruction of traditional downtowns" (line 34).
   H. "'affordable' housing on the edge of town" (line 53).
   J. "an integrated system of planning decisions and regulations" (lines 87–88).

13. The last paragraph differs from the first paragraph in that in the last paragraph the author:

   A. asks a question and then answers it.
   B. uses more statistics to support his arguments.
   C. incorporates more emotional language.
   D. offers solutions rather than stating a problem.

14. In the passage, the author answers all of the following questions EXCEPT:

   F. How long has sprawl been happening in US cities?
   G. Is development synonymous with progress?
   H. What is one major reason that people in the United States use automobiles so much?
   J. What should communities do to combat sprawl?

15. The author states that one superstore may do all of the following EXCEPT:

   A. have more retail space than an entire downtown.
   B. lead to serious downtown renovations.
   C. make the downtown area into a ghost town.
   D. shift the center of gravity away from downtown.

16. The statistics cited by the author in the tenth paragraph (lines 67–79) are used to illustrate the concept that:

   F. allowing mixed uses of land leads to environmental destruction.
   G. current zoning laws help create a compact, walkable environment.
   H. land-use regulations now in effect increase the overall costs of transportation.
   J. Americans spend too much of their budgets on food and health care.

17. One form of sprawl the author describes is retail development that:

   A. adjoins existing downtown areas.
   B. utilizes historic buildings.
   C. turns roads into strip malls.
   D. promotes a sense of community around a superstore.

18. As it is used in line 51, the word *detached* most nearly means:

   F. objective.
   G. set apart.
   H. broken apart.
   J. taken away.

19. The author uses the statement "The game isn't being played on a level field" (line 64) most nearly to mean that:

   A. cities needlessly duplicate essential services.
   B. higher taxes for some people make their lives more difficult.
   C. marketplace forces are at work.
   D. governmental decisions influence marketplace forces.

20. The phrase *mixed uses* (line 67) most likely refers to:

   F. having large parking lots around even larger stores.
   G. preserving and restoring historic neighborhoods.
   H. ensuring that automobiles cannot be driven to the various local businesses.
   J. allowing one area to contain various types of development.

Passage III

HUMANITIES: This passage is adapted from the essay "My Life with a Field Guide" by Diana Kappel-Smith (©2002 by Phi Beta Kappa Society).

I was seventeen when it started. My family was on vacation, and one day we went on a nature walk led by a young man a few years older than I. Probably I wanted to get his attention—I'm sure I did—so I
5 pointed to a flower and asked, "What's that?"

"Hmmm? Oh, just an aster," he said.

Was there a hint of a sniff as he turned away? There was! It was just an aster and I was just a total ignoramus!

10 And I remember the aster. Its rays were a brilliant purple, its core a dense coin of yellow velvet. It focused light as a crystal will. It faced the sun; it was the sun's echo.

Later that day, a book with a green cover lay on
15 the arm of a chair under an apple tree. It was the same volume that our guide had carried as he marched us through the woods. The book had been left there, by itself. It was a thing of power. In the thin summer shadow of the tree, quivering, like a veil, the book was
20 revealed, and I reached for it. A FIELD GUIDE TO WILD FLOWERS—PETERSON & McKENNY, its cover said. Its backside was ruled like a measuring tape, its inside was full of drawings of flowers. By the end of that week I had my own copy. I have it still.

25 Over the next several years this field guide would become my closest companion, a slice of worldview, as indispensable as eyes or hands. I didn't arrive at this intimacy right away, however. This wasn't going to be an easy affair for either of us.

30 I'll give you an example of how it went. After I'd owned the Peterson's for about a week, I went on a hike with some friends up a little mountain, taking the book along. Halfway up the mountain, there by the trailside was a yellow flower, a nice opportunity to take my new
35 guide for a test drive. "Go on ahead!" I said to my hiking companions, "I'll be a minute . . ." Famous last words.

I had already figured out the business of the book's colored tabs. I turned in an authoritative way to
40 the Yellow part and began to flip through. By the time the last of my friends had disappeared up the trail, I'd arrived at a page where things looked right. Five petals? Yes. Pinnate leaves? Whatever. Buttercup? There are, amazingly, *eleven* buttercups. Who would
45 have thought? However hard I tried to make it so, my item was not one of them. Next page. Aha! this looked more like it. Bushy cinquefoil? Nope, leaves not *quiiite* right, are they? As the gnats descended, I noticed that there were six more pages ahead, each packed with
50 five-petaled yellow flowers—St. John's wort loose-strifes, puccoons.

Why I persisted in carrying it around and consulting its crowded pages at every opportunity, I have no idea. The book was stubborn; well, I was stubborn, too;
55 that was part of it. And I had no choice, really, not if I wanted to *get in*. A landscape may be handsome in the aggregate, but this book led to the particulars, and that's what I wanted. A less complete guide would have been easier to start with, but more frustrating in the
60 end. A more complete book would have been impossible for me to use. So I persisted in wrestling with the Peterson's, and thus by slow degrees the crowd of plant stuff in the world became composed of individuals. As it did, the book changed: its cover was stained by
65 water and snack food, the spine grew invitingly lax, and some of the margins sprouted cryptic annotations.

By the time the next summer came, I had fully discovered the joy of the hunt, and every new species had its trophy of data—name and place and date—to be
70 jotted down. If I'd found a flower before, I was happy to see it again. I often addressed it with enthusiasm: *Hi there, Solidago hispida!* I discovered early on that a plant's Latin name is a name of power by which the plant can be uniquely identified among different spoken
75 tongues, across continents, and through time. The genus name lashes it firmly to its closest kin, while its species name describes a personal attribute—*rubrum* meaning red, *officinale* meaning medicinal, *odoratus* meaning smelly, and so on. It all makes such delightful
80 sense!

My friend Julie and I identified individual plants in our rambles, but from the particulars we began to know wholes. Bogs held one community, montane forests held another, and the plants they held in
85 common were clues to intricate dramas of climate change and continental drift. So from plant communities it followed that the grand schemes of things, when they came our way, arrived rooted in real place and personal experience: quaternary geology, biogeography,
90 evolutionary biology all lay on the road that we had begun to travel.

21. The passage is best described as being told from the point of view of someone who is:

   A. tracing her developing interest in identifying flowers and in the natural world.
   B. reexamining the event that led her to a lifelong fascination with asters.
   C. reviewing her relationships with people who have shared her interest in flowers.
   D. describing how her hobby of identifying flowers became a profitable career.

22. As portrayed by the author, the young man responded to her question about the flower with what is best described as:

    F. acceptance.
    G. surprise.
    H. condescension.
    J. anger.

23. What name, if any, does the author report assigning to the yellow flower she came across during a mountain hike?

    A. St. John's wort
    B. Loosestrife
    C. Puccoon
    D. The passage doesn't name the flower.

24. Looking back at her early experiences with the Peterson's, the author most strongly implies that the guide was:

    F. daunting at first, but in retrospect preferable to either a more or a less complete guide.
    G. easy to use in the beginning, but more frustrating in the end than a more complete guide would have been.
    H. impossible for her to follow until she started pairing it with a different guide written for beginners.
    J. appealing initially until she realized how poorly illustrated its crowded pages were.

25. As it is used in line 56, the phrase *get in* most nearly means:

    A. arrive at a physical location.
    B. be chosen for group membership.
    C. truly understand the subject.
    D. be friendly with someone.

26. The passage best supports which of the following conclusions about Julie?

    F. She has more experience than the author has in identifying flowers.
    G. She owns a house that's close to either a bog or a montane forest.
    H. She sees value in understanding the various communities of plants.
    J. She stopped using the Peterson's as her primary source of flower information.

27. The author states that the Peterson's became her closest companion over a period of several:

    A. days.
    B. weeks.
    C. months.
    D. years.

28. In the context of the passage, the author's statement in lines 56–58 most nearly means that she:

    F. learned to understand landscapes by looking at their overall patterns rather than their details.
    G. found that landscapes lost their appeal the more she tried to understand them logically.
    H. hoped to paint attractive portraits of landscapes by paying careful attention to details.
    J. sought a deeper knowledge of landscapes through learning about their individual parts.

29. The details in lines 64–66 primarily serve to suggest the:

    A. poor craftsmanship the publishing company used in producing the Peterson's.
    B. transformation the author's copy of the Peterson's underwent as a result of heavy use.
    C. strange writing the author often encountered in reading the Peterson's.
    D. carelessness with which the author used the Peterson's, much to her later regret.

30. The author refers to *Solidago hispida* as an example of a flower that she:

    F. had great trouble identifying the first time she stumbled upon it.
    G. hopes to finally come across on one of her nature walks.
    H. was pleased to encounter again after she had learned to identify it.
    J. feels has an inappropriate name given the plant's characteristics.

Passage IV

NATURAL SCIENCE: This passage is adapted from the article "When Research Is a Snow Job" by Sarah Boyle (©2002 by National Wildlife).

The figure is beyond comprehension: Every year, 1,000,000,000,000,000,000,000,000 (1 septillion) snowflakes fall worldwide. As the crystals fall, they encounter different atmospheric conditions that produce
5 flakes with unique attributes. The more complex those conditions are, the more elaborate the crystals.

Kenneth Libbrecht is a physicist at the California Institute of Technology. Along with the work of scientists at the U.S. Department of Agriculture's Agricul-
10 tural Research Service (ARS), his research is uncovering new information about the magical world of snow crystals—information that has practical applications in such diverse areas as agriculture and the production of electricity.

15 Snow crystals are individual crystals—usually in a hexagonal form—while snowflakes are collections of two or more snow crystals. Beginning as condensed water vapor, a crystal typically grows around a nucleus of dust. Its shape depends on how the six side facets—
20 or faces—grow in relation to the top and bottom facets. If they grow relatively tall, the crystal appears column-like; if the side facets are short compared to the length of the bottom and top facets, the crystal looks platelike.

Currently Libbrecht is trying to crack the problem
25 of why the crystal facets' growth varies with temperature. He believes this may have something to do with the ice surface's "quasi-liquid" layer, which affects how water molecules stick to the surface.

By manipulating the temperature and humidity
30 within an incubation chamber (and by adding an electric current or various gases at times), Libbrecht creates "designer" snowflakes in his lab. Such experiments are helping him determine how crystals form.

William Wergin, a retired ARS research biologist,
35 and a colleague, Eric Erbe, were using scanning electron microscopy to look at biological problems relating to agriculture. To avoid the laborious procedure that using such equipment usually entails, the two scientists decided to freeze the tissue they were working with and
40 look at it in the frozen state.

"One day it happened to be snowing," says Wergin, "and we were looking for a specimen. We imaged some snowflakes and were very surprised to see what we did." It was the first time anyone had
45 attempted to image snow crystals with scanning electron microscopy, which provides precise detail about the crystals' shape, structural features and metamorphosed conditions (crystals often change once on the ground depending on the surrounding environment).

50 Wergin called another ARS colleague, hydrologist Albert Rango, to see if the snow crystal magnifications had any applications for his research. Rango now uses Wergin's electron microscopy data, along with microwave satellite data, in the Snowmelt Runoff
55 Model to predict the amount of water available in a winter snowpack. For western states such as Colorado, Montana, Utah and Wyoming, about 75 percent of the annual water supply comes from snowmelt. Snowmelt water is critical to crop irrigation and hydroelectric
60 power, as well as recreation and domestic water supplies, fisheries management and flood control.

Before employing the scanning electron microscopy results, the forecasted amounts of snowpack water were inaccurate whenever the size and shape of the
65 snow crystals varied much from the norm. "The more we know about crystals," notes Rango, "the easier it will be to use microwave satellite data for predictions of the snow water equivalent."

Currently, forecasts using the model are about
70 90 percent accurate. A 1980 study estimated that improving the prediction by 1 percent would save $38 million in irrigation and hydropower in the western United States.

Rango is also looking ahead at climate change pre-
75 dictions. "Following the estimates that have been made about what will happen by 2100, things are definitely warming up," he says. Temperature increases will likely result in a reduction in stream flow as overall snow accumulation decreases, winter precipitation runs
80 off as rain, and water evaporates at a quicker rate. The gap between water supply and demand will magnify even more, greatly increasing water's economic value, anticipates Rango.

Not only does the crystal research help gauge
85 snowmelt, it is also useful in predicting avalanches, designing artificial snow, and, perhaps in the near future, examining air pollution. "You can put snow in a scanning electron microscope and tell which elements are present, such as sulfur and nitrogen," says Wergin.
90 "You can then see what kind of pollution is in the area and possibly track the source."

31. It can reasonably be inferred from the passage that the information about the scientific study of snow is presented primarily to:

A. emphasize the importance of communication among scientists.
B. explain how snow crystal facets influence the snowpack in some western states.
C. showcase the varied uses of the scanning electron microscope.
D. demonstrate some of the practical applications of the study of snow crystals.

32. According to the passage, the use of scanning electron microscopy can save money by:

    F. encouraging scientists to make estimates of water requirements far into the future.
    G. allowing forecasters to predict more accurately the quantity of water in the snowpack.
    H. helping agricultural researchers to identify biological problems.
    J. increasing the water supply for Colorado, Montana, Utah, and Wyoming by 75 percent.

33. It can reasonably be inferred that the phrase *metamorphosed conditions* (lines 47–48) refers to the:

    A. temperature and humidity at which crystals form.
    B. process by which snow crystals develop from a speck of dust and water vapor.
    C. state of snow crystals after they reach the ground.
    D. major changes in environmental conditions.

34. According to the passage, the addition of electron microscopy data to the Snowmelt Runoff Model allows scientists using the model to include in their predictions detailed information about:

    F. microwave satellite data.
    G. structural variations of snow crystals.
    H. locations having the most snowfall.
    J. biological problems related to agriculture.

35. According to Rango, one reason that water's economic value is likely to increase by the year 2100 is that:

    A. more water will be polluted by then.
    B. less water will be wasted due to more accurate predictions of the water supply.
    C. the sulfur and nitrogen content in snow is likely to increase.
    D. predicted climate changes will reduce overall snow accumulation.

36. According to the passage, snowflakes have infinite variety because:

    F. enormous numbers of snow crystals fall worldwide.
    G. falling snow crystals meet with varied atmospheric conditions.
    H. snow crystals fall at various rates, creating unique snowflakes.
    J. complexities in the atmosphere slow snow crystal development.

37. The passage states that snowflakes differ from snow crystals in that snowflakes:

    A. grow around a nucleus of dust.
    B. combine to form snow crystals.
    C. grow in relation to top and bottom facets.
    D. are composed of more than one crystal.

38. The term *"designer" snowflakes* (line 32) refers directly to the fact that:

    F. no two snowflakes are alike.
    G. Libbrecht produces the snowflakes in his lab.
    H. snowflakes are part of the grand design of nature.
    J. Libbrecht's snowflakes exhibit special beauty.

39. As it is used in line 59, the word *critical* most nearly means:

    A. evaluative.
    B. faultfinding.
    C. vital.
    D. acute.

40. The passage states that research about snow crystals has helped scientists do all of the following EXCEPT:

    F. extract pollutants from snow.
    G. gauge snowmelt.
    H. design artificial snow.
    J. predict avalanches.

Passage V

LITERARY NARRATIVE: This passage is adapted from the short story "Elba" by Marly Swick (©1991 by the University of Iowa). Fran is the narrator of the story.

Mother, who wanted to keep her, always thought of her as some wild little bird, but I knew she was a homing pigeon. I knew that at some point in her flight path, sooner or later, she would make a U-turn. A sort
5 of human boomerang. So even though I had long since stopped expecting it, I was not surprised when I walked down the gravel drive to the mailbox, which I'd painted papaya yellow to attract good news, and found the flimsy envelope with the Dallas postmark. I didn't
10 know a soul in Dallas, or Texas for that matter, but the handwriting reminded me of someone's. My own.

I walked back inside the house.

"Still raining?" Mother asked. She was sitting in her new electric wheelchair in front of the TV, painting
15 her fingernails a neon violet.

"Just let up," I said. "Sun's poking through. You know anyone in Dallas, Mother?"

"Not so as I recall." She dabbed at her pinky with a cottonball. Mother was vain about her hands. I was
20 used to how she looked now, but I noticed people staring in the doctor's waiting room. She had lost some weight and most of her hair to chemotherapy, and I guess people were startled to see these dragon-lady nails on a woman who looked as if she should be lying
25 in satin with some flowers on her chest.

"Why do you ask?" she said.

I opened the envelope and a picture fluttered into my lap. It was a Polaroid of a sweet-faced blond holding a newborn baby in a blue blanket. Before I
30 even read the letter I knew. I knew how those Nazis feel when suddenly, after twenty or thirty uneventful years, they are arrested walking down some sunny street in Buenos Aires. It's the shock of being found after waiting so long.

35 "What's that?" Mother said.

I wheeled her around to face me and handed her the Polaroid. She studied it for a minute and then looked up, speechless for once, waiting for me to set the tone.

40 "That's her," I said. "Her name's Linda Rose Caswell."

We looked at the picture again. The blond woman was seated on a flowered couch, her wavy hair just grazing the edge of a dime-a-dozen seascape in a cheap gilt frame.

45 Mother pointed to the envelope. "What's she say?"

I unfolded the letter, a single page neatly written.

"She says she's had my name and address for some time but wanted to wait to contact me until after the birth. The baby's name is Blake and he weighs eight
50 pounds, eight ounces, and was born by cesarean. She says they are waiting and hoping to hear back from me soon."

"That's it?"

I nodded and handed her the letter. It was short
55 and businesslike, but I could see the ghosts of all the long letters she must have written and crumpled into the wastebasket.

"I guess that makes you a great-grandmother," I said.

60 "What about you?" she snorted, pointing a Jungle Orchid fingernail at me. "You're a grandmother."
We shook our heads in disbelief. I sat silently, listening to my brain catch up with my history. Forty years old and I felt as if I had just shaken hands with
65 Death. I suppose it's difficult for any woman to accept that she's a grandmother, but in the normal order of things, you have ample time to adjust to the idea. You don't get a snapshot in the mail one day from a baby girl you gave up twenty-four years ago saying,
70 Congratulations, you're a grandma!"

"It's not fair," I said. "I don't even feel like a mother."

"Well, here's the living proof." Mother tapped her nail against the glossy picture. "She looks just like you. Only her nose is more aristocratic."

75 "I'm going to work." My knees cracked when I stood up. "You be all right here?"

Mother nodded, scrutinizing the picture in her lap. "You going to write to her?"

"Of course I am," I bristled. "I may be some
80 things, but I am not rude."

"You going to invite them here? Her and the baby?" She swiveled her eyes sideways at me.

"I haven't thought that far," I said.

"Well, don't put it off." She slid her eyes back to
85 the television. "She's been waiting twenty-five years. You worried she's going to be trouble or ask for money? For all we know, she's married to a brain surgeon with his and her Cadillacs."

"She didn't mention any husband at all," I said,
90 getting drawn into it despite myself.

"Maybe you're worried she'll be disappointed in you," she said, "You know, that she's had this big fantasy for all these years that maybe you were Grace Kelly or Margaret Mead and who could live up to that?
95 No one. But you don't have to, Fran, that's the thing. You're her flesh-and-blood mother and that's enough. That's all it'll take."

41. Fran would most likely agree with which of the following statements about her relationship with Linda Rose?

   A. Their lives are still connected despite long separations of time and distance.
   B. They have built up too much resentment toward each other to have a good relationship now.
   C. Fran's dreams of a perfect daughter will interfere with any real relationship she might have with Linda Rose.
   D. The two of them have enough in common that it won't be difficult for them to get close.

42. Fran's mother can most accurately be characterized as:

   F. arrogant and cruel.
   G. strong-willed and caring.
   H. friendly but withdrawn.
   J. loving but embittered.

43. Which of the following statements does NOT describe one of Fran's reactions to the news that she is a grandmother?

   A. She wishes she had had time to prepare for the news.
   B. She looks forward to inviting Linda Rose and her son, Blake, over for a visit.
   C. She feels suddenly older now that the label of grandmother applies to her.
   D. She protests that this change in her life is unfair.

44. The main point of the first paragraph is that:

   F. Fran believed Linda Rose would someday try to contact her.
   G. Linda Rose acted like a wild bird when she was young.
   H. Fran finds the arrival of a letter from Linda Rose surprising.
   J. Linda Rose's handwriting reminds Fran of her own handwriting.

45. The main point of the last paragraph is that Fran's mother believes:

   A. Linda Rose has few illusions about Fran.
   B. Linda Rose might cause trouble or ask for money.
   C. Fran shouldn't worry about disappointing Linda Rose.
   D. Fran shouldn't write to Linda Rose until Fran is emotionally prepared.

46. According to the passage, when Fran looks at her mother, Fran feels:

   F. surprised by how weak and old her mother looks.
   G. embarrassed by the gaudy colors of nail polish her mother uses.
   H. pity that so many people stare at her mother in public.
   J. accustomed to her mother's frailness and unusual fingernails.

47. Which of the following statements most accurately expresses Fran's feelings when she hands her mother the letter from Linda Rose?

   A. Fran is disappointed about getting such a short letter after so many years of no news from Linda Rose.
   B. Fran welcomes the good news about the birth of her grandson, Blake.
   C. Fran is offended by the letter's cold, businesslike tone.
   D. Fran knows how hard it must have been for Linda Rose to write the letter.

48. It can logically be inferred from the passage that the reason it has been a long time since Fran and Linda Rose have seen each other is because:

   F. Linda Rose left home to get married.
   G. arguments between Fran and Linda Rose drove Linda Rose away.
   H. Linda Rose chose to live with her father.
   J. as a child Linda Rose was adopted by another family

49. A reasonable conclusion Fran and her mother draw about Linda Rose from her letter and picture is that Linda Rose:

   A. lives near the coast of Texas with her husband.
   B. enjoys and collects fine paintings.
   C. bears a strong resemblance to Fran.
   D. cares little about how she or her house looks.

50. According to the passage, the reason why Fran's mother warns Fran not to put off contacting Linda Rose is that Fran's mother:

   F. wants to see her new great-grandson before she dies.
   G. knows Fran tends to delay making hard decisions.
   H. knows how long Linda Rose has been waiting to see Fran.
   J. suspects Linda Rose is in some sort of trouble.

Passage VI

SOCIAL SCIENCE: This passage is adapted from a book titled *How Courts Govern America* by Richard Neely (©1981 by Richard Neely).

Government is a technical undertaking, like the building of rocketships or the organizing of railroad yards. Except possibly on the local level, the issues which attract public notice usually involve raising

5 money (taxes), spending money (public works), foreign wars (preventing them or arguing for fighting easy ones), education, public morals, crime in the streets, and, most important of all, the economy. When times are bad or there is a nationwide strike or disaster,

10 interest in the economy becomes all-consuming. However, the daily toiling of countless millions of civil servants in areas such as occupational health and safety, motor vehicle regulation, or control of navigable waterways escapes public notice almost completely.

15 Furthermore, even with regard to high-visibility issues, significant communication between the electorate and public officials is extremely circumscribed. Most serious political communication is limited to forty-five seconds on the network evening news. In

20 days gone by, when the only entertainment in town on a Wednesday night was to go to the county courthouse to listen to a prominent politician give a theatrical tirade against Herbert Hoover, an eloquent speaker could pack the courthouse and have five thousand people lined up

25 to the railroad tracks listening to the booming loud-speakers.

The political orator of yesteryear has been replaced by a flickering image on the tube, unlocking the secrets of the government universe in forty-five-

30 second licks. Gone forever are Lincoln–Douglas type debates on courthouse steps. Newspapers take up the slack a little, but very little. Most of what one says to a local newspaper (maybe not *The New York Times*) gets filtered through the mind of an inexperienced

35 twenty-three-year-old journalism school graduate. Try sometime to explain the intricacies of a program budget, which basically involves solving a grand equation composed of numerous simultaneous differential functions, to a reporter whose journalism school

40 curriculum did not include advanced algebra, to say nothing of calculus.

But the electorate is as interested in the whys and wherefores of most technical, non-emotional political issues as I am in putting ships in bottles: they do not

45 particularly care. Process and personalities, the way decisions are made and by whom, the level of perquisites, extramarital sexual relations, and, in high offices, personal gossip dominate the public mind, while interest in the substance of technical decisions is

50 so minimal. Reporters focus on what sells papers or gets a high Nielsen rating; neither newspapers nor television stations intend to lose their primary value as entertainment. Since the populace at large is more than willing to delegate evaluation of the technical aspects of

55 government to somebody else, it inevitably follows that voting is a negative exercise, not a positive one. Angry voters turn the rascals out and, in the triumph of hope over experience, let new rascals in. What voters are unable to do—because they themselves do not under-

60 stand the technical questions—is tell the rascals how to do their jobs better.

Serious coverage of goings-on in government is deterred by the fact that government is so technical that even career civil servants cannot explain what is

65 happening. In 1978 I attended a seminar on federal estate and gift tax, where the Internal Revenue Service lawyers responsible for this area frankly confessed that they did not understand the Tax Reform Act of 1976. Intricate technical issues such as taxation, arms control,

70 and nuclear power are difficult to understand for professionals, to say nothing of the most diligent layman.

That anything gets done by a political body at all is to be applauded as a miracle rather than accepted as a matter of course. When we recognize that in the federal

75 government, with its millions of employees, there are but five hundred and thirty-seven elected officials, put into office to carry out the "will" of a people who for the most part know little and care less about the technical functioning of their government, the absurdity of

80 the notion of rapid democratic responsiveness becomes clear. The widely held tenet of democratic faith that elected officials, as opposed to bureaucrats or the judiciary are popularly selected and democratically responsive is largely a myth which gives a useful legiti-

85 macy to a system. In fact, however, far from democratic control, the two most important forces in political life are indifference and its direct byproduct, inertia.

51. One of the main points that the author seeks to make in the passage is that American citizens:

A. cannot understand government because they read too many newspapers and watch too much television.

B. have little chance of improving government because they do not understand the important details of government.

C. can control elected officials' technical decisions through elections, but have no control over the bureaucrats.

D. used to have a responsive government before television cut back on news and began to concentrate on entertainment.

52. The author asserts that local newspaper reporters are often:

    F. inexperienced and insufficiently educated.
    G. inexperienced but well educated.
    H. young but experienced.
    J. young and well educated.

53. The author uses the description of the tax seminar in 1978 to make the point that some governmental issues are:

    A. so technical that not even career civil servants can understand them.
    B. so technical that only career civil servants can understand them.
    C. more technical than they used to be before the passage of the Tax Reform Act.
    D. too technical for anyone other than an Internal Revenue Service tax lawyer to understand.

54. When the author asserts that *indifference* is a central fact of American political life (line 87), he most likely means that citizens are:

    F. not concerned about the technical, but important, details of government.
    G. completely taken in by the myth that government is responsive to democratic control.
    H. more responsive to elected government officials than to unelected bureaucrats.
    J. not prepared to concede legitimacy to a government unless it is democratically elected.

55. According to the passage, when is voter interest in the economy greatest?

    A. When national elections are held
    B. When interesting personalities are leaders
    C. When there are bad economic times
    D. When there are no other interesting issues

56. As it is used in line 17, the word *circumscribed* means:

    F. technical.
    G. limited.
    H. entertaining.
    J. serious.

57. According to the passage, the news story under which of the following headlines would attract the greatest number of readers?

    A. Department of Interior Announces End of National Park Fees
    B. New Accounting Procedures in Federal Budget
    C. New Federal Safety Regulations Due Out Today
    D. Senator Smith Claims "I Never Made a Nickel On It"

58. The passage makes the claim that television news coverage is heavily influenced by Nielsen ratings because:

    F. those ratings place great emphasis on technical details.
    G. their competitors, the newspapers, get very high ratings.
    H. the Federal Communications Commission requires Nielsen ratings.
    J. television is primarily an entertainment medium.

59. In the fourth paragraph, the phrase "the triumph of hope over experience" (lines 57–58) is an expression of the belief that:

    A. newly elected officials will govern better than the ones just defeated.
    B. expertise in a technical field is a qualification for holding office.
    C. if the voters get angry enough, elected officials will do a better job.
    D. newspapers and television will eventually provide better news coverage.

60. In the passage, the argument is made that citizens are unable to tell government officials how to do their jobs better because citizens:

    F. don't vote in every election.
    G. have a tendency to elect rascals.
    H. don't read enough newspapers or see enough television.
    J. don't understand the technical details of government.

Passage VII

HUMANITIES: This passage is adapted from Bharati Mukherjee's essay "A Four-Hundred Year-Old Woman," which appears in the anthology *The Writer on Her Work* (©1991 by Janet Sternburg).

I was born into a class that did not live in its native language. I was born into a city that feared its future, and trained me for emigration. I attended a school run by Irish nuns, who regarded our walled-off school
5 compound in Calcutta as a corner of England. My "country"—called in Bengali *desh*—I have never seen.

It is the ancestral home of my father and is now in Bangladesh. Nevertheless, I speak his dialect of Bengali, and think of myself as "belonging" to
10 Faridpur, the tiny village that was his birthplace. The political entity to which I gave my first allegiance—India—was not even a sovereign nation when I was born.

My horoscope, cast by a neighborhood astrologer
15 when I was a week-old infant, predicted that I would be a writer, that I would cross oceans and make my home among aliens. Brought up in a culture that places its faith in horoscopes, it never occurred to me to doubt it.

The astrologer meant to offer me a melancholy future;
20 to be destined to leave India was to be banished from the sources of true culture. The nuns at school, on the other hand, insinuated that India had long outlived its glories, and that if we wanted to be educated, modern women, we'd better hit the trail westward. All my girl-
25 hood, I straddled the seesaw of contradictions. I have found my way to the United States after many transit stops. The unglimpsed phantom Faridpur and the all too real Manhattan have merged as "desh." I am an American. I am an American writer, in the
30 American mainstream, trying to extend it. This is a vitally important statement for me—I am not an Indian writer, not an expatriate. I am an immigrant; my investment is in the American reality, not the Indian. It took me ten painful years, from the early seven-
35 ties to the early eighties, to overthrow the smothering tyranny of nostalgia. The remaining struggle for me is to make the American readership, meaning the editorial and publishing industries as well, acknowledge the same fact. The foreign-born, the Third World immi-
40 grant with non-Western religions and non-European languages and appearance, can be as American as any steerage passenger from Ireland, Italy, or the Russian Pale.

My literary agenda begins by acknowledging that
45 America has transformed *me*. It does not end until I show how I (and the hundreds of thousands like me) have transformed America.

I've had to sensitize editors as well as readers to the richness of the lives I'm writing about. The most
50 moving form of praise I receive from readers can be summed up in three words: I never knew. Meaning, I see these people (call them Indians, Filipinos, Koreans, Chinese) around me all the time and *I never knew* they had an inner life. I never knew they schemed and
55 cheated, suffered, cared so passionately. When even the forms of praise are so rudimentary, the writer knows she has an inexhaustible fictional population to enumerate. Perhaps even a mission.

I have been blessed with an enormity of material:
60 the rapid and dramatic transformation of the United States since the early 1970s. Within that perceived perimeter, however, I hope to wring surprises. Yet my imaginative home is also in the tales told by my mother and grandmother, the world of the Hindu
65 epics. For all the hope and energy I have placed in the process of immigration and accommodation—I'm a person who couldn't ride a public bus when she first arrived, and now I'm someone who watches tractor pulls on obscure cable channels—there are parts of
70 me that remain Indian. The form that my stories and novels take inevitably reflects the resources of Indian mythology—shape-changing, miracles, godly perspectives. My characters can, I hope, transcend the strait-jacket of simple psychologizing. The people I write
75 about are culturally and politically several hundred years old: consider the history they have witnessed (colonialism, technology, education, liberation, civil war). They have shed old identities, taken on new ones, and learned to hide the scars. They may sell you news-
80 papers, or clean your offices at night.

Writers (especially American writers weaned on affluence and freedom) often disavow the notion of a "literary duty" or "political consciousness," citing the all-too-frequent examples of writers ruined by their
85 shrill commitments. Glibness abounds on both sides of the argument, but finally I have to side with my "Third World" compatriots: I do have a duty, beyond telling a good story. My duty is to give voice to continents, but also to redefine the nature of *American*.

61. One of the main arguments the author is trying to make in the passage is that:

   A. until recently, foreign-born residents have not wanted to be involved in defining the American reality.
   B. non-Western immigrants are changing the definition of what it means to be an American.
   C. the United States immigration policy is inherently unfair.
   D. America has changed the political affiliations of most non-Western immigrants.

62. Considering the information given in the first three paragraphs (lines 1–33), which of the following is the most accurate description of the author's girlhood and early adulthood?

    F. She grew up and was educated in Calcutta, moved to the United States, and lived in Manhattan.
    G. She was born in Calcutta, was educated in England by Irish nuns, then moved to Manhattan.
    H. She was raised in Bangladesh, educated by Irish nuns in Calcutta, moved first to England and some time later arrived in the United States.
    J. She was born in Faridpur, was educated in Calcutta, then moved to Manhattan.

63. The author sees her "literary agenda" (line 44) and her "mission" (line 58) to be:

    A. raising the political consciousness of recent immigrants to the United States.
    B. creating characters whose cultural heritage is not easily identifiable.
    C. reinterpreting, through her stories, what it means to be an American.
    D. finding an audience for her stories and novels.

64. Which of the following statements from the passage is an acknowledgment by the author that she was changed by America?

    F. "The astrologer meant to offer me a melancholy future" (line 19).
    G. "All my girlhood, I straddled the seesaw of contradictions" (lines 24–25).
    H. "I'm someone who watches tractor pulls on obscure cable channels" (lines 68–69).
    J. "My characters can, I hope, transcend the straitjacket of simple psychologizing" (lines 73–74).

65. The author refers to the village of Faridpur as a "phantom" (line 27) because:

    A. it is a part of the Indian mythology her mother told her about.
    B. she considers Manhattan, not Bangladesh, to be her home.
    C. even though it was once part of India, it is now part of Bangladesh.
    D. even though she considers it to be her ancestral home, she has never been there.

66. When the author says that she is "trying to extend it" (line 30), she most likely means that she:

    F. wants to see people from non-European ethnicities included in what is considered mainstream American.
    G. prefers to be part of both the Indian and the American cultures.
    H. is trying to find a way to make her home in the United States permanent.
    J. is working to change regulations so that many more Indian immigrants can live in the United States.

67. The author implies that she had to "sensitize editors" (line 48) because those editors:

    A. did not understand that many Asian Americans were already reading her work.
    B. gave superficial praise to her work, but would not publish her novels.
    C. were overtly discriminatory when it came to non-Western writers.
    D. tended to view the people she wrote about as one-dimensional.

68. According to the passage, by reading her stories, many of the author's readers learned that:

    F. good fiction writing obscures cultural differences among characters.
    G. they have much more in common with the author's characters than they ever realized.
    H. stories about immigrants to the United States generally have many more characters than do other types of stories.
    J. because of their immigrant status, people from non-Western countries have developed a stronger inner life than have most native-born Americans.

69. The first paragraph states that, at the time of the author's birth, India was:

    A. engaged in a war with England.
    B. not an independent country.
    C. still part of Bangladesh.
    D. governed by the Irish.

70. When the author says that the people she writes about "are culturally and politically several hundred years old" (lines 75–76), she most likely means that her characters:

    F. have cultural and political viewpoints that are repressive and outdated.
    G. have rejected Bengali, British, Irish, and American values.
    H. have experienced an incredible amount of change in just one lifetime.
    J. are really her mother's and grandmother's ancestors.

Passage VIII

NATURAL SCIENCE: This passage is adapted from the essay "Were Dinosaurs Dumb?" by Stephen Jay Gould (©1980 by Stephen Jay Gould).

The discovery of dinosaurs in the nineteenth century provided, or so it appeared, a quintessential case for the negative correlation of size and smarts. With their pea brains and giant bodies, dinosaurs became a
5 symbol of lumbering stupidity. Their extinction seemed only to confirm their flawed design.
Dinosaurs were not even granted the usual solace of a giant—great physical prowess. Dinosaurs have usually been reconstructed as slow and clumsy. In
10 the standard illustration, *Brontosaurus* wades in a murky pond because he cannot hold up his own weight on land. . . .

Dinosaurs have been making a strong comeback of late, in this age of "I'm OK, You're OK." Most paleon-
15 tologists are now willing to view them as energetic, active, and capable animals. The Brontosaurus that wallowed in its pond a generation ago is now running on land, while pairs of males have been seen twining their necks about each other in elaborate sexual combat
20 for access to females (much like the neck wrestling of giraffes). Modern anatomical reconstructions indicate strength and agility, and many paleontologists now believe that dinosaurs were warm blooded. . . .

The idea of warm-blooded dinosaurs has captured
25 the public imagination and received a torrent of press coverage. Yet another vindication of dinosaurian capability has received very little attention, although I regard it as equally significant. I refer to the issue of stupidity and its correlation with size. The revisionist
30 interpretation, which I support . . . does not enshrine dinosaurs as paragons of intellect, but it does maintain that they were not small brained after all. They had the "right-sized" brains for reptiles of their body size.

I don't wish to deny that the flattened, minuscule
35 head of large-bodied *Stegosaurus* houses little brain from our subjective, top-heavy perspective, but I do wish to assert that we should not expect more of the beast. First of all, large animals have relatively smaller brains than related, small animals. The correlation of
40 brain size with body size among kindred animals (all reptiles, all mammals for example) is remarkably regular. As we move from small to large animals, from mice to elephants or small lizards to Komodo dragons, brain size increases, but not so fast as body size. In
45 other words, bodies grow faster than brains, and large animals have low ratios of brain weight to body weight. In fact, brains grow only about two-thirds as fast as bodies. Since we have no reason to believe that large animals are consistently stupider than their smaller rel-
50 atives, we must conclude that large animals require relatively less brain to do as well as smaller animals. If we do not recognize this relationship, we are likely to underestimate the mental power of very large animals, dinosaurs in particular. . . .

55 If behavioral complexity is one consequence of mental power, then we might expect to uncover among dinosaurs some signs of social behavior that demand coordination, cohesiveness and recognition. Indeed we do, and it cannot be accidental that these signs were
60 overlooked when dinosaurs labored under the burden of a falsely imposed obtuseness. Multiple trackways have been uncovered, with evidence for more than twenty animals traveling together in parallel movement. Did some dinosaurs live in herds? At the Davenport Ranch
65 sauropod trackway, small footprints lie in the center and larger ones at the periphery. Could it be that some dinosaurs traveled much as some advanced herbivorous mammals do today, with large adults at the borders sheltering juveniles in the center? . . .

70 But the best illustration of dinosaurian capability may well be the fact most often cited against them— their demise. . . .

The remarkable thing about dinosaurs is not that they became extinct, but that they dominated the earth
75 for so long. Dinosaurs held sway for 100 million years while mammals, all the while, lived as small animals in the interstices of their world. After 70 million years on top, we mammals have an excellent track record and good prospects for the future, but we have yet to dis-
80 play the staying power of dinosaurs.

People, on this criterion, are scarcely worth mentioning—5 million years perhaps since *Australopithecus*, a mere 50,000 for our own species, *Homo sapiens*. Try the ultimate test within our system of values: Do you
85 know anyone who would wager a substantial sum even at favorable odds on the proposition that *Homo sapiens* will last longer than *Brontosaurus*?

71. In the context of the passage as a whole, it is most reasonable to infer that the phrase "the *Brontosaurus* that wallowed in its pond a generation ago is now running on land" (lines 16–18) means that:

A. the *Brontosaurus* evolved from living in the water to living on land.
B. scientists' understanding of the *Brontosaurus's* lifestyle has changed within the last generation.
C. standard illustrations of dinosaurs still inaccurately depict their lifestyles.
D. the *Brontosaurus* eventually learned to hold up its own weight on land.

72. The passage suggests that some fossil evidence about dinosaur behavior has been overlooked in the past because scientists:

    F. had preconceived ideas about the intelligence of dinosaurs.
    G. believed that mammals were not capable of social formations.
    H. did not have the current data about dinosaur brain size.
    J. did not have the necessary equipment to discover the social patterns of dinosaurs.

73. What does the passage offer as evidence that dinosaurs may have exhibited complex behaviors?

    A. Modern anatomical reconstructions indicating strength and agility
    B. Fossils revealing that dinosaurs labored under severe burdens
    C. Footprints of varying sizes indicating that dinosaurs traveled with advanced herbivorous mammals
    D. Multiple trackways in which footprint size and location indicate social order

74. In the context of the passage, what does the author mean when he states that "people … are scarcely worth mentioning" (lines 81–82)?

    F. Compared to the complex social behavior of dinosaurs, human behavior seems simple.
    G. Compared to the longevity of dinosaurs, humans have been on earth a very short time.
    H. Compared to the size of dinosaurs, humans seem incredibly small.
    J. Compared to the amount of study done on dinosaurs, study of human behavior is severely lacking.

75. According to the passage, what is the revisionist interpretation concerning the relationship between intelligence and physical size?

    A. Dinosaurs actually had relatively large brains.
    B. Dinosaurs were paragons of intellect.
    C. Dinosaurs were relatively small brained.
    D. Dinosaurs' brains were appropriately sized.

76. What does the author suggest in lines 34–38 when he states that *Stegosaurus* has a small brain from "our subjective, top-heavy perspective"?

    F. Humans are unusually smart in their judgment of other species.
    G. The human physical construction is deformed by the largeness of the skull.
    H. It is unfair to judge other species by human standards.
    J. Not all species have a brain as small relative to body weight as do humans.

77. The passage states that the ratio of brain weight to body weight in larger animals, as compared to smaller animals, is:

    A. higher.
    B. lower.
    C. the same.
    D. overestimated.

78. According to the passage, which of the following correctly states the relationship of brain size to body size?

    F. The brain grows at two-thirds the rate of body growth.
    G. At maturity, the brain weighs an average of one-third of body weight.
    H. Large animals are not consistently less intelligent than smaller animals.
    J. Brain size is independent of body size.

79. The author states that the best illustration of dinosaurs' capability is their dominance of the earth for:

    A. 100,000 years.
    B. 5 million years.
    C. 70 million years.
    D. 100 million years.

80. As it is used in line 82, the term *Australopithecus* most nearly means:

    F. the last of the dinosaurs, which became extinct 5 million years ago.
    G. the first *Homo sapiens,* who appeared on earth 50,000 years ago.
    H. an early version of humankind, but a different species.
    J. a physically larger species of human with a much smaller brain.

Passage IX

LITERARY NARRATIVE: This passage is adapted from the novel *Monkey Bridge* by Lan Cao (©1997 by Lan Cao). The story is set in the late 1970s in Virginia, where the narrator and her mother have moved from Vietnam after the fall of Saigon.

I discovered soon after my arrival in Virginia that everything, even the simple business of shopping the American way, unsettled my mother's nerves. From the outside, it had been an ordinary building that held no
5 promises or threats. But inside, the A & P brimmed with unexpected abundance. Metal stands overflowed with giant oranges and meticulously arranged grapefruits. Columns of canned vegetables and fruits stood among multiple shelves as people well rehearsed to the
10 demands of modern shopping meandered through florescent aisles. I remembered the sharp chilled air against my face, the way the hydraulic door made a sucking sound as it closed behind.

My mother did not appreciate the exacting orderli-
15 ness of the A & P. She could not give in to the precision of previously weighed and packaged food, the bloodlessness of beef slabs in translucent wrappers, the absence of carcasses and pigs' heads. When we were in Saigon, there were only outdoor markets. "Sky mar-
20 kets," they were called, vast, prosperous expanses in the middle of the city where barrels of live crabs and yellow carps and booths of ducks and geese would be stacked side by side with cardboard stands of expensive silk fabric. It was always noisy there—a voluptuous
25 mix of animal and human sounds. The sharp acrid smell of gutters choked by the monsoon rain. The odor of horses, partially camouflaged by the scent of guavas and bananas.

My mother knew the vendors and the shoppers by
30 name and would take me from stall to stall to expose me to her skills. They were all addicted to each other's oddities. My mother would feign indifference and they would inevitably call out to her. She would heed their call and they would immediately retreat into sudden
35 apathy. They knew my mother's slick bargaining skills, and she, in turn, knew how to navigate with grace through their extravagant prices and rehearsed huffiness. Theirs had been a mating dance, a match of wills.

Every morning, we drifted from vendor to vendor.
40 Tables full of shampoo and toothpaste were pocketed among vegetable stands one day and jars of herbs the next. The market was randomly organized, and only the mighty and experienced like my mother could navigate its patternless paths.

45 But with a sense of neither drama nor calamity, my mother's ability to navigate and decipher simply became undone in our new life. She preferred the improvisation of haggling to the conventional certainty of discount coupons, the primordial messiness and fish-
50 mongers' stink of the open-air market to the aroma-free order of individually wrapped fillets.

Now, a mere three and a half years or so after her last call to the sky market, the dreadful truth was simply this: we were going through life in reverse, and I was
55 the one who would help my mother through the hard scrutiny of ordinary suburban life. I would have to forgo the luxury of adolescent experiments and temper tantrums, so that I could scoop my mother out of harm's way and give her sanctuary. Now, when we stepped into
60 the exterior world, I was the one who told my mother what was acceptable or unacceptable behavior.

All children of immigrant parents have experienced these moments. When it first occurs, when the parent first reveals the behavior of a child, is a defining
65 moment. Of course, all children eventually watch their parents' astonishing return to the vulnerability of childhood, but for us the process begins much earlier than expected.

"We don't have to pay the moment we decide to
70 buy the pork. We can put as much as we want in the cart and pay only once, at the checkout counter." It took a few moments' hesitation for my mother to succumb to the peculiarity of my explanation.

"I can take you in this aisle," a store clerk offered
75 as she unlocked a new register to accommodate the long line of customers. She gestured us to "come over here" with an upturned index finger, a disdainful hook we Vietnamese use to summon dogs. My mother did not understand the ambiguity of American hand
80 gestures. In Vietnam, we said "Come here" to humans differently, with our palm up and all four fingers waved in unison—the way people over here waved goodbye.

"Even the store clerks look down on us," my mother grumbled. This was a truth I was only begin-
85 ning to realize: it was not the enormous or momentous event, but the gradual suggestion of irrevocable and protracted change that threw us off balance and made us know in no uncertain terms that we would not be returning to the familiarity of our former lives.

81. At the time of the events of the story, the narrator is:

A. an adult remembering how hard it was on her mother when the two of them visited the United States from Saigon.

B. an adult planning to take her mother back to their native Saigon after an unsuccessful trip to the United States.

C. an adolescent imagining what it had been like when her mother moved to the United States years ago.

D. an adolescent trying to ease her mother's adjustment to life in the United States.

82. It can reasonably be inferred from the passage as a whole that the narrator views her mother's bargaining skills as ones that were developed:

F. to a degree that was exceptional even in Saigon but that have no apparent outlet in the United States.

G. to a degree that is commonplace in the competitive sky markets but that is exceptional in the United States.

H. to a lesser degree than those of most sky market shoppers in Saigon but to a degree that seems exceptional in the United States.

J. solidly and irrevocably over years of shopping in Saigon, putting her at an advantage in the challenging circumstances of her adopted home.

83. It can reasonably be inferred from the passage that when shopping at the sky market the narrator's mother viewed which of the following as something disagreeable to overcome?

A. The primordial messiness

B. The extravagant prices

C. The odors of animals

D. The other shoppers

84. The passage states that the narrator's mother finds all of the following aspects of shopping at the A & P troubling EXCEPT the:

F. orderliness of the place.

G. absence of carcasses.

H. hurried shoppers.

J. system of paying for merchandise.

85. It can reasonably be inferred that the narrator views her mother's approach to shopping at the sky market with a mixture of:

A. anxiety and huffiness.

B. surprise and embarrassment.

C. impatience and amusement.

D. respect and nostalgia.

86. The passage states that the narrator became aware of her mother's particular way of behaving in the sky markets as a result of:

F. talking to the vendors who knew her mother years ago.

G. her mother's vivid descriptions of the sky market and the things she purchased there.

H. her mother's deliberate attempts to display her shopping skills to her daughter.

J. tagging along defiantly on shopping trips against the wishes of her strong-willed mother.

87. The distinction the narrator makes between children in general and the children of immigrants in particular is that:

A. children of immigrants inevitably have to watch their parents return to a state of childlike vulnerability while other children may not.

B. the inevitable shift from being the vulnerable child to protecting the vulnerable parent takes place sooner for children of immigrants than for other children.

C. children of immigrants anticipate assuming the role of protectors of their parents, while other children are taken by surprise by the inevitable responsibility.

D. children of immigrants are misunderstood by their parents to a greater degree than are other children.

88. Which of the following statements best describes the way the seventh paragraph (lines 62–68) functions in the passage as a whole?

F. It provides the first indication that making the transition to another culture has been difficult for the narrator and her mother.

G. It sets up a contrast between the narrator's view of what it takes to adjust to a new culture and what she thought it would take before she left Saigon.

H. It shows the narrator making connections between the experiences she describes elsewhere in the passage and the experiences of the children of immigrants in general.

J. It divides the passage into two parts, one focused on the narrator, the other focused on children of immigrants in general.

89. The statement "They were all addicted to each other's oddities" (lines 31–32) functions in the passage to support the narrator's view that:

A. there was a consistent dynamic between the sky market vendors and her mother.

B. the sky markets were in someways not as appealing as the American supermarkets.

C. sky market shoppers purchased items they didn't need just for the enjoyment of bargaining.

D. people shopped at the sky markets because the items for sale were so unusual.

90. The narrator refers to "temper tantrums" (lines 57–58) as behavior she would have to view as:

F. one of the best ways she could use to get her mother's undivided attention.

G. a luxury she could not afford in her new relationship with her mother.

H. a part of her character that she inherited from her headstrong mother.

J. an understandable reaction on her mother's part to a confusing new set of circumstances.

Passage X

SOCIAL SCIENCE: This passage is adapted from Joseph Ellis's biography *American Sphinx: The Character of Thomas Jefferson* (©1997 by Joseph J. Ellis).

The most famous section of the Declaration of
Independence, which has become the most quoted
statement of human rights in recorded history as well as
the most eloquent justification of revolution on behalf
5 of them, went through the Continental Congress
without comment and with only one very minor change.
These are, in all probability, the best-known fifty-eight
words in American history: "We hold these truths to be
self-evident; that all men are created equal; that they
10 are endowed by their Creator with certain inherent and
inalienable Rights; that among these are life, liberty
and the pursuit of happiness; that to secure these rights,
governments are instituted among men, deriving their
just powers from the consent of the governed." This is
15 the seminal statement of the American Creed, the
closest approximation to political poetry ever produced
in American culture. In the nineteenth century Abraham
Lincoln, who also knew how to change history with
words, articulated with characteristic eloquence the
20 quasi-religious view of Thomas Jefferson as the original American oracle: "All honor to Jefferson—to the
man who, in the concrete pressure of a struggle for
national independence by a single people, had the cool-
ness, forecast, and capacity to introduce into a merely
25 revolutionary document, an abstract truth, and so to
embalm it there, that today and in all coming days, it
shall be a rebuke and a stumbling block to the very harbingers of reappearing tyranny and oppression."

No serious student of either Jefferson or the
30 Declaration of Independence has ever claimed that he
foresaw all or even most of the ideological consequences of what he wrote. But the effort to explain
what was in his head has spawned almost as many
interpretations as the words themselves have generated
35 political movements. Jefferson himself was accused of
plagiarism by enemies or jealous friends on so many
occasions throughout his career that he developed a
standard reply. "Neither aiming at originality of principle or sentiment, nor yet copied from any particular
40 and previous writing," he explained, he drew his ideas
from "the harmonizing sentiments of the day, whether
expressed in letters, printed essays or in the elementary books of public right, as Aristotle, Cicero, Locke,
Sidney, etc."

45 This is an ingeniously double-edged explanation,
for it simultaneously disavows any claims to originality
and yet insists that he depended upon no specific texts
or sources. The image it conjures up is that of a
medium, sitting alone at the writing desk and making
50 himself into an instrument for the accumulated wisdom
and "harmonizing sentiments" of the ages. It is only a
short step from this image to Lincoln's vision of

Jefferson as oracle or prophet, receiving the message
from the gods and sending it on to us and then to the
55 ages. Given the character of the natural rights section of
the Declaration, several generations of American interpreters have felt the irresistible impulse to bathe the
scene in speckled light and cloudy mist, thereby
implying that efforts to dispel the veil of mystery rep-
60 resent some vague combination of sacrilege and
treason.

Any serious attempt to pierce through this veil
must begin by recovering the specific conditions inside
that room on Market and Seventh streets in June 1776.
65 Even if we take Jefferson at his word, that he did not
copy sections of the Declaration from any particular
books, he almost surely had with him copies of his own
previous writings, to include *Summary View*, *Causes
and Necessities* and his three drafts of the Virginia con-
70 stitution. This is not to accuse him of plagiarism, unless
one wishes to argue that an author can plagiarize himself. It is to say that virtually all the ideas found in the
Declaration and much of the specific language had
already found expression in those earlier writings.

75 Recall the context. The Congress is being overwhelmed with military reports of imminent American
defeat in New York and Canada. The full Congress is in
session six days a week, and committees are meeting
throughout the evenings. The obvious practical course
80 for Jefferson to take was to rework his previous drafts
on the same general theme. While it seems almost sacrilegious to suggest that the creative process that produced the Declaration was a cut-and-paste job, it strains
credulity and common sense to the breaking point to
85 believe that Jefferson did not have these items at his
elbow and draw liberally from them when drafting the
Declaration.

91. It can reasonably be inferred from the passage that the
author believes that Jefferson was:

A. a mysterious character whose attempts at originality were very patriotic.

B. a brilliant yet practical man, neither plagiarizer nor
prophet, writing under pressure.

C. a politician who deserves more attention for his
writing than he gets.

D. an average man who has been represented as a
quasi-religious leader by later generations.

92. Details in the passage suggest that the author's personal position on the question of Jefferson's alleged plagiarism is that the:

    F. idea of Jefferson copying from his own writings is only common sense.
    G. notion of Jefferson copying from past writings is in fact sacrilegious.
    H. concept of the Declaration as a cut-and-paste job strains credulity.
    J. claim that the Declaration is related in some way to *Causes and Necessities* strains common sense.

93. It can reasonably be inferred that one of the functions of the first sentence (lines 1–6) is to:

    A. point out that Jefferson's words have been used to justify revolutions as well as to promote human rights.
    B. establish that the author believes that the Continental Congress should have commented on and reworked the Declaration.
    C. emphasize the author's surprise at the eventual fame achieved by this section of the Declaration.
    D. suggest that equally eloquent works were probably produced before the beginning of recorded history.

94. Which of the following statements best summarizes Lincoln's thoughts about what Jefferson achieved when he wrote the Declaration (lines 21–28)?

    F. Even during the fight for independence, Jefferson's cool intelligence allowed him to write a statement that has been used against revolutionaries ever since.
    G. Even during a revolution, Jefferson was calm enough to change a merely political document into a statement that predicted the rise of future tyrants.
    H. Even under pressure of war, Jefferson was able to write a document that not only announced a revolution but also spoke against oppression for all time.
    J. Even under pressure of war, Jefferson was able to write a document that both proclaimed abstract truths and dared tyrants to continually reappear.

95. The main function of the second paragraph (lines 29–44) in relation to the passage as a whole is to:

    A. redirect the passage toward a discussion of various interpretations of the Declaration.
    B. establish the passage's claim that Jefferson receives a great deal of serious scholarly attention for many of his writings.
    C. shift the passage's focus toward an inquiry into the sources of the ideas expressed in the Declaration.
    D. emphasize the passage's point that interpreters disagree about why the Declaration was written.

96. In saying "Even if we take Jefferson at his word, that he did not copy sections of the Declaration from any particular books" (lines 65–67), the author implies that he thinks Jefferson:

    F. may not have been totally honest when he said that no parts of the Declaration were copied from any previous writing.
    G. may have in fact copied some of Abraham Lincoln's writings when drafting the Declaration.
    H. should not be believed because his character has been hidden behind a veil of mystery for so long.
    J. cannot be accused of plagiarizing parts of the Declaration because it was written so long ago.

97. Use of the phrase *characteristic eloquence* (line 19) to describe Abraham Lincoln's words indicates the author's:

    A. use of irony to describe words written by Lincoln that the author finds difficult to believe.
    B. belief that Lincoln was usually a persuasive, expressive speaker and writer.
    C. notion that Lincoln was a bit of a character because of his controversial opinions.
    D. feelings of regret that Lincoln's words are so often difficult for modern readers to understand.

98. According to lines 29–32, students of Jefferson and of the Declaration think that Jefferson:

    F. carefully contrived to write ambiguously about freedom.
    G. anticipated most of the ideological outcomes of what he wrote.
    H. never foresaw most of the ideological outcomes of what he wrote.
    J. wrote the Declaration from memory without consulting other works.

99. The author thinks Jefferson's reply to accusations of plagiarism was "ingeniously double-edged" (line 45) because Jefferson claimed that:

    A. he wrote alone, while also implying that he copied from his own previous writings.
    B. his work was prophetic, yet he made no claim to originality.
    C. he was a prophet, and he later influenced Lincoln to agree with that claim.
    D. his writing was not new, yet he maintained he had not copied from any particular text.

100. The author uses the description of what was happening in the country when Jefferson was writing the Declaration (lines 75–79) to suggest that Jefferson:

    F. felt great urgency to get the Declaration written, and didn't have much time to do so.
    G. was depressed by news of American defeats and so lacked energy to draft a new document.
    H. knew the Declaration could solve the problems of the nation and finished it in a hurry.
    J. worried that the war was moving closer to home and felt he should take his time writing the Declaration.

Passage XI

HUMANITIES: This passage is adapted from the essay "Spaced Out: The *Star Trek* Literary Phenomenon: Where No TV Series Has Gone Before" by Michael M. Epstein, which appeared in *Television Quarterly* (©1996 by The National Academy of Television Arts and Sciences).

On September 8, 1966, when NBC premiered its new futuristic series, *Star Trek*, few were watching. Conceived by television writer Gene Roddenberry as part American Western, part science fiction, and part
5 contemporary morality play, *Star Trek* languished for two and a half years before being canceled as a ratings flop in January 1969.

Two years later, *Star Trek* somehow had captured the imagination and viewer loyalty of millions of
10 Americans who "discovered" the show anew in syndicated reruns. *Star Trek*'s meteoric rise to popularity was unprecedented for a television program. By January 1972, the show was airing in over one hundred local markets in America and seventy more around the
15 world.

Perhaps more than other television series, *Star Trek* benefited greatly from being the right show at the right time. In middle-class America, social and political change in the late 1960s made it increasingly
20 difficult for people to unite in common purpose. Civil rights struggles, the Vietnam War, and the rise of a culturally empowered youth movement, among other things, divided many Americans by race, gender, age, and politics.

25 Although television news programs helped focus the country on the rifts that had begun to percolate on campuses, in city streets, and around dining room tables, as a rule entertainment programming avoided conflict and controversy. Escapist comedy about suburban
30 witches, genies, and rural townspeople was standard fare. Network drama emphasized law, order, and conformity, whether on the police beat, in a courtroom, or out on the great Western frontier.

Star Trek was different. Created in the optimistic
35 afterglow of John F. Kennedy's inauguration of the space race, *Star Trek*'s exploration of the "final frontier" was a theme that resonated with millions of idealistic and awestruck Americans who looked at the Apollo moon landings as a crowning, positive achieve-
40 ment for humankind. Still, as Gene Roddenberry often claimed, *Star Trek* was less about the future than the present.

Indeed, it was precisely because of its futuristic storyline that *Star Trek* was able to address many of the
45 contemporary social problems that other programs shunned. *Star Trek*'s visionary episodes on race relations, nuclear deterrence, multiculturalism, and ecology

(among others) were not threatening to those who saw it as fantastic science fiction. For those who saw the
50 program as a window into current controversy, *Star Trek* offered insight and added perspective to continued American cultural and political change in the 1970s. Either way, the show's wide appeal in syndication was such that, by 1977, *Star Trek* had become the most-
55 watched off-network series drama of all time.

In nearly thirty years, Gene Roddenberry's fantasy space concept has spawned four prime-time series, continued syndication, a cartoon, eight major motion pictures, countless toys, games, and computer software.
60 Nearly overlooked, however, is the unparalleled impact *Star Trek* has had on an industry that has only recently become television friendly: publishing. Since the early 1970s, when the first novels hit bookshelves, the world of *Star Trek* has exploded in print like no other pheno-
65 menon in American popular culture. *Star Trek* fan volumes, cast memoirs, and novels continue to appear—and in record numbers.

Of all the "classic" and contemporary shows available to a critic, none illustrates the scope of America's
70 cultural evolution as eloquently as the saga of *Star Trek* and its next-generation spin-offs. In a culture that has undergone dramatic and far-reaching change in the last thirty years, *Star Trek* sweetens the often bitter alienation of contemporary change with the type of famil-
75 iarity and constancy that only a show with a thirty-year history can offer.

Star Trek offers viewers the paradox of a program that combines provocative insight into changing cultural values with the reassuring comfort that the
80 "known" universe of Starfleet, Klingons, and phasers can nonetheless survive intact, and even grow. Because of its active fandom, *Star Trek* has become a television phenomenon like no other in American culture. And just as the original *Star Trek* has
85 found new expression in series such as *The Next Generation*, *Deep Space Nine*, and *Voyager*, I suspect fans will find new ways to indulge or express their private affection for *Star Trek* by reading—and writing—books in greater numbers. As America goes boldly into
90 the next millennium, so will *Star Trek* in print, on television, and in formats yet to come.

101. The main purpose of the passage can best be described as an effort to:

A. explain how and why *Star Trek* has endured.

B. illustrate what American society was like at the time the original *Star Trek* series was created.

C. discuss how *Star Trek*'s storyline has changed over its thirty-year history.

D. describe the different forms that *Star Trek* has taken, such as television series, films, and novels.

102. The author's attitude toward the subject of the passage can best be characterized as:

F. amused tolerance.
G. detached interest.
H. warm appreciation.
J. mild skepticism.

103. It can be reasonably inferred that the author believes *Star Trek* first became a success in:

A. 1966.
B. 1969.
C. 1971.
D. 1977.

104. According to the fourth paragraph (lines 25–33), compared to television news programs of the time period, entertainment programming is described as:

F. more willing to examine the rifts developing in American society.
G. more willing to portray violent conflict and controversy.
H. less willing to promote the principles of conformity and order.
J. less willing to present a realistic picture of contemporary life.

105. As described in the passage, the effect *Star Trek* has had on the publishing industry can best be summarized by which of the following statements?

A. *Star Trek*'s impact can be safely overlooked because the publishing industry remains unfriendly to television.
B. *Star Trek* made an impact with its first novels, but that impact has lessened over time.
C. *Star Trek*'s tremendous impact has been primarily limited to novels.
D. *Star Trek* has had a deep impact with its extensive and popular range of books.

106. When the author states that *Star Trek* was "the right show at the right time" (lines 17–18), he most likely means that the series benefited from:

F. the unsettled social and political conditions.
G. the general popularity of syndicated reruns.
H. an increasing appetite for escapist entertainment.
J. the increasingly empowered middle class.

107. The passage indicates that *Star Trek* creator Gene Roddenberry's primary purpose in creating the series was to:

A. show how different life would be in the future.
B. promote the space program and the exploration of space.
C. offer a lighthearted alternative to serious entertainment.
D. comment on problems facing people in the present.

108. According to the author, the primary benefit of the original *Star Trek*'s futuristic storyline was that it allowed the series' writers to:

F. offer perspectives and insights that were unthreatening.
G. invent fantastic and entertaining science fiction worlds.
H. easily develop related spin-offs, such as films and new series.
J. avoid controversial topics, such as nuclear deterrence and multiculturalism.

109. The author calls some of the original *Star Trek*'s episodes "visionary" in line 46 most likely because they:

A. presented issues that weren't problems at the time but that now are.
B. dealt with complex themes with imagination and foresight.
C. offered dreamy and unrealistic solutions to difficult problems.
D. appealed to a wide audience through syndication.

110. The "paradox" mentioned in line 77 most directly refers to what the author sees as the conflicting ideas of:

F. cultural values and entertainment.
G. familiarity and change.
H. comfort and the *Star Trek* universe.
J. survival and being provocative.

Passage XII

NATURAL SCIENCE: This passage is adapted from *An Anthropologist on Mars* by Oliver Sacks (©1995 by Oliver Sacks). Johann Wolfgang von Goethe was an eighteenth-century German poet and philosopher; Hermann von Helmholtz was a nineteenth-century scientist and philosopher.

Goethe's color theory, his *Farbenlehre* (which he regarded as the equal of his entire poetic opus), was, by and large, dismissed by all his contemporaries and has remained in a sort of limbo ever since, seen as the
5 whimsy, the pseudoscience, of a very great poet. But science itself was not entirely insensitive to the "anomalies" that Goethe considered central, and Helmholtz, indeed, gave admiring lectures on Goethe and his science, on many occasions—the last in 1892. Helmholtz
10 was very conscious of "color constancy"—the way in which the colors of objects are preserved, so that we can categorize them and always know what we are looking at, despite great fluctuations in the wavelength of the light illuminating them. The actual wavelengths
15 reflected by an apple, for instance, will vary considerably depending on the illumination, but we consistently see it as red, nonetheless. This could not be, clearly, a mere translation of wavelength into color. There had to be some way, Helmholtz thought, of "discounting the
20 illuminant"—and this he saw as an "unconscious inference" or "an act of judgement" (though he did not venture to suggest where such judgement might occur). Color constancy, for him, was a special example of the way in which we achieve perceptual constancy gen-
25 erally, make a stable perceptual world from a chaotic sensory flux—a world that would not be possible if our perceptions were merely passive reflections of the unpredictable and inconstant input that bathes our receptors.

30 Helmholtz's great contemporary, James Clerk Maxwell, had also been fascinated by the mystery of color vision from his student days. He formalized the notions of primary colors and color mixing by the invention of a color top (the colors of which fused,
35 when it was spun, to yield a sensation of grey), and a graphic representation with three axes, a color triangle, which showed how any color could be created by different mixtures of the three primary colors. These prepared the way for his most spectacular demonstration,
40 the demonstration in 1861 that color photography was possible, despite the fact that photographic emulsions were themselves black and white. He did this by photographing a colored bow three times, through red, green, and violet filters. Having obtained three "color-
45 separation" images, as he called them, he now brought these together by superimposing them upon a screen, projecting each image through its corresponding filter (the image taken through the red filter was projected with red light, and so on). Suddenly, the bow burst
50 forth in full color. Clerk Maxwell wondered if this was how colors were perceived in the brain, by the addition of color-separation images or their neural correlates [what functions in the brain as a color-separation

image], as in his magic-lantern demonstrations.
55 Clerk Maxwell himself was acutely aware of the drawback of this additive process: color photography had no way of "discounting the illuminant," and its colors changed helplessly with changing wavelengths of light.

60 In 1957, ninety-odd years after Clerk Maxwell's famous demonstration, Edwin Land—not merely the inventor of the instant Land camera and Polaroid, but an experimenter and theorizer of genius—provided a photographic demonstration of color perception even
65 more startling. Unlike Clerk Maxwell, he made only two black-and-white images (using a split-beam camera so they could be taken at the same time from the same viewpoint, through the same lens) and superimposed these on a screen with a double-lens projector. He used
70 two filters to make the images: one passing longer wavelengths (a red filter), the other passing shorter wavelengths (a green filter). The first image was then projected through a red filter, the second with ordinary white light, unfiltered. One might expect that this
75 would produce just an overall pale-pink image, but something "impossible" happened instead. The photograph of a young woman appeared instantly in full color—"blonde hair, pale blue eyes, red coat, bluegreen collar, and strikingly natural flesh tones," as Land later
80 described it. Where did these colors come from, how were they made? They did not seem to be "in" the photographs or the illuminants themselves. These demonstrations, overwhelming in their simplicity and impact, were color "illusions" in Goethe's sense, but illusions
85 that demonstrated a neurological truth—that colors are not "out there" in the world, nor (as classical theory held) an automatic correlate of wavelength, but, rather, are *constructed by the brain*.

111. According to the passage, regarding Goethe's color theory, Helmholtz expressed which of the following attitudes?

A. Disbelief
B. Respect
C. Amusement
D. Skepticism

112. It can be inferred that in Clerk Maxwell's 1861 demonstration a color image would not have been produced from black-and-white film emulsions without the use of color:

    F. filters.
    G. triangles.
    H. tops.
    J. slides.

113. As described in the passage, Goethe's contemporaries for the most part regarded him as a:

    A. mediocre poet whose most important work was as a scientist.
    B. theorist whose attempts at poetry were commendable but insignificant.
    C. leading poet whose contributions to science were less noteworthy.
    D. leading theorist who overturned previously standard approaches to scientific inquiry.

114. The tendency to perceive objects as having a given color, such as the perception of an apple as "red" even if it is "red" only in certain lighting, is an example of what Helmholtz refers to as:

    F. split-beam filtering.
    G. sensory flux.
    H. color separation.
    J. color constancy.

115. According to lines 14–17, the wavelengths reflected by the apple vary considerably as a result of:

    A. the differences between the viewer's right and left eye.
    B. the distance between the apple and the eyes.
    C. a viewer's ability to perceive red in different light.
    D. variations in the source of light reaching the apple.

116. The term *illuminant*, as it is used in line 20 and elsewhere in the passage, refers to which of the following?

    F. Camera flash equipment
    G. A color theorist
    H. Light that makes an object visible
    J. Light before it passes through a filter

117. What about the nature of color perception is described as a preoccupation of Helmholtz's? The way in which:

    A. varying wavelengths of light stabilize the appearance of an object.
    B. humans arrive at a notion of what the color of an object is.
    C. humans undergo changes in color awareness as they age.
    D. one color becomes another when images are superimposed.

118. According to the passage, the relationship between primary colors and other colors can be best described by which of the following statements?

    F. All colors are either primary colors or can be created by a combination of primary colors.
    G. The human eye perceives primary colors first, then other colors.
    H. Primary colors were the first colors captured on film by the camera; other colors were captured by later, more sophisticated, equipment.
    J. Primary colors emerge as a result of blending non-primary colors along the axes of Clerk Maxwell's triangle.

119. Clerk Maxwell demonstrated that color photography was possible even though at the time of his demonstrations:

    A. illuminants were thought to be stable rather than variable.
    B. photographic emulsions were available only in black-and-white.
    C. the general public rejected the new technology as stunts with no practical application.
    D. professional photographers were reluctant to abandon the established black-and-white aesthetic.

120. The two images that became the single image in Land's photograph of a woman were obtained by using:

    F. a screen lit from the front and back.
    G. flickering light sources.
    H. one lens in two cameras.
    J. one camera with one divided lens.

Passage XIII

LITERARY NARRATIVE: This passage is adapted from the short story "Golden Glass" by Alma Villanueva (©1982 by Bilingual Press).

It was his fourteenth summer. He was thinning out, becoming angular and clumsy, but the cautiousness, the old-man seriousness he'd had as a baby, kept him contained, ageless and safe. His humor, always dry
5 and to the bone since a small child, let you know he was watching everything.

He seemed always to be at the center of his own universe, so it was no surprise to his mother to hear Ted say: "I'm building a fort and sleeping out in it all
10 summer, and I won't come in for anything, not even food. Okay?"

This had been their silent communion, the steady presence of love that flowed regularly, daily—food. The presence of his mother preparing it, his great
15 appetite and obvious enjoyment of it—his nose smelling everything, seeing his mother more vividly than with his eyes.

He watched her now for signs of offense, alarm, and only saw interest. "Where will you put the fort?"
20 Vida asked.

She trusted him to build well and not ruin things, but of course she had to know where.

"I'll build it by the redwoods, in the cypress tree. Okay?"

25 "Make sure you keep your nails together and don't dig into the trees. I'll be checking. If the trees get damaged, it'll have to come down."

The cypress was right next to the redwoods, making it seem very remote. Redwoods do that—they
30 suck up sound and time and smell like another place. So he counted the footsteps, when no one was looking, from the fort to the house. He couldn't believe it was so close; it seemed so separate, alone—especially in the dark, when the only safe way of travel seemed flight
35 (invisible at best).

Ted had seen his mother walk out to the bridge at night, looking into the water, listening to it. He knew she loved to see the moon's reflection in the water. She'd pointed it out to him once by a river where they
40 camped, her face full of longing. Then, she swam out into the water, at night, as though trying to touch the moon. He wouldn't look at her. He sat and glared at the fire and roasted another marshmallow the way he liked it: bubbly, soft and brown (maybe six if he could get
45 away with it). Then she'd be back, chilled and bright, and he was glad she went. Maybe I like the moon too, he thought, involuntarily, as though the thought weren't his own—but it was.

He built the ground floor directly on the earth,
50 with a cover of old plywood, then scattered remnant rugs that he'd asked Vida to get for him. He concocted a latch and a door. He brought his sleeping bag, some pillows, a transistor radio, some clothes, and moved in for the summer.

55 He began to build the top floor now but he had to prune some limbs out of the way. Well, that was okay as long as he was careful. So he stacked them to one side for kindling and began to brace things in place. It felt weird going up into the tree, not as safe as his
60 small, contained place on the ground.

Vida noticed Ted had become cheerful and would stand next to her, to her left side, talking sometimes. But she realized she mustn't face him or he'd become silent and wander away. So she stood listening, in the
65 same even breath and heart beat she kept when she spotted the wild pheasants with their long, lush tails trailing the grape arbor, picking delicately and greedily at the unpicked grapes in the early autumn light. So sharp, so perfect, so rare to see a wild thing at peace.

70 Ted was taking a makeup course and one in stained glass. There, he talked and acted relaxed; no one expected any more or less. The colors of the stained glass were deep and beautiful, and special—you couldn't waste this glass. The sides were sharp, the cuts
75 were slow and meticulous with a steady pressure. The design's plan had to be absolutely followed or the beautiful glass would go to waste, and he'd curse himself.

The stained glass was finished and he decided to place it in his fort facing the back fields. In fact, it
80 looked like the back fields—trees and the sun in a dark sky. During the day the glass sun shimmered a beautiful yellow, the blue a much better color than the sky outside: deeper, like night.

He was so used to sleeping outside now he didn't
85 wake up during the night, just like in the house. One night, toward the end when he'd have to move back with everyone (school was starting, frost was coming and the rains), Ted woke up to see the stained glass full of light. The little sun was a golden moon and the
90 inside glass sky and the outside sky matched.

In a few days he'd be inside, and he wouldn't mind at all.

---

121. The passage establishes that Vida and Ted have all of the following traits in common EXCEPT:

A. a willingness to accommodate the requests each makes of the other.

B. a response to elements of nature.

C. a perception of others that surfaces in humor.

D. an awareness of what delights the other.

122. Which of the following is NOT an accurate description of the passage?

    F. A story about a teenager whose summer experiences building and occupying a fort near his house have a positive effect on his relationship with his mother

    G. A glimpse at what connects a mother and a son and what separates them as the boy tests his own limits with a summer project

    H. A look at how two characters—one grown, one young—behave when each perceives the fragility of someone or something he or she holds dear

    J. A portrait of two family members whose painful disagreements force one to seek shelter outside the home until they reach an understanding

123. In both the twelfth paragraph (lines 61–69) and the thirteenth paragraph (lines 70–77) the author is portraying characters who:

    A. feel compelled to act carefully in order to avoid shattering something precious.

    B. are frustrated to the point of indignation that success seems always slightly out of reach.

    C. are at first excited by a project but later lose interest as others get involved.

    D. discover that a personal weakness in some situations can be a personal strength in others.

124. It can most reasonably be inferred that as it is used in line 69 the term *wild thing* refers not only to a pheasant but also to:

    F. Ted as Vida somewhat reverently sees him.

    G. Vida as seen by Ted when she visits the fort.

    H. Ted as he imagines himself to be.

    J. What Vida wishes Ted would cease to be.

125. Which of the following best describes the difference between Ted as a little boy and Ted at the time he builds and occupies the fort?

    A. By the time Ted builds the fort he has lost the light-hearted manner he had as a child and has become more of a brooder who avoids the company of others.

    B. As a teenager Ted is physically clumsier and more angular than he was as a child, but he retains the humor, cautiousness, and seriousness that distinguished him at an early age.

    C. As a child Ted was constantly observing others for indications of how he should behave, but as a teenager he looks more to nature for guidance.

    D. As a child Ted was outgoing in a way that appealed to adults, but as a teenager he was introspective in a way that alarmed them.

126. The passage indicates that Vida was not surprised by Ted's decision to build a fort because she:

    F. knew that more often than not he was inclined to take projects she had started a step farther.

    G. sensed that it fit with his tendency to approach life as if he were self-contained.

    H. had noticed that ever since their camping trip he had been putting more and more distance between himself and her.

    J. had noticed that he no longer worried that his fascination with nature would interfere with his longstanding craving for the company of others.

127. As it is used in the passage, the term *silent communion* (line 12) refers to the:

    A. way that without using words Ted communicates his disappointments to Vida.

    B. promise Ted made to himself that he would not return to the house all summer, even for food.

    C. way a thought shifted in Ted's mind from feeling like someone else's to feeling like his own.

    D. exchange of warm emotions between Ted and Vida during the preparation and sharing of food.

128. Which of the following best describes the way the seventh paragraph (lines 25–27) functions in the passage?

    F. It reinforces the image of Vida established elsewhere in the passage as someone whose skeptical nature disheartens Ted on the brink of new projects.

    G. It foreshadows events described later in the passage that lead to the dismantling of the tree house once Ted is back in school.

    H. It reveals that Vida takes an interest in Ted's project to the extent that she determines ways in which he needs to carry it out to avoid problems.

    J. It reveals that Vida's willingness to shift responsibility to her son for his actions is greater than his willingness to accept such responsibility.

129. According to the passage, Ted attributes which of the following characteristics to the redwoods?

    A. They make ideal supports for a fort because they are strong and tall.

    B. They create a sense of remoteness by absorbing time and sound and by smelling like another place.

    C. They lend a feeling of danger to whatever surrounds them because they themselves are endangered.

    D. They grace their surroundings with a serenity that softens disturbing emotions like fear of the dark.

130. Ted felt that in comparison to the ground floor of the fort, going up into the tree to build the top floor seemed:

    F. safer because the top floor was less accessible to intruders.

    G. safer because the branches provided him with a sense of privacy.

    H. less safe because the place felt bigger and more exposed.

    J. less safe because the top floor was made of cypress instead of redwood.

Passage XIV

SOCIAL SCIENCE: This passage is adapted from *Biomimicry: Innovation Inspired by Nature* by Janine M. Benyus (©1997 by Janine M. Benyus).

If anybody's growing biomass, it's us. To keep our system from collapsing on itself, industrial ecologists are attempting to build a "no-waste economy." Instead of a linear production system, which binges on virgin
5 raw materials and spews out unusable waste, they envision a web of closed loops in which a minimum of raw materials comes in the door, and very little waste escapes. The first examples of this no-waste economy are collections of companies clustered in an ecopark
10 and connected in a food chain, with each firm's waste going next door to become the other firm's raw material or fuel.

In Denmark, the town of Kalundborg has the world's most elaborate prototype of an ecopark. Four
15 companies are co-located, and all of them are linked, dependent on one another for resources or energy. The Asnaesverket Power Company pipes some of its waste steam to power the engines of two companies: the Statoil Refinery and Novo Nordisk (a pharmaceutical
20 plant). Another pipeline delivers the remaining waste steam to heat thirty-five hundred homes in the town, eliminating the need for oil furnaces. The power plant also delivers its cooling water, now toasty warm, to fifty-seven ponds' worth of fish. The fish revel in the
25 warm water, and the fish farm produces 150 tons of sea trout and turbot each year.

Waste steam from the power company is used by Novo Nordisk to heat the fermentation tanks that produce insulin and enzymes. This process in turn creates
30 700,000 tons of nitrogen-rich slurry a year, which used to be dumped into the fjord. Now, Novo bequeaths it free to nearby farmers—a pipeline delivers the fertilizer to the growing plants, which are in turn harvested to feed the bacteria in the fermentation tanks.

35 Meanwhile, back at the Statoil Refinery, waste gas that used to go up a smokestack is now purified. Some is used internally as fuel, some is piped to the power company, and the rest goes to Gyproc, the wallboard market next door. The sulfur squeezed from the gas
40 during purification is loaded onto trucks and sent to Kemira, a company that produces sulfuric acid. The power company also squeezes sulfur from its emissions, but converts most of it to calcium sulfate (industrial gypsum), which it sells to Gyproc for wallboard.

45 Although Kalundborg is a cozy co-location, industries need not be geographically close to operate in a food web as long as they are connected by a mutual desire to use waste. Already, some companies are designing their processes so that any waste that falls on
50 the production-room floor is valuable and can be used by someone else. In this game of "designed offal," a

process with lots of waste, as long as it's "wanted waste," may be better than one with a small amount of waste that must be landfilled or burned. As author
55 Daniel Chiras says, more companies are recognizing that "technologies that produce by-products society cannot absorb are essentially failed technologies."

So far, we've talked about recycling within a circle of companies. But what happens when a product
60 leaves the manufacturer and passes to the consumer and finally to the trash can? Right now, a product visits one of two fates at the end of its useful life. It can be buried in a landfill or incinerated, or it can be recaptured through recycling or reuse.

65 Traditionally, manufacturers haven't had to worry about what happens to a product after it leaves their gates. But that is starting to change, thanks to laws now in the wings in Europe (and headed for the United States) that will require companies to take back their
70 durable goods such as refrigerators, washers, and cars at the end of their useful lives. In Germany, the take-back laws start with the initial sale. Companies must take back all their packaging or hire middlemen to do the recycling. Take-back laws mean that manufacturers
75 who have been saying, "This product can be recycled," must now say, "We recycle our products and packaging."

When the onus shifts in this way, it's suddenly in the company's best interest to design a product that will
80 either last a long time or come apart easily for recycling or reuse. Refrigerators and cars will be assembled using easy-open snaps instead of glued-together joints, and for recyclability, each part will be made of one material instead of twenty. Even simple things, like the snack
85 bags for potato chips, will be streamlined. Today's bags, which have nine thin layers made of seven different materials, will no doubt be replaced by one material that can preserve freshness and can easily be remade into a new bag.

131. According to the passage, waste emissions from the Asnaesverket Power Company are used to help produce all of the following EXCEPT:

   A. insulin.
   B. heating oil.
   C. plant fertilizer.
   D. industrial gypsum.

132. When the author says "our system" (lines 1–2), she is most likely referring to a production system in:

    F. Denmark in which four companies are co-located in one small town and are linked by their dependence on energy resources.

    G. the United States that produces recyclable durable goods such as refrigerators, washers and cars.

    H. the United States and Europe in which products are developed with few virgin raw materials and leave little or no waste.

    J. the United States and Europe that uses too many virgin raw materials and produces too much unused waste.

133. The main purpose of the second, third, and fourth paragraphs (lines 13–44) is to show:

    A. how four companies depend on each other for resources and the recycling of waste.

    B. that Denmark is one of the world's leaders in developing new sources of energy.

    C. that one town's need for energy can be eliminated through recycling.

    D. that a no-waste economy saves money.

134. It is reasonable to infer that the author's proposed solution to what she sees as the problem of an increasing amount of biomass is to:

    F. change the process by which manufacturers produce their products.

    G. make consumers responsible for recycling the products they buy.

    H. encourage traditional businesses to compete with new, innovative businesses.

    J. encourage companies that produce similar products to cluster together in ecoparks.

135. Based on the passage, which of the following pairs of industries is shown to depend directly on one another for the production of their products?

    A. Statoil and Gyproc

    B. Asnaesverket and fish farmers

    C. Novo Nordisk and plant farmers

    D. Statoil and Novo Nordisk

136. The main function of the sixth paragraph (lines 58–64) in relation to the passage as a whole is most likely to provide:

    F. evidence to support Daniel Chiras's statement in lines 54–57.

    G. a transition between the two main points discussed in the passage.

    H. a conclusion to the author's discussion about a no-waste economy.

    J. a summary of the author's main argument.

137. According to the passage, take-back laws in Germany shift the responsibility for recycling from the:

    A. local government to the manufacturer.

    B. manufacturer to the local government.

    C. manufacturer to the consumer.

    D. consumer to the manufacturer.

138. According to the passage, the common element for companies that want to be part of a food web is their mutual interest in:

    F. relocating their operations to a common geographic area in Europe.

    G. providing industrial waste to private homes and farming operations.

    H. eliminating the need for raw materials.

    J. using industrial waste as raw materials.

139. The author uses the term "designed offal" (line 51) to indicate that:

    A. companies can design ways in which their waste products can be used.

    B. industrial ecologists have designed ways to reduce waste products.

    C. technology has not kept pace with how to dispose of waste products.

    D. companies can learn to design more efficient landfill spaces.

140. According to Daniel Chiras, a failed technology is one that:

    F. cannot reuse its own waste.

    G. produces more waste than it uses.

    H. produces waste that is unusable.

    J. makes durable goods such as refrigerators.

Passage XV

PROSE FICTION: This passage is adapted from the novel *Monkey King* by Patricia Chao (©1997 by Patricia Chao).

It's my tenth birthday. Ma doesn't get a cake or presents because we're busy getting ready to go to visit our Nai-nai in San Diego. That is, my sister, Marty, and I are going while Ma and Daddy spend the summer in
5 Taiwan, where my father has a teaching job. In the front of the tunnel to the plane Ma hands us over to the stewardess, who wears white gloves. Marty cries but I don't.

During the flight the stewardess keeps coming over with children's magazines, coloring books, mag-
10 netic tic-tac-toe. Not that we need distractions; we sit quietly, buckling our seat belts when the sign says to. Most of the way I read *Eight Cousins*, feeling my sister's hot skull pressed against my shoulder as she sleeps.

15 My Nai-nai is so glad to see us, she has tears in her eyes. "*Ni kan!*" she says to her cousin Su-yi, who has come to the airport too because our grandmother doesn't drive. Nai-nai used to live with Su-yi, but now she has a separate house on the same street.

20 Ma has warned us not to tire Nai-nai out. But my grandmother is inexhaustible. Mornings, when she comes to wake us, she's already dressed, hair up, face powdered, lipstick on. The first night when she tucks us in Marty asks, "When do you go to bed?" and Nai-nai
25 answers: "Very, very late. Old lady doesn't need much sleep."

Over my grandmother's shoulder I am watching the curtains, patterned with cobalt and fuchsia prim-roses, dancing over the open window. I have brought
30 Piggy, although I am way too old. Marty left her doll on her pillow at home. Nai-nai doesn't make fun of me. "Poor old man," she says, when she notices Piggy's tat-tered chest. She looks in her drawers and finds a baby T-shirt I can dress him in.

35 Marty and I play softball and kickball with the kids on our street. Sometimes we go to the beach, along with a lot of other kids in bathing suits, crowded into the back of a station wagon that smells like hot rubber and coconut lotion. It is the most beautiful ocean I have
40 ever seen, with all different kinds of blue in it, rolling like fluted glass toward us.

I tell the other kids about the Gulf of Mexico, where Aunty Mabel and Uncle Richard live. There were things waiting there in that warm flat water, crabs
45 who'd clamp your toes no matter how carefully you stepped. Then I tell them about the beach in Monterey, where I was born, with all the wildflowers in the spring, and of course the seals.

Marty and I get very tan, and Nai-nai scolds us.
50 But she softens when she sees how hungry we are after our days at the beach, how we wolf everything down, no matter how strange. When we first got here we were picky, polite. Nai-nai corrected the way Marty held her chopsticks and made her cry. Our grandmother serves
55 the meal in courses, unlike Ma, who sets everything down on the table at once.

Now we compromise. Marty is allowed to use a fork, and Nai-nai sometimes gives in to our pleas at the grocery store. One night she even makes hamburgers,
60 following the recipe from *Joy of Cooking*, although we forget to get buns so we have to have them on toast.

On the first rainy day, Nai-nai climbs the steplad-der and takes out boxes from the top shelf of her bed-room closet. They are filled with presents from her
65 admirers, back in her youth when she was a lieder singer. She kept everything: dried sprays of orchids, brittle and black-edged; a collection of music boxes from Switzerland; perfume, never opened, the bottoms of the crystal flasks coated brown. I imagine the per-
70 fume to be like orange juice concentrate: if you added water it would be as good as fresh.

She shows us photographs of our parents' wed-ding. "Handsome couple," she says. My mother doesn't look too different, except for more makeup and wavy
75 hair, but my father is unrecognizable. The man in the picture has dark, thick hair and a smooth, confident face, as if nothing bad had ever happened to him.

My hair is long but I am not allowed to wear it loose except at night. Nai-nai washes it for me in the
80 kitchen sink. I force myself to stand very still, although I get a crick in my neck and the water from the spray nozzle tickles.

Once, after my hair had dried enough to brush out,
Nai-nai puts it up into a bun like hers. I watch her in the
85 dresser mirror, trying to memorize the motions, but my
grandmother is too fast. When she's done she gives me
the hand mirror so that I can examine the back of my
head. I see that she has anchored the bun with a single
pale green hairpin, like an arrow through a valentine.

90   "It's jade," my grandmother says, patting my
shoulder. "You keep."

141. The narrator's use of sensory details, such as the color
of the curtains and the smell of the station wagon, most
strongly suggests that:

   A. she is too young to comprehend her world in anything but sensory images.

   B. the separation from her parents is so upsetting that
she is strikingly aware of her physical surroundings.

   C. the routine nature of the trip causes her to fully
notice small changes in her surroundings since her
last visit.

   D. vivid images best represent what she appreciates
about the experiences of her trip.

142. It can reasonably be inferred from the passage that the
narrator views the children who live on Nai-nai's street
as:

   F. spoilsports unwilling to participate in activities
that would make the summer days even more
enjoyable.

   G. friends who often vocalize what intrigues them
about the ocean's beautiful appearance.

   H. companions with whom to share the memorable
stories of her life.

   J. children who have been deprived of the wonderful
opportunity to play on the beach.

143. As depicted in the eighth and ninth paragraphs
(lines 49–61), the relationship between the girls and
their grandmother is best described by which of the
following statements?

   A. The girls are reluctantly adjusting to their grandmother's ways.

   B. The girls and their grandmother are learning to
accept each other in new ways.

   C. The grandmother is exhausted from trying to
entertain and care for the girls.

   D. The grandmother, though loving, is rigid about
what she considers correct.

144. Details in the tenth paragraph (lines 62–71) most
strongly suggest that the grandmother:

   F. hopes the girls will pursue careers as singers or
actors.

   G. hopes the girls will keep and preserve the presents
she received as a lieder singer.

   H. exaggerates the experiences in her life in a way the
narrator enjoys.

   J. has a lively past she wants the girls to learn about.

145. The narrator's imaginative way of viewing her surroundings is best revealed by her description of the:

   A. baby T-shirt.

   B. stewardess's white gloves.

   C. coconut lotion.

   D. perfume.

146. Which of the following statements about why the narrator and Marty will spend the summer with Nai-nai is
supported by the passage?

   F. They are taking a special trip planned for the narrator's birthday.

   G. Their parents will be in Taiwan, so the girls need a
place to stay.

   H. Their parents believe it is important for the girls to
learn more about Nai-nai's past.

   J. Nai-nai lives by the ocean, where there is more to
do in the summer than at their parents' house.

147. Which of the following statements most nearly cap-
tures the sentiment behind the narrator's comment
"Nai-nai doesn't make fun of me" (line 31)?

   A. "Nai-nai knows how it feels to be laughed at."

   B. "Nai-nai knows why I would like a baby T-shirt."

   C. "Nai-nai understands why I ask when she goes to
bed."

   D. "Nai-nai understands why I bring Piggy."

148. It can reasonably be inferred from the passage that
which of the following events happened first in the
narrator's life?

   F. She visited Aunty Mabel and Uncle Richard.

   G. She visited Nai-nai at Su-yi's house.

   H. She lived in Monterey.

   J. She lived in Taiwan.

149. In line 75, the narrator describes her father as "unrecognizable," which most nearly suggests that she:

   A. does not recognize her father because he has often
been away from home.

   B. is aware of the changes in her father's appearance.

   C. is unsure that the man in the picture is her father.

   D. does not recognize her father because to her surprise he looks younger now than he does in the
picture.

150. It can most reasonably be inferred from the passage
that the narrator's father:

   F. has faced many instances of misfortune in his life.

   G. becomes distressed when Marty cries before the
trip.

   H. views his wedding day as the turning point of his
life.

   J. has contemplated moving to San Diego with his
family.

Passage XVI

SOCIAL SCIENCE: This passage is adapted from the article "No Longer Alone: The Scientist Who Dared to Say Animals Think" by Emily Eakin (©2001 by The New York Times).

Donald Griffin was at the Central Park Zoo watching the polar bears nuzzle a synthetic log smeared with peanut butter. Dr. Griffin observed as Gus, 800 pounds, tried to fit his nose into an enticingly sticky knothole.
5 To the untutored eye it looked like just another feeding time at the zoo, but at Central Park the exercise with the log and snack goes by the grander name of "animal enrichment" and is intended to stimulate the bears' minds as well as their appetites. It's a concept for
10 which the bears have Dr. Griffin, 85, in large part to thank.

Twenty-five years ago he published a short book suggesting that humans didn't have the monopoly on thoughts and feelings. Animals, he argued, most likely
15 had them, too.

Other scientists were appalled. According to the behaviorist doctrine that held sway at the time, animals were little more than "stimulus response automata," robots with a central nervous system. The idea that an
20 ant or an elephant might have thoughts, images, experiences or beliefs was not just laughable; it was seditious.

But over the last decade alone a flood of new data have emerged that would seem to have turned the tide definitively in Dr. Griffin's favor. In Arizona an
25 African Gray parrot named Alex can identify colors and shapes as well as any preschooler. In Georgia a bonobo ape named Kanzi converses with his trainer via computer keyboard and watches Tarzan movies on television. Researchers at the Massachusetts Institute of
30 Technology published evidence suggesting that rats dream. Animal enrichment programs featuring mental puzzles disguised as toys and treats have become a standard part of daily life at zoos. And in the spring of 2001 the University of Chicago Press issued an updated
35 edition of Dr. Griffin's 1992 book, *Animal Minds*.

If Dr. Griffin views these developments as vindication, he is too modest to say so. "We know so very little," he said. "Scientists, including me, have come to be very cautious. Early work on primate gestures and
40 facial expressions was grossly misinterpreted."

In fact the recent findings appear to have only intensified the debate over animal consciousness. Lately, experts on the human mind—philosophers and psychologists—have been weighing in alongside the
45 scientists. For if it turns out that animals can think, then the idea that consciousness is unique to humans—a basic assumption in Western thought—becomes impossible to maintain.

Clearly Gus, Alex and Kanzi aren't automatons,
50 but just how conscious are they? Do they experience pain, desire and other sensations the way humans do?

(Philosophers call this *phenomenal consciousness*.) Are they capable of thinking about their experiences? (Philosophers call this *self-consciousness*.) Do they
55 have beliefs? What about remembering the past? Do earthworms have some form of consciousness? What about salamanders? Is it even possible to study an animal's inner life? The range of opinion on these questions is nearly as great as the number of possible
60 answers. Tufts University philosopher Daniel C. Dennett declared the state of thinking on animal consciousness a "mess."

On the one hand there are the pro-consciousness philosophers like Colin McGinn, a professor at Rutgers
65 University, and Peter Singer, a professor of bioethics at Princeton and a leading animal rights advocate. These scholars believe that most if not all animals have phenomenal consciousness. "I think it's plain common sense that animals have conscious states," Mr. McGinn
70 said. "Animals way down to insects have phenomenal consciousness. It's a primitive feature of the biological world."

On the other hand there are the skeptics like Mr. Dennett and Herbert Terrace, a psychologist at
75 Columbia University. What "are you seeing when you see sentience in a creature?" Mr. Dennett asked in a 1995 essay. "It is in fact ridiculously easy to induce powerful intuitions of not just sentience but full-blown consciousness (ripe with malevolence or curiosity or
80 friendship) by exposing people to quite simple robots made to move in familiar mammalian ways at mammalian speeds."

Dr. Griffin appears mildly amused by the debate his work has helped unleash. During his visit to the
85 Central Park Zoo he gave a talk to donors and trustees. "Daniel Dennett calls the pursuit of animal consciousness a 'wild goose chase,'" he told the audience with a chuckle. "But there are no neurons or synapses in the human brain that aren't also in animals. It's as difficult
90 to disprove animal consciousness as it is to prove it."

151. The passage most strongly suggests that animal enrichment programs at zoos are designed primarily to do which of the following?

A. Offer the animals mental stimulation they might otherwise have had in the wild
B. Trick the animals into eating well-balanced diets
C. Encourage the animals to be more tolerant of humans
D. Prepare the animals for potential release into their natural habitats

152. Gus the polar bear's behavior with the synthetic log in the first paragraph would most likely be explained by Daniel Dennett and Herbert Terrace as which of the following?

    F. Physical response to an external stimulus
    G. Mental stimulation for animal enrichment
    H. Evidence of phenomenal consciousness
    J. An example of self-consciousness

153. The examples supplied in the fourth paragraph (lines 22–35) appear most to undermine the position held by:

    A. the passage's author.
    B. Donald Griffin.
    C. Colin McGinn.
    D. Daniel Dennett.

154. The passage indicates that animal rights advocates would be most likely to agree with which of the following statements?

    F. Some animal species ought to be called stimulus response automata.
    G. Animal enrichment programs are well intentioned but ultimately ineffective.
    H. Most animal species have some degree of phenomenal consciousness.
    J. The behaviorist doctrine provides ample support for animal rights.

155. The passage most strongly suggests that today's controversy over whether animals think was prompted by which of the following?

    A. Early scientific work on primate gestures
    B. A book written by Donald Griffin in the 1970s
    C. A parrot that can identify colors
    D. Programs at the Central Park Zoo

156. The main idea of the quotation from Daniel Dennett's essay in the ninth paragraph (lines 73–82) is that:

    F. robots can be built to act extremely similar to humans.
    G. mammals are quite capable of curiosity and friendship.
    H. people can easily infer attributes of consciousness from nonconscious things.
    J. insects are much less likely than mammals to have phenomenal consciousness.

157. The primary function of the last paragraph is to:

    A. suggest that even without definite proof, Donald Griffin is not willing to relinquish his theory.
    B. summarize in detail the evidence used by Donald Griffin in support of his theory.
    C. illustrate Donald Griffin's resentment of Daniel Dennett's philosophical position.
    D. imply that Donald Griffin is prepared to provide new evidence countering Daniel Dennett's statements.

158. According to the passage, stimulus response automata are:

    F. puzzles disguised as toys.
    G. robots with a central nervous system.
    H. parrots that can identify colors.
    J. machines made to move like mammals.

159. According to the passage, Donald Griffin believes that scientists' early work on primate gestures and facial expressions was:

    A. overly cautious.
    B. badly misconstrued.
    C. somewhat laughable.
    D. largely satisfactory.

160. According to the passage, the experience of pain and desire by humans is called which of the following by philosophers?

    F. Phenomenal consciousness
    G. Stimulus response
    H. Primate gestures
    J. Sentience

Passage XVII

HUMANITIES: This passage is adapted from "Reading Blind" by Margaret Atwood (©1989 by Margaret Atwood). It was originally published as the introduction to *The Best American Short Stories 1989.*

Our first stories come to us through the air. We hear voices.

Children grow up within a web of stories. We listen before we can read. Some of our listening is more
5 like listening in, to the voices of the adult world, on the radio or the television or in our daily lives. Often it's an overhearing of things we aren't supposed to hear, eavesdropping on gossip or family secrets. From all these scraps of voices, from the whispers and shouts
10 that surround us, even from the silences, the unfilled gaps in meaning, we patch together for ourselves an order of events, a plot or plots; these, then, are the things that happen, these are the people they happen to, this is the forbidden knowledge.

15 We have all been little pitchers with big ears, shooed out of the kitchen when the unspoken is being spoken, and we have probably all been tale-bearers, blurters at the dinner table, unwitting violators of adult rules of censorship. Perhaps this is what writers are:
20 those who never kicked the habit. We remained tale-bearers. We learned to keep our eyes open, but not to keep our mouths shut.

Two kinds of stories we first encounter form our idea of what a story is and color the expectations we
25 bring to stories later. Perhaps it's from the collisions between these two kinds of stories—what is often called "real life" (and which writers greedily think of as their "material") and what is sometimes dismissed as "mere literature" or "the kinds of things that happen
30 only in stories"—that original and living writing is generated. A writer with nothing but a formal sense will produce dead work, but so will one whose only excuse for what is on the page is that it really happened. Anyone who has been trapped in a bus beside a nonstop
35 talker graced with no narrative skill or sense of timing can testify to that. Expressing yourself is not nearly enough. You must express the story.

Perhaps all I want from a good story is what children want when they listen to tales.

40 They want their attention held, and so do I. I always read to the end, out of some adult sense of duty owed; but if I start to fidget and skip pages, and wonder if conscience demands I go back and read the middle, it's a sign that the story has lost me, or I have lost it.

45 They want to feel they are in safe hands, that they can trust the teller. With children this may mean simply that they know the speaker will not betray them by closing the book in the middle, or mixing up the heroes and the villains. With adult readers it's more compli-
50 cated than that, and involves many dimensions, but there's the same element of keeping faith. Faith must be kept within the language—even if the story is funny, its language must be taken seriously—with the concrete details of locale, mannerism, clothing; with the shape
55 of the story itself. A good story may tease, as long as this activity is not used as an end in itself. If there's a promise held out, it must be honored. Whatever is hidden behind the curtain must be revealed at last, and it must be at one and the same time completely unex-
60 pected and inevitable. It's in this last respect that the story comes closest to resembling two of its oral predecessors, the riddle and the joke. Both, or all three, require the same mystifying buildup, the same surprising twist, the same impeccable sense of timing. If we
65 guess the riddle at once, or if we can't guess it because the answer makes no sense—if we see the joke coming, or if the point is lost because the teller gets it muddled—there is failure. Stories can fail in the same way.

But anyone who has ever told, or tried to tell, a
70 story to children will know that there is one thing without which none of the rest is any good. Young children have little sense of dutifulness or of delaying anticipation. They are longing to hear a story, but only if you are longing to tell one. They will not put up with your
75 lassitude or boredom: If you want their full attention, you must give them yours. You need a sense of urgency.

Urgency does not mean frenzy. The story can be a quiet story. But it must be urgently told. It must be told with as much intentness as if the teller's life depended
80 on it. And, if you are a writer, so it does, because your life as the writer is only as long, and as good, as the story itself. Most of those who hear it or read it will never know you, but they will know the story. Their act of listening is its reincarnation.

85 From listening to the stories of others, we learn to tell our own.

161. It can reasonably be inferred that the primary purpose of this passage is to:

A. persuade readers to stop being tale-bearers and instead be good listeners.

B. present one author's attempt to stop writers from being nonstop talkers and instead practice the craft of a storyteller.

C. instruct readers to practice oral storytelling in order to become good writers.

D. present a viewpoint on the art of storytelling and the relationship between the author and the audience.

162. Which of the following best describes the way the first paragraph functions in relation to the passage as a whole?

   F. It offers an assertion that is the basis for the author's discussion of storytelling.

   G. It introduces an opinion that is later contradicted by the author's personal experience.

   H. It presents a confusing image that is not explained by supporting details in the following paragraphs.

   J. It supports the essay's assertion that writing is easy because stories come to us through air.

163. When the writer refers to "adult rules of censorship" in lines 18–19, she is most likely referring to rules determined by:

   A. a sense of propriety derived from maturity and social experience.

   B. the laws that protect the personal privacy of citizens in a democracy.

   C. the customs and habits practiced by the tellers of tales.

   D. a shared understanding formed between children who are tale-bearers.

164. In the fourth paragraph (lines 23–37), the author says that a writer must be able to "express the story." It can reasonably be inferred that which of the following is NOT a part of that ability?

   F. Possessing literary and narrative skill

   G. Retelling events because they occurred

   H. Pacing the telling of the story

   J. Combining real experience with fiction

165. According to the passage, what the author calls "real life" (line 27) and "mere literature" (line 29) differ from one another in that:

   A. real life, unlike mere literature, supplies believable action that interests adults but that bores younger audiences.

   B. real life is associated with daily, actual events, while mere literature is often dismissed as events that only occur in fiction.

   C. mere literature, unlike real life, provides the details that writers greedily think of as their own material.

   D. mere literature truly expresses the meaning behind real-life experience, while real life produces formal, dead work.

166. According to the author's comparison, successful stories written for adults and successful tales told to children:

   F. possess no similar attributes.

   G. are equally easy to compose.

   H. have little to do with "real life."

   J. share several important characteristics.

167. The author states that good stories share all of the following characteristics with jokes and riddles EXCEPT a:

   A. mystifying buildup.

   B. surprise twist.

   C. predictable ending.

   D. sense of timing.

168. Based on the passage, a child's experience of overhearing the voices of the adult world is significant because it:

   F. later prevents the child as a writer from being able to distinguish reality and fantasy.

   G. invites the adult censorship that discourages the child in his or her later formation as a writer.

   H. provides a child with information later used to create meaning in the child's life.

   J. enables a child to create a new world of his or her own by tuning out the voices of the adult world.

169. The author states that when she reads a story, her adult response to the story is that she:

   A. feels obligated to read it to the end.

   B. refuses to finish it if it loses her.

   C. no longer feels guilty if she skips pages.

   D. expects it to have a happy ending with all its elements revealed.

170. When the author describes a good story as requiring "a sense of urgency" (line 76), she is most directly referring to the concept that a writer has to:

   F. tell the story with her or his full attention.

   G. make sure that the story is exciting and fast paced.

   H. immediately reveal the plot with intentness.

   J. relate the story out of a sense of duty.

Passage XVIII

NATURAL SCIENCE: This passage is adapted from *Just Six Numbers: The Deep Forces That Shape the Universe* by Martin Rees (©2000 by Martin Rees).

The Sun is fuelled by conversion of hydrogen (the simplest atom, whose nucleus consists of one proton) into helium (the second-simplest nucleus, consisting of two protons and two neutrons). Attempts to harness
5 fusion as a power source ('controlled fusion') have so far been stymied by the difficulty of achieving the requisite temperatures of many millions of degrees. It is even more of a problem to confine this ultra-hot gas physically in a laboratory—it would obviously melt any
10 solid container—and it has instead to be trapped by magnetic forces. But the Sun is so massive that gravity holds down the overlying cooler layers, and thereby 'keeps the lid on' the high-pressure core. The Sun has adjusted its structure so that nuclear power is generated
15 in the core, and diffuses outward, at just the rate needed to balance the heat lost from the surface—heat that is the basis for life on Earth.

This fuel has kept the Sun shining for nearly five billion years. But when it starts to run out, in another
20 five billion years or so, the Sun's core will contract, and the outer layers expand. For a hundred million years—a brief interval relative to its overall lifetime—the Sun will brighten up and expand into the kind of star known as a 'red giant', engulfing the inner planets
25 and vaporizing any life that remains on Earth. Some of its outer layers will be blown off, but the core will then settle down as a white dwarf, shining with a dull blue glow, no brighter than a full moon today, on the parched remains of the Solar System.

30 Astrophysicists have computed what the inside of our Sun should be like, and have achieved a gratifying fit with its observed radius, brightness, temperature and so forth. They can tell us confidently what conditions prevail in its deep interior; they can also calculate how
35 it will evolve over the next few billion years. Obviously these calculations can't be checked directly. We can, however, observe other stars *like* the Sun that are at different stages in their evolution. Having a single 'snapshot' of each star's life is not a fatal handicap if we
40 have a large sample, born at different times, available for study. In the same way, a newly landed Martian wouldn't take long to infer the life-cycle of humans (or of trees), by observing large numbers at different stages. Even among the nearby stars, we can discern
45 some that are still youngsters, no more than a million years old, and others in a near-terminal state, which may already have swallowed up any retinue of planets that they once possessed. Such inferences are based on the assumption that atoms and their nuclei are the same
50 everywhere.

Astrophysicists can compute, just as easily as the Sun's evolution, the life-cycle of a star that is (say) half, twice, or ten times the mass of the Sun. Smaller stars burn their fuel more slowly. In contrast, stars ten
55 times as heavy as the Sun—the four blue Trapezium stars in the constellation of Orion, for instance—shine thousands of times more brightly, and consume their fuel more quickly. Their lifetimes are much shorter than the Sun's, and they expire in a more violent way, by
60 exploding as supernovae. They become, for a few weeks, as bright as several billion suns. Their outer layers, blown off at 20,000 kilometres per second, form a blast wave that ploughs into the surrounding interstellar gas.

65 Supernovae represent cataclysmic events in the life of the stars, involving some 'extreme' physical processes; so supernovae naturally fascinate astronomers. But only one person in ten thousand is an astronomer. What possible relevance could these stellar
70 explosions thousands of light-years away have to all the others, whose business lies purely on or near the Earth's surface? The surprising answer is that they are fundamental to everyone's environment. Without them, we would never have existed. Supernovae have created
75 the 'mix' of atoms that the Earth is made of and that are the building blocks for the intricate chemistry of life. Ever since Darwin, we've been aware of the evolution and selection that preceded our emergence, and of our links with the rest of the biosphere. Astronomers now
80 trace our Earth's origins back to stars that died before the Solar System formed. These ancient stars made the atoms of which we and our planet are composed.

171. The primary purpose of the passage is to:

A. encourage readers to become aware of specific stars and constellations in other solar systems.
B. showcase new information astrophysicists have learned through direct observation of the Sun's core.
C. convince readers that the work of astrophysicists is inconclusive with respect to the origin of Earth and its inhabitants.
D. describe the evolution and demise of stars and the effects their deaths have for the planets and life.

172. The passage mentions astrophysicists calculating all of the following about stars EXCEPT:

F. what the inside of the Sun should be like.
G. how the Sun will evolve over the next few billion years.
H. what the life cycle of a star bigger or smaller than the Sun is.
J. how long the Sun will emit a dull blue glow.

173. Information in the first paragraph indicates that "controlled fusion" requires all of the following EXCEPT:

   A. the transformation of atomic nuclei.
   B. ultra-hot temperatures.
   C. the Sun as the fuel source.
   D. magnetic containment of helium.

174. According to the passage, what is the last described event in the Sun's life cycle?

   F. It will shine thousands of times more brightly.
   G. Its core will become a white dwarf.
   H. Its outer layers will be ejected from the Solar System.
   J. It will explode as a supernova.

175. In the context of the third paragraph (lines 30–50), lines 38–41 primarily serve to emphasize the:

   A. ability of astrophysicists to locate stars that have the same features and birth date as the Sun.
   B. difficulty of getting clear photographs of the Sun as it undergoes changes in its structure.
   C. method used by astrophysicists to verify computations about the Sun.
   D. fatal mistakes astrophysicists make when observing large sample sets over an extended period of time.

176. Which of the following questions is NOT answered by information given in the passage?

   F. What is one characteristic of a white dwarf?
   G. What assumption do astrophysicists make in order to compute the evolution of the Sun?
   H. Why is the Sun so massive in comparison to Earth?
   J. Why are astronomers fascinated by supernovae?

177. The main purpose of the last paragraph is to:

   A. stress the significance of supernovae to humans and to the formation of Earth.
   B. present a detailed account of cataclysmic events in the Solar System.
   C. expose the flaws of Darwin's theories of evolution and selection.
   D. persuade readers to become amateur astronomers.

178. As it is used in lines 70–71, the phrase *all the others* most likely refers to:

   F. the stellar explosions near Earth.
   G. the planets in the Solar System.
   H. astrophysicists and astronomers.
   J. most people on Earth.

179. The author would most likely agree with which of the following statements?

   A. Fusion will not be used as a power source in the future because of opposition by industrial leaders.
   B. The age of stars is inferred by calculating their proximity to the Sun.
   C. The Trapezium stars in the constellation Orion will have a longer life span than the Sun.
   D. Earth and its inhabitants are made up of particles from primordial stars.

180. The passage most nearly indicates that attempts to harness fusion as a power source have been:

   F. remarkably successful.
   G. unsuccessful to date.
   H. hindered by financial issues.
   J. inconsistent across trials.

Passage XIX

PROSE FICTION: This passage is adapted from the novel *Toning the Sweep* by Angela Johnson (©1993 by Angela Johnson).

The narrator is visiting her grandmother, Ola, to help her prepare to move. Martha is Ola's friend and neighbor.

I think about how everybody Ola knows here has a story. Daddy says that everybody has one and their stories are all a part of us. If Ola loves these people, then they must be a part of me too. It must be true about all
5 of us being a part of one another like Daddy says.

Ola hums on the porch while Mama eats an apple and labels boxes. I go over to the phone by the refrigerator and call Martha. When she picks up, her voice rings out and is so familiar. I tell her Ola's idea about
10 making a movie.

Martha Jackson's hair is the color of coal and she must be about my grandmama's age. She cuts her hair short, and sometimes it sticks straight up, but she doesn't care.

15 She's probably one of the tallest people I know, and walks like she's swimming. Martha looks at you for a long time before she decides to speak.

She's leaning on a Joshua tree in Ola's front yard, saying, "It's like poetry and eating to me now. You let
20 the camera become part of you. Like your head and your eyes. If the camera were to fall out of your hands, it should be like your head falling off in the middle of a conversation."

"I don't know if the camera can ever be that spe-
25 cial to me, Martha," I say. "I just got used to the camera my dad gave me four years ago. I can remember to take off the lens cap sometimes."

Martha smiles. "This is a thing to get used to—that's all. No magic, no special real training. Turn the
30 camera on and shoot."

I take the camera and start taping a crow that's landed on the back porch. I figure it's a start. The crow gets real interested in me filming him and stops pecking

at the old apple core he's found near the garbage cans.
35 He hops off the porch and checks me and the camera out till he sees something else off over by some brush.

Martha's watching me with a smirk when I turn back to her with the camera. "I guess you'll do okay by yourself now." She looks at me for a long time, then
40 says, "Let's talk about Ola."

I start shooting and say to myself, "A part of me," and hope that the thing is going and the lens cap hasn't been on the whole time I've been taping the crow. I zoom in on Martha leaning against the Joshua tree. She
45 stares into the camera.

"I met Ola in the late summer of 1964 'cause there was no other way around it."

A pot falls in the kitchen, and we can hear Ola laughing—then she stops. I keep the camera running.

50 "Like I was saying," Martha starts to whisper, but changes her mind and speaks even louder. "I couldn't help but meet her. There's about five hundred people that live out here, and she happens to be my closest neighbor. She was playing her music loud one night,
55 and I was sitting out in my yard."

Ola comes out the screen door and sits down by Martha Jackson. Two people couldn't be more different in looks. I have them both in the frame.

Ola's short and delicate—like she'd break if you
60 held her arm too tight. She wouldn't break, though. She hands Martha a glass of iced tea and sits cross-legged on the ground.

I press the pause button, then change my mind. I sit down on a lawn chair and ask, "What did you two
65 think of each other when you first met?" It's easier to ask what I'd usually think of as a nosy question from behind a camera.

Martha whispers, "I thought she had the worst accent of anybody that I'd ever heard. It grew on me,
70 though, and I got used to it. I liked her car and the way the fool painted the house yellow the day after she and Diane moved in."

Ola spills a little iced tea and says, "No, you didn't. You yelled from the road that this shade of
75 yellow didn't look good from where you stood, and what was it called?" Ola looks at the camera and tells me, "Your mama was so embarrassed, Emmie, she begged me to stop painting it yellow and just make it gray or something. Your mama always took things so
80 much to heart."

"What did you say to Martha then?"

"I told her I didn't know who she was, but if she had enough energy to yell from the road at a perfect stranger, she probably had enough strength to pick up a
85 brush."

Martha tilts her head back and laughs. "So I did."

Ola gets up and goes into the house without making a sound. I don't think that Martha even knows she's gone, 'cause her eyes are closed.

90   I want to make this movie on my own. Martha makes me want to know all of Ola's friends. I want to know who they are and what they've done. I'll put them all in front of the camera, and when the movie's done, it can be my gift to Ola. The other gifts I've given her are
95 things she could put on the wall or wear. I figure this will be better than all that. I'll give her memories of her people.

181. Based on the passage, Ola and Martha can reasonably be said to share all of the following traits EXCEPT a:

A. sense of humor.
B. capacity for brutal honesty.
C. great vitality and liveliness.
D. tendency to pause before speaking.

182. Which of the following statements does the passage support regarding the idea for the movie?

F. Though the original idea was Ola's, the narrator and Martha embraced it.
G. Although the narrator came up with the idea, she needed Martha's encouragement to continue.
H. Ola proposed the idea to Martha, who recruited the narrator to make the movie.
J. The narrator suggested the idea to Ola, who had to be talked into it by Martha.

183. The narrator's two references to a camera's lens cap (lines 27 and 42) primarily serve to suggest her:

A. expanding knowledge of camera terminology.
B. continuing desire to uncover her artistic vision.
C. ongoing insecurity about her skill with a camera.
D. growing eagerness to use a camera to tell stories.

184. Viewed in the context of the passage, Martha's smirk (line 37) most likely reflects a feeling of:

F. mild weariness.
G. sharp condescension.
H. profound relief.
J. slight amusement.

185. As presented by the participants, the initial meeting between Ola and Martha can best be described as:

A. a misunderstanding that escalates into harsh words until the two agree to keep their distance from each other.
B. a potentially bitter confrontation that, because of the personalities of the two people, turns into a cooperative effort.
C. a friendly, relaxed get-together between two families made even more enjoyable by music and a shared task.
D. an accidental encounter that slowly turns unpleasant due to a dispute that Ola's daughter helps resolve.

186. Martha clearly recommends that the narrator use a camera in which of the following ways?

F. Scientifically
G. Cautiously
H. Intuitively
J. Secretly

187. It can most reasonably be inferred that Diane is the name of:

A. the narrator.
B. the narrator's mother.
C. one of Ola's neighbors.
D. one of Martha's best friends.

188. In terms of the development of the narrator as a character, the last paragraph primarily serves to:

F. establish motivation for her actions.
G. provide background details about her past.
H. elaborate on her relationship with Martha.
J. undermine the reliability of her account.

189. In the first paragraph, the main conclusion the narrator reaches is that:

A. Daddy is usually right in his assessments of people.
B. Ola is a wonderful storyteller who entertains everyone she knows.
C. Ola shares a close bond with her neighbors.
D. people everywhere are connected to each other by stories and love.

190. The narrator's statement "She wouldn't break, though" (line 60) most nearly means that in the narrator's opinion, Ola is:

F. too stubborn to change her opinions very often.
G. too guarded to show her feelings.
H. stronger than she appears to be.
J. more active than many people half her age.

Passage XX

SOCIAL SCIENCE: This passage is adapted from the article "The Trouble with Fries" by Malcolm Gladwell (©2001 by The Condé Nast Publications Inc.).

It is entirely possible, right now, to make a delicious French fry that does not carry with it a death sentence. A French fry can be much more than a delivery vehicle for fat.

5   Is it really that simple, though? Consider the cautionary tale of the efforts of a group of food scientists at Auburn University more than a decade ago to come up with a better hamburger. The Auburn team wanted to create a leaner beef that tasted as good as regular
10 ground beef. They couldn't just remove the fat, because that would leave the meat dry and mealy. They wanted to replace the fat. The goal of the Auburn scientists was to cut about two-thirds of the fat from normal ground beef, which meant that they needed to find something
15 to add to the beef that would hold an equivalent amount of water—and continue to retain that water even as the beef was being grilled. Their choice? Seaweed, or, more precisely, carrageenan. They also selected some basic flavor enhancers, designed to make up for the lost
20 fat "taste." The result was a beef patty that was roughly three-quarters water, twenty per cent protein, five per cent or so fat, and a quarter of a per cent seaweed. They called it AU Lean.

It didn't take the Auburn scientists long to realize
25 that they had created something special. They began doing blind taste comparisons of AU Lean burgers and traditional twenty-per-cent-fat burgers. Time after time, the AU Lean burgers won. Next, they took their invention into the field. They recruited a hundred families
30 and supplied them with three kinds of ground beef for home cooking over consecutive three-week intervals— regular "market" ground beef with twenty per cent fat, ground beef with five per cent fat, and AU Lean. The families were asked to rate the different kinds of beef,
35 without knowing which was which. Again, the AU Lean won hands down.

What the Auburn team showed was that, even though people love the taste and feel of fat—and naturally gravitate toward high-fat food—they can be
40 fooled into thinking there is a lot of fat in something when there isn't. When the group tried to lower the fat in AU Lean below five per cent, people didn't like it anymore. But, within the relatively broad range of between five and twenty-five per cent, you can add
45 water and some flavoring and most people can't tell the difference.

What's more, people appear to be more sensitive to the volume of food they consume than to its calorie content. Barbara Rolls, a nutritionist at Penn State, has
50 demonstrated this principle with satiety studies. She feeds one group of people a high-volume snack and another group a low-volume snack. Even though the two snacks have the same calorie count, she finds that people who eat the high-volume snack feel more satis-
55 fied. Eating AU Lean, in short, isn't going to leave you with a craving for more calories; you'll feel just as full.

For anyone looking to improve the quality of fast food, all this is heartening news. It means that you should be able to put low-fat cheese and low-fat may-
60 onnaise in a fast-food hamburger without anyone's complaining. It also means that there's no particular reason to use twenty-per-cent-fat ground beef in a fast-food burger. In 1990, using just this argument, the Auburn team suggested to McDonald's that it make a
65 hamburger out of AU Lean. Shortly thereafter, McDonald's came out with the McLean Deluxe. Other fast-food houses scrambled to follow suit. Nutritionists were delighted. And fast food appeared on the verge of a revolution.

70 Only, it wasn't. The McLean was a flop, and four years later it was off the market. What happened? Part of the problem appears to have been that McDonald's rushed the burger to market before many of the production kinks had been worked out. More important,
75 though, was the psychological handicap the burger faced. People liked AU Lean in blind taste tests because they didn't know it was AU Lean; they were fooled into thinking it was regular ground beef. But nobody was fooled when it came to the McLean Deluxe. It was sold
80 as the healthy choice—and who goes to McDonald's for health food?

This is sobering news for those interested in improving the American diet. For years, the nutrition movement in this country has made transparency one of
85 its principal goals: it has assumed that the best way to help people improve their diets is to tell them precisely what's in their food, to label certain foods good and certain foods bad. But transparency can backfire, because sometimes nothing is more deadly for our taste
90 buds than the knowledge that what we are eating is good for us.

191. The author most nearly portrays the Auburn scientists as:

A. severe critics of the fast-food industry's practices.
B. enthusiastic promoters of their promising work.
C. diligent researchers uninterested in the practical application of their work.
D. clever innovators more interested in nutrition than in how food tastes.

192. It can reasonably be inferred from the passage that changing which of the following conditions of the experiment described in lines 28–36 would have had the biggest effect on the outcome?

   F. Altering the order in which the families received the three kinds of ground beef
   G. Using two hundred families instead of one hundred in the study
   H. Telling the families which kind of ground beef they were getting each time
   J. Lengthening the time the families used each type of ground beef

193. The statement in lines 61–63 most likely represents the view of all of the following groups EXCEPT:

   A. McDonald's officials introducing the McLean Deluxe to the public.
   B. the Auburn scientists, who had research to support these conclusions.
   C. nutritionists who saw the potential health benefits of AU Lean.
   D. fast-food company executives at the time this article was published.

194. According to the passage, carrageenan's role in AU Lean was as a:

   F. flavor enhancer.
   G. substitute for fat.
   H. source of protein.
   J. replacement for seaweed.

195. The author implies that for an AU Lean hamburger to seem as satisfying as a hamburger made from regular ground beef, the most important factor would be keeping which of the following the same?

   A. Volume
   B. Calorie content
   C. Percent of fat
   D. Method of cooking

196. The author indicates that the main cause of the failure of the McLean Deluxe was that:

   F. McDonald's failed to promote it through advertising.
   G. it was rushed to market before production problems were solved.
   H. people believed that it was made from "market" hamburger.
   J. people knew that it was supposed to be good for them.

197. The author most likely intends the question in lines 80–81 to be read:

   A. rhetorically; he believes the answer is self-evident and negative.
   B. ironically; he finds it surprising that people really wanted the healthy choice.
   C. genuinely; he is unsure about whether people enjoy healthy fast food.
   D. critically; he objects to fast-food restaurants selling AU Lean.

198. It can reasonably be inferred from the last paragraph that the author thinks that, in the future, the nutrition movement should:

   F. make its goals more transparent.
   G. reconsider its goal of transparency.
   H. label foods as either good or bad.
   J. tell people exactly what is in their food.

199. According to the passage, which of the following elements makes up the highest percent of AU Lean?

   A. Fat
   B. Seaweed
   C. Water
   D. Protein

200. According to information in the fourth paragraph (lines 37–46), which of the following comparisons between a 20-percent-fat hamburger and an 8-percent-fat hamburger with added water and flavorings would most people make?

   F. The 20-percent-fat hamburger would taste slightly better.
   G. The 8-percent-fat hamburger would taste slightly better.
   H. The 8-percent-fat hamburger would taste significantly better.
   J. The two hamburgers would taste the same.

Passage XXI

HUMANITIES: This passage is adapted from *The Piano Shop on the Left Bank* by Thad Carhart (©2001 by Thad Carhart).

No one knows exactly when the piano was invented. The generally accepted date is around 1700. There is little doubt, however, about its inventor, an instrument maker in Florence, Italy, named Bartolomeo
5 Cristofori, who developed a way of making a struck string resound loudly. Before Cristofori, keyboard instruments were unsatisfactory for different reasons: clavichords, whose strings are struck, were small and delicate, and their greatly reduced volume made them
10 suitable only for small gatherings. Harpsichords, while larger and therefore considerably louder, had one overriding limitation: since the string is plucked, the force with which the key is depressed is unrelated to the volume of the sound produced. Dynamic control of
15 each note was not possible.

What was needed—and what Cristofori invented—was an instrument as large and robust as the big harpsichords that would also allow the dynamic range that before had only been available on the flimsy clavi-
20 chords. The first piano was described by a contemporary musician in 1711 as a *"gravicembalo col piano e forte,"* a "harpsichord with soft and loud." This was the essential breakthrough, but it took decades for the seed to find fertile ground, and it did so not in Italy but in
25 eighteenth-century Germany.

German instrument makers incorporated Cristofori's breakthrough into a series of increasingly powerful keyboard instruments that were true pianos. Johann Sebastian Bach was impressed by the first piano
30 he tried, but he pointed out limitations that still needed to be worked on: a heavy action and a treble that was not loud enough. Two of his sons, Carl Philipp Emanuel and Johann Christian, championed the instrument in the next generation; by the time Johann Christian Bach
35 gave England's first solo piano performance in 1768, the triumph of this new keyboard instrument over the harpsichord was assured.

The role of the keyboard as a solo instrument came to the fore musically. It was no longer just another part
40 of the ensemble, and its unique volume freed it from the confines of the drawing room to which the harpsichord had almost always been consigned. Haydn and Mozart both wrote masterful sonatas for the new instrument, its keyboard was greatly expanded, and its
45 dynamic range—the single feature that most distinguished it from the harpsichord—was exploited fully. A whole new technique stressing fluidity was developed for the piano, and Mozart wrote: "It should flow like oil." Solo concerts became the norm rather than the
50 exception, and a class of instrumentalists with technique and power arrived on the scene.

What had been a tinkerer's offshoot among harpsichord makers became an industry in its own right. London and Vienna were its focal points. The two capi-
55 tals gave rise to distinct schools of piano building, the principal difference having to do with how the action—the intricate mechanism that activates the hammers to strike the strings—was conceived and assembled. Viennese pianos were generally softer, with a refined
60 singing tone that allowed the melody to come to the fore; the pianos themselves had delicate cabinetry. English pianos, on the other hand, had a more robust tone, with a stronger action and greater tension in the strings; they had solid cases and sturdy frames. The great Vien-
65 nese composers of the classical era—Haydn, Mozart, Beethoven—played Viennese pianos, but the transition to the stronger instruments of the English school can be seen in Beethoven's last piano sonatas.

Beethoven was known for the increasing dynamic
70 contrasts in his works for piano, from whisper to thunder, and he sometimes destroyed the fragile Viennese pianos when playing his music. He had a strong influence on the direction of piano manufacture, and as early as 1796 he expressed his frustration with the overly
75 delicate styles of playing that were a holdover from harpsichords.

In 1818, Broadwood, the pre-eminent English manufacturer of the day, offered him a grand piano that incorporated all of the latest features: stronger case and
80 frame, trichord stringing, more responsive action. This piano, too, Beethoven damaged with the fervor of his playing (a contemporary reported that "the broken strings were jumbled up like a thorn bush in a storm"), but he remained attached to it until his death in 1827.
85 He imagined music unlike anything his contemporaries were writing; the *Hammerklavier* sonata from this period still strikes many as a revelation of the piano's extreme limits of power and expressiveness.

201. Which of the following statements best describes how the second paragraph (lines 16–25) functions in relation to the first paragraph?

A. It moves further back in time to provide background for the circumstances described in the first paragraph.

B. It focuses on the general public's reaction to the developments described in the first paragraph.

C. It provides the other side of the argument presented in the first paragraph.

D. It describes the solution to the problem presented in the first paragraph.

202. Which of the following questions is NOT answered by the passage?

F. Who invented the piano?

G. What were keyboard instruments like before 1700?

H. What are the beginning and ending dates of the classical era?

J. What is *action* as it relates to keyboard instruments?

203. Based on the passage, the author would most likely agree that both Beethoven and Cristofori were:

A. tremendous innovators in ways that dramatically affected the music world.

B. world-class musicians who gained recognition in their time.

C. contributors to the advancement of the piano who were appreciated only after their deaths.

D. musicians who found more fame outside their native countries than inside.

204. For purposes of the passage, the significance of eighteenth-century Germany is that it was there:

F. Cristofori had his breakthrough.

G. instrument makers improved upon ideas of piano making that had originated in Italy.

H. the best harpsichords and clavichords were originally produced.

J. the first major split occurred among piano makers over the best way to design keyboards.

205. As it is used in line 27, the phrase *Cristofori's breakthrough* most nearly refers to the:

A. instrument maker's decision to let leading musicians initiate changes to standard piano design.

B. creation of pianos whose strings could be plucked loudly or softly, depending on the effect desired.

C. piano's release from the confines of the drawing room to larger performance spaces.

D. development of a keyboard instrument that offered the dynamic range of the clavichord and the loudness of the harpsichord.

206. It can most reasonably be inferred from the passage that which of the following was a direct expression of others' deep respect for Beethoven?

F. The grand piano manufactured by Broadwood whose strings the composer damaged

G. The way Viennese pianos were built before the classical era

H. The sonatas written and performed by Haydn and Mozart

J. The piano schools established in London and Vienna

207. As it is used in line 88, the phrase *extreme limits* most nearly means:

A. harsh rules.

B. far reaches.

C. high notes.

D. drastic shortcomings.

208. According to the passage, Johann Sebastian Bach's reaction to the first piano he played was:

F. disapproval of its loudness, accompanied by appreciation of its fluidity.

G. mild irritation over the singing quality of the notes.

H. genuine respect, accompanied by observations about problems.

J. amusement that the fervor of his playing damaged the strings.

209. According to the passage, the piano was better suited than the harpsichord to:

A. solo performances.

B. drawing room concerts.

C. delicate cabinetry.

D. church music.

210. According to the passage, the *Hammerklavier* sonata is a composition by Beethoven that:

F. sounds as dramatic on the clavichord as on the piano.

G. reveals the composer's remarkable awareness and use of the piano's full capacities.

H. gained more favor in England than in Vienna until Vienna imported English pianos.

J. first inspired Mozart to compose for piano.

Passage XXII

NATURAL SCIENCE: This passage is adapted from *Great Waters: An Atlantic Passage* by Deborah Cramer (©2001 by Deborah Cramer).

Relative newcomers to the marine world, bluefin tuna and swordfish have evolved into some of the sea's most highly developed fishes. While the cod, haddock, flounder, and plaice who dwell year-round in the North
5 Sea and the Gulf of Mexico are cold-blooded, their body temperatures rising and falling in synchrony with the surrounding water, thus limiting their geographic range, swordfish and bluefin, exquisitely adapted to live in the vastness of the sea, are free from the bound-
10 aries imposed by temperature. The swordfish who sur-face at the shelf edge have swum up from the depths, rising hundreds of feet through the water each evening as the sun sets, following their prey of fish and squid. A temperature difference of 36 degrees Fahrenheit, as
15 great as the swing between winter and summer, night and day, separates cold deep from warm surface. Swordfish exit one realm and swim into the other in under an hour.

Moving between such extremes would stun the
20 nervous system of a cold-blooded fish, but these ocean princes make their own heat, warming themselves in the deep cold. The burner of the swordfish lies behind its eyes, below its brain, a dark mass of tissue sur-rounded by insulating fat, heavy with blood, and loaded
25 with energy-producing mitochondria. With warm brain and eyes, swordfish can chase their food in waters deep and shallow, near and distant. By night, they feed at the surface, at the edge of the deep water. By day, they move onto shallow banks, like Georges or the Grand
30 Banks, and dive down to feed, slashing through schools of menhaden and mackerel with their long, sharp swords.

Bluefin tuna thrive in waters as cold as 40 degrees Fahrenheit and as warm as 75 degrees Fahrenheit but
35 unlike swordfish, they do not possess organs whose chief function is to produce heat. Instead they retain the heat they generate swimming. Other bony fish quickly lose their heat to the sea, for their red muscle lies near their skin, close to the cold water. In bluefin, who can
40 weigh as much as 1,000 pounds, red muscles are housed deep within the body, near the backbone. Warm venous blood flowing away from muscles heats cold blood coming in through the arteries, enabling bluefin to retain 98 percent of their body heat, giving them free
45 rein to forage in cold waters and to dip in and out of the Gulf Stream, where sea temperatures plummet as much as 27 degrees Fahrenheit across one nautical mile. In cold water, the bluefin, separated from the chill by only a taut skin, maintains an internal temperature of
50 80 degrees Fahrenheit.

Coincident with the relocation of its red muscle, bluefin developed the unique style of swimming for which they are so aptly named (*Thunnus thynnus,* from the Greek meaning to dart or lunge forward). While the
55 bodies of other fish undulate through the water as they swim, the crescent-shaped tail of the bluefin propels its rigid body forward. Retractable fins, small scales, and recessed eyes further enable bluefin to thrust quickly through thick and heavy seas, easily overcoming
60 water's drag and resistance. With their warm bodies, rapid metabolism, and sleek design, bluefin excel at both short sprints and long-distance travel. They zoom in on prey in short, quick bursts of speed, and they can cruise at two body lengths per second, easily making
65 long-distance endurance swims along an entire ocean basin. Engineers who design underwater robotics dream of replicating the sleek body of this 8-foot-long, 700-pound fish who rushes without ceasing through the breadth and depth of the sea.

70 Swordfish and bluefin travel throughout the Atlantic with tremendous speed, but from moment to moment, day to day, month to month, their migrations are not well charted. In the winter of 1997, when the warm Gulf Stream edged shoreward toward the coast of
75 Cape Hatteras, pressing against cold water rushing south in the Labrador Current, giant bluefin gathered in the warmth along the boundary. The following year, when the Gulf Stream moved offshore and the chilly Labrador Current filled the waters of coastal Cape Hat-
80 teras, bluefin wintered in waters unknown to people. Some bluefin, fattened in American coastal waters during the summer and fall, follow the currents across the sea during the winter. How they navigate, no one really knows. They could be guided by internal com-
85 passes of magnetite chips embedded in their skulls, by the warmth, salinity, or motion of the current, by pat-terns of polarized light received by the pineal window in their heads, or by prey leaving their scent as an oily, odorous slick in the water.

211. The main purpose of the passage is to:

A. propose that research be conducted to confirm which navigational method swordfish and bluefin actually use.

B. persuade the reader that swordfish are superior to bluefin in their adaptation to ocean life.

C. speculate on the reasons why two fish have devel-oped certain specialized traits.

D. describe two fishes' adaptations to the ocean envi-ronment, including specialized traits and physical features.

212. The author's attitude regarding swordfish and bluefin can best be described as one of:

F. appreciation for the advanced, unique abilities of the two fish.

G. concern that their adaptations put other fish at a disadvantage.

H. confusion over how their adaptations evolved so quickly beyond other fish.

J. neutrality when comparing their abilities to those of other fish.

213. The passage indicates that the body temperature of a cold-blooded fish is primarily determined by the:

    A. limits of its geographic range.
    B. speed at which it swims.
    C. type of prey it consumes.
    D. temperature of its surrounding water.

214. According to the passage, the most significant difference between the temperature-regulation systems of swordfish and bluefin is that swordfish:

    F. generate heat from a specialized organ, while bluefin retain heat generated from swimming.
    G. have a heat-producing organ located behind their eyes, while the bluefin's is near its backbone.
    H. retain heat generated by mitochondria, while bluefin retain heat generated by ocean currents.
    J. retain most of the heat they generate, while bluefin lose most of the heat they generate.

215. It can reasonably be concluded from the passage that the body of a bluefin remaining rigid while swimming is related to the fact that its red muscles are:

    A. moved sparingly in order to conserve body heat.
    B. frozen stiff from the icy-cold water of the ocean.
    C. restricted from movement by its super-tight skin.
    D. located deep within its body near the backbone.

216. It can most reasonably be inferred from the passage that the waters in and near the Gulf Stream pose a challenge to most species of fish primarily because these waters:

    F. are home to a large number and variety of predators.
    G. represent a wide range of temperatures.
    H. contain strong and swirling currents.
    J. force fish into unfamiliar ocean regions.

217. According to the passage, the Greek-derived name for bluefin refers to the:

    A. bluefin's constant internal temperature.
    B. powerful crescent-shaped tail of the bluefin.
    C. bluefin's lunging swimming style.
    D. sound the bluefin produces while swimming.

218. The main purpose of the last paragraph is to:

    F. explain that charting the Gulf Stream would help accurately predict the migration patterns of swordfish and bluefin.
    G. highlight the fact that researchers do not yet fully understand the migrations of swordfish and bluefin.
    H. reiterate that the territory of swordfish and bluefin is the entire Atlantic Ocean.
    J. remind the reader of the speed and depth at which swordfish and bluefin travel.

219. The passage supports the idea that all of the following fish dwell in the North Sea and the Gulf of Mexico year round EXCEPT:

    A. cod.
    B. haddock.
    C. plaice.
    D. bluefin.

220. According to the passage, the heat a swordfish generates is primarily intended to:

    F. attract cold-blooded prey seeking warmth.
    G. maintain the warmth of its eyes and brain.
    H. increase its speed by keeping large muscles warm.
    J. strengthen its long, sharp sword with warm blood.

Passage XXIII

PROSE FICTION: This passage is adapted from the novel *Night Water* by Helen Elaine Lee (©1996 by Helen Elaine Lee).

There had been no words for naming when she was born. She was "Girl Owens" on the stamped paper that certified her birth, and at home, she had just been "Sister," that was all. When asked to decide, at six,
5 what she would be called, she had chosen "Sunday," the time of voices, lifted in praise.

That was one piece of the story, but other parts had gone unspoken, and some had been buried, but were not at rest. She was headed back to claim them, as
10 she had taken her name.

She could smell the burnt, sweet odor of the paper mill that sprawled across the edge of town, and as the train got closer, she remembered all that she saw. She felt herself entering the greens and reds and browns of
15 her own paintings, pulling aside her brushstrokes as if they were curtains and stepping through. There were autumn trees on fire everywhere, and she moved beyond the surface of color and texture into the hidden layers of the past, from which she had learned to speak
20 her life with paint.

The train passed through the part of town where she grew up. She watched as they left behind the neat, compact frame houses and hollow storage buildings. She was going back to piece together their family story
25 of departure and return. She saw it all from the inside out, as native and exile, woman and child. From all that she remembered and all that she was. She was Girl Owens and Sister. She was Sunday, and she was headed home.

30 Waiting for Sunday's arrival, Delta Owens stepped out onto the front porch. She hoped she would be able to find the right way to approach Sunday, with whom she had only been in touch by mail for five years. She had tried to demonstrate a persistent bond with the help
35 of words put together by experts, choosing for each birthday and holiday an oversized greeting card, depending on its ornate script and polished rhyme to express what she had never been able to say. Each one she had signed "Always, Delta" before addressing the
40 envelope carefully and mailing it off to Chicago. She had heard back irregularly, receiving wood block prints or splashes of paint on wefts of heavy paper with ragged edges or on see-through skins. Each one she had turned round and round, looking for right-side up with
45 the help of the signature. Each one she had saved. Though she hadn't known what, specifically, to make of any of them, she knew their appearance said something about the habit of love.

They had kept up contact despite the differences
50 that had accumulated over the years and finally erupted in accusations and insults after Nana's death. In the wide, post-funeral quiet, after the visitors had gone home, they had both uttered things huge and unerasable.

55 She had always known how Sunday felt about home. "I'm in a little box," she had often complained while growing up, trying to express to Delta how different she felt, how she was of it, but would never be able to stay. And Delta, who had fought anyone who
60 criticized her sister, had listened and comforted her, but hadn't really understood. Sunday was the one she was different from.

"This place pulls you down and holds you," Sunday had said. "Delta, don't you see, it pulls you
65 down and holds you, silent and safe."

What Sunday said that night was condemnation of a place, but Delta absorbed it all. She was of Wake County and caught in that understanding of herself. Intoxicated with saying what had long been felt, they
70 both spoke freely and all barriers fell. Most of the things Sunday said had not surprised Delta, but one indictment had left her open-mouthed: "You don't even see my painting," Sunday had accused, "you don't even see me at all."

75 Delta had laughed callously at the accusation, for she knew, though she couldn't have said it, that for most of her life she had seen little else. She had answered by calling her a misfit who thought she was better than the folks she had left behind. And it was
80 Delta's recognition of her own rancor, as much as the substance of what they said, that staggered and disgraced her. She hadn't even realized all the things for which she couldn't forgive Sunday, hadn't known her own smallness until she found herself measuring her
85 sister out loud.

Finally, the rush of words had ended, and they had silently straightened up and gone upstairs without repairing their trespasses. Sunday had gathered and packed her things in a wild, tearful stupor of regret and
90 relief, while Delta cried herself to sleep with bitter remorse.

Delta pushed that night from her mind, hoping that this visit might help them leave behind their troubled history.

221. Which of the following statements offers the best short summary of this passage?

A. A painter, Sunday, returns to her hometown to attend Nana's funeral and to visit her sister Delta, whom she hasn't seen for some time.
B. Two sisters try unsuccessfully to resolve their differences when one of them returns to her hometown for a visit.
C. Two sisters contemplate their relationship to each other and to their hometown just prior to a reunion between them.
D. Two sisters argue over their childhood differences after one of them considers moving from Chicago back to Wake County.

222. The main conflict in this passage could best be described as:

F. Delta's struggle over her inability to express herself adequately in her paintings.
G. Sunday's internal conflict over whether she should stay away from or go back to her hometown.
H. the tension between two sisters, Delta and Sunday, who have differing views of the world.
J. the hostility between two sisters, Delta and Sunday, each of whom wants control over the other.

223. In this passage, the reader gains the most information about how Sunday feels about Wake County from:

A. Sunday's words as remembered by Delta.
B. Sunday's thoughts.
C. the words Delta speaks to Sunday.
D. Delta's description of Sunday's artwork.

224. The point of view from which this story is told changes at the beginning of line:

F. 21.
G. 30.
H. 55.
J. 66.

225. In the passage, Sunday defines herself as a painter and someone who has broken free of childhood constraints, while Delta tends to define herself as:

A. a homemaker, caregiver, and skilled writer in competition with her artistic sister.
B. a person who differs from the other residents of Wake County.
C. a woman who has always differed from her sister.
D. someone who is trying to become more worldly.

226. The first paragraph reveals all of the following details EXCEPT:

F. who suggested that Sunday choose her own name.
G. what name had been printed on Sunday's birth certificate.
H. what the name Sunday represented to Sunday herself.
J. at what point "Sister" acquired the name Sunday.

227. As it is used in line 26, the phrase *native and exile* most directly refers to:

A. the point of view of an artist versus that of her sister.
B. Sunday's love for and conflict with her sister Delta.
C. the period of time when Sunday was called "Sister" and the period of time after she became Sunday.
D. Sunday's childhood in Wake County and her adulthood in Chicago.

228. According to the passage, how did Delta interpret the paintings on paper and the block prints that Sunday sent to her?

F. She believed they indicated Sunday's lack of skill as a painter.
G. She thought they were Sunday's way of showing that she cared about her sister.
H. She felt they represented Sunday's acceptance that Delta would never leave Wake County.
J. She believed they were proof that Sunday was a misfit.

229. According to the passage, Delta had once accused Sunday of:

A. not appreciating Delta's artistic talents.
B. thinking Sunday was better than the people who lived in Wake County.
C. disgracing the family when she moved away from Wake County.
D. creating paintings that had almost no significance in the real world.

230. In the context of lines 79–85, the word *smallness* (line 84) most nearly means:

F. pettiness.
G. willfulness.
H. diminutive size.
J. lack of artistic talent.

Passage XXIV

SOCIAL SCIENCE: This passage is adapted from Michael J. Sandel's article "America's Search for a New Public Philosophy" (©1996 by The Atlantic Monthly Company). The author argues that our current conception of democracy underlies many of our social and economic problems.

The central idea of the public philosophy by which we live is that freedom consists in our capacity to choose our ends for ourselves. Politics should not try to form the character or cultivate the virtue of its citizens,
5 for to do so would be to "legislate morality." Government should not affirm, through its policies or laws, any particular conception of the good life; instead it should provide a neutral framework of rights within which people can choose their own values and ends.

10 The aspiration to neutrality finds prominent expression in our politics and law. Although it derives from the liberal tradition of political thought, its province is not limited to those known as liberals, rather than conservatives, in American politics; it can
15 be found across the political spectrum. Liberals invoke the ideal of neutrality when opposing school prayer or restrictions on abortion or attempts by certain groups to bring their morality into the public square. Conservatives appeal to neutrality when opposing attempts
20 by government to impose certain moral restraints—for the sake of workers' safety or environmental protection or distributive justice—on the operation of the market economy.

The ideal of free choice also figures on both sides
25 of the debate over the welfare state. Republicans have long complained that taxing the rich to pay for welfare programs for the poor is a form of coerced charity that violates people's freedom to choose what to do with their own money. Democrats have long replied that
30 government must assure all citizens a decent level of income, housing, education, and health care, on the grounds that those who are crushed by economic necessity are not truly free to exercise choice in other domains. Despite their disagreement about how gov-
35 ernment should act to respect individual choice, both sides assume that freedom consists in the capacity of people to choose their own ends.

So familiar is this vision of freedom that it might seem a permanent feature of the American political tra-
40 dition. But as a reigning public philosophy, it is a recent arrival, a development of the past half century. Its distinctive character can best be seen by comparison with a rival public philosophy that it gradually displaced: a version of republican political theory.

45 Central to republican theory is the idea that liberty depends on sharing in self-government. This idea is not by itself inconsistent with liberal freedom. Participating in politics can be one among the ways in which people choose to pursue their individual ends. According to
50 republican political theory, however, sharing in self-rule involves something more. It involves deliberating with fellow citizens about the common good and helping to shape the destiny of the political community. But to deliberate well about the common good requires
55 more than the capacity to choose one's ends and to respect others' rights to do the same. It requires a knowledge of public affairs and also a sense of belonging, a concern for the whole, a moral bond with the community whose fate is at stake. To share in self-
60 rule therefore requires that citizens possess, or come to acquire, certain civic virtues. But this means that republican politics cannot be neutral toward the values and ends its citizens espouse. The republican conception of freedom, unlike the liberal conception, requires
65 a formative politics, a politics that cultivates in citizens the qualities of character that self-government requires.

Both the liberal and the republican understandings of freedom have been present throughout our political experience, but in shifting measure and relative impor-
70 tance. In recent decades the civic, or formative, aspect of our politics has given way to a procedural republic, concerned less with cultivating virtue than with enabling persons to choose their own values. This shift sheds light on our present discontent. For despite its
75 appeal, the liberal vision of freedom lacks the civic resources to sustain self-government. The public philosophy by which we live cannot secure the liberty it promises, because it cannot inspire the sense of community and civic engagement that liberty requires.

231. Which of the following offers the best description of republican political theory as it is defined in this passage?

  A. Citizens should be able to choose their own values, and should respect others' right to do the same.
  B. Citizens need to participate in politics and to care for their community in order to enjoy true liberty.
  C. Citizens need to be neutral about their values and beliefs in order that others not be offended.
  D. Citizens must understand that choosing their own values is inconsistent with liberal freedom.

232. According to the passage, in order for citizens to "deliberate well about the common good" (line 54) citizens must possess all of the following EXCEPT:

  F. knowledge of public affairs.
  G. a neutral framework of rights.
  H. concern for fellow citizens.
  J. a sense of civic engagement.

233. The main point of the second paragraph (lines 10–23) is that:

   A. liberals and conservatives have essentially the same value systems.
   B. liberals and conservatives find governmental neutrality appealing for different reasons.
   C. conservatives are more interested in the nation's economy than are liberals.
   D. liberals are responsible for the idea that the U.S. government should be neutral.

234. The main point of the fifth paragraph (lines 45–66) is that:

   F. liberal and republican theories each demand that citizens take part in politics.
   G. liberal and republican theories each have their good points and their bad points.
   H. republican politicians tend to be more virtuous and compassionate than liberal politicians.
   J. republican theory requires that citizens demonstrate a concern for the common good.

235. As it is used in line 65, the phrase *formative politics* refers to a type of politics that:

   A. promotes important civic virtues.
   B. is consistent with liberal freedom.
   C. is part of a procedural republic.
   D. is distinct from self-rule.

236. If the last paragraph were deleted, what critical piece of information would be lost?

   F. What the author sees as the features that distinguish between procedural and liberal republics
   G. What the author sees as the centerpiece of republican political theory
   H. What the author sees as the central weakness of our current public philosophy
   J. What the author sees as the difference between liberal and republican political theories

237. As it is used in lines 68–69, the phrase *political experience* most nearly means:

   A. country's history.
   B. voting patterns.
   C. presidential campaigns.
   D. elective office.

238. The main point being made in lines 10–15 is that:

   F. a belief in citizens' rights to choose their own values is shared by people with different politics.
   G. liberals and conservatives can be found across the political spectrum.
   H. the aspiration to neutrality is guaranteed by the Constitution and supported by republican theory.
   J. the liberal tradition in American politics is somewhat limited in its theoretical background.

239. The last paragraph most strongly suggests that a "procedural republic" is a republic:

   A. known for having good political procedures.
   B. that has developed a formative politics.
   C. based upon many rules and regulations.
   D. with a neutral framework of rights.

240. The author of the passage claims that the liberal vision of freedom cannot provide liberty because that vision:

   F. gives citizens too many choices to consider.
   G. does not teach citizens to care about community.
   H. inspires moral neutrality, which is anti-government.
   J. depends too heavily on the concept of legislating morality.

Passage XXV

HUMANITIES: This passage is adapted from *Bowman's Store: A Journey to Myself* by Joseph Bruchac (©1997 by Joseph Bruchac). The author and his grandfather, Jesse Bowman, are Abenaki Indians.

I remember my grandfather's garden. It was around back, between my grandparents' house and the small two-room building we used for storing things.

Another of my earliest memories is walking
5 through the furrows of that newly plowed garden with my grandfather—who seemed taller than the biggest trees then—holding my hand. I could barely walk, even on level ground, but he wouldn't let me fall. I wore the same kind of overalls that he did, and people were
10 already calling me "Jess's Shadow."

That was how Lawrence Older put it one day when he was buying gasoline at my grandparents' filling station. "Jess," Larry said, with a twinkle in his eye, "that grandson of yours stays so close to you he don't
15 hardly leave room enough for your shadow."

Jess's Shadow? I didn't quite understand that name. My name was Sonny. I knew that for sure. That was the name my grandparents called me by. I never heard either of them speak to me or about me by any
20 other name.

I remember the day—I could not have been more than two and a half years old—when my grandfather said to me, "Sonny, cup out yer hands." I held them out together, trying to make a really good cup. Carefully,
25 taking the seeds out from the cloth sack he had slung over his shoulder, he filled my hands with kernels of golden corn. I stood there holding those seeds for him, watching as he took them, four at a time, to plant them.

"Yer turn now," he said when those seeds were
30 gone, and he held out one leathery hand filled with corn. I'd watched really carefully, so I knew what to do. I did it so well that my grandfather allowed that I was already better at it than he was. Then, as I planted my first hills of corn, he talked to me about things. He
35 always talked more when he was in his garden.

There in his garden, as he spaded or began to hoe, he would talk about the different plants, about the birds we heard singing, about how we had to watch for the woodchucks or the rabbits or the raccoons. Sometimes
40 he would talk about the old way of plowing with a team of horses, and he would tell me the names of the horses he'd loved—the last of them dead and gone a decade before I was born. He told me how, as their plows cut their way down into the rich earth that was the same
45 color as his face, he and his father used to turn up arrowheads.

"Indian arrowheads," he would say.

He had a name for that work of preparing his garden for the sweet corn and green beans and butternut
50 squash we always put in. I never heard anyone else say it just the way he did until I met Grampa's younger brother Jack, many years later, when I was a grown man. "Fitting the ground to plant." That is what Grampa called it. This is what Jack called it. This is
55 what their father, Lewis Bowman, had called it. Fitting the ground to plant.

Another spring day, perhaps a year later, I was following my grandfather while he worked in the garden. He had made a small hoe for me that year, and I was, as
60 always, trying to do exactly what he did. Then he stopped hoeing. I stopped too and waited. I remember that I heard a bird sing just then, a long ululating song.

"Oriole," my grandfather said. Then he bent over and picked something up. He brushed soil from it and
65 went down on one knee next to me.

I leaned close to look at the dark, blocky piece of flint that filled my grandfather's broad hand.

"Indian," my grandfather said. "Axhead."

He hefted it first in one hand and then the other.
70 He did it with the same care that my grandmother used when she was gathering eggs in the henhouse and putting them into the basket hung over her arm. Then he placed that axhead into my hands.

Thirty years after that day when my grandfather
75 put the stone axhead in my hands, I understood at last why, as I held that stone, my mind had filled with images of tall corn swaying in the wind, images of women dancing as they held the season's harvest in their hands. Hearing a friend tell the story of the
80 coming of corn was the last stroke of the hoe that fit my own mind to the earth my grandfather had given to me. And I knew that as long as my hands had the strength to hold a hoe, I would work that garden where corn had been cared for by my grandparents and by my great-
85 grandparents before them. I would listen to that land just as it had once been listened to by other men and women, generations of Abenaki people and Mohawk people whose stories were told in a tongue as old as the soil. Spring would find me preparing the earth for the
90 Corn Maiden, find me fitting the ground of my grandfather's garden to plant.

241. Which of the following statements best describes the nature of this passage?

A. A grandson learns to appreciate his grandfather, whom he had always had difficulty understanding before.
B. An adult reflects on time spent with his grandfather and comes to understand more fully what he learned from him.
C. A grown man looks back with nostalgia on his relationship with his grandfather and on a garden that no longer exists.
D. A grandson recounts childhood memories that bring back strong and often unpleasant emotions from his years spent with his grandfather.

242. The perspective from which the narrator relates the passage shifts most dramatically beginning with line:

    F. 16.
    G. 21.
    H. 57.
    J. 74.

243. It can reasonably be inferred that within the passage, the nickname Jess's Shadow represents all of the following about the narrator EXCEPT his:

    A. strong emotional bond with his grandfather.
    B. close physical proximity to his grandfather when the narrator was young.
    C. conscious imitation of his grandfather.
    D. feeling of being protected from other people by his grandfather.

244. In the fifth and sixth paragraphs (lines 21–35), the narrator approaches planting corn with his grandfather with what is best characterized as:

    F. a reluctant willingness to participate in an activity the narrator knows is important to his grandfather.
    G. a great enthusiasm that causes the narrator to be slightly careless in his work.
    H. an interest in every detail of the process in an effort to do the best job possible.
    J. a genuine interest in the work that fades as the work becomes more difficult.

245. The scene revealed in the tenth through fourteenth paragraphs (lines 57–73) is best described by which of the following?

    A. An older man shares with his grandson a symbol of their common heritage.
    B. Two people are brought closer together by their love of birds.
    C. A young child comes to value a small hoe given to him by his grandfather.
    D. The discovery of an Indian axhead leads a grandfather to a new appreciation of his past.

246. The images in lines 4–8 are used primarily to convey the narrator's sense as a young child of being:

    F. overly controlled by his grandfather.
    G. watched over by his awe-inspiring grandfather.
    H. puzzled by his grandfather's height.
    J. impressed by the size of his grandfather's garden.

247. The narrator suggests that Lawrence Older's comment, quoted in lines 13–15, was intended to express:

    A. amusement.
    B. concern.
    C. dismay.
    D. elation.

248. According to the passage, the narrator initially reacts to being called Jess's Shadow with confusion because:

    F. his parents had given him the name Sonny.
    G. he is no longer certain whether his name is Sonny or Jess's Shadow.
    H. he is unsure whether Lawrence Older was referring to him or to someone else.
    J. Sonny is the only name he remembers his grandparents using for him.

249. The narrator describes the term "fitting the ground to plant" as one that was:

    A. commonly used by people in the community where his grandfather lived.
    B. invented by his grandfather and used by the narrator.
    C. traditionally used by people in his grandfather's family.
    D. unfamiliar to the narrator until he was a grown man.

250. The author includes the fourteenth paragraph (lines 69–73) primarily to:

    F. introduce the character of the grandmother, who up to this point has been absent from the narrative.
    G. describe the type of work that the narrator's grandparents often had to do.
    H. establish that the narrator and his grandfather would often exchange small but meaningful gifts.
    J. portray the reverence with which the grandfather treated the object he had unearthed.

Passage XXVI

NATURAL SCIENCE: This passage is adapted from the book *Eggs: Nature's Perfect Package* by Robert Burton (©1987 by Robert Burton).

Birds are 'glorified reptiles' and some biologists believe that they are indeed no more than reptiles with feathers. It is not surprising, therefore, that birds' eggs are similar to those of reptiles. The main interest in
5 birds' eggs from an evolutionary point of view is the adaptation of the eggs of different species to particular lifestyles.

In both reptile and bird eggs, there is a large yolk which not only supplies the needs of the embryo but
10 will also sustain the newly hatched animal until it can feed. In birds' eggs, after the egg cell—consisting mainly of a ball of yolk—has been fertilized, it moves down the oviduct where it collects the albumen or 'egg white' and takes on its shell. The albumen is mainly a
15 filler for protecting the embryo, but it also supplements the yolk as a valuable source of protein and a reservoir of water. Between the albumen and the shell are two parchment-like shell membranes. When they are first formed they fit quite loosely, but during the next stage,
20 known as 'plumping', water and salts fill out the albumen until the membranes are taut. The shell is then attached firmly onto the outer membrane, as can be seen when peeling a hard-boiled egg.

The innermost layer of albumen is thick and forms
25 a hammock slung between the ends of the shell to keep the yolk suspended in the centre. Within it are two twisted cords called chalazae, which act as bearings to allow the yolk and embryo to rotate freely when the egg is turned by the parent bird in the nest. Chalazae are
30 presumably unnecessary in reptile eggs because they are never turned, and some, such as those of tortoises, will not hatch if they are turned accidentally.

The shell takes 15 to 16 hours to form in a domestic hen. It consists of crystals of calcite, a form of cal-
35 cium carbonate, strengthened with protein fibres which also attach it to the underlying membrane. The amount of calcium needed for each egg is about 2 grams. As no more than 25 milligrams are circulating in the blood of the hen, the balance must be mobilized from her
40 reserves. She cannot absorb enough calcium from her food while making the egg, so she has to remove it from her bones. Birds have developed a special kind of bone, called medullary bone, which females lay down in the marrow cavity of existing bones during the
45 weeks before laying commences and use as a source of calcium when the eggshells are being formed. Some birds even have difficulty in laying down this reserve because their diet is deficient in calcium. Shortage of calcium affects the breeding of scavenging birds, such
50 as vultures, which have a diet of pure meat; to over-come this problem some species switch to hunting small animals, which they swallow whole, during the breeding season. Another example of the ingenious methods used by birds to provide calcium for their eggs

55 can be seen on the Arctic tundra, where insect-eating sandpipers swallow the bones of long-dead lemmings; as a result there is more calcium in each clutch of eggs than there is in the adult's entire skeleton.

The shell of a hen's egg is peppered with 10,000
60 tiny pores, just visible to the naked eye as small depres-sions in the shell. These pores are used for the passage of oxygen, carbon dioxide and water vapour. Unlike a lung, however, the flow of gases cannot be regulated and relies purely on diffusion through the pores.
65 Nevertheless, the flow must be finely attuned to the needs of the embryo. As development proceeds, more oxygen is required, but the loss of water must be kept low. The eggshell's role in regulating gas flow and water loss is shown by the arrangement of pores in dif-
70 ferent eggs—quite simply, diffusion depends on the size and number of the pores. Of all the eggs studied, from the 1-gram eggs of warblers to the 1.5-kilogram ostrich eggs, the weight of the egg and hence its meta-bolic requirements is directly proportional to the total
75 cross-sectional area of the pores.

Birds' eggs are uniform in shape when compared with the eggs of reptiles, but there are significant varia-tions from the standard oval. Owls' eggs are noticeably more spherical than normal, while those of swifts and
80 swallows are longer and more elliptical, although it is not obvious why this should be. Many waders have eggs shaped like old-fashioned spinning tops, blunt at one end and tapering sharply at the other. The reason for this is clear: there are usually four in a clutch and,
85 being large for the size of the parent, they fit under its body better when packed points inward in the nest.

251. Which of the following best describes the content of the passage?
   A. A point by point comparison between the eggs of birds and those of reptiles
   B. A technical discussion of the development of birds' eggs, including some references for com-parison sake to those of reptiles
   C. An examination of how recent studies have shown that birds' eggs are less like reptile eggs than was previously thought
   D. A discussion of how from an evolutionary stand-point birds' eggs have become more adapted to their environment than reptile eggs have

252. Which of the following statements about the eggshell of a domestic hen is NOT supported by the passage?
   F. It contains about 10,000 tiny pores, which are vis-ible to the naked eye.
   G. It takes about 15 hours to form.
   H. It consists of crystals of calcite.
   J. It contains about 15 grams of calcium.

253. Which of the following statements best explains how the last paragraph functions in the passage as a whole?

   A. It summarizes the main points made about eggs in the preceding paragraphs.
   B. It introduces a comparison between reptile eggs and bird eggs.
   C. It brings the issue of shape into the discussion of significant features of an egg.
   D. It focuses attention on what puzzles biologists most about the design and function of eggs.

254. What explanation, if any, does the passage provide for why a parent bird turns the eggs in the nest?

   F. In some species, the parent turns the egg to maximize the exposure of the pores to oxygen and water.
   G. The parent bird turns the egg to ensure the equal distribution of its body heat to the entire clutch.
   H. The parent bird turns the egg as one of many measures it takes to determine if the egg is developing properly.
   J. The passage provides no explanation for this behavior.

255. The passage indicates that from the inside out a bird's egg is made up of the following elements in the following order:

   A. yolk, chalazae-containing albumen, two shell membranes, shell.
   B. yolk, egg cell, inner shell, parchment membranes, outer shell.
   C. yolk, parchment membrane, cell membrane, albumen, inner shell, chalazae, outer shell.
   D. yolk, chalazae, parchment membranes, albumen, shell.

256. As it is used in line 20, the word *plumping* refers to the:

   F. phase in which the adult female bird increases her nutrient intake in preparation for egg-laying.
   G. formation of two parchment-like membranes around the fertilized egg cell.
   H. stage during which increased levels of water and salts expand the albumen in a developing egg.
   J. adjustments a nesting bird makes in its plumage to maximize its ability to warm a clutch of eggs.

257. Which of the following best describes the form and function of the chalazae as they are described in the passage?

   A. A hammock inside the shells of birds and reptiles that protects the developing embryo
   B. Two twisted cords that allow the yolk and embryo in a bird's egg to rotate freely when the egg is moved
   C. Two small vessels that allow the exchange of nutrients and waste between the yolk and the embryo in a bird's egg
   D. Two thin layers of protein that protect the embryo in bird and reptile eggs once plumping has occurred

258. According to the passage, protein fibers in the eggshells of birds serve to:

   F. deliver crystals of calcite to the bones of the developing embryo.
   G. facilitate the movement of life-sustaining gases to the embryo.
   H. strengthen the shell and attach it to the underlying membrane.
   J. suspend the yolk in a hammock-like feature for protective purposes.

259. Which of the following best describes the medullary bone and its significance in bird development?

   A. It is the lower of two hollow bones that together form the legs of a bird.
   B. It is a calcium-rich bone in small Arctic mammals that become the preferred prey of breeding Arctic birds.
   C. It is a pliable bone that temporarily encases the spinal cord in developing bird and reptile embryos until it is replaced by a stronger bone.
   D. It is a supplemental bone that forms inside a hen's existing bones prior to egg-laying to serve as a source of calcium.

260. What advantage, if any, does the passage suggest is offered by the shape of the eggs of waders?

   F. The shape provides protection from certain kinds of egg-eating predators that don't recognize the wader egg as an egg.
   G. The shape allows the egg to be positioned efficiently along with other eggs underneath the nesting adult wader.
   H. The shape provides the embryo the space it needs to extend and thereby strengthen its developing wings.
   J. The passage does not indicate what advantage the shape of these eggs provides.

Passage XXVII

PROSE FICTION: This passage is adapted from the novel *The Bonesetter's Daughter* by Amy Tan (©2001 by Amy Tan).

The setting of the passage is a small town in China during the early part of the twentieth century. The capital city of China, now known in English as Beijing, formerly was called Peking.

When I was growing up, nearly two thousand people lived in Immortal Heart. It was crowded, packed from one edge of the valley to the other. We had a brick maker, a sack weaver, and a dye mill. We had twenty-
5 four market days, six temple fairs, and a primary school that GaoLing and I went to when we were not helping our family at home. We had all kinds of peddlers who went from house to house, selling fresh bean curd and steamed buns, twisted dough and colorful candies. A
10 few coppers, that was all you needed to make your stomach as happy as a rich man's.

The Liu clan had lived in Immortal Heart for six centuries. For that amount of time, the sons had been inkstick makers who sold their goods to travelers. They
15 had lived in the same courtyard house that had added rooms, and later wings, when one mother four hundred years ago gave birth to eight sons, one a year. The family home grew from a simple three-pillar house to a compound with wings stretching five pillars each.

20 All in all, our family was successful but not so much that we caused great envy. We ate meat or bean curd at almost every meal. We had new padded jackets every winter, no holes. We had money to give for the temple, the opera, the fair. But the men of our family
25 also had ambitions. They were always looking for more. They said that in Peking, more people wrote important documents. Those important documents required more good ink. Peking was where more of the big money was. Around 1920, Father, my uncles, and
30 their sons went there to sell the ink. From then on, that was where they lived most of the time, in the back room of a shop in the old Pottery-Glazing District.

In our family, the women made the ink. We stayed home. We all worked—me, GaoLing, my aunts and girl
35 cousins, everybody. Even the babies and Great-Granny had a job of picking out stones from the dried millet we boiled for breakfast. We gathered each day in the inkmaking studio. According to Great-Granny, the studio began as a grain shed that sat along the front
40 wall of the courtyard house. Over the years, one generation of sons added brick walls and a tile roof. Another strengthened the beams and lengthened it by two pillars. The next tiled the floors and dug pits for storing the ingredients. Then other descendants made a cellar
45 for keeping the inksticks away from the heat and cold.

Because our ink was the best quality, we had to keep the tables and the floors clean year-round. With the dusty yellow winds from the Gobi Desert, this was not easy to do. The window openings had to be covered
50 with both glass and thick paper. In the summer, we hung netting over the doorways to keep out the insects. In the winter, it was sheep hides to keep out the snow.

I can still smell the ingredients of our ink. There were several kinds of fragrant soot: pine, cassia, cam-
55 phor, and the wood of the chopped-down Immortal Tree. There was also a glue of sticky paste mixed with many oils. Then we added a sweet poisonous flower that helped resist insects and rats. That was how special our ink was, all those lasting smells.

60 We made the ink a little at a time. If a fire broke out, as it had a couple of hundred years before, all the supplies and stock would not be lost at once. Each of us had at least one part in a long list of things to do. First there was burning and grinding, measuring and
65 pouring. Then came stirring and molding, drying and carving. And finally, wrapping and counting, storing and stacking. One season I had to wrap, only that. My mind could wander, but my fingers still moved like small machines. Another season I had to use very fine
70 tweezers to pluck bugs that had fallen onto the sticks. Whenever GaoLing did this, she left too many dents. Precious Auntie's job was to sit at a long table and press the sooty mixture into the stone molds. When the ink was dry, she used a long, sharp tool to carve the
75 good-luck words and drawings into the sticks. Her cal-ligraphy was even better than Father's.

It was boring work, but we were proud of our secret family recipe. It yielded just the right color and hardness. An inkstick of ours could last ten years or
80 more. It did not dry out and crumble, or grow soggy with moisture. And if the sticks were stored in the cool-ness of a root cellar, as ours were, they could last from

one great period of history into another. Those who used our ink said the same. It didn't matter how much
85 heat or moisture or dirt from fingers soaked into the page, their words lasted, black and strong.

261. The point of view from which the passage is told is best described as that of:

    A. a child living in a small town in China.
    B. an adult remembering her childhood in China.
    C. an inkmaker describing the century-old production process she still uses.
    D. a great-grandmother whose family makes ink.

262. According to the passage, the men in the family lived in Peking most of the time because they:

    F. wanted to write important documents in the capital.
    G. made pottery in the Pottery-Glazing District.
    H. were ambitious salesmen in the Pottery-Glazing District.
    J. produced ink in the Pottery-Glazing District.

263. According to the passage, the family's ink studio consisted of a:

    A. refurbished shed, pits, and a cellar.
    B. house, a courtyard, and a cellar.
    C. refurbished shed, a courtyard, and a cellar.
    D. storeroom, a house, and pits.

264. It can most reasonably be inferred from the passage that one ingredient being burned (lines 64–65) to make the ink was:

    F. millet or another grain.
    G. roots from the cellar.
    H. wooden beams from the compound.
    J. wood from the Immortal Tree.

265. The main purpose of the last paragraph is to:

    A. explain the importance of storing inksticks in a cool place.
    B. show that the family refused to share its recipe for making ink, which remained a secret.
    C. illustrate the lasting quality of the Liu clan's ink.
    D. indicate that Chinese history is divided into a series of "great periods."

266. As it is used in line 10, the word *coppers* most likely refers to:

    F. ink-storage containers.
    G. metal cooking pots.
    H. police officers.
    J. coins.

267. The passage makes clear that the house grew from a simple house to a compound because:

    A. the family business required more and more space.
    B. one mother in the family had borne many sons.
    C. the storage of ink ingredients had taken up several rooms.
    D. everybody in the family worked in the inkmaking studio.

268. The narrator makes clear that one mark of success for her family was:

    F. eating dried millet for breakfast every day.
    G. owning sheep hides to provide warmth in winter.
    H. having bean curd or meat at almost every meal.
    J. giving birth to a son each year for many years.

269. Which of the following does the passage suggest had happened about two hundred years earlier?

    A. The family had added a secret fragrance to the ink.
    B. The ink and its ingredients had been damaged or lost in a fire.
    C. The family had experimented with yellow-colored ink.
    D. There had been an invasion of pests that had ruined the ink.

270. Which of the following comparisons regarding calligraphy does the narrator make?

    F. The narrator's calligraphy was better than GaoLing's.
    G. Precious Auntie's calligraphy was better than Father's.
    H. Great-Granny's calligraphy was better than the narrator's.
    J. Father's calligraphy was the best of all the family members'.

Passage XXVIII

SOCIAL SCIENCE: This passage is adapted from the article "High Over Kitty Hawk, Looking for a Profit" by Paul Hoffman (©2003 by The New York Times Company).

The foggy lens of history has been kind to Wilbur and Orville Wright. We regard the boys from Dayton, Ohio, as American heroes who flew the first airplane and ushered in the age of air travel. At the time, though,
5 the brothers' achievement was barely recognized—and their motives were far from visionary.

On Dec. 17, 1903, the Wrights took turns making short ascents over the dunes of Kill Devil Hills, four miles south of Kitty Hawk, N.C., in a propeller-driven
10 biplane powered by an internal combustion engine. They each got airborne twice—with Wilbur going the farthest, 852 feet in 59 seconds—before a gust flipped the plane while it was on the ground.

But what was really so historic about the flight?
15 The Wrights were certainly not the first people to rise above the Earth. Balloonists had been doing that for more than a century. In June 1783, Joseph and Etienne Montgolfier, paper makers from Annonay, France, demonstrated in a public square the first hot-air balloon
20 capable of carrying a load as heavy as a human being.

The Wrights were also not the first to pilot a heavier-than-air craft. In 1849, Sir George Cayley, a British physicist, constructed a three-winged glider that lifted a 10-year-old child a few feet. After four years of
25 further experimentation, Cayley enlarged his "boy glider" into an adult-size craft and sent a grown man through the air for several hundred feet.

Nor were the Wright brothers the first to achieve powered flight. In 1901, a Brazilian named Alberto
30 Santos-Dumont entertained all of Paris by making a 14-mile trip over the city, including a revolution of the Eiffel Tower, in a cigar-shaped balloon powered by a car engine.

The Wrights were not even the first to leave the
35 ground in a powered plane. In 1874, Felix du Temple, a French naval officer, watched the steam-powered plane he devised speed down a ski-jump-like ramp and sputter through the air with a young sailor at the helm.

Of course, it is one thing to be hurled through the
40 air for a few fleeting moments—what aviation historians call a "hop"—and quite another to make a controlled flight under one's own power. Control is what the Wright brothers so ably and singularly demonstrated. While other aviation pioneers concentrated on
45 how to power a plane—not a difficult task by the time automobile engines had come into their own—the Wrights focused on how to stabilize it.

Many early aviation pioneers employed horizontal and vertical rudders to keep their experimental aircraft
50 from veering right or left or unintentionally diving or rising. But only the Wrights appreciated another necessity: preventing the plane from suddenly rolling because of a difference in wind on the left and right wings. They ingeniously countered roll by "wing-
55 warping"—using flexible wing tips with wire controls so that the pilot can bring the right wing into the wind at a different inclination from the left one, creating lift.

Thus while the brothers' flights were remarkable, they were hardly bolts from the blue. Rather, their
60 achievement was a vital step in a long progression toward controlled flight. And by no means did their success make them overnight celebrities: in 1903 hardly anyone heard about their flights, and those who did were not inclined to believe the tale.

65 The Wright brothers chose the Outer Banks of North Carolina not just for the favorable winds, but also for the remoteness. They wanted to fly in near secrecy because they weren't sure they could patent their plane, and wanted to profit from it before others
70 knocked off the design. Yet, they expected the press to hail them as the conquerors of the air.

But reporters were skeptical. Six days before Kitty Hawk, a crowd of official witnesses and Washington bigwigs had gathered to watch what was supposed to be
75 the maiden flight of the giant Aerodrome designed by Samuel Langley, the head of the Smithsonian Institution. The plane was catapulted from a houseboat in the Potomac but instead of rising into the air plunged into the frigid waters. News reporters could not accept that
80 two bicycle mechanics with little money had succeeded while the dean of American science, financed with government money, had failed.

The few newspapers that wrote about Kitty Hawk got everything wrong. The Dayton Daily News
85 described the Wrights' aircraft as a dirigible and planted the story under the headline "Dayton Boys Emulate Great Santos-Dumont." The first eyewitness account of their subsequent flights was published more than two years after Kitty Hawk, in an obscure maga-
90 zine called *Gleanings in Bee Culture*.

271. The point of view from which the passage is told is best described as that of:

A. a writer with a historical perspective who wants to correct misconceptions about early flight.

B. a relative of the Wright brothers who wants to build a monument in their honor.

C. an inventor who wants to illustrate how difficult it is to invent something important.

D. an observer of the initial Kitty Hawk flight who is critical of how it was reported, both then and later.

272. What does the passage indicate was the main difference between the Wright brothers' aircraft and the works of other inventors?

   F. The Wright brothers succeeded in flying when other inventors had failed.
   G. Other inventors used balloons, not heavier-than-air craft.
   H. No other inventors had used both horizontal and vertical rudders.
   J. The Wright brothers prevented the rolling of a plane while other inventors had concentrated on powering a plane.

273. According to the passage, what was one reason reporters were skeptical that the Wright brothers had successfully flown?

   A. The first story of the Wright brothers' flight was not published for two years.
   B. It was widely assumed that the Wright brothers wanted to profit from their ideas.
   C. A leader in science with government funding had failed to have his own plane fly.
   D. Balloonists had already been flying for more than a century.

274. The main purpose of the last paragraph is to show that the Wright brothers:

   F. were successful in their attempt to fly.
   G. had merely duplicated what Alberto Santos-Dumont had done earlier.
   H. were originally from Dayton, Ohio.
   J. were initially poorly covered by the media.

275. The main purpose of the second paragraph (lines 7–13) is to:

   A. argue that more people should admire the Wright brothers for their accomplishments.
   B. explain why it took two years for the first eyewitness account of the Wright brothers' initial flight to be published.
   C. detail the first successful flights of the Wright brothers near Kitty Hawk.
   D. clarify that it took many more years before the airplane was perfected.

276. As it is used in line 31, the word *revolution* most nearly means:

   F. political rebellion.
   G. radical change.
   H. circular course.
   J. pivotal invention.

277. The passage makes clear that it became easier for inventors to power their aircraft after:

   A. the Wright brothers flew near Kitty Hawk.
   B. automobile engines had been developed.
   C. they started adding horizontal and vertical rudders.
   D. Sir George Cayley perfected his "boy glider."

278. The statement "they were hardly bolts from the blue" (line 59) most strongly suggests that flights like the Wright brothers' were:

   F. unsurprising.
   G. improbable.
   H. unusual.
   J. remarkable.

279. The passage makes clear that one personal reason the Wright brothers had for testing their aircraft where they did was to:

   A. avoid the negative publicity that would come if their plane failed to fly.
   B. keep away anyone who couldn't help if something went wrong during the test flight.
   C. maintain confidentiality despite the many interviews they had previously given.
   D. make money from their invention by isolating it from potential imitators.

280. It can most reasonably be inferred from the tenth paragraph (lines 65–71) that the author believes:

   F. the Wright brothers shouldn't have expected to be praised by the press.
   G. North Carolina was too windy for flying experimental aircraft safely.
   H. secrecy is necessary for inventors.
   J. reporters can't be trusted to get their information correct.

Passage XXIX

HUMANITIES: This passage is adapted from the article "The Comics" by M. Thomas Inge (©1990 by Smithsonian Institution).

Comic art has much in common with all the other forms of literary and visual communication of the twentieth century. As in fiction, the elements of narrative, characterization, and setting are important in accom-
5 plished comic art; and as in poetry, ideas must be developed within a very short period of reading time, a few seconds for a comic strip and fifteen minutes or less for a comic book story. As in drama, a story or incident must be staged before our eyes within the artificial
10 strictures of a box-like frame and with all the limitations of a play in terms of compressed time, dialogue, and plot development. As in a motion picture, such visual devices as cutting, framing, close-ups, and montage are used by the comic artist, and the point-of-view
15 is free to roam the world over to places known and fantastic.

Although the comics share a good deal with other forms of artistic expression, they differ in distinct ways and provide a method of communication which is ulti-
20 mately unique. For one thing, comics depend for their effectiveness on a balanced combination of word and picture, the one depending fully on the other for maximum effect. Thus some commentators have suggested that in comic strip art, if either the picture or the text is
25 not essential to understanding, then a proper balance is lacking.

There are other essential features of comic art, which distinguish it from other art forms. For example, comic strips appear on a daily basis in newspapers
30 delivered to homes, while comic books appear on a monthly basis in special serial publications sold at newsstands or comic book shops (and more recently a few bookstores). Both are usually printed on inexpensive paper, and while comic books generally appear in
35 color, comic strips have traditionally been in color only on Sundays.

Another distinguishing feature is that most comic strips and books feature a set of recurring characters with whom the reader becomes familiar over a period
40 of time, with an occasional retelling of their past histories in capsule form. It is the accumulative weight of familiarity over several months or years of reading experience with the characters through which the development of personality occurs, although many characters
45 remain essentially the same throughout their lifetimes. Especially in humor, a set of stock and stereotyped players is essential to the daily comic routines, formulaic repetition being one of those techniques which most often make people laugh (as in Charlie Brown's
50 unsuccessful attempt to kick the football held annually by Lucy in the *Peanuts* comic strip).

Time is also treated differently in that generally it has no effect on the lives of characters in the comics. They do not grow old chronologically (with the notable
55 exception of *Gasoline Alley* in which several generations of a family have grown old along with the readers). The dramatic narrative is open-ended and the action, whenever the reading experience begins, is always somewhere in the middle. Thus comics charac-
60 ters inhabit a world that has no beginning and no end, that remains constant and is shored up against the usual influences of change and deterioration. Only in the case of politically satiric strips, such as *Doonesbury, Bloom County,* or *Pogo,* are immediately contemporary events
65 and personalities reflected or depicted in the comics.

Since comics characters inhabit a world of silence, due to the restrictions of the printed page which cannot allow for motion and sound, dialogue and noise require a special set of conventions. Words are usually spoken
70 in cloud-like puffs of smoke called balloons. Because of the limited amount of space, dialogue must be kept to an absolute minimum and the joke or story told with the fewest words possible, a continual challenge to the skills of the writer of a comic. As for sounds, the comic
75 artist must resort to the poetic device of onomatopoeia, and while many traditional words such as *slam, bang, sock, smash,* or *bump* will serve the situation, new word coinages have proven necessary. Thus the comics have enriched American English by such contributions as
80 *wow, plop, zowie, bam,* and *whap.* In order to convey ideas which cannot be expressed with words, the comic artist has also developed a vocabulary of visual symbols, such as bubble balloons for silent thoughts, stars to show pain, drops of water to express labor or worry,
85 or radiating lines to convey pride or enlightenment. It is remarkable how effective these conventions are in creating the impression of a loud and noisy medium.

---

281. Suppose a reader had composed the following summary of the passage:

> Comic art has been an important part of U.S. culture for decades, reflecting the historical and aesthetic changes within the country and its changing values.

Would this be an effective summary of the passage?

A. Yes, because the passage focuses on how comic artists have used their art to reflect the changing culture.

B. Yes, because the passage focuses on how comic artists have developed their own storytelling methods over many decades.

C. No, because the passage focuses on the established practices that comic artists have traditionally used in comic art.

D. No, because the passage focuses on the connections between comic art and film.

282. The primary purpose of the first paragraph is to:

    F. compare the elements of comic art to elements of other artistic forms.

    G. describe the various techniques used in a wide variety of artistic forms.

    H. introduce the history and development of comic art as a form of artistic expression.

    J. define the limitations of various forms of artistic expression.

283. It can reasonably be inferred from the passage that the author believes which of the following about the publication materials used in comic art?

    A. High-quality paper is necessary in the publication of the best comic art.

    B. The use of color in comic art enhances the distinction between pictures and words.

    C. Whether color or good paper is used in comic art is irrelevant to its artistic quality.

    D. The use of recyclable paper is necessary for the purest forms of comic art.

284. The passage makes all of the following points about time and the comics EXCEPT that:

    F. comic strips and comic books appear in print on a regular schedule.

    G. readers can slow the pace of a story line by the speed at which they read the comics.

    H. the dramatic narrative is open ended and the action is always somewhere in the middle.

    J. the passage of time usually has little effect on the characters' lives.

285. Which of the following questions does the passage NOT answer?

    A. What elements do comic art and literary art share?

    B. Are stock characters used in humorous comic strips?

    C. How is the effect of sound created in comic art?

    D. What drawing styles are most popular in comic art?

286. As it is used in lines 69 and 86, the word *conventions* most nearly means:

    F. gatherings of comic artists.

    G. stereotypical situations.

    H. common courtesies.

    J. customary practices.

287. The passage mentions which one of the following poetic devices as having been used by comic artists to create linguistic effects?

    A. Rhyme

    B. Onomatopoeia

    C. Metaphor

    D. Hyperbole

288. According to the passage, balance must be achieved in comics between:

    F. word and picture.

    G. humor and drama.

    H. sound and silence.

    J. stereotyped and original characters.

289. The passage states that the development of the personalities of characters in comic art occurs as a result of:

    A. dialogue.

    B. descriptive character sketches.

    C. familiarity over time.

    D. stereotypes.

290. According to the passage, direct references to current real-world events and personalities are found only in which type of comic?

    F. Political satire

    G. Family

    H. Horror

    J. Science fiction

Passage XXX

NATURAL SCIENCE: This passage is adapted from *The Blind Watchmaker* by Richard Dawkins (©1986 by Richard Dawkins).

The South American and the African weakly electric fish are quite unrelated to each other, but both live in the same kinds of waters in their respective continents, waters that are too muddy for vision to be effec-
5 tive. The physical principle that they exploit—electric fields in water—is even more alien to our consciousness than that of bats and dolphins. We at least have a subjective idea of what an echo is, but we have almost no subjective idea of what it might be like to perceive
10 an electric field. We didn't even know of the existence of electricity until a couple of centuries ago.

It is easy to see on the dinner plate that the muscles down each side of any fish are arranged as a row of segments, a *battery* of muscle units. In most fish they
15 contract successively to throw the body into sinuous waves, which propel it forward. In electric fish, both strongly and weakly electric ones, they have become a battery in the electric sense. Each segment (cell) of the battery generates a voltage. These voltages are con-
20 nected up in series along the length of the fish so that, in a strongly electric fish such as an electric eel, the whole battery generates as much as 1 amp at 650 volts. An electric eel is powerful enough to knock a man out. Weakly electric fish don't need high voltages or cur-
25 rents for their purposes, which are purely information gathering ones.

The principle of electrolocation, as it has been called, is fairly well understood at the level of physics though not, of course, at the level of what it feels like
30 to be an electric fish. The following account applies equally to African and South American weakly electric fish: the convergence is that thorough. Current flows from the front half of the fish, out into the water in lines that curve back and return to the tail end of the
35 fish. There are not really discrete 'lines' but a continuous 'field,' an invisible cocoon of electricity surrounding the fish's body. However, for human visualization it is easiest to think in terms of a family of curved lines leaving the fish through a series of portholes spaced
40 along the front half of the body, all curving round in the water and diving into the fish again at the tip of its tail. The fish has what amounts to a tiny voltmeter monitoring the voltage at each 'porthole.' If the fish is suspended in open water with no obstacles around, the
45 lines are smooth curves. The tiny voltmeters at each porthole all register the voltage as 'normal' for their porthole. But if some obstacle appears in the vicinity, say a rock or an item of food, the lines of current that happen to hit the obstacle will be changed. This will
50 change the voltage at any porthole whose current line is affected, and the appropriate voltmeter will register the fact. So in theory a computer, by comparing the pattern of voltages registered by the voltmeters at all the portholes, could calculate the pattern of obstacles around
55 the fish. This is apparently what the fish brain does. Once again, this doesn't have to mean that the fish are

clever mathematicians. They have an apparatus that solves the necessary equations, just as our brains unconsciously solve equations every time we catch a
60 ball.

It is very important that the fish's own body is kept absolutely rigid. The computer in the head couldn't cope with the extra distortions that would be introduced if the fish's body were bending and twisting
65 like an ordinary fish. Electric fish have, at least twice independently, hit upon this ingenious method of navigation, but they have had to pay a price: they have had to give up the normal, highly efficient, fish method of swimming, throwing the whole body into serpentine
70 waves. They have solved the problem by keeping the body stiff as a poker, but they have a single long fin all the way along the length of the body. Then instead of the whole body being thrown into waves, just the long fin is. The fish's progress through the water is rather
75 slow, but it does move, and apparently the sacrifice of fast movement is worth it: the gains in navigation seem to outweigh the losses in speed of swimming. Fascinatingly, the South American electric fish have hit upon almost exactly the same solution as the African ones,
80 but not quite. Both groups have developed a single long fin that runs the whole length of the body, but in the African fish it runs along the back whereas in the South American fish it runs along the belly.

291. Which of the following questions about the South American and African weakly electric fish does the passage NOT directly answer?

A. What do they use electrolocation for?
B. What effect does their differing fin location have?
C. What do the voltmeters on the fish do?
D. Why do they swim more slowly than ordinary fish?

292. The author does all of the following in the second paragraph (lines 12–26) EXCEPT:

F. contrast electric fish to other types of fish.
G. compare strongly electric fish to weakly electric fish.
H. begin to explain electrolocation.
J. give an example of a weakly electric fish.

293. According to the author's simplified description in the passage, the flow of electric current generated by the weakly electric fish enters the water from the:

A. tip of the tail and is reabsorbed into the head.
B. head and is reabsorbed into the portholes.
C. portholes and is reabsorbed into the portholes.
D. portholes and is reabsorbed into the tip of the tail.

294. According to the passage, a weakly electric fish would know if there were a rock in its path because the:

   F. lines of current the fish generates would be in a smooth curve around the fish.

   G. fish would receive a small shock when the current it generates contacted the rock.

   H. current the fish generates would create a sound when it contacted objects.

   J. affected lines of current generated by the fish would produce detectable changes in voltage.

295. The main focus of the last paragraph is on the way weakly electric fish differ from ordinary fish in terms of:

   A. the length of their bodies.

   B. how they swim.

   C. how they use sight.

   D. the complexity of their brains.

296. The passage indicates that weakly electric fish have developed a system of navigation using electric fields because:

   F. as predators, it gives them an advantage over other fish.

   G. it helps keep them on course during lengthy migrations.

   H. they are nocturnal creatures and swim only in the dark.

   J. their habitats are muddy and therefore visibility is limited.

297. As it is used in line 14, the word *battery* most nearly refers to the:

   A. arrangement of fish muscles.

   B. electric field produced by fish muscles.

   C. energy that propels fish forward.

   D. different kinds of muscles contained in fish.

298. According to the passage, an electric eel is a type of:

   F. South American weakly electric fish.

   G. African weakly electric fish.

   H. strongly electric fish.

   J. dangerous water snake.

299. The author indicates that he chooses to describe the electric field emitted by the weakly electric fish as a "family of curved lines" (line 38) because:

   A. that is the precise scientific terminology for the phenomenon.

   B. this image is relatively easy for people to visualize.

   C. cocoons are made from curved lines.

   D. each line supports the others, like family members support each other.

300. According to the passage, successful navigation for weakly electric fish requires:

   F. frequent breaks in motion.

   G. an unobstructed swimming area.

   H. a rigid body.

   J. rapid water currents.

Chapter 11:
Answers and Explanations

Check your answers to the questions in chapter 10 with the following answer key. If you missed a question, review the answer explanations on the pages following the answer key.

Answer Key

1.	A	50.	H	99.	D
2.	G	51.	B	100.	F
3.	A	52.	F	101.	A
4.	H	53.	A	102.	H
5.	C	54.	F	103.	C
6.	G	55.	C	104.	J
7.	B	56.	G	105.	D
8.	F	57.	D	106.	F
9.	A	58.	J	107.	D
10.	J	59.	A	108.	F
11.	A	60.	J	109.	B
12.	J	61.	B	110.	G
13.	D	62.	F	111.	B
14.	F	63.	C	112.	F
15.	B	64.	H	113.	C
16.	H	65.	D	114.	J
17.	C	66.	F	115.	D
18.	G	67.	D	116.	H
19.	D	68.	G	117.	B
20.	J	69.	B	118.	F
21.	A	70.	H	119.	B
22.	H	71.	B	120.	J
23.	D	72.	F	121.	C
24.	F	73.	D	122.	J
25.	C	74.	G	123.	A
26.	H	75.	D	124.	F
27.	D	76.	H	125.	B
28.	J	77.	B	126.	G
29.	B	78.	F	127.	D
30.	H	79.	D	128.	H
31.	D	80.	H	129.	B
32.	G	81.	D	130.	H
33.	C	82.	F	131.	B
34.	G	83.	B	132.	J
35.	D	84.	H	133.	A
36.	G	85.	D	134.	F
37.	D	86.	H	135.	C
38.	G	87.	B	136.	G
39.	C	88.	H	137.	D
40.	F	89.	A	138.	J
41.	A	90.	G	139.	A
42.	G	91.	B	140.	H
43.	B	92.	F	141.	D
44.	F	93.	A	142.	H
45.	C	94.	H	143.	B
46.	J	95.	C	144.	J
47.	D	96.	F	145.	D
48.	J	97.	B	146.	G
49.	C	98.	H	147.	D

148.	H	199.	C	250.	J
149.	B	200.	J	251.	B
150.	F	201.	D	252.	J
151.	A	202.	H	253.	C
152.	F	203.	A	254.	J
153.	D	204.	G	255.	A
154.	H	205.	D	256.	H
155.	B	206.	F	257.	B
156.	H	207.	B	258.	H
157.	A	208.	H	259.	D
158.	G	209.	A	260.	G
159.	B	210.	G	261.	B
160.	F	211.	D	262.	H
161.	D	212.	F	263.	A
162.	F	213.	D	264.	J
163.	A	214.	F	265.	C
164.	G	215.	D	266.	J
165.	B	216.	G	267.	B
166.	J	217.	C	268.	H
167.	C	218.	G	269.	B
168.	H	219.	D	270.	G
169.	A	220.	G	271.	A
170.	F	221.	C	272.	J
171.	D	222.	H	273.	C
172.	J	223.	A	274.	J
173.	C	224.	G	275.	C
174.	G	225.	C	276.	H
175.	C	226.	F	277.	B
176.	H	227.	D	278.	F
177.	A	228.	G	279.	D
178.	J	229.	B	280.	F
179.	D	230.	F	281.	C
180.	G	231.	B	282.	F
181.	D	232.	G	283.	C
182.	F	233.	B	284.	G
183.	C	234.	J	285.	D
184.	J	235.	A	286.	J
185.	B	236.	H	287.	B
186.	H	237.	A	288.	F
187.	B	238.	F	289.	C
188.	F	239.	D	290.	F
189.	D	240.	G	291.	B
190.	H	241.	B	292.	J
191.	B	242.	J	293.	D
192.	H	243.	D	294.	J
193.	D	244.	H	295.	B
194.	G	245.	A	296.	J
195.	A	246.	G	297.	A
196.	J	247.	A	298.	H
197.	A	248.	J	299.	B
198.	G	249.	C	300.	H

Explanatory Answers

Passage I

Question 1. The best answer is **A** because the passage identifies Shades Bowen as one of the other local musicians in the "bullpen" (lines 5–6) and goes on to state that, of those local musicians, Everett Payne "was the one being invited to sit in" (line 15) and play with the band that night. In this context, "the one" indicates that only Everett was sitting in, and no mention is made in the passage of any other musician sitting in.

The best answer is NOT:

B because although the passage indicates that Everett Payne is "not long out of the army" (lines 14–15), the passage makes no mention of Shades Bowen having been in the army as well.

C because although the passage refers to all the people in the "bullpen" as "young locals" (line 9), the passage makes no mention of Shades Bowen's age.

D because the passage states that Everett Payne joined Shades Bowen in the "bullpen" (lines 5–7) where "young locals gathered . . . each Sunday evening, hoping for a chance to perform" (lines 9–10). This indicates that Shades Bowen was a local musician himself, and there is no indication in the passage that Shades Bowen had any role in deciding which other local musicians were allowed to play with the band.

Question 2. The best answer is **G** because the statement in question (line 62) describes the audience's physical reaction to Everett Payne's performance. This performance is described in great detail in the preceding paragraph (lines 48–61) as being impressive enough to warrant such a reaction.

The best answer is NOT:

F because the statement in question (line 62) refers to the audience's physical reaction to the improvisational passages that Payne played after he had taken his time "paying his respects to the tune as written" (lines 48–49). This indicates that the audience reaction was not based on "initial expectations" but rather on later developments in the playing of the song "Sonny Boy Blue."

H because the statement in question (line 62) supports, rather than counteracts, the narrator's description of Payne's performance.

J because there is no mention in the passage that Payne is well known by the audience.

Question 3. The best answer is **A** because the passage describes the jazz show as "winding down" (lines 1–2) near the end of the second set. This implies that the second set is the final set of the show.

The best answer is NOT:

B because there is no description in the passage of the first set or of the length of either the first or the second set.

C because the narrator mentions that the show is "winding down" (lines 1–2), which suggests that there will be no third set.

D because the passage states that the jazz show is "nearing the end of the second set" (line 1) when the musicians in the "bullpen" were called up to play. If the *entire* second set was performed solely by musicians from the "bullpen," then they would not be "called up to play" only toward the end of that set.

Question 4. The best answer is **H** because the passage states that when the purists first heard Payne's choice of music, they "slouched deeper in their chairs in open disgust" (lines 36–37).

The best answer is NOT:

F because although the passage mentions the silence following Payne's performance (lines 81–83), there is no specific mention of the audience reacting to Payne's choice of music with silence.

G because the audience's in-suck of breath (line 62) is in response to Payne's performance, not to his choice of music.

J because the purists stood up at the end of Payne's performance "in languid praise" (line 88) of Payne, not as a reaction to Payne's choice of music.

Question 5. The best answer is **C** because the narrator describes how she watched as Payne "slowly mounted the bandstand and conferred with the bassist and drummer" (lines 26–27).

The best answer is NOT:

A because Payne did not move quickly to the bandstand. Rather, the narrator describes him as moving with "a deliberate pause between each step" (lines 18–19).

B because the narrator describes Payne as sitting down to play "without in any way acknowledging the audience" (line 30).

D because the narrator says that Payne sat down at the piano "without announcing the name of the tune he intended playing" (lines 28–29).

Question 6. The best answer is **G** because the purists are described as reacting negatively to Payne because of his choice of song (lines 35–37), suggesting intolerance. They are also described as usually refusing "to applaud even genius" (line 88), implying snobbishness.

The best answer is NOT:

F because although the term *purist* in the context of a jazz audience suggests that they may be knowledgeable about jazz music, the purists in this audience are described as reacting negatively to Payne because of his choice of song (lines 35–37), suggesting that they are intolerant rather than open-minded.

H because the passage makes no mention of whether or not the purists are educated. Additionally, the purists are not portrayed as rational, as they usually refuse to acknowledge a praiseworthy performance (lines 87–88).

J because although the purists may be "uninhibited" in that they visibly react or do not react to performances as they please, the passage makes no mention of their "inexperience" regarding jazz. In fact, the opposite impression is created by the purists' initial disgust at the prospect of hearing a "hokey" (line 38), or old-fashioned, tune such as "Sonny Boy Blue." Moreover, the term *purist* in general denotes someone devoted to the most essential or "pure" expression of a particular idea or practice, and such devotion usually indicates a deep familiarity with the object of their devotion rather than "inexperience."

Question 7. The best answer is **B** because the narrator refers to Bach and the blues as being the "bedrock" on which Payne had been trained (lines 76–77).

The best answer is NOT:

A because there is nothing in the passage to suggest that Everett did anything to avoid representing Bach and the blues when he played piano.

C because the narrator describes Bach and the blues as being "earthbound" (line 76) and "the bedrock" (line 76) of Payne's musical inspiration. Moreover, the narrator contrasts these influences, which Payne hears through "his other ear" (line 75) with "the true music of the spheres" (lines 72–73), which he hears through "his right ear directed skyward" (line 68).

D because the passage does not imply that Everett is limited to "Tin Pan Alley" tunes. Rather, the passage states that Everett "recast" and "reinvented" the Tin Pan Alley tune "Sonny Boy Blue" "in an image all his own" (lines 60–61).

Question 8. The best answer is **F** because the passage indicates that Payne first played the song "at a slower tempo than was called for" (line 41).

The best answer is NOT:

G because there is no indication in the passage that Payne spoke with anyone other than the bassist and the drummer.

H because although the passage states that Payne conferred with the bassist and the drummer (line 27), there is no mention in the passage that either the bassist or the drummer had any reaction to what Payne said to them.

J because when Payne first played "Sonny Boy Blue," he played the song "straight through as written" (line 39). The passage also states that throughout Payne's performance, he "continued to acknowledge the little simple-minded tune" (lines 59–60).

Question 9. The best answer is **A** because Hattie speculates that Payne's talent "had to do . . . with the way he held his head . . . tilted" (lines 65–67).

The best answer is NOT:

B because the narrator never mentions the simplemindedness of the tune as being related to Payne's musical ideas and feelings. Rather, the characterization of "Sonny Boy Blue" as a "little simple-minded tune" (lines 59–60) creates a contrast between Payne's elaborate and inventive improvisations and the simple and overly familiar song that he chooses as a vehicle for those improvisations.

C because although the narrator mentions Payne's formality in playing through the parts of "Sonny Boy Blue" the first time (lines 42–43), the narrator does not identify this formality as the source of the musical ideas and feelings showcased in Payne's improvisations.

D because the passage makes no mention of any connection Payne feels with his audience. Rather, the passage states that Payne does not even acknowledge his audience before playing (line 30).

Question 10. The best answer is **J** because the passage states that Payne's performance seemed to Hattie "a joyous, terrifying roller coaster of a ride" (lines 78–79).

The best answer is NOT:

F because although the passage states that Payne's rendition of the song began slowly and formally (lines 41–43), the passage goes on to contrast this beginning with a lengthy improvisational section described in terms that indicate that Hattie found the performance as a whole anything but formal (lines 48–61).

G because there is no indication in the passage that Hattie considers Payne's musical performance absent-minded. Instead, she describes his body "moving absentmindedly through space" as he approaches the bandstand to play (lines 20–21).

H because the narrator does not describe Payne's performance of "Sonny Boy Blue" as resembling a song played in church. Rather, she describes the audience reacting to Payne's performance "as if they were in church and weren't supposed to clap" (lines 82–83).

Passage II

Question 11. The best answer is A because the passage as a whole presents a cohesive argument that sprawl is both unpleasant and harmful (lines 9–10, 25–27, 33–37, 44–47, 59–61, 74–79); that its destructive effects are too often ignored (lines 11–16); that characterizations of sprawl as either inevitable or desirable are flawed (lines 17–19, 52–54, 62–66); that policies currently in place encourage sprawl to continue (lines 19–22, 66–74); and that there are a set of alternative policies that, if adopted, would resist sprawl and reduce these harmful effects (lines 80–91). The overall effect of these linked propositions is to persuade the reader that a choice must be made between a proven harm and a beneficial alternative. Moreover, the language used to describe sprawl throughout the passage is consistently negative, including, for example, the initial identification of sprawl as a "destructive, soulless, ugly mess" (lines 9–10). In contrast to these descriptions, communities without sprawl are described as "places that people care about" (line 35) or characterized as representing a "compact walkable environment" (70–71). Drawing a contrast between attractive and unattractive descriptions, as this passage does, is a common tactic of persuasive rhetoric.

> **The best answer is NOT:**
>
> **B** because although the author explains what sprawl is, the main purpose of the passage is not merely to explain what sprawl is but to argue for measures that would control sprawl and "knit communities together" (line 89).
>
> **C** because although the author does describe sprawl throughout the passage, these descriptions are more often colorful and emotional than they are precise and exact. For example, sprawl is initially characterized as a "destructive, soulless mess" (lines 9–10). By contrast, communities without sprawl are described as "places that people care about" (line 35) or characterized as representing a "compact walkable environment" (lines 70–71). Drawing a contrast between attractive and unattractive descriptions, as this passage does, is a common tactic of persuasive rather than descriptive rhetoric. Therefore the principal aim of the passage is persuasive rather than descriptive.
>
> **D** because the passage does not tell a story. Rather, it informs the reader of a problem and urges the reader not only to see sprawl as a problem as well but also to take measures to solve the problem.

Question 12. The best answer is J because after describing the effect of sprawl on communities, and criticizing policies that encourage sprawl, the author proposes the adoption of policies that discourage sprawl, such as "downtown housing and mixed-use zoning" (lines 85–86) and goes on to explain that "the goal should be an integrated system of planning decisions and regulations that knit communities together instead of tearing them apart" (lines 87–90). Therefore, in the context of the sentence in which it appears and in the context of the entire passage, the establishment of "an integrated system of planning decisions and regulations" is clearly something that the author would like to see happen.

The best answer is NOT:

F because the full sentence in question reads "Too many developers follow standard formulas, and too many government entities have adopted laws and policies that constitute powerful incentives for sprawl" (lines 19–22). The author's opposition to the laws in question is signaled within the sentence by the assertion that "too many government entities" enact them. In the context of the sentence in which it appears and in the context of the author's criticism of sprawl throughout the passage, the enactment of "laws . . . that provide powerful incentives for sprawl" is not something that the author would like to see happen.

G because "the destruction of traditional downtowns" (line 34) is presented as an end result of sprawl and as something that "is corroding the very sense of community that helps bind us together as a people and as a nation" (lines 35–37). In the context of the sentence in which it appears and in the context of the author's criticism of sprawl throughout the passage, "the destruction of traditional downtowns" is not something that the author would like to see happen.

H because the author explains that " 'affordable' housing on the edge of town" (line 53) is only more affordable for developers (line 55), and that the construction of this housing, which is a familiar form of sprawl (lines 48–50), requires "higher taxes for needless duplication of services and infrastructure" (lines 59–60). In the context of the sentence in which it appears and in the context of the author's criticism of sprawl throughout the passage, construction of this housing is not something that the author would like to see happen.

Question 13. **The best answer is D** because in the first paragraph the author defines sprawl as a problem, and in the last paragraph, the author offers possible solutions to this problem, including "sensible land-use planning" (line 82), "mixed-use zoning" (lines 85–86), and "an integrated system of planning decisions and regulations" (lines 87–88).

The best answer is NOT:

A because the author does not ask a question at any point in the final paragraph. Rather, the author offers solutions to the problem explained throughout the passage.

B because the author mentions no specific statistics in the final paragraph.

C because the final paragraph does not incorporate more emotional language than the first. If anything, the opposite may be true. In the first paragraph, the author uses emotionally loaded language to encourage the reader to agree that the "destructive, soulless, ugly mess called sprawl" (lines 9–10) is a serious problem. By contrast, the last paragraph, while arguing that "our communities should be shaped by choice, not by chance" (lines 80–81), uses more precise and less emotional language to describe possible solutions to the problem of sprawl, such as "an integrated system of planning decisions and regulations" (lines 87–88). This less emotional language encourages the reader to agree that these solutions may be effective.

Question 14. **The best answer is F** because the passage makes no mention of how long the problem of sprawl has been happening in US cities.

The best answer is NOT:

G because the author answers this question in lines 17–18: "Development that destroys communities isn't progress. It's chaos."

H because the author argues that current zoning laws, which make construction of a "walkable environment" impossible, "are a major reason why 82 percent of all trips taken in the United States are taken by car" (lines 69–74).

J because the author offers solutions to the problem of what to do to combat sprawl in the final paragraph in the passage.

Question 15. **The best answer is B** because the passage does not support the idea that the opening of a superstore leads to downtown renovations. Rather, the passage states that, after a superstore opens in a small town, "downtown becomes a ghost town" (lines 46–47).

The best answer is NOT:

A because the author states that "in many small towns, a single new superstore may have more retail space than the entire downtown business district" (lines 42–44).

C because the author states that, after a superstore opens in a small town, "downtown becomes a ghost town" (lines 46–47).

D because the author states that, when a superstore opens in a small town, "the retail center of gravity shifts away from Main Street" (lines 45–46).

Question 16. **The best answer is H** because the statistics in question (lines 73–76) show that a significant majority of all trips taken in the United States are taken by car, and that American families spend a significant portion of their budget on transportation expenses. The author argues that these statistics regarding automobile transportation and its costs represent the effects of land use regulations that make it impossible to construct a "compact walkable environment" (lines 69–71).

The best answer is NOT:

F because the statistics in question (lines 73–76) do not support the idea that mixed-use zoning leads to environmental destruction. Rather, they show that a significant majority of all trips taken in the United States are taken by car, and that American families spend a significant portion of their budget on transportation. According to the author, the dependence on automobile transportation is a result of current zoning laws "prohibiting mixed uses" (line 67). Because this dependence on automobile transportation is associated with sprawl, which is associated with environmental destruction throughout the passage, the statistics in question support the argument that it is the prohibition of mixed-use zoning, rather than mixed-use zoning itself, that creates environmental destruction (line 67).

G because the statistics in question (lines 73–76) show that a significant majority of all trips taken in the United States are taken by car, and that American families spend a significant portion of their budget on transportation expenses. The author argues that these statistics regarding automobile transportation and its costs represent the effects of land-use regulations that make it impossible to construct a "compact walkable environment" (lines 69–71).

J because the statistics in question do not support the idea that Americans spend too much of their budgets on food and health care. Rather, the passage states that "the average American household now allocates more than 18 percent of its budget to transportation expenses" and that this is "more than it spends for food and three times more than it spends for health care" (lines 74–79). This strongly suggests that Americans spend too much on transportation, rather than suggesting that they spend too much on food and health care.

Question 17. **The best answer is C** because the passage refers to "retail development that transforms roads into strip malls" (lines 38–39).

The best answer is NOT:

A because the author discusses the type of sprawl that develops far away from town centers (line 30), not adjacent to them.

B because the author argues that the development of sprawl leads to the neglect of historic buildings in towns (lines 26–27), not that sprawl leads to the utilization of these buildings.

D because the author argues that the construction of superstores is part of a process whereby "the retail center of gravity shifts away from Main Street" and "downtown becomes a ghost town" (lines 45–47). This strongly suggests that superstores are associated with the destruction, rather than the promotion, of a sense of community in the towns in which they are constructed.

Question 18. **The best answer is G** because the sentence is describing how residential subdivisions are driven "by the American dream of a detached home in the middle of a grassy lawn" (lines 50–52). Since a grassy lawn surrounds the home being referred to, it is reasonable to assume there is space between the home and other structures. In other words, the home is "set apart."

The best answer is NOT:

F because although the word *detached* can indicate an objective point of view, *detached* is used in this context to describe a house, which does not have a point of view.

H because the passage does not provide a clear sense of what "broken apart" would mean in the context of this sentence.

J because there is nothing in the passage to suggest that the home being referred to was "taken away" from another location.

Question 19. The best answer is D because the statement in question is preceded by, and is intended to counter, the claim made by some people that "sprawl is merely the natural product of marketplace forces at work" (lines 62–63). Therefore, the author is arguing that people who make this claim "fail to recognize" (line 63) that those market forces are influenced by governmental decisions. The author's rhetoric here assumes that the reader will recognize "a level playing field" as a popular expression for conditions governed purely by market forces, and will understand that a playing field that "isn't level" (line 64) refers to conditions in which governmental decisions *do* influence market forces.

The best answer is NOT:

A because the "needless duplication of services and infrastructure" (line 60) referred to in the passage is identified as a *result* of sprawl, whereas the phrase "the game isn't being played on a level field" (line 64) is used to identify the influence of governmental decisions on market forces, and not market forces alone, as a *cause* of sprawl.

B because the "higher taxes" (line 59) referred to in the passage are identified as a *result* of sprawl, whereas the phrase "the game isn't being played on a level field" (line 64) is used to identify the influence of governmental decisions on market forces, and not market forces alone, as a *cause* of sprawl.

C because the phrase "the game isn't being played on a level field" (line 64) is used to identify the influence of governmental decisions on market forces, and not market forces alone, as a cause of sprawl. The author's rhetoric here assumes that the reader will recognize "a level playing field" as a popular expression for conditions governed purely by market forces, and will understand that a playing field that "isn't level" (line 64) refers to conditions in which governmental decisions do influence market forces.

Question 20. The best answer is **J** because the passage identifies zoning laws that prohibit "mixed uses" (line 67) as a primary cause of the separation of urban commercial zones and residential subdivisions described in the three paragraphs that immediately precede the sentence in question (lines 48–66). That separation of commercial and residential land use is contrasted, in the following sentences, with "the sort of compact walkable environment that attracts us to older neighborhoods and historic communities all over the world" (lines 70–72). Therefore the phrase "mixed uses" can be understood as referring to zoning that allows one area to contain various types of development.

The best answer is NOT:

F because the passage identifies both large parking lots (lines 3–4) and large retail stores (lines 38–42) as being characteristic of sprawl, which is encouraged by the prohibition of "mixed uses" (line 67). Furthermore, parking lots and retail stores are both understood to be commercial uses of land, and therefore the phrase "mixed uses" is unlikely to refer to them.

G because although the passage states that the prohibition of "mixed uses" (line 67) makes it "impossible—even illegal—to create the sort of compact walkable environment that attracts us to older neighborhoods and historic communities" (lines 69–72), the phrase "mixed uses" itself is not directly associated with historic preservation in any way. Rather, "mixed uses" refers to the designation of land use as residential, commercial, or industrial under zoning laws.

H because although "mixed uses" (line 67) are understood within the context of the passage as encouraging the creation of a "walkable environment" (line 71), there is no association between the phrase "mixed uses" and the prohibition of driving or parking.

Passage III

Question 21. The best answer is A because the passage begins with the narrator's description of an incident in which she first became interested in identifying flowers and in the natural world (lines 1–24), and the remainder of the passage describes how this early interest developed into a larger part of her life.

The best answer is NOT:

B because although the identification of an aster is part of the incident (lines 1–24) that leads to the narrator's lifelong interest in flowers and the natural world, there is no mention in the passage of the author having a lifelong fascination for asters in particular. Rather, the incident in question leads to a lifelong fascination with identifying flowers in general.

C because although the author briefly mentions hiking with companions (lines 31–32) and identifying flowers with a friend (lines 81–82), the primary focus of the passage is on the author's individual interest in flowers and how that interest developed.

D because the author does not discuss her career in the passage.

Question 22. The best answer is H because the author describes the young man's answer to her question as containing "the hint of a sniff" (line 7), which indicates that she detected disdain or condescension in the tone of the young man's answer.

The best answer is NOT:

F because there is nothing in the passage to suggest that the guide treated the author with acceptance. Rather, his reaction to her question about the flower is described as containing "the hint of a sniff" (line 7), which indicates disdain or condescension, qualities that are incompatible with acceptance.

G because there is no mention in the passage of the guide being surprised by the author's question. Rather, his reaction is described as containing "the hint of a sniff" (line 7), which indicates disdain or condescension and not surprise.

J because there is no mention in the passage of the guide becoming angry with the author. Rather, his reaction to her question about the flower is described as containing "the hint of a sniff" (line 7), which indicates disdain or condescension and not anger.

Question 23. The best answer is **D** because although the author describes her efforts to identify a yellow flower on a particular hike (lines 30–51), she does not name the flower in question. Rather, she uses the description of this incident to explain her developing "intimacy" (line 28) with the book *A Field Guide to Wild Flowers.*

The best answer is NOT:

A because although the author mentions St. John's wort, loosestrife, and puccoon as "five-petaled yellow flowers" (lines 50–51) similar to the one she is trying to identify, she does not identify the flower in question as St. John's wort.

B because although the author mentions St. John's wort, loosestrife, and puccoon as "five-petaled yellow flowers" (lines 50–51) similar to the one she is trying to identify, she does not identify the flower in question as loosestrife.

C because although the author mentions St. John's wort, loosestrife, and puccoon as "five-petaled yellow flowers" (lines 50–51) similar to the one she is trying to identify, she does not identify the flower in question as puccoon.

Question 24. The best answer is **F** because the author states that though daunting at first, the book was neither too frustrating as a more basic book would have become nor too daunting as a more complex one would have been (lines 58–61).

The best answer is NOT:

G because the author indicates that the book was not easy to use in the beginning. Rather, it was difficult for her, but she "persisted in wrestling" (line 61) with the book until it became easier.

H because the author makes no mention in the passage of any other guide she used.

J because the author makes no negative statements about the illustrations in the guide.

Question 25. **The best answer is C** because the sentence in question reads "I had no choice, really, not if I wanted to *get in*" (lines 55–56), and the surrounding sentences indicate that the matter she had no choice in was the use of the field guide, which "led to the particulars" (line 57), or deepened her understanding, of the landscape. Therefore, in this context, to "get in" to a subject can be understood as meaning to fully understand that subject.

The best answer is NOT:

A because the sentence in question reads "I had no choice, really, not if I wanted to *get in*" (lines 55–56), and there is no indication in the surrounding lines that the matter she has no choice in is her arrival in a specific location. Rather, she wants to figuratively, and not literally, arrive at a deeper understanding of the landscape, and she has no choice but to use the field guide in order to do so (lines 55–58).

B because the sentence in question reads "I had no choice, really, not if I wanted to *get in*" (lines 55–56), and there is no indication in the surrounding lines or the passage as a whole that the matter she has no choice in has anything to do with membership in any group. Rather, she wants to figuratively, and not literally, "get in" to a deeper understanding of the landscape, and she has no choice but to use the field guide in order to do so (lines 55–58).

D because the sentence in question reads "I had no choice, really, not if I wanted to *get in*" (lines 55–56), and there is no indication in the surrounding lines or the passage as a whole that the matter she has no choice in has anything to do with being friendly with someone. Rather, she wants to figuratively, and not literally, "get in" to a deeper understanding of the landscape, and she has no choice but to use the field guide in order to do so (lines 55–58).

Question 26. **The best answer is H** because the author states that she and Julie began to see that their understanding of plant communities was valuable because it led to a greater understanding of larger issues such as "climate change and continental drift" (lines 85–86).

The best answer is NOT:

F because there is no information in the passage about Julie's level of experience in identifying plant life.

G because there is no information in the passage about Julie owning a house near a bog.

J because there is no information in the passage about whether or not Julie used the Peterson's guide.

Question 27. The best answer is D because the author states that "over the next several years this field guide would become my closest companion" (lines 25–26), specifying that she measures the period in question in "years."

The best answer is NOT:

A because the author states that "over the next several years this field guide would become my closest companion" (lines 25–26), specifying "years" and not days as the way in which she measures the period in question.

B because the author states that "over the next several years this field guide would become my closest companion" (lines 25–26), specifying "years" and not weeks as the way in which she measures the period in question.

C because the author states that "over the next several years this field guide would become my closest companion" (lines 25–26), specifying "years" and not months as the way in which she measures the period in question.

Question 28. The best answer is J because the author's statement that "a landscape may be handsome in the aggregate, but this book led to the particulars, and that's what I wanted" (lines 56–58) contrasts the surface appeal of a landscape seen at a distance with the deeper knowledge of a landscape that only comes from familiarity with the "particulars," or individual parts, and specifies that this deeper knowledge of the landscape is what she sought.

The best answer is NOT:

F because the author's statement that "a landscape may be handsome in the aggregate, but this book led to the particulars, and that's what I wanted" (lines 56–58) specifies that she was more interested in the deeper knowledge of the landscape that comes from familiarity with the "particulars," or individual parts, than she was in an understanding of a landscape that might come from looking at its overall patterns.

G because although the passage does relate the way in which the field guide helps the author break landscapes down logically into their "particulars" (line 57), or individual parts, there is no indication that this made landscapes lose their appeal. Rather, she states that this kind of understanding was "what [she] wanted" (line 58) and that the logically ordered classifications in the field guide all made "such delightful sense" (lines 79–80).

H because there is no indication in the passage that the deeper understanding of landscapes that she sought through knowledge of their "particulars" (line 57), or individual parts, was in any way related to painting portraits of those landscapes.

Question 29. The best answer is B because the details in question describe the ways in which the field guide "changed" (line 64) as she figuratively, and not literally, "persisted in wrestling" (line 61) with it "by slow degrees" (line 62). In this context, these details indicate that this transformation occurred because of heavy use over a long period of time.

The best answer is NOT:

A because there is no indication that the transformation of the book described by the details in question (lines 64–66) takes place because of poor craftsmanship. Rather, the details in question describe the ways in which the field guide "changed" (line 64) as she, figuratively and not literally "persisted in wrestling" (line 61) with it "by slow degrees" (line 62). In this context, these details indicate that this transformation occurred because of heavy use over a long period of time.

C because the passage implies that the "cryptic annotations" (line 66) in the guide were made by the author herself.

D because the details in question describe the ways in which the field guide "changed" (line 64) as she, figuratively and not literally "persisted in wrestling" (line 61) with it "by slow degrees" (line 62). Although this indicates that the book's condition was transformed because of heavy use, there is no specific indication of carelessness and no mention anywhere in the passage of any regret the author has regarding her use of the field guide.

Question 30. The best answer is H because the author mentions *Solidago hispida* in order to exemplify her practice of addressing flowers that she has encountered before by their Latin name after she has learned to identify them (lines 70–72).

The best answer is NOT:

F because the passage makes no mention of any trouble the author had initially identifying *Solidago hispida*.

G because the author mentions *Solidago hispida* as an example of a flower she has addressed in the past with great enthusiasm, meaning she has already come across the flower in her nature walks.

J because there is no indication anywhere in the passage that the author feels the name *Solidago hispida* is inappropriate. Rather, the author mentions *Solidago hispida* only in order to exemplify her practice of addressing flowers by their Latin name (lines 70–72).

Passage IV

Question 31. The best answer is D because the passage states that information gained from the study of snow crystals "has practical applications in such diverse areas as agriculture and the production of electricity" (lines 12–14). Specific details about these practical applications are presented in the final five paragraphs (lines 50–91) of the passage.

The best answer is NOT:

A because although the passage does mention the fact that scientists have communicated with each other during the course of studying snow crystals (lines 50–54), communication is secondary to the main point of the passage, which is to explain the practical applications of such a study.

B because although the passage does discuss the role of snow crystal facets in the formation of snow crystals (lines 19–23) and also discusses the winter snowpack in some Western states (lines 56–61), the passage makes no specific connection between the snow crystal facets and the snowpack and does not indicate that either one is the primary reason for presenting information about the scientific study of snow.

C because although the passage does tell the story of the first time a scanning electron microscope was used in the scientific study of snow (lines 34–49), it tells this story in the context of presenting information about the practical applications of the scientific study of snow and does not explicitly discuss the varied uses of the scanning electron microscope.

Question 32. The best answer is G because the passage states that "before employing the scanning electron microscopy results, the forecasted amounts of snowpack water were inaccurate" (lines 62–64) and that "improving the prediction [of snowpack water] by 1 percent would save $38 million" in costs (lines 71–72). Improving a prediction can be understood as making that prediction more accurate, which establishes a connection between the use of the scanning electron microscope and saving money.

The best answer is NOT:

F because although the passage mentions future predictions in the context of less snowfall expected (lines 75–80), those future predictions are not linked to any money saved.

H because as the passage states, the two scientists (who were looking at biological problems) froze the tissue they were using in order "to avoid the laborious procedure" (lines 37–38) that the use of scanning electron microscopes usually entailed. The passage does not state that the scientists were saving money by using these microscopes when looking for these biological problems.

J because although the passage states that snowmelt accounts for 75 percent of the annual water supply of these western states (lines 56–58), the passage mentions nothing about increasing the water supply of these states as a means of saving money.

Question 33. The best answer is C because the phrase in question is immediately followed by a statement in parentheses explaining that "crystals often change once on the ground depending on the surrounding environment" (lines 48–49). Because *metamorphosed* means "changed," and *conditions* and *environment* have similar meanings, we can read the parenthetical statement as clarifying the fact that "metamorphosed conditions" refers to the state of snow crystals after they reach the ground.

The best answer is NOT:

A because the passage does not establish a direct connection between the phrase "metamorphosed conditions" (lines 47–48) and the temperature and humidity at which crystals form. Rather, the phrase in question is immediately followed by a statement in parentheses explaining that "crystals often change once on the ground depending on the surrounding environment" (lines 48–49). Read in context, the parenthetical statement, which makes no mention of the temperature and humidity at which crystals form, can be understood as defining the phrase "metamorphosed conditions."

B because the passage does not establish a direct connection between the phrase "metamorphosed conditions" (lines 47–48) and the process by which snow crystals develop from a speck of dust and water vapor. Rather, the phrase in question is immediately followed by a statement in parentheses explaining that "crystals often change once on the ground depending on the surrounding environment" (lines 48–49). Read in context, the parenthetical statement, which makes no mention of the formation of snow crystals, can be understood as defining the term "metamorphosed conditions."

D because the phrase in question (lines 47–48) is immediately followed by a statement in parentheses explaining that "crystals often change once on the ground depending on the surrounding environment" (lines 48–49). This clarification indicates that the phrase "metamorphosed conditions" refers to changes in the snowflake that occur as a result of changes in the environment and not directly to changes in the environment.

Question 34. The best answer is G because the passage explains that "before employing the scanning electron microscopy results, the forecasted amounts of snowpack water were inaccurate whenever the size and shape of the snow crystals varied much from the norm" (lines 62–65). This indicates that the addition of scanning electron microscopy data allowed scientists using the model to include more detailed information about structural variations in snow crystals in their predictions, making those predictions more accurate.

The best answer is NOT:

F because the passage does not specify that the addition of scanning microscopy data allowed scientists using the Snowmelt Runoff Model to include more detailed information about microwave satellite data. Rather, the passage states that Albert Rango "now uses Wergin's electron microscopy data, along with microwave satellite data, in the Snowmelt Runoff Model to predict the amount of water available in a winter snowpack" (lines 52–56). This indicates that scanning electron microscopy data and microwave satellite data are used in conjunction with each other, not that one allows the inclusion of more detailed information about the other.

H because the passage makes no mention of electron microscopy in helping provide detailed information about locations having the highest amount of snowfall.

J because although the passage mentions that William Wergin and Eric Erbe were looking for biological problems related to agriculture (lines 34–37), there is no mention of biological problems in the discussion of the Snowmelt Runoff Model, which occupies the last five paragraphs of the passage (lines 50–91).

Question 35. The best answer is D because the passage states that, because of temperature increases, less snow will fall, thus "greatly increasing water's economic value" (lines 77–82).

The best answer is NOT:

A because although the passage mentions an increased ability to track water pollution via the use of crystal research (lines 90–91), the passage makes no mention of an increase of pollution as a cause of an increase in water's value.

B because the passage makes no mention of water conservation leading to an increase in water's value.

C because although the passage mentions the ability of scanning electron microscopes to detect sulfur and nitrogen in snow (lines 87–89), the passage makes no mention of a predicted increase in sulfur and nitrogen levels in snow.

Question 36. The best answer is G because the passage states that "as the crystals fall, they encounter different atmospheric conditions that produce flakes with unique attributes" (lines 3–5).

The best answer is NOT:

F because although the passage does state that 1 septillion snowflakes fall worldwide each year (lines 1–3), the passage does not make any connection between that enormous number and the infinite variety of snowflakes. Rather, the passage states that "as the crystals fall, they encounter different atmospheric conditions that produce flakes with unique attributes" (lines 3–5).

H because the passage makes no connection between the rate at which snowflakes fall and the infinite variety of snowflakes. Rather, the passage states that "as the crystals fall, they encounter different atmospheric conditions that produce flakes with unique attributes" (lines 3–5).

J because although the passage does state that more complex atmospheric conditions produce more elaborate and therefore more varied snow crystals (lines 5–6), the passage makes no connection between those complex atmospheric conditions and the speed at which snow crystals develop, and the passage makes no connection between the speed at which snow crystals develop and the infinite variety of snowflakes.

Question 37. The best answer is D because the passage states that "snowflakes are collections of two or more snow crystals" (lines 16–17).

The best answer is NOT:

A because the passage does not state that snowflakes grow around a nucleus of dust. Rather, the passage states that "snowflakes are collections of two or more snow crystals" (lines 16–17) and that a crystal "typically grows around a nucleus of dust" (lines 18–19).

B because the snowflakes do not combine to form snow crystals. Rather, according to the passage, the opposite is true: snow crystals combine to form snowflakes (lines 16–17).

C because although the passage states that the shape of a snow crystal "depends on how the six side facets—or faces—grow in relation to the top and bottom facets" (lines 19–20), there is no mention of any direct relation between top and bottom facets and the growth of snowflakes.

Question 38. The best answer is **G** because the passage specifies that the physicist Kenneth Libbrecht "creates 'designer' snowflakes in his lab" (lines 31–32).

The best answer is NOT:

F because the passage makes no connection between the term "'designer' snowflakes" (line 32) and the fact that no two snowflakes are alike. Rather, the passage specifies that the physicist Kenneth Libbrecht "creates 'designer' snowflakes in his lab" (lines 31–32).

H because the passage makes no mention of the grand design of nature. Rather, the passage specifies that the physicist Kenneth Libbrecht "creates 'designer' snowflakes in his lab" (lines 31–32).

J because although the passage does state that the physicist Kenneth Libbrecht "creates 'designer' snowflakes in his lab" (lines 31–32), the passage makes no mention of the beauty of Libbrecht's snowflakes.

Question 39. The best answer is **C** because the sentence in question states that "snowmelt water is critical to crop irrigation and hydroelectric power, as well as recreation and domestic water supplies, fisheries management and flood control" (lines 58–61). In context, this is understood to mean that snowmelt water is vital, or very important, to these processes and practices.

The best answer is NOT:

A because the sentence in question states that "snowmelt water is critical to crop irrigation and hydroelectric power, as well as recreation and domestic water supplies, fisheries management and flood control" (lines 58–61). In this context *critical* cannot be read as meaning "evaluative" because snowmelt water cannot evaluate anything or anyone.

B because the sentence in question states that "snowmelt water is critical to crop irrigation and hydroelectric power, as well as recreation and domestic water supplies, fisheries management and flood control" (lines 58–61). In this context *critical* cannot be read as meaning "faultfinding" because snowmelt water cannot find fault with anything or anyone.

D because the sentence in question states that "snowmelt water is critical to crop irrigation and hydroelectric power, as well as recreation and domestic water supplies, fisheries management and flood control" (lines 58–61). In context, the adjective *critical* is understood to mean that snowmelt water is vital, or very important, to these processes and practices. Although it is also an adjective and can sometimes be understood to mean vital or important, *acute* cannot be substituted for *critical* in this sentence because it would be neither grammatical nor logical to say "water is *acute* to crop irrigation."

Question 40. The best answer is **F** because although the passage does state that research about snow crystals has helped scientists to identify and possibly track the source of pollutants in snow (lines 90–91), the passage does not make any connection between research about snow crystals and the extraction of pollutants *from* snow.

The best answer is NOT:

G because one meaning of *gauge* is "to measure," and the term *snowmelt* refers to water generated by a melting snowpack; therefore, when the passage states that research about snow crystals has helped scientists to "predict the amount of water available in a winter snowpack" (lines 55–56), that statement means that research about snow crystals has helped scientists to gauge (measure) the probable amount of snowmelt. Lines 84–85 specifically state that "the crystal research help[s] gauge snowmelt."

H because the passage states that, in the process of conducting research about snow crystals, physicist Kenneth Libbrecht "creates 'designer' snowflakes in his lab" (lines 31–32).

J because the passage states that research about snow crystals "is also useful in predicting avalanches" (line 85).

Passage V

Question 41. The best answer is **A** because Fran describes Linda Rose as "a homing pigeon" (lines 2—3) and "a sort of human boomerang" (lines 4–5) who'd "make a U-turn" (line 4) back to Fran despite a twenty-five-year wait. Though Fran had "long since stopped expecting" word from Linda Rose, she was still "not surprised" when she got it (lines 5–6). Fran experienced "the shock of being found after waiting so long" (lines 33–34), which again suggests she'd been expecting to hear from Linda Rose.

The best answer is NOT:

B because the passage doesn't support the idea that Fran and Linda Rose have built up resentment toward each other.

C because the passage doesn't support the idea that Fran has dreams of a perfect daughter. It's Fran's mother who brings up—and dismisses—the idea that Linda Rose has unrealistic expectations about Fran being "Grace Kelly or Margaret Mead" (lines 96–97).

D because there's no indication in the passage that Fran and Linda Rose share much of anything beyond a biological tie, similar handwriting (see lines 9–11), and physical appearance (see lines 76–77).

Question 42. The best answer is G because "strong-willed" and "caring" best describe Fran's mother. She has "dragon-lady nails" (lines 23–24) in defiance of her chemotherapy. She "snorted" (line 60) a response to Fran's comment about her being a great-grandmother. She also firmly tells Fran not to put off contacting Linda Rose, who's "been waiting for twenty-five years" (line 85) for a meeting. But Fran's mother also cares deeply about Fran and tries to reassure her by saying, "You're [Linda Rose's] flesh-and-blood mother and that's enough. That's all it'll take" (lines 96–97).

The best answer is NOT:

F because while Fran's mother might (with some difficulty) be described as arrogant, she isn't cruel. While Fran's mother "snorted" a response to Fran and though she firmly tells Fran not to put off contacting Linda Rose, her love for Fran and her concern for Linda Rose's feelings also come through.

H because while Fran's mother might be described as friendly, she isn't withdrawn, as revealed by her nails, her snort, and her firm warning to Fran.

J because while Fran's mother is loving, there's no evidence in the passage that she's embittered.

Question 43. This is a NOT question, which asks you to find the answer choice that is *not* supported by the passage. **The best answer is B** because Fran's reactions to learning she's a grandmother don't include looking forward to inviting Linda Rose and Blake over for a visit. When Fran's mother asks if Fran is going to invite Linda Rose and the baby, Fran replies, "I haven't thought that far" (line 83). The remainder of the passage suggests that Fran is nervous about such a visit. The other three answer choices are supported by the passage.

The best answer is NOT:

A because Fran notes that "in the normal order of things, you have ample time to adjust to the idea" of being a grandmother (lines 67–68). In Fran's case, however, she simply gets "a snapshot in the mail one day" (line 68) letting her know she's a grandmother.

C because Fran notes that upon getting the news about being a grandmother, she feels "as if I had just shaken hands with Death" (lines 64–65).

D because in line 71, Fran says being a grandmother is "not fair" because she doesn't "even feel like a *mother*."

Question 44. The best answer is F because the first paragraph is built around Fran's lack of surprise that Linda Rose contacted her. Fran calls Linda Rose "a homing pigeon" (lines 2–3) and "a sort of human boomerang" (lines 4–5) who she knew "sooner or later … would make a U-turn" back to her (line 4). The paragraph closes with Fran's suspicion, based on the familiarity of the handwriting, that the letter in the mailbox is from Linda Rose. Fran claims that while she had "long stopped expecting" such a letter, she "was not surprised" when she got it (lines 5–6).

The best answer is NOT:

G because the first paragraph doesn't claim that Linda Rose acted like a wild bird, just that Fran's mother "always thought of her as some wild little bird" (lines 1–2). In any case, the first paragraph doesn't focus on Linda Rose's behavior as a child.

H because the passage states that Fran "was not surprised" when she got the letter from Linda Rose.

J because while Linda Rose's handwriting reminds Fran of her own, this isn't the main point of the last paragraph. It's just a detail supporting the paragraph's main idea.

Question 45. The best answer is C because the last paragraph focuses on Fran's mother's efforts to reassure Fran. Fran's mother brings up the idea of Linda Rose having a "big fantasy" (lines 92–93) that Fran is Grace Kelly or Margaret Mead and says "no one" (line 95) could live up to that. She goes on to say, though, that as Linda Rose's "flesh-and-blood mother," Fran has "all it'll take" to have a good relationship with Linda Rose (lines 95–97).

The best answer is NOT:

A because neither Fran nor her mother has seen Linda Rose for a quarter century, so they can only guess about what Linda Rose thinks.

B because the only reference to the idea that Linda Rose might cause trouble or ask for money occurs in the twenty-seventh paragraph (lines 87–91), not in the last paragraph.

D because in the last paragraph, Fran's mother tries to reassure Fran in an effort to encourage her to invite Linda Rose and Blake for a visit in the near future.

READING • EXPLANATORY ANSWERS

Question 46. The best answer is J because Fran says that while her mother "had lost some weight and most of her hair to chemotherapy" (lines 21–22), Fran "was used to how she looked now" (lines 19–20).

The best answer is NOT:

F because rather than being surprised, Fran says she "was used to" her mother's appearance (lines 19–20).

G because there's no support in the passage for the idea that Fran is embarrassed by the nail polish colors her mother uses. Fran merely notes that her mother "was vain about her hands" (line 19) and had painted her nails "Jungle Orchid" (lines 60–61).

H because while Fran says she's "noticed people staring" at her mother (lines 20–21), there's no evidence in the passage that Fran feels pity for her mother as a result.

Question 47. The best answer is D because in thinking about the letter she receives from Linda Rose, Fran notes, "I could see the ghosts of all the long letters she must have written and crumpled into the wastebasket" (lines 55–57), suggesting Fran sympathizes with Linda Rose.

The best answer is NOT:

A because while Fran acknowledges that the letter was "short" (line 54), she feels sympathy, not disappointment.

B because soon after handing her mother the fetter from Linda Rose, Fran comments, "Forty years old and I felt as if I had just shaken hands with Death" (lines 63–65)—hardly a happy reaction.

C because while the letter was "businesslike" (line 55), Fran sympathizes with Linda Rose and doesn't feel offended.

Question 48. The best answer is **J** because details in the passage suggest Fran had put Linda Rose up for adoption a quarter century ago. Fran says her mother had "wanted to keep" Linda Rose (line 1), which implies that Fran didn't. More directly, Fran notes upon receiving the letter and photograph from Linda Rose that a person doesn't usually "get a snapshot in the mail one day from a baby girl you gave up twenty-four years ago saying, 'Congratulations, you're a grandma!' " (line 70).

The best answer is NOT:

F, G, or **H** because there's no evidence in the passage that the reason it's been such a long time since Fran and Linda Rose have seen each other is that Linda Rose left home to get married (**F**), that arguments between the two drove Linda Rose away (**G**), or that Linda Rose chose to live with her father (**H**).

Question 49. The best answer is **C** because after looking at the picture Linda Rose sends, Fran's mother says to Fran, "She looks just like you. Only her nose is more aristocratic" (lines 73–74).

The best answer is NOT:

A because when Fran's mother suggests that Linda Rose may be "married to a brain surgeon with his and her Cadillacs" (lines 87–88), Fran replies, "She didn't mention any husband at all" (line 92) in the letter.

B because the passage's only reference to a piece of art is to the "dime-a-dozen seascape in a cheap gilt frame" (lines 43–44) behind Linda Rose in the picture.

D because there's no evidence in the passage that either the letter or the picture reveals that Linda Rose cares little about how she or her house looks.

Question 50. The best answer is **H** because after telling Fran not to put off contacting Linda Rose and inviting her and the baby for a visit, Fran's mother says Linda Rose has "been waiting twenty-five years" (line 85).

The best answer is NOT:

F because Fran's mother never directly expresses the desire to see her new great-grandson before she dies.

G because there's no evidence in the passage that Fran generally tends to delay making hard decisions.

J because while Fran's mother wonders aloud whether Linda Rose is "going to be trouble or ask for money" (lines 89–90), she only does this because she thinks Fran might use this as an excuse to put off contacting Linda Rose and inviting her and the baby for a visit. Fran's mother goes on to say, "For all we know, [Linda Rose is] married to a brain surgeon with his and her Cadillacs" (lines 90–91).

Passage VI

Question 51. The best answer is **B** because the author argues throughout the passage, and particularly in the fourth paragraph (lines 42–61), that people's lack of understanding of important details about government keeps them from improving government. He contends that people "do not particularly care" (lines 44–45) about "the whys and wherefores of most technical, non-emotional political issues" (lines 42–44) and are "more than willing to delegate evaluation of the technical aspects of government to somebody else" (lines 53–55). For the author, this means that "angry voters turn the rascals out and, in the triumph of hope over experience, let new rascals in" (lines 56–58) but that the voters are unable to "tell the rascals how to do their jobs better" (lines 60–61) because the voters "themselves do not understand the technical questions" (lines 59–60).

The best answer is NOT:

A because the author doesn't argue that American citizens read too many newspapers or watch too much television.

C because while the author does contend that people have a certain control over elected officials through voting, he also claims that voters are unable to affect how officials do their jobs while in office because the voters "themselves do not understand the technical questions." The author also doesn't directly address whether people can control bureaucrats.

D because there's no evidence in the passage that television has cut back on news to focus on entertainment. Furthermore, the author undermines the idea that Americans ever had a truly responsive government when he repeats but dismisses "the widely held tenet of democratic faith that elected officials, as opposed to bureaucrats or the judiciary, are popularly selected and democratically responsive" (lines 81–84).

Question 52. The best answer is **F** because the author contends that a typical local newspaper reporter is "an inexperienced twenty-three-year-old journalism school graduate" (lines 34–35) whose "journalism school curriculum did not include advanced algebra, to say nothing of calculus" (lines 39–41)—leaving the reporter ill prepared to understand "the intricacies of a program budget, which basically involves solving a grand equation composed of numerous simultaneous differential functions" (lines 36–39).

The best answer is NOT:

G because while the author contends that the reporters are often inexperienced, he doesn't think they're well educated.

H or **J** because while the author contends that the reporters are often young, he also calls them "inexperienced" (ruling out **H**) and not well educated (ruling out **J**).

Question 53. The best answer is **A** because according to the author, even the "Internal Revenue Service lawyers" at the tax seminar who were experts on federal estate and gift tax laws "frankly confessed that they did not understand the Tax Reform Act of 1976" (lines 66–68). The author uses this example to make the point that "government is so technical that even career civil servants cannot explain what is happening" (lines 63–65).

The best answer is NOT:

B or **D** because even the civil servants couldn't understand the law.

C because the author doesn't use the example to make the broad claim that some governmental issues are more technical than they used to be before passage of the act, nor is the timing of the act relevant here.

Question 54. The best answer is **F** because the author contends that Americans "for the most part know little and care less about the technical functioning of their government" (lines 77–79). Such indifference helps reduce the idea of elected officials being "democratically responsive" (lines 83–84) to (more or less) the status of "a myth" (line 84).

The best answer is NOT:

G or **J** because the author doesn't specifically claim that people are completely taken in by the myth that government is responsive to democratic control (**G**) or that people are prepared to concede legitimacy only to a democratically elected government (**J**). In any case, he uses the word *indifference* to refer directly to the idea that Americans are largely ignorant of and unconcerned about technical governmental issues.

H because the idea that citizens are responsive to either elected officials or bureaucrats isn't discussed in the passage.

Question 55. The best answer is **C** because the author states that "interest in the economy becomes all-consuming" when "times are bad, or there is a nationwide strike or disaster" (lines 8–10).

The best answer is NOT:

A, **B**, or **D** because the author doesn't claim that voter interest in the economy is greatest when national elections are held (**A**), when interesting personalities are leaders (**B**), or when there are no other interesting issues (**D**).

Question 56. **The best answer is G** because *limited* is the best synonym for *circumscribed* in context. The author states that "most serious political communication" between public officials and voters "is limited to forty-five seconds on the network evening news" (lines 18–19) even when the issues are known to voters. Furthermore, in the third paragraph (lines 27–41), the author stresses the limited knowledge communicated by television and local newspapers on serious and complicated political issues.

The best answer is NOT:

F because *technical* makes no sense in context. Since people "for the most part know little and care less about the technical functioning of their government" (lines 77–79), it's not likely that communication between public officials and voters would be extremely technical.

H because *entertaining* makes no sense in context given the fact that people are largely ignorant of and unconcerned about technical governmental issues.

J because *serious* is not the best synonym in context. Lines 15–17 set up a contrast between the seriousness of the political issues and the "extremely circumscribed," or limited, communication between public officials and voters on those issues.

Question 57. **The best answer is D** because the author states, "Process and personalities, the way decisions are made and by whom, the level of perquisites, extramarital sexual relations, and, in high offices, personal gossip dominate the public mind" (lines 45–48). It can reasonably be inferred, then, that a news story with a headline about Senator Smith denying he improperly made money would attract the greatest number of readers.

The best answer is NOT:

A, **B**, or **C** because news stories with headlines about park fees (**A**), accounting procedures (**B**), and safety regulations (**C**)—"the substance of technical decisions" (line 49)—would, based on the passage, draw comparatively few readers.

Question 58. The best answer is **J** because the author claims that "reporters focus on what sells papers or gets a high Nielsen rating" (lines 50–51). Since "neither newspapers nor television stations intend to lose their primary value as entertainment" (lines 51–53), it's clear that Nielsen ratings in some way measure how "entertaining" television news coverage is to the public, which is why television news coverage is heavily influenced by them.

The best answer is NOT:

F or **H** because there's no evidence in the passage that Nielsen ratings place great emphasis on technical details (**F**) or that the Federal Communications Commission requires Nielsen ratings (**H**).

G because lines 50–51, which distinguish between selling newspapers and getting high Nielsen ratings, suggest that Nielsen ratings are relevant only to television.

Question 59. The best answer is **A** because the author states, "Angry voters turn the rascals out and, in the triumph of hope over experience, let new rascals in" (lines 56–58). The "new rascals" are newly elected officials who the angry voters hope will do a better job than the "rascals" they just voted out of office.

The best answer is NOT:

B or **D** because in context, the phrase "the triumph of hope over experience" has nothing to do with the belief that expertise in a technical field is a qualification for holding office (**B**) or that newspapers and television will eventually provide better news coverage (**D**). **C** because in context, the phrase "the triumph of hope over experience" relates to the hope that new officials will outperform old officials, not to the hope that a sufficient amount of anger will make a given group of officials do a better job.

Question 60. The best answer is **J** because the author states, "What voters are unable to do because they themselves do not understand the technical questions is tell the rascals how to do their jobs better" (lines 58–61).

The best answer is NOT:

F or **H** because the passage never argues that citizens are unable to tell government officials how to do their jobs better because citizens don't vote in every election (**F**) or read enough newspapers or see enough television (**H**).

G because while the author does suggest that citizens have a tendency to elect rascals, he doesn't say that this tendency is why citizens can't tell government officials how to do their jobs better. The real reason is that citizens don't understand the technical questions.

Passage VII

Question 61. The best answer is **B** because throughout the passage, the author makes the argument that non-Western immigrants are changing the definition of what it means to be an American. About herself, she says, "I am an American writer, in the American mainstream, trying to extend it" (lines 29–30). She says she's tried to make Americans aware that "the foreign-born, the Third World immigrant with non-Western religions and non-European languages and appearance, can be as American as any steerage passenger from Ireland, Italy, or the Russian Pale" (lines 39–43). The author feels it's part of her "literary agenda" (line 44) to "show how I (and the hundreds of thousands like me) have transformed America" (lines 46–47). She concludes, "I do have a duty, beyond telling a good story. My duty is to give voice to continents, but also to redefine the nature of *American*" (lines 87–89).

The best answer is NOT:

A or **C** because the author never argues in the passage that until recently, foreign-born residents haven't wanted to be involved in defining the American reality (**A**) or that the United States immigration policy is inherently unfair (**C**).

D because while the author does suggest that America can change immigrants—"America has transformed *me*" (line 45)—she doesn't make the stronger, more specific argument that America has changed the political affiliations of most non-Western immigrants.

Question 62. The best answer is **F** because lines 3–5 reveal that the author attended school in Calcutta, while lines 26–28 indicate she moved to the United States and lived in "the all too real Manhattan."

The best answer is NOT:

G because lines 3–5 indicate that the school run by Irish nuns was in Calcutta (even though the nuns considered it "a corner of England").

H because the passage doesn't say that the author was raised in Bangladesh or that she moved to England before moving to the United States.

J because the author says she's never been to Faridpur, her father's birthplace: "My 'country'—called in Bengali *desh*—I have never seen. It is the ancestral home of my father and is now in Bangladesh" (lines 5–8).

Question 63. The best answer is **C** because the author repeatedly claims that her agenda or mission is to reinterpret, through her stories, what it means to be an American. About herself, she says, "I am an American writer, in the American mainstream, trying to extend it" (lines 29–30). She says she's tried to make Americans aware that "the foreign-born, the Third World immigrant with non-Western religions and non-European languages and appearance, can be as American as any steerage passenger from Ireland, Italy, or the Russian Pale" (lines 39–43). The author feels it's part of her "literary agenda" (line 44) to "show how I (and the hundreds of thousands like me) have transformed America" (lines 46–47). She concludes, "I do have a duty, beyond telling a good story. My duty is to give voice to continents, but also to redefine the nature of *American*" (lines 87–89).

The best answer is NOT:

A or **B** because the author never says in the passages that her agenda and mission are to raise the political consciousness of recent immigrants to the United States (**A**) or to create characters whose cultural heritage isn't easily identifiable (**B**).

D because while the author undoubtedly wants to find an audience for her stories and novels, she says her agenda or mission is to reinterpret what it means to be an American.

Question 64. The best answer is **H** because the author notes that as part of her "process of immigration and accommodation" to the United States, she's gone from being "a person who couldn't ride a public bus when she first arrived" to being "someone who watches tractor pulls on obscure cable channels" (lines 66–69).

The best answer is NOT:

F because line 19 refers to a horoscope "cast by a neighborhood astrologer when [the author] was a week-old infant" living in Calcutta (lines 14–15).

G because lines 24–25 refer to the author's girlhood in Calcutta, where she had to deal with such "contradictions" hearing native people praise India and the Irish nuns at her school condemn it (see lines 19–24).

J because lines 73–74 deal with how the author creates her fictional characters and thus have no direct relationship to the idea that she's been changed by America.

Question 65. The best answer is **D** because the author says, "My 'country'—called in Bengali *desh*—I have never seen. It is the ancestral home of my father and is now in Bangladesh. Nevertheless, I … think of myself as 'belonging' to Faridpur, the tiny village that was his birthplace" (lines 5–10).

The best answer is NOT:

A because Faridpur is a real place that, based on the passage at least, has no role in Indian mythology.

B because in lines 27–28, the author says, "The unglimpsed phantom Faridpur and the all too real Manhattan have merged as 'desh,'" meaning both Faridpur and Manhattan are in some sense her home now.

C because while it's true that Faridpur is now part of Bangladesh, this isn't why she refers to Faridpur as a "phantom"—it's a "phantom" because she's never seen it.

Question 66. The best answer is **F** because of the context in which the phrase "trying to extend it" appears. The author writes, "I am an American writer, in the American mainstream, trying to extend it" (lines 29–30), with *it* being the American mainstream. Soon after, she says her "remaining struggle" (line 36) as a writer is to convince American readers, editors, and publishers that "the foreign-born, the Third World immigrant with non-Western religions and non-European languages and appearance, can be as American as any steerage passenger from Ireland, Italy, or the Russian Pale" (lines 39–43). Thus, through her stories, she's trying to extend the boundaries of the American mainstream to include people of non-European ethnicities.

The best answer is NOT:

G because the author says she's not part of both Indian and American cultures: "I am an immigrant; my investment is in the American reality, not the Indian" (lines 32–33).

H or **J** because there's no evidence in the passage that the author is trying to find a way to make her home in the United States permanent (**H**)—she implies, in fact, that it already is, or is working to change immigration regulations (**J**).

Question 67. The best answer is **D** because when the author says she's "had to sensitize editors as well as readers to"—that is, make them aware of—"the richness of the lives I'm writing about" (lines 48–49), she's implying that these editors had previously tended to view the people she writes about in one-dimensional, stereotypical terms.

The best answer is NOT:

A, **B**, or **C** because there's no evidence in the passage that the author is implying that the editors didn't understand that many Asian Americans were already reading her work (**A**), that the editors gave her work superficial praise but refused to publish her novels (**B**), or that the editors were overtly (openly) discriminatory when it came to non-Western writers (**C**).

Question 68. The best answer is **G** because the author implies that many readers come unexpectedly to see themselves in her stories' characters. Adopting the voice of some of her readers, the author says, "… I see these people (call them Indians, Filipinos, Koreans, Chinese) around me all the time and I never knew they had an inner life. I never knew they schemed and cheated, suffered, cared so passionately" (lines 51–55). In other words, these readers gain from "the richness of the lives [she's] writing about" (line 49) a sense that "these people" have the same kinds of dreams, feelings, and experiences as the readers themselves do.

The best answer is NOT:

F because lines 51–55 show how readers come to see characters in the author's stories as distinct individuals from diverse cultural backgrounds.

H because there's no evidence in the passage that stories about immigrants to the United States generally have many more characters than other types of stories do.

J because the author never claims that immigrants from non-Western countries have developed a stronger inner life than have native-born Americans, only that non-Western immigrants have an inner life, just like everyone else.

Question 69. The best answer is **B** because the author states in the first paragraph that "the larger political entity to which I gave my first allegiance—India—was not even a sovereign [independent] nation when I was born" (lines 10–13).

The best answer is NOT:

A, C, or **D** because the first paragraph doesn't state that at the time of the author's birth, India was engaged in a war with England (**A**), still part of Bangladesh (**C**), or governed by the Irish (**D**).

Question 70. The best answer is **H** because immediately after the quoted phrase, the author writes, "consider the history [the characters] have witnessed (colonialism, technology, education, liberation, civil war). They have shed old identities, taken on new ones, and learned to hide the scars" (lines 76–79).

The best answer is NOT:

F because the author isn't being critical of her characters' cultural and political viewpoints; rather, she's saying that the people she writes about have seen and experienced a great deal in a short amount of time, making them seem "older" than they actually are.

G or **J** because the author doesn't make the specific claim that her characters have rejected Bengali, British, Irish, and, American values (**G**) or that her characters are really her mother's and grandmother's ancestors (**J**).

Passage VIII

Question 71. The best answer is **B** because lines 16–18 are introduced by the author's claim that "most paleontologists are now willing to view [dinosaurs] as energetic, active, and capable animals" (lines 14–16) despite earlier theories that dinosaurs were stupid, slow, and clumsy. It's reasonable, then, that what follows in lines 16–18 is a description of scientists' changing understanding of *Brontosaurus* lifestyle.

The best answer is NOT:

A or **D** because the words "a generation ago" and "now" in lines 16–18 indicate that the author is describing the present and recent past, not the time when *Brontosaurus* lived.

C because there's no evidence in the passage that the author believes standard illustrations of dinosaurs still inaccurately depict their lifestyles. "The standard illustration" of *Brontosaurus* mentioned in line 10 refers to an outdated image based on earlier scientific beliefs. Lines 16–22 (especially the reference to "modern anatomical reconstructions") suggest that illustrations have changed along with scientists' beliefs about dinosaurs.

Question 72. The best answer is **F** because the author indicates that "signs of social behavior that demand coordination, cohesiveness and recognition" (lines 57–58) in dinosaurs "were overlooked when dinosaurs labored under the burden of a falsely imposed obtuseness" (lines 59–61). In other words, when scientists thought dinosaurs were unintelligent, they failed to see evidence of complex social behaviors, such as "multiple trackways" (line 61) and hints that adult dinosaurs flanked young, immature dinosaurs during travel in order to protect them.

The best answer is NOT:

G because there's no evidence in the passage that scientists ever believed mammals were incapable of social formations.

H because there's no indication in the passage that the information in the fourth paragraph (lines 34–54) about brain and body sizes is new to scientists.

J because the passage doesn't say that any particular equipment was needed to identify the "multiple trackways" and the evidence that adult dinosaurs protected young, immature ones while traveling. It was mainly a matter of looking at fossilized footprints without the preconceived notion that dinosaurs were unintelligent.

Question 73. The best answer is D because the author describes "signs of social behavior that demand coordination, cohesiveness and recognition" (lines 57–58) in dinosaurs. These include "multiple trackways . . . with evidence for more than twenty animals traveling together in parallel movement" (lines 61–63), suggesting some dinosaurs may have lived in herds, and "small footprints" in a sauropod trackway that "lie in the center" with "larger ones at the periphery" (lines 65–66), suggesting adult dinosaurs may have flanked young, immature dinosaurs during travel in order to protect them.

The best answer is NOT:

A because while the author mentions "modern anatomical reconstructions" that "indicate strength and agility" in dinosaurs (lines 21–22), he doesn't use these as evidence of complex behaviors in dinosaurs.

B because in lines 60–61, the author is referring to old scientific misinterpretations, not to fossil evidence, when he mentions that at one time "dinosaurs labored under the burden of a falsely imposed obtuseness."

C because the author doesn't say that dinosaurs traveled with advanced herbivorous mammals, only that some evidence suggests that some dinosaurs may have traveled "much as some advanced herbivorous mammals do today, with large adults at the borders sheltering juveniles in the center" (lines 67–69).

Question 74. The best answer is G because the author states that while "dinosaurs held sway for 100 million years" (line 75), people have a much shorter history: "5 million years perhaps since *Australopithecus*, a mere 50,000 for our own species, *Homo sapiens*" (lines 82–83).

The best answer is NOT:

F because while the author does see "signs of social behavior that demand coordination, cohesiveness and recognition" in dinosaurs (lines 57–58), he nowhere suggests that human behavior seems simple in comparison to the complexity of dinosaur social behavior.

H because while the author does call dinosaurs "very large animals" (line 53), he doesn't claim that humans seem incredibly small in comparison.

J because nowhere in the passage does the author contend that study on human behavior is severely lacking in comparison to the amount of study done on dinosaurs.

Question 75. The best answer is D because the author claims that the revisionist interpretation of the relationship between dinosaur intelligence and physical size is that dinosaurs "had the 'right-sized' brains for reptiles of their body size" (lines 32–33).

The best answer is NOT:

A because, according to the author, the revisionist position isn't that dinosaurs had relatively large brains, but rather that they had appropriately sized brains.

B because the author states, "The revisionist interpretation, which I support, . . . does not enshrine dinosaurs as paragons of intellect" (lines 29–31).

C because the author states that revisionists claim dinosaurs "were not small brained after all" (line 32).

Question 76. The best answer is H because the author says the revisionist position he endorses is that dinosaurs "had the 'right-sized' brains for reptiles of their body size" (lines 32–33), a point people are likely to miss if they judge dinosaurs by human standards of brain size, body size, and intelligence. In fact, people wrongly used to see dinosaurs as "a symbol of lumbering stupidity" (lines 4–5).

The best answer is NOT:

F because the author suggests just the opposite—that humans, with their "subjective, top-heavy perspective," are likely to misjudge dinosaurs and, by implication, other nonhuman species.

G because while the author does say that humans are "top-heavy," he never claims that the human physical construction is deformed by the largeness of the skull. Instead, he uses the idea of people being "top-heavy" to question humans' ability to judge dinosaurs and other nonhuman species.

J because the idea that humans are "top-heavy" undercuts the idea that humans have a small brain relative to their body weight.

Question 77. The best answer is B because the passage states that relative to smaller animals, "large animals have low ratios of brain weight to body weight" (lines 45–46).

The best answer is NOT:

A or **C** because lines 45–46 rule out the possibility that the ratio is higher in larger animals (**A**) or the same in both larger and smaller animals (**C**).

D because there's no evidence in the passage that the ratio is overestimated.

Question 78. The best answer is F because the passage states, "In fact, brains grow only about two-thirds as fast as bodies" (lines 47–48).

The best answer is NOT:

G because even though brains grow about two-thirds as fast as bodies, this doesn't mean that at maturity, the brain weighs an average of one-third of body weight.

H because while the passage does say that "we have no reason to believe that large animals are consistently stupider than their smaller relatives" (lines 48–50), this speaks to the relationship of intelligence to body size, not brain size to body size.

J because the passage does not say that brain size is independent of body size, but instead asserts that there is a relationship.

Question 79. The best answer is D because the author states, "Dinosaurs held sway for 100 million years" (line 75), which the author finds "remarkable" (line 73).

The best answer is NOT:

A, B, or C because dinosaurs dominated Earth for 100 million years, not just 100,000 years (**A**), 5 million years (**B**), or 70 million years (**C**).

Question 80. The best answer is H because the author begins the last paragraph by stating that compared to the longevity of dinosaurs, "people … are scarcely worth mentioning" (lines 81–82) and immediately after notes that it's been only 5 million years since the emergence of *Australopithecus* and only 50,000 years since "our own species, *Homo sapiens*," emerged (line 83). It's clear from this that *Australopithecus* was human (a "person"), but not a modern human (*H. sapiens*).

The best answer is NOT:

F because *Australopithecus* wasn't a dinosaur.

G because *Australopithecus* was different from *H. sapiens* and appeared on Earth 5 million years ago.

J because there's no evidence in the passage that *Australopithecus* was a physically larger species of human or that it had a much smaller brain.

Passage IX

Question 81. The best answer is D because the narrator indicates that "now" (line 52) she "would have to forgo the luxury of adolescent experiments and temper tantrums" (lines 56–58), which indicates that the narrator is an adolescent. She takes on adult responsibilities so that she "could scoop [her] mother out of harm's way and give her sanctuary" (lines 58–59) in the United States.

The best answer is NOT:

A because the narrator is not an adult and because she and her mother are not merely visiting the United States: it has been "three and a half years or so" (line 52) since the mother's last trip to the sky market.

B because the narrator is not an adult and because there's no indication in the passage that the narrator and her mother plan to return to Saigon.

C because rather than imagining her mother's move to the United States, the narrator relates her own and her mother's shared experiences in Vietnam and the United States.

Question 82. The best answer is F because in Saigon, vendors recognized the "slick bargaining skills" (line 35) of the narrator's mother, who could "navigate with grace through their extravagant prices and rehearsed huffiness" (lines 36–38) and who was "mighty and experienced" (line 43). The narrator says, however, that "my mother's ability to navigate and decipher simply became undone in our new life" (lines 46–47) in the United States.

The best answer is NOT:

G or **H** because the mother's skills were not commonplace (G) or below average (H) in the Saigon sky markets, nor were her skills exceptional in the United States.

J because the mother's skills didn't give her an advantage in the United States, her adopted home; in fact, they were of no use there.

Question 83. The best answer is B because the narrator says that in dealing with the Saigon sky market vendors, her mother "knew how to navigate with grace through their extravagant prices and rehearsed huffiness" (lines 36–38).

The best answer is NOT:

A or **C** because the narrator says that her mother preferred "the primordial messiness and fishmongers' stink of the open-air market to the aroma-free order of individually wrapped fillets" (lines 49–51) found at the A & P.

D because while the narrator's mother "knew … the shoppers by name" (lines 29–30), there's no evidence in the passage that she found her fellow sky market shoppers to be something disagreeable to overcome.

Question 84. This is an EXCEPT question, which asks you to find the answer choice that is *not* supported by the passage.

The best answer is H because the narrator states that the other A & P shoppers "meandered" (line 10) rather than hurried through the store. The other three answer choices are supported by the passage.

> **The best answer is NOT:**
>
> **F** because lines 14–15 state, "My mother did not appreciate the exacting orderliness of the A & P."
>
> **G** because the narrator states that at the A & P, her mother "could not give in to . . . the absence of carcasses and pigs' heads" (lines 15–18).
>
> **J** because when the narrator explains to her mother that they don't need to pay for pork as soon as they decide to buy it, instead paying for everything at once at the checkout counter, the narrator says, "It took a few moments' hesitation for my mother to succumb to the peculiarity of my explanation" (lines 71–73).

Question 85. The best answer is D because the narrator views her mother's approach to sky market shopping with respect and nostalgia. The narrator describes her mother's "slick bargaining skills" (line 35) and calls her "mighty and experienced" (line 43). It has been "three and a half years or so after her [mother's] last call to the sky market" (lines 52–53), and the narrator is fondly looking back in order to set up a contrast with "the hard scrutiny of ordinary suburban life" (lines 55–56) in the United States through which she has to guide her mother.

> **The best answer is NOT:**
>
> **A, B,** or **C** because there's no evidence in the passage that the narrator views her mother's approach to sky market shopping with anxiety or huffiness (**A**), surprise or embarrassment (**B**), or impatience or amusement (**C**).

Question 86. The best answer is H because the narrator says her mother "would take me from stall to stall" in the sky markets "to expose me to her skills" (lines 30–31).

> **The best answer is NOT:**
>
> **F** because the passage doesn't state that the narrator talked to the vendors.
>
> **G** because the narrator learned about her mother's sky market behavior directly, by accompanying her "from stall to stall" (line 30), and not through her mother's descriptions.
>
> **J** because the narrator didn't have to tag along defiantly on shopping trips against her mother's wishes; her mother wanted her to come.

Question 87. The best answer is **B** because the narrator says, "Of course, all children eventually watch their parents' astonishing return to the vulnerability of childhood, but for us [children of immigrant parents] the process begins much earlier than expected" (lines 65–68). Having experienced this shift, the narrator took on adult responsibilities so that she "could scoop [her] mother out of harm's way and give her sanctuary" (lines 58–59) in the United States.

The best answer is NOT:

A because the narrator says that "all children," not just children of immigrants, "eventually watch their parents' astonishing return to the vulnerability of childhood."

C because the narrator contends that children of immigrants are taken by surprise when "the process" of parents reverting to childlike vulnerability "begins much earlier than expected."

D because the passage provides no evidence that children of immigrants are misunderstood by their parents to a greater degree than are other children.

Question 88. The best answer is **H** because the passage's first six paragraphs (lines 1–61) describe the narrator's disconcerting experiences shopping with her mother at the A & P, which leads into the assertion in the seventh paragraph (lines 62–68) that "all children of immigrant parents have experienced these moments" (lines 62–63) when a parent acts like a child. The seventh paragraph goes on to contend that for children of immigrant parents, the parents' return to childlike vulnerability "begins much earlier than expected" (lines 67–68).

The best answer is NOT:

F because the seventh paragraph is not the first place in which the narrator indicates that adjusting to another culture has been difficult for her and her mother. For example, the passage's opening sentence (lines 1–3) says, "I discovered soon after my arrival in Virginia that everything, even the simple business of shopping the American way, unsettled my mother's nerves."

G because neither the seventh paragraph nor the rest of the passage discusses what the narrator, before leaving Saigon, thought it would take to adjust to a new culture.

J because while the seventh paragraph does discuss children of immigrant parents in general, the narrator relates details about her experiences both before and after the seventh paragraph.

READING • EXPLANATORY ANSWERS

Question 89. The best answer is **A** because the third paragraph (lines 29–38), in which the quoted statement appears, illustrates a consistent relationship, or dynamic, between the sky market vendors and the narrator's mother. As an example of the "oddities" to which her mother and the vendors were "addicted," the narrator says, "My mother would feign indifference and they would inevitably call out to her" (lines 32–33). The paragraph concludes, "Theirs had been a mating dance, a match of wills" (line 38).

The best answer is NOT:

B because while "oddities" may seem negative, the quoted statement and the third paragraph as a whole reflect a positive relationship between the sky market vendors and the narrator's mother; in contrast, the mother found American supermarkets unappealing.

C because there's no evidence in the passage that sky market shoppers purchased items they didn't need at the markets.

D because "oddities" doesn't refer to the unusualness of the items for sale at the sky markets but rather to the behaviors of the sky market vendors and the narrator's mother.

Question 90. The best answer is **G** because the narrator says, "I would have to forgo the luxury of adolescent experiments and temper tantrums" (lines 56–58) in order to protect her mother.

The best answer is NOT:

F because the narrator says she had to "forgo" tantrums, not "use" tantrums.

H because there's no evidence in the passage that temper tantrums were a part of the narrator's character inherited from her mother.

J because the temper tantrums mentioned in lines 57–58 are ones that the narrator, not her mother, would have to "forgo."

Passage X

Question 91. The best answer is B because throughout the passage, the author reveals his belief that Jefferson was brilliant yet practical and writing under pressure. The author calls the natural rights section of Jefferson's Declaration "the seminal statement of the American Creed, the closest approximation to political poetry ever produced in American culture" (lines 15–17). He stresses Jefferson's practicality by mentioning that "virtually all the ideas found in the Declaration and much of the specific language had already found expression in those earlier writings" (lines 72–74) of Jefferson, but the author doesn't want to "accuse [Jefferson] of plagiarism" (line 70) for this borrowing. The author provides details highlighting the pressure under which Jefferson worked: "The Congress is being overwhelmed with military reports of imminent American defeat in New York and Canada. The full Congress is in session six days a week, and committees are meeting throughout the evenings" (lines 75–79). This led Jefferson to take "the obvious practical course" (line 79), which was to draw from his previous writings in composing the Declaration.

The best answer is NOT:

A because the author tries to "pierce through" the "veil" (line 62) of mystery surrounding Jefferson. The author also presents a complex notion of Jefferson's originality, which isn't reflected in the idea of Jefferson merely making attempts at originality.

C because the author contends that Jefferson has received a great deal of deserved praise for the Declaration. Everyone from Abraham Lincoln to "several generations of American interpreters" (lines 56–57) has praised Jefferson and the Declaration.

D because the author views Jefferson as anything but ordinary and because the passage never identifies Jefferson as a quasi-religious leader.

Question 92. The best answer is **F** because in the last paragraph, the author reminds readers of the high-pressure circumstances under which the Declaration was written and says, "The obvious practical course for Jefferson to take was to rework his previous drafts on the same general theme" (lines 79–81). He dismisses the idea that Jefferson didn't draw from his older works, saying it "strains credulity and common sense to the breaking point" (lines 83–84).

The best answer is NOT:

G because while the author asserts that "it seems almost sacrilegious to suggest that the creative process that produced the Declaration was a cut-and-paste job" (lines 81–83), in trying to recover "the specific conditions inside that room on Market and Seventh streets in June 1776" (lines 63–64), the author shows he wants to question assumptions about how Jefferson composed the Declaration.

H because the idea that the Declaration was wholly original is what, in the author's mind, "strains credulity."

J because the author believes that in writing the Declaration, Jefferson "almost surely had with him copies of his own previous writings, to include *Summary View, Causes and Necessities* and his three drafts of the Virginia constitution" (lines 67–70).

Question 93. The best answer is **A** because in the passage's first sentence (lines 1–6), the author calls the natural rights section of the Declaration "the most quoted statement of human rights in recorded history as well as the most eloquent justification of revolution on behalf of them."

The best answer is NOT:

B because while the author notes in lines 1–6 that the Continental Congress made no comment and only one slight change to the natural rights section, he doesn't suggest in lines 1–6 or elsewhere in the passage that the Congress should have commented on or reworked the Declaration.

C because in neither lines 1–6 nor elsewhere in the passage does the author express surprise at the eventual fame of the natural rights section, which he calls "the seminal statement of the American Creed, the closest approximation to political poetry ever produced in American culture" (lines 15–17).

D because the author offers no indication in either lines 1–6 or elsewhere in the passage that equally eloquent works were probably produced before the beginning of recorded history.

Question 94. The best answer is H because in Lincoln's words, Jefferson wrote under "the concrete pressure of a struggle for national independence by a single people" (lines 22–23), yet he had the ability "to introduce into a merely revolutionary document, an abstract truth, and so to embalm it there" permanently, for "today and in all coming days" (lines 24–26). This truth forever serves as "a rebuke and a stumbling block to the very harbingers of reappearing tyranny and oppression" (lines 27–28).

The best answer is NOT:

F because Lincoln doesn't describe Jefferson's statement as having been used against revolutionaries ever since its writing. Indeed, the statement was itself part of a "revolutionary document."

G because Lincoln describes the natural rights section of the Declaration as a permanent "rebuke and a stumbling block to the very harbingers of reappearing tyranny and oppression," not as a predictor of the rise of future tyrants.

J because Lincoln mentions only a single "abstract truth" in the natural rights section and doesn't claim that the section dared tyrants to continually reappear, only that it acted as "a rebuke and a stumbling block" whenever the first signs of tyranny revealed themselves.

Question 95. The best answer is C because the author signals that the second paragraph (lines 29–44) and the rest of the passage will focus on "the effort to explain what *was* in [Jefferson's] head" (lines 32–33) as he wrote the Declaration. The rest of the second paragraph presents Jefferson's standard response to those who accused him of plagiarism, which reinforces the notion that sources of ideas will be the subject of the rest of the passage.

The best answer is NOT:

A because while the second paragraph does allude to numerous "interpretations" (line 34), these are interpretations of "what *was* in [Jefferson's] head" (line 33) when he wrote the Declaration.

B because while the second paragraph does mention that Jefferson receives a great deal of scholarly attention, the focus of the paragraph and passage is on the process Jefferson used to put together the Declaration.

D because, again, while the second paragraph does allude to numerous "interpretations," nowhere does the paragraph or passage suggest anyone has doubts about why the Declaration was written.

Question 96. The best answer is **F** because the phrase "even if" (line 65) implies that the author doubts Jefferson was being totally honest about not copying from any previous writing—an implication reinforced in lines 72–74 when the author says that "virtually all the ideas found in the Declaration and much of the specific language had already found expression in [Jefferson's] earlier writings."

The best answer is NOT:

G because Lincoln was a nineteenth-century political figure (see lines 17–28), while Jefferson wrote the Declaration in the late eighteenth century (see lines 62–64), making it impossible for Jefferson to have copied from Lincoln.

H because the phrase "even if" implies some doubt, but it isn't a clear-cut assertion that Jefferson shouldn't be believed. Furthermore, the author declines "to accuse [Jefferson] of plagiarism" (line 70).

J because while the author doesn't accuse Jefferson of plagiarism, this isn't because Jefferson wrote the Declaration so long ago but because the author thinks that at worst Jefferson "plagiarize[d] himself" (lines 71–72), something the author doubts is even truly possible.

Question 97. The best answer is **B** because, as used in line 19, *characteristic* most nearly means "usually," and *eloquence* translates to "persuasive" and "expressive." That the author is being sincere in his praise for Lincoln is made clear when he says that Lincoln, like Jefferson, "also knew how to change history with words" (lines 18–19).

The best answer is NOT:

A because there's nothing ironic or negative about the author's view of Lincoln, as expressed in the passage.

C because calling Lincoln "a bit of a character" would be patronizing, which is clearly not the author's intent. In addition, Lincoln's view of Jefferson "as the original American oracle" (lines 20–21) is the standard view of "several generations of American interpreters" (lines 56–57), which means, in this case anyway, that Lincoln's opinion is not controversial.

D because there's no evidence in the passage that the author feels Lincoln's words are often difficult for modern readers to understand.

Question 98. The best answer is **H** because lines 29–32 state, "No serious student of either Jefferson or the Declaration of Independence has ever claimed that he foresaw all or even most of the ideological consequences of what he wrote."

The best answer is NOT:

G because according to lines 29–32, students of Jefferson or of the Declaration do not claim that Jefferson anticipated most of the ideological outcomes of what he wrote.

F or **J** because there's no evidence in lines 29–32 that students of Jefferson or of the Declaration think Jefferson purposely wrote ambiguously about freedom (**F**) or that he wrote the Declaration from memory without consulting other works (**J**).

Question 99. The best answer is **D** because in lines 45–48, the author explains that by calling Jefferson's explanation "ingeniously double-edged," he means that the explanation "simultaneously disavows any claims to originality"—thus, the writing wasn't new—"and yet insists that he depended upon no specific texts or sources"—thus, the writing wasn't copied from any particular text.

The best answer is NOT:

A, **B**, or **C** because the phrase "ingeniously double-edged" doesn't mean that Jefferson claimed to have written alone and copied from his own previous writings (**A**), that Jefferson felt his work was prophetic (**B**), or that Jefferson claimed he was a prophet or an influence on Lincoln (**C**).

Question 100. The best answer is **F** because lines 75–79 help create a sense of urgency about the writing of the Declaration, with the Continental Congress "being overwhelmed with military reports of imminent American defeat in New York and Canada," being "in session six days a week" as a full group, and meeting in committees "throughout the evenings." This situation led Jefferson to take "the obvious practical course" (line 79) writing the Declaration, which "was to rework his previous drafts on the same general theme" (lines 80–81).

The best answer is NOT:

G because there's no evidence in lines 75–79 or elsewhere in the passage that Jefferson was depressed by news of American defeats or that he lacked energy to draft a new document.

H because while Jefferson finished the Declaration in a hurry, there's no evidence in lines 75–79 or elsewhere in the passage that Jefferson knew the Declaration could solve the problems of the nation.

J because while lines 75–79 suggest that the war was moving closer to home, they also describe an urgent situation that would have made it impossible for Jefferson to take his time writing the Declaration.

READING • EXPLANATORY ANSWERS

Passage XI

Question 101. The best answer is **A** because claims and supporting details presented throughout the passage explain how and why *Star Trek* has endured: it "captured the imagination and viewer loyalty of millions of Americans" (lines 8–10), it was "the right show at the right time" (lines 17–18), and its space-exploration theme "resonated with millions of idealistic and awestruck Americans" (lines 37–38). The seventh paragraph (lines 56–67) and last paragraph highlight ways in which the show has endured. For instance, *Star Trek* "has spawned four prime-time series, continued syndication, a cartoon, eight major motion pictures, countless toys, games, and computer software" (lines 57–59), it has "exploded in print like no other phenomenon in American popular culture" (lines 64–65), and it "has become a television phenomenon like no other in American culture" (lines 82–84).

The best answer is NOT:

B because while the passage does describe what American society was like at the time the original *Star Trek* was created, particularly in the third paragraph (lines 16–24), the author only does this to put *Star Trek* into historical context.

C because the author doesn't discuss how *Star Trek's* storyline has changed over its thirty-year history. The passage, in fact, suggests that little has changed in the " 'known' universe of Starfleet, Klingons, and phasers" (line 80).

D because while the passage does mention the different forms *Star Trek* has taken, it doesn't describe any of these in detail.

Question 102. The best answer is **H** because the language the author uses throughout the passage—for example, "visionary episodes" (line 46), "eloquently" (line 70), and "provocative insight" (line 78)—shows his warm appreciation for *Star Trek*.

The best answer is NOT:

F because there's no evidence in the passage that the author is amused by *Star Trek*, and his appreciation for it goes well beyond tolerance.

G because the author's interest in *Star Trek* is not detached, but rather quite passionate.

J because there's no evidence in the passage that the author is mildly skeptical about *Star Trek*. On the contrary, the author is deeply enthusiastic about *Star Trek*, and he concludes with a strong note of optimism about *Star Trek's* future: "As America goes boldly into the next millennium, so will *Star Trek* in print, on television; and in formats yet to come" (lines 89–91).

READING • EXPLANATORY ANSWERS

Question 103. The best answer is C because two years after *Star Trek's* cancellation in 1969—in other words, 1971—"*Star Trek* somehow had captured the imagination and viewer loyalty of millions of Americans who 'discovered' the show anew in syndicated reruns" (lines 8–11).

The best answer is NOT:

A because "few were watching" (line 2) when *Star Trek* premiered in 1966.

B because *Star Trek* was "canceled as a ratings flop in January 1969" (lines 6–7).

D because while the passage states that "by 1977, *Star Trek* had become the most-watched off-network series drama of all time" (lines 54–55), the year 1977 was not when *Star Trek* first became a success—that was 1971.

Question 104. The best answer is J because the fourth paragraph (lines 25–33) indicates that entertainment programming during the time period was generally less willing than news programming to present a realistic picture of contemporary life. The author states, "Although television news programs helped focus the country on the rifts that had begun to percolate … as a rule entertainment programming avoided conflict and controversy" (lines 25–29). In addition, "Escapist comedy about suburban witches, genies, and rural townspeople was standard fare" (lines 29–31).

The best answer is NOT:

F or G because they reverse the actual relationship: entertainment programming was generally less, not more, willing than news programming to examine the rifts developing in American society (F) and to display violent conflict and controversy (G).

H because the fourth paragraph implies entertainment programming was generally more, not less, willing than news programming to promote the principles of conformity and order: "network drama emphasized law, order, and conformity" (lines 31–32), whereas "television news programs helped focus the country on the rifts that had begun to percolate."

Question 105. **The best answer is D** because the author claims *Star Trek* has had an "unparalleled impact" (line 60) on the publishing industry and that this impact has come in the diverse forms of "fan volumes, cast memoirs, and novels" (lines 65–66).

The best answer is NOT:

A because the author feels *Star Trek* has had an "unparalleled impact" on the publishing industry and that the industry has "recently become television friendly" (lines 61–62).

B because while the author traces the impact of *Star Trek* on publishing back to "the early 1970 s, when the first novels hit bookshelves" (lines 62–63), the author contradicts the idea of a lessening impact by noting that *Star Trek* books "continue to appear—and in record numbers" (lines 66–67).

C because the author doesn't claim *Star Trek's* impact on publishing has been primarily limited to novels.

Question 106. **The best answer is F** because the series, with its "visionary episodes on race relations, nuclear deterrence, multiculturalism, and ecology (among others)" (lines 46–48), came out during a period in which "social and political change" (lines 18–19) was not otherwise dealt with by most entertainment programming, which "avoided conflict and controversy" (lines 28–29).

The best answer is NOT:

G because while *Star Trek* had a "wide appeal in syndication" (line 53), there's no evidence in the passage that syndicated reruns in general were popular.

H because the author portrays *Star Trek*, with its "visionary episodes" on serious topics, as the opposite of escapist entertainment. The author does acknowledge that some people viewed *Star Trek* as "fantastic science fiction" (line 49), but the author himself believes *Star Trek* was "a window into current controversy" that "offered insight and added perspective to continued American cultural and political change in the 1970s" (lines 51–52).

J because the author makes no reference to an increasingly empowered middle class, only to "a culturally empowered youth movement" (lines 21–22) and to a middle class divided by "social and political change" (lines 18–19).

Question 107. The best answer is **D** because the author reports Roddenberry's claim that "*Star Trek* was less about the future than the present" (lines 41–42), which the author takes to mean that "precisely because of its futuristic storyline . . . *Star Trek* was able to address many of the contemporary social problems that other programs shunned" (lines 43–46).

The best answer is NOT:

A because, as the above quotations show, Roddenberry wasn't primarily concerned with showing how different life would be in the future.

B because while the author does note that *Star Trek* was "created in the optimistic afterglow of John F. Kennedy's inauguration of the space race" (lines 34–36), he doesn't claim that promoting the space program and the exploration of space was Roddenberry's main purpose in creating *Star Trek*.

C because with its "visionary episodes on race relations, nuclear deterrence, multiculturalism, and ecology (among others)" (lines 46–48), *Star Trek* was, in the author's view, anything but light entertainment.

Question 108. The best answer is **F** because the author states that "it was precisely because of its futuristic storyline that *Star Trek* was able to address many of the contemporary social problems that other programs shunned" (lines 43–46). The author claims that *Star Trek's* episodes dealing with present-day social problems "were not threatening to those who saw it as fantastic science fiction" (lines 48–49); for those who wanted to see *Star Trek* as a commentary on social problems, the series "offered insight and added perspective" (line 51).

The best answer is NOT:

G because the passage indicates that the main benefit of the futuristic storyline wasn't to enable writers to invent fantastic and entertaining science fiction (even if some people saw the series as "fantastic science fiction") but rather to offer unthreatening perspectives and insights.

H because while *Star Trek* "has spawned . . . eight major motion pictures" (lines 57–59) and "series such as *The Next Generation, Deep Space Nine,* and *Voyager*" (lines 85–86), the author doesn't claim that the ease with which related spin-offs could be developed was the primary benefit of the original show's futuristic storyline.

J because the series addressed, rather than avoided, controversial topics such as multiculturalism and nuclear deterrence.

Question 109. The best answer is **B** because the original *Star Trek's* "episodes on race relations, nuclear deterrence, multiculturalism, and ecology (among others)" (lines 46–48) were visionary because they dealt with contemporary social problems in a way that, like the series generally, "offered insight and added perspective" (line 51).

The best answer is NOT:

A because the passage indicates that the visionary episodes addressed "contemporary social problems" (line 45) and "current controversy" (line 50).

C because while the series did deal with difficult problems, nowhere does the author claim that the series offered solutions that were dreamy and unrealistic—a claim that would be inconsistent with the praiseful tone of the passage.

D because although the original *Star Trek* did have "wide appeal in syndication" (line 53), this fact is not directly relevant to the author's claim that some of the series' episodes were visionary.

Question 110. The best answer is **G** because the ideas of familiarity and change are at the heart of the paradox described by the author. He presents as conflicting the ideas of "changing cultural values" (lines 78–79) and the familiar, " 'known' universe of Starfleet, Klingons, and phasers" (line 80).

The best answer is NOT:

F because although the author does mention "changing cultural values," he doesn't describe the ideas of cultural values and entertainment as conflicting.

H because the author sees the ideas of comfort and the *Star Trek* universe as compatible, not conflicting: in times of "changing cultural values," people can take "reassuring comfort" (line 79) in the fact that the familiar *Star Trek* universe "can nonetheless survive intact, and even grow" (line 81).

J because the author doesn't present the ideas of survival and being provocative as conflicting, as evidenced by *Star Trek*, whose universe "can . . . survive intact, and even grow" despite the fact that the series offers "provocative insight" (line 78).

Passage XII

Question 111. The best answer is B because, according to the passage, Helmholtz had respect for Goethe's color theory: "Helmholtz . . . gave admiring lectures on Goethe and his science, on many occasions" (lines 7–9) and he, like Goethe, was interested in the idea of "color constancy" (line 10). Helmholtz was unusual in his respect for Goethe's color theory, as it "was, by and large, dismissed by all [Goethe's] contemporaries and has remained in a sort of limbo ever since, seen as the whimsy, the pseudoscience, of a very great poet" (lines 2–5).

The best answer is NOT:

A, C, or **D** because the reference to Helmholtz's "admiring lectures on Goethe and his science" rules out disbelief (**A**), amusement (**C**), and skepticism (**D**) as Helmholtz's attitude.

Question 112. The best answer is F because Clerk Maxwell showed how color photography was possible despite black-and-white emulsions "by photographing a colored bow three times, through red, green, and violet filters" (lines 42–44), then superimposing the "three 'color-separation' images" (lines 44–45) on a screen, "projecting each image through its corresponding filter" (line 47), which allowed the bow to "burst forth in full color" (lines 49–50).

The best answer is NOT:

G because the passage doesn't indicate that Clerk Maxwell's color triangle—"a graphic representation with three axes" that "showed how any color could be created by different mixtures of the three primary colors" (lines 35–38)—had any role in his 1861 demonstration.

H because the passage doesn't indicate that Clerk Maxwell's color top—which helped formalize "the notions of primary colors and color mixing" (lines 32–33)—had any role in his 1861 demonstration.

J because the passage doesn't mention color slides as being part of Clerk Maxwell's 1861 demonstration. Clerk Maxwell used "three 'color-separation' images" and three color filters, but these aren't the same as color slides.

Question 113. The best answer is **C** because the passage says Goethe was generally viewed by his contemporaries as "a very great poet" whose attempt at a color theory was "whimsy" and "pseudoscience" (line 5).

The best answer is NOT:

A or **B** because in ranking Goethe's science above his poetry, they say essentially the opposite of what the passage says about the general view of Goethe among his contemporaries.

D because by noting that Goethe's color theory was widely dismissed, the passage contradicts the idea that Goethe was generally viewed as a leading theorist who overturned previously standard approaches to scientific inquiry.

Question 114. The best answer is **J** because the passage defines color constancy as "the way in which the colors of objects are preserved, so that we can categorize them and always know what we are looking at, despite great fluctuations in the wavelength of the light illuminating them" (lines 10–14). Color constancy means, in this case, that a "red" apple looks "red" regardless of the wavelength of the light reflected by the apple.

The best answer is NOT:

F because the only mention in the passage of "split-beam" is in reference to Land's "split-beam camera" (line 66).

G because the only mention in the passage of "sensory flux" is in reference to the "chaotic sensory flux" (lines 25–26) from which "a stable perceptual world" (line 25)—including stable perceptions of color—must somehow be drawn.

H because the idea of color separation relates to the multiple images, taken through red, green, and violet filters, that Clerk Maxwell "brought … together by superimposing them upon a screen, projecting each image through its corresponding filter" (lines 45–47), thus demonstrating that "color photography was possible, despite the fact that photographic emulsions were themselves black and white" (lines 40–42).

Question 115. **The best answer is D** because the passage states that "the actual wavelengths reflected by an apple, for instance, will vary considerably depending on the illumination" (lines 14–16), or light reaching the apple.

The best answer is NOT:

A or **B** because there's no evidence in lines 14–17 to support the idea that the wavelengths reflected by an apple vary considerably as a result of differences between a viewer's two eyes (**A**) or the distance between the apple and the eyes (**B**).

C because while a viewer has the ability to perceive an apple as red in different lights according to Helmholtz's idea of "color constancy" (line 10), this isn't the reason the wavelengths reflected by an apple vary considerably. This stable perception of color is possible despite considerable variance in the wavelengths reflected by an apple.

Question 116. **The best answer is H** because the word *illuminant*, as it is used in line 20, refers to light that makes an object visible. Lines 14–16 indicate that "the actual wavelengths reflected by an apple, for instance, will vary considerably depending on the illumination," or light reaching the apple. Helmholtz felt people had some way of "discounting the illuminant" (lines 19–20), by which he meant some way of seeing an apple as red regardless of the wavelength of the light reflected by the apple.

The best answer is NOT:

F or **G** because there's no evidence in the passage to support the idea that the word *illuminant*, as it is used in line 20, refers to camera flash equipment (**F**) or to a color theorist (**G**).

J because while the word *illuminant*, as it is used in line 20, does refer to light, it doesn't refer specifically to light before it passes through a filter; instead, it refers more generally to light that makes an object visible.

Question 117. The best answer is B because the passage describes Helmholtz as being interested in " 'color constancy'—the way in which the colors of objects are preserved, so that we can categorize them and always know what we are looking at, despite great fluctuations in the wavelength of the light illuminating them" (lines 10–14).

The best answer is NOT:

A because although Helmholtz was interested in "color constancy," he believed that people continually saw an apple as red despite, not because of, varying wavelengths of light: "the actual wavelengths reflected by an apple, for instance, will vary considerably depending on the illumination, but we consistently see it as red, nonetheless" (lines 14–17).

C because there's no evidence in the passage that Helmholtz was preoccupied with the notion that humans undergo changes in color awareness as they age.

D because in the passage, Clerk Maxwell and Land—not Helmholtz—were the people interested in superimposing images.

Question 118. The best answer is F because the passage states that "any color could be created by different mixtures of the three primary colors" (lines 37–38).

The best answer is NOT:

G because there's no evidence in the passage that the human eye perceives primary colors first and then other colors.

H because the passage doesn't provide a sequence listing the order in which colors were first captured on film.

J because it's basically the opposite of what the passage says.

Question 119. The best answer is **B** because the passage says Clerk Maxwell's "most spectacular demonstration [was] the demonstration in 1861 that color photography was possible, despite the fact that photographic emulsions were themselves black and white" (lines 39–42).

The best answer is NOT:

A because there's no evidence in the passage that illuminants were thought to be stable rather than variable in Clerk Maxwell's time. On the contrary, Clerk Maxwell was Helmholtz's "great contemporary" (line 30), meaning he lived in Helmholtz's time, and Helmholtz knew there were "great fluctuations in the wavelength of the light illuminating" objects (lines 13–14).

C because there's no evidence in the passage that in Clerk Maxwell's time, the general public rejected the new technology of color photography as a stunt with no practical application.

D because there's no evidence in the passage that professional photographers in Clerk Maxwell's time were reluctant to abandon the established black-and-white aesthetic when presented with color photography.

Question 120. The best answer is **J** because for the demonstration, Land made "two black and-white images (using a split-beam camera so they could be taken at the same time from the same viewpoint, through the same lens)" (lines 66–68).

The best answer is NOT:

F because although Land used a screen in the demonstration (see lines 65–69), there's no evidence in the passage that the screen was lit from the front and back.

G because there's no evidence in the passage that the light sources flickered in the demonstration.

H because while Land did use a single lens to obtain his two images, there's no evidence in the passage that this lens was in two cameras.

Passage XIII

Question 121. This is an EXCEPT question, which asks you to find the answer choice that is *not* supported by the passage.

The best answer is C because neither Vida nor Ted has a perception of others that surfaces in humor. The other three answer choices are supported by the passage.

The best answer is NOT:

A because Vida and Ted share a willingness to accommodate each other's requests. When Ted asks Vida if it's OK if he builds and moves into a fort for the summer, she doesn't respond with "offense" or "alarm," but only with "interest" (lines 18–19). Vida sets the rules Ted has to follow: "Make sure you keep your nails together and don't dig into the trees" (lines 25–26). Though Ted never directly says he'll obey, the fact that he builds and is allowed to keep the fort suggests that he does.

B because Vida and Ted share a response to elements of nature. For example, the eighth paragraph (lines 28–35) illustrates Ted's response to the redwoods, while the ninth paragraph (lines 36–48) shows Ted's and Vida's responses to the moon.

D because Vida and Ted know what delights the other. They have a "silent communion" (line 12) through food, which Vida prepares knowing Ted's "great appetite and obvious enjoyment of it" (lines 14–15). Ted, for his part, knows Vida "loved to see the moon's reflection in the water" (line 38) and that she seemed to want to "touch the moon" (lines 41–42).

Question 122. This is a NOT question, which asks you to find the answer choice that is *not* supported by the passage. **The best answer is J** because nothing in the passage indicates Ted and Vida have painful disagreements that force Ted to move out. When Ted asks Vida if it's OK if he builds and moves into a fort for the summer, she doesn't respond with "offense" or "alarm," but only with "interest" (lines 18–19). The passage lists the reasons why Ted moves back into the house—"school was starting, frost was coming and the rains" (lines 87–88)— but these reasons don't include reaching an understanding with Vida. The other three answer choices are supported by the passage.

The best answer is NOT:

F because the passage shows Ted's relationship with Vida improving after he builds and occupies the fort: "Vida noticed Ted had become cheerful and would stand next to her, to her left side, talking sometimes" (lines 61–62), which leads Vida to think of him as "a wild thing at peace" (line 69).

G because the passage shows what connects and separates Vida and Ted and how Ted tests his limits. Ted and Vida are connected by, among other things, food (see lines 12–17) and their fondness for the moon (see lines 36–48). They're separated by physical distance, when Ted moves out into the fort, and by emotional distance, since Vida "realized she mustn't face [Ted] or he'd become silent and wander away" (lines 63–64). The passage implies in many ways that Ted is testing his limits, such as by showing him asking for privacy and privileges from Vida (see, for example, lines 9–11) and working on the upper floor of the fort (see lines 55–60).

H because the passage shows how Vida and Ted behave when each sees the fragility of someone or something held dear. To observe Ted, Vida "stood listening, in the same even breath and heart beat she kept when she spotted the wild pheasants" (lines 64–66). Ted would "curse himself" if he wasted the "beautiful glass" (lines 76–77).

Question 123. The best answer is **A** because in the twelfth paragraph (lines 61–69), the author says Vida avoided facing Ted and remained still to keep from disturbing "a wild thing at peace" (line 69), while in the thirteenth paragraph (lines 70–77), the author describes Ted making cuts in glass that "were slow and meticulous with a steady pressure" (line 75) and carefully following the design in order to avoid wasting the glass.

The best answer is NOT:

B because Vida is neither frustrated nor unsuccessful in the twelfth paragraph, while the thirteenth paragraph only says Ted became frustrated when he failed, not that success was always slightly out of reach for him.

C or **D** because neither the twelfth nor the thirteenth paragraph shows a character losing interest in a project as others get involved (**C**) or discovering a personal weakness in some situations becoming a personal strength in others (**D**).

Question 124. The best answer is **F** because the twelfth paragraph (lines 61–69) shows Vida carefully and reverently observing Ted in the same way she used with the wild pheasants. She "realized she mustn't face him or he'd become silent and wander away" (lines 63–64). She "stood listening" to Ted "in the same even breath and heart beat she kept when she spotted the wild pheasants" (lines 64–66) in order to avoid disturbing Ted. When the paragraph concludes, "So sharp, so perfect, so rare to see a wild thing at peace" (lines 68–69), it's clear the phrase *wild thing* refers both to the pheasants and to Ted.

The best answer is NOT:

G because the phrase refers to Ted, not Vida.

H because the phrase refers to how Vida sees Ted, not to how Ted sees himself.

J because the twelfth paragraph shows Vida appreciates how Ted "had become cheerful and would stand next to her, to her left side, talking sometimes" (lines 61–62), and she respects that Ted is like a wild thing, even though it means she has to act carefully around him.

Question 125. The best answer is B because the passage describes the teenage Ted as "thinning out, becoming angular and clumsy" and retaining "the cautiousness, the old-man seriousness he'd had as a baby" (lines 1–3) as well as his sense of humor, "always dry and to the bone since a small child" (lines 4–5).

The best answer is NOT:

A because Ted had always been cautious and serious, not lighthearted, and because Ted "had become cheerful" (line 61) and more talkative, not brooding and isolated, since moving into the fort.

C because while the passage says Ted even as a small child "let you know he was watching everything" (lines 5–6), it doesn't say that he watched others for indications of how he should behave or that as a teenager he looked to nature for such guidance.

D because Ted was cautious and serious, not outgoing, as a child, and because no adult, including Vida, is alarmed by Ted's introspection as a teenager. When Ted watches Vida "for signs of offense, alarm," he "only saw interest" in his plan for building and moving into a fort for the summer (lines 18–19).

Question 126. The best answer is G because the passage states that to Vida, Ted "seemed always to be at the center of his own universe, so it was no surprise to his mother" to hear Ted's plan to build and move into a fort for the summer (lines 7–11).

The best answer is NOT:

F because the passage presents the fort as Ted's project, not as something Vida started.

H or J because there's no evidence in the passage that Ted had put more and more distance between himself and Vida since the camping trip (H) or that he had a longstanding craving for the company of others (J).

Question 127. The best answer is **D** because the passage describes the *silent communion* as "the steady presence of love that flowed regularly, daily" (lines 12–13) through food: "the presence of his mother preparing it, his great appetite and obvious enjoyment of it—his nose smelling everything, seeing his mother more vividly than with his eyes" (lines 14–17).

The best answer is NOT:

A because Ted isn't disappointed but instead pleased by the food and his mother's preparation of it.

B because while Ted does promise not to return to the house all summer, even for food (see lines 9–11), he makes this promise aloud to Vida, and in any case this promise isn't what the phrase *silent communion* refers to.

C because while Ted's thought about liking the moon does shift from seeming like someone else's to seeming like his own (see lines 46–48), this shift isn't what the phrase *silent communion* refers to.

Question 128. The best answer is **H** because the seventh paragraph (lines 25–27) illustrates both Vida's interest in Ted's project and her concerns about it. Earlier, the passage says Vida showed "interest" (line 19) in Ted's plan and that "she trusted him to build well and not ruin things" (line 21). The seventh paragraph shows Vida anticipating possible problems with the proposed fort and indicating how to avoid them: "Make sure you keep your nails together and don't dig into the trees. I'll be checking. If the trees get damaged, it'll have to come down."

The best answer is NOT:

F or **J** because there's no evidence in the passage that Vida has a skeptical nature or that Ted feels disheartened (**F**) or that Vida wants to give Ted more responsibility than Ted himself wants to take on (**J**).

G because the passage never says the fort was dismantled, only that Ted would have to move back inside "in a few days" (line 91).

Question 129. The best answer is B because in Ted's view, redwoods "suck up sound and time and smell like another place" (line 30), making the cypress near the redwoods seem like a "very remote" location (line 29) for the fort.

The best answer is NOT:

A because the passage doesn't say that Ted will use the redwoods as supports for the fort, only that Ted will build the fort "by the redwoods, in the cypress trees" (line 23).

C because while the passage does say that the site for the fort "seemed so separate, alone—especially in the dark, when the only safe way of travel seemed flight (invisible at best)" (lines 33–35), it doesn't say that this was because redwoods are endangered.

D because as lines 33–35 show, the redwoods increased, rather than softened, disturbing emotions such as fear of the dark.

Question 130. The best answer is H because lines 58–60 state, "It felt weird going up into the tree, not as safe as his small, contained place on the ground."

The best answer is NOT:

F or **G** because Ted feels less, not more, safe going up into the tree to build the top floor.

J because there's no evidence in the passage that Ted built any of the fort from redwood or cypress; the only building material mentioned by name is plywood (see lines 49–51).

READING · EXPLANATORY ANSWERS

Passage XIV

Question 131. This is an EXCEPT question, which asks you to find the answer choice that is *not* supported by the passage.

The best answer is B because the passage doesn't mention waste emissions from the Asnaesverket Power Company being used to help produce heating oil. The other three answer choices are supported by the passage.

The best answer is NOT:

A because lines 27–29 state, "Waste steam from the power company is used by Novo Nordisk to heat the fermentation tanks that produce insulin and enzymes."

C because the process described in lines 27–29 "creates 700,000 tons of nitrogen-rich slurry a year" (lines 29–30), which Novo Nordisk gives to farmers for use as plant fertilizer.

D because lines 41–44 state, "The power company also squeezes sulfur from its emissions, but converts most of it to calcium sulfate (industrial gypsum), which it sells to Gyproc for wallboard."

Question 132. The best answer is **J** because "our system" (lines 1–2) is "a linear production system, which binges on virgin raw materials and spews out unusable waste" (lines 4–5). That "our system" is the system of the United States and Europe is implied in the seventh paragraph (lines 65–77) when the author mentions that environmental reform in the form of take-back laws is coming to these two regions.

The best answer is NOT:

F because while the passage does discuss four linked, co-located Denmark companies (see lines 13–44), the phrase "our system" refers to a wasteful system found in the United States and Europe.

G because the author implies that a system that produces recyclable durable goods such as refrigerators, washers, and cars is only "headed for the United States" (lines 68–69) via take-back laws yet to be passed. In any case, the phrase "our system" refers to a wasteful system found in both the United States and Europe.

H because it's the opposite of "our system," as described in the passage.

Question 133. The best answer is **A** because the second, third, and fourth paragraphs (lines 13–44) are mainly a case study of an ecopark in Kalundborg, Denmark. The three paragraphs show how the four companies in the ecopark depend on each other for resources and the recycling of waste. For example, the Asnaesverket Power Company sends waste steam to the Statoil Refinery and Novo Nordisk for use as a power source (see lines 16–20), while Statoil sends purified waste gas to Asnaesverket and Gyproc (see lines 35–39).

The best answer is NOT:

B because nowhere in the three paragraphs does the author indicate Denmark is one of the world's leading developers of new sources of energy or even that the sources of energy being used by the four companies in the ecopark are new.

C because while the passage does say that waste steam from the power company is used "to heat thirty-five hundred homes in the town, eliminating the need for oil furnaces" (lines 21–22), this isn't the same as saying that the town's need for energy can be eliminated through recycling. The town still needs energy; it just gets some of its energy needs met by an unusual source.

D because the three paragraphs aren't clear on whether a no-waste economy saves money, so saving money can't be their main focus.

Question 134. The best answer is **F** because the author says, "To keep our system from collapsing on itself" due to increasing amounts of biomass, "industrial ecologists are attempting to build a 'no-waste economy'" (lines 1–3), which she describes as "a web of closed loops in which a minimum of raw materials comes in the door, and very little waste escapes" (lines 6–8).

The best answer is NOT:

G because through her description in the seventh and last paragraphs (lines 65–89) of take-back laws and their impact, the author suggests that manufacturers, not consumers, should be held responsible for recycling many kinds of products.

H because the notion of having traditional businesses compete with new, innovative businesses doesn't directly come up in the passage. Instead, the author focuses on changes that can take place in all kinds of companies, traditional and new.

J because while the four Kalundborg companies described in the second, third, and fourth paragraphs (lines 13–44) are co-located in an ecopark, the author says that "industries need not be geographically close to operate in a food web as long as they are connected by a mutual desire to use waste" (lines 45–48). Also, the four Kalundborg companies aren't producing similar products.

Question 135. **The best answer is C** because Novo Nordisk's fermentation process produces "700,000 tons of nitrogen-rich slurry a year" (line 30), which is given free as fertilizer to farmers, whose plants "are in turn harvested to feed the bacteria in the fermentation tanks" (lines 33–34).

The best answer is NOT:

A because while purified waste gas from Statoil Refinery is sent to Gyproc (see lines 35–39), the passage doesn't show how, if at all, Statoil depends directly on Gyproc.

B because while the Asnaesverket Power Company "delivers its cooling water, now toasty warm, to fifty-seven ponds' worth of fish" (lines 23–24), the passage doesn't show how, if at all, Asnaesverket depends directly on fish farmers.

D because the passage doesn't show any direct relationship between Statoil and Novo Nordisk.

Question 136. **The best answer is G** because in the sixth paragraph (lines 58–64), the author uses phrases such as "so far" (line 58), "but what happens" (line 59), and "right now" (line 61) to signal a transition between the two main points in the passage: "recycling within a circle of companies" (lines 58–59) and the final fate of products once they leave the manufacturer.

The best answer is NOT:

F because the sixth paragraph doesn't provide any evidence to support Daniel Chiras's statement in lines 54–57; the discussion in the sixth paragraph is on products, not by-products.

H because the sixth paragraph offers no conclusion to the author's discussion about a no-waste economy; instead, the paragraph shifts gears between two points related to the idea of a no-waste economy.

J because while the sixth paragraph does provide something of a summary ("so far . . ."), the paragraph goes on to introduce the passage's second main point, which concerns the final fate of products once they leave the manufacturer.

Question 137. The best answer is **D** because the author says the German take-back laws "start with the initial sale," meaning "companies must take back all their packaging or hire middlemen to do the recycling" (lines 72–74). This fits in with the author's general discussion in the seventh paragraph (lines 65–77) of take-back laws, which "will require companies to take back their durable goods such as refrigerators, washers, and cars at the end of their useful lives" (lines 69–71).

The best answer is NOT:

A or **B** because there's no evidence in the passage that German take-back laws shift the responsibility of recycling from the local government to the manufacturer (**A**) or from the manufacturer to the local government (**B**).

C because it reverses the actual relationship.

Question 138. The best answer is **J** because lines 45–48 state that "industries need not be geographically close to operate in a food web as long as they are connected by a mutual desire to use waste."

The best answer is NOT:

F because, as the above quotation shows, companies need not relocate their operations to a common geographic area in Europe to be part of a food web.

G because while the Asnaesverket Power Company and Novo Nordisk do provide industrial waste to private homes and farming operations (see lines 16–34), the passage doesn't say that all companies that want to be part of a food web have to do this.

H because food webs, as described in the passage, don't eliminate the need for raw materials. Instead, one company's waste becomes another company's raw material, as when sulfur removed from Statoil Refinery's waste gas during purification is sent to Kemira for use in sulfuric acid production (see lines 35–41).

Question 139. The best answer is A because the author says "designed offal" results when companies design their processes in such a way that "any waste that falls on the production-room floor is valuable and can be used by someone else" (lines 49–51).

The best answer is NOT:

B because "designed offal" doesn't necessarily involve reducing waste products: "in this game of 'designed offal,' a process with lots of waste, as long as it's 'wanted waste,' may be better than one with a small amount of waste that must be landfilled or burned" (lines 51–54).

C because "designed offal" is a success story, not a failure of technology to keep pace with how to dispose of waste products.

D because while the author does mention landfills (see lines 51–54 and 62–64), she never discusses the idea of making landfill spaces more efficient. Her focus is on keeping products out of landfills.

Question 140. The best answer is H because in lines 56–57, Daniel Chiras is quoted as saying that "technologies that produce by-products society cannot absorb are essentially failed technologies."

The best answer is NOT:

F or G because Chiras's quotation deals with whether society as a whole, and not a particular technology, can make use of waste. The "designed offal" example described in lines 48–54 suggests that how much waste a particular technology produces isn't the most important factor in evaluating the environmental impact of the technology: a technology might produce more waste than it uses but still be environmentally sound so long as someone can use the waste

J because Chiras doesn't say in the passage that a failed technology is one that produces durable goods such as refrigerators. The passage, on the contrary, indicates that durable goods can be produced with a greatly reduced environmental impact (see lines 59–84).

Passage XV

Question 141. The best answer is D because the word *appreciate* has multiple meanings, one of which is to grasp, comprehend, or recognize the value of something. The narrator's use of vivid sensory details suggests that they have left a strong impression on her.

The best answer is NOT:

A because, as the opening line of the passage states, the narrator has just turned ten. She reads a book *Eight Cousins* for most of the trip, which shows that she is able to focus on reading and that she has not been rattled by the experience of parting with her mother temporarily.

B because the narrator is not upset. Rather, she is depicted as unfazed by the trip to see her grandmother.

C because while the narrator uses words like *now* and *first* that signal change over time, these changes occur over the course of one summer. There is no indication that this is a recurring trip

Question 142. The best answer is H because the narrator portrays the other children who live on Nai-nai's street as companions who join her, crowding together in the back of a station wagon or playing a game.

F because there is no indication that the narrator has a negative attitude toward the children who live on Nai-nai's street. She is comfortable crowding together with these kids in the back of a station wagon and joining them in softball and kickball games.

G because the narrator observes that the ocean is the most beautiful one she has ever seen. She describes her experience of viewing the Gulf of Mexico, but there is no indication that the other children enjoy sharing stories about the ocean.

J because the children all crowd together in the back of a station wagon to head to the beach. There is no indication that the other children have been deprived of the opportunity to go to the beach. The narrator describes the Gulf of Mexico, but that is only because it is a body of water that she has seen that the other children likely have not (lines 42–47).

Question 143. **The best answer is B** because the girls are growing accustomed to their grandmother and vice-versa. This is conveyed when the narrator says "now we compromise" (line 57). For example, Nai-nai initially scolds the girls for staying out in the sun, but she "softens when she sees how hungry" the girls are (lines 49–50).

The best answer is NOT:

A because this answer choice does not include that the grandmother is becoming accustomed to the girls' ways. For example, "one night she [Nai-nai] even makes hamburgers" (line 59).

C because the grandmother does not seem exhausted by the girls' ways. Nai-nai is depicted as being full of energy.

D because the grandmother softens over the course of the summer. She is initially rigid about the use of chopsticks, for example, but she later allows Marty to use a fork.

Question 144. **The best answer is J** because these presents from her admirers (flowers, music boxes, and perfume) remind Nai-nai of her experiences as a lieder singer. She shows these mementos to her granddaughters in order to convey the depth of her audience's admiration.

The best answer is NOT:

F because there is no indication that the grandmother hopes that the girls will pursue careers as singers or actors. She is simply sharing mementos that remind her of her own experiences as a lieder singer.

G because while "she kept everything" (line 66), there is no indication that she expects the girls to treasure these sentimental items.

H because the grandmother does not seem to be exaggerating her experiences as a lieder singer. The flowers, music boxes, and perfume are gifts from admirers. The grandmother's story does not seem to be embellished.

Question 145. The best answer is D because the narrator says, "I imagine the perfume to be like orange juice concentrate: if you added water, it would be as good as fresh" (lines 69–71). The narrator draws an abstract comparison between the old perfume and orange juice concentrate. This imaginative imagery conveys how dried up and condensed the perfume has become.

The best answer is NOT:

A because although the baby T-shirt is worn by the narrator's toy Piggy, it is Nai-nai who dresses the toy in this T-shirt after noticing its tattered chest. The fact that the narrator still has such a toy suggests that the ten-year-old is maturing but that she still holds on to some of her childhood wonder.

B because the description of the stewardess's white gloves is straightforward and literal rather than figurative: "Ma hands us over to the stewardess, who wears white gloves" (lines 6–7).

C because the narrator is straightforwardly describing the smell of the station wagon when she says it "smells like hot rubber and coconut lotion" (lines 38–39).

Question 146. The best answer is G because the introductory paragraph indicates that "my sister, Marty, and I are going while Ma and Daddy spend the summer in Taiwan, where my father has a teaching job" (lines 3–5).

The best answer is NOT:

F because while it is the narrator's tenth birthday, this is not the reason for the trip. In fact, the trip seems to distract the narrator's mother from even celebrating the narrator's birthday. The text indicates that "Ma doesn't get a cake or presents because we're busy getting ready to go to visit our Nai-nai in San Diego" (lines 1–3).

H because the parents do not express any desire for the girls to learn about their grandmother's past. The girls do end up learning a good deal about their grandmother's life experiences, including her time working as a lieder dancer, but this happens incidentally while they are spending time with their grandmother. It is not the stated purpose of the trip.

J because while it is true that Nai-nai lives by the ocean, there is no indication that there is *more* to do at Nai-nai's home. The narrator describes how she rides bikes and goes to the beach at Nai-nai's, but it is possible that there is even *more* to do back home.

Question 147. **The best answer is D** because the narrator has only just turned ten years old. She is embarrassed that she has this toy, as shown when she says, "I have brought Piggy, although I am way too old" (lines 29–30). She is on the cusp of adolescence. Her parents are far away, and this toy brings her comfort. Piggy's tattered chest and Nai-nai calling Piggy "poor old man" (lines 32–33) further indicate that the narrator has had Piggy for quite some time.

The best answer is NOT:

A because there is no indication that Nai-nai has ever been laughed at. We learn that Nai-nai was a lieder dancer, but we only learn of her admirers who gave her gifts. We never learn of any negative experiences Nai-nai faced during her career as a lieder dancer.

B because Nai-nai places the baby T-shirt on Piggy after noticing his tattered chest. There is no indication that the narrator particularly likes this baby T-shirt.

C because Marty does ask Nai-nai *when* she goes to bed, but this is just because the girls are in awe of how early Nai-nai wakes up (lines 21–25).

Question 148. **The best answer is H** because the narrator says, "I tell them about the beach in Monterey, where I was born" (lines 46–47). The narrator's ability to recall details about her life in Monterey, including the wildflowers and the seals, shows that she lived there after her birth (lines 47–48).

The best answer is NOT:

F because Monterey is where the narrator spent her early childhood. She did visit her Aunty Mabel and Uncle Richard later on in her childhood (lines 42–46)

G because it is unclear if the narrator ever visited Nai-nai when she "used to live with Su-yi" (lines 18–19).

J because her father is teaching in Taiwan for the summer, but there is no indication that the narrator has ever been to Taiwan (lines 4–5).

Question 149. The best answer is B because the narrator uses hyperbole: an exaggeration that is not intended to be interpreted literally. In other words, the narrator actually *does* recognize her father, but she is taken aback by how much his appearance has changed over time. She states that, "The man in the picture has dark, thick hair and a smooth, confident face, as if nothing bad had ever happened to him" (lines 75–77). This implies that her father's hair is now gray, white, or balding and that he has been wearied by life's experiences.

The best answer is NOT:

A because there is no indication that her father regularly lives apart from the family.

C because "my father is unrecognizable" is an excessively literal interpretation. This line is intended hyperbolically, not literally. The narrator does recognize her father.

D because it is clear that her father looks young in the photograph from his wedding day, and it would not be logical for him to look *younger* now, years later. Dark, thick hair is typically associated with youth. It is implied that the father's hair is now gray, white, or balding.

Question 150. The best answer is F because when the narrator looks at a photograph of her father from his wedding day, she says he is "unrecognizable" (line 75). She describes the man in the photograph as having "a smooth, confident face, as if nothing bad had ever happened to him" (lines 76–77). This implies that her father has experienced hardships that have aged him physically and mentally.

The best answer is NOT:

G because the narrator's father is not present when Marty cries as she boards the airplane. The narrator's mother is traveling to visit the narrator's father in Taiwan.

H because there is no indication that his marriage has been a turning point. The narrator's description of the man in the photograph implies that at some point after his marriage, the man experienced hardships, but it is not clear when or why those difficulties occurred.

J because the narrator and Marty are flying *to* San Diego in order to spend the summer with their Nai-nai (lines 2–3). Therefore, readers know that the family does not live in San Diego. The father is just temporarily living in Taiwan to teach for the summer, so it seems likely that he typically lives with his family during the regular school year (lines 4–5).

READING • EXPLANATORY ANSWERS

Passage XVI

Question 151. The best answer is **A** because, as the passage states, this practice "is intended to stimulate the bears' minds as well as their appetites" (lines 8–9). Animal enrichment programs such as "mental puzzles designed as treats" echo animals' experiences in the wild in the sense that animals are challenged to interact with their environment to achieve a goal (lines 31–32).

The best answer is NOT:

B because the passage does not suggest that animals are being *tricked* into eating well-balanced diets.

C because the passage does not suggest that the animal enrichment programs are designed to improve the relationships between animals and their caretakers. Increased tolerance of human beings may be an unintended outcome of the enrichment programs, but it is not the primary goal.

D because there is no indication that these programs are designed to prepare the animals for release.

Question 152. The best answer is **F** because Dennett and Terrace are described as skeptics about animal phenomenal consciousness (line 73). Dennett and Terrace believe that animals are merely displaying a physical response to an external stimulus.

The best answer is NOT:

G because Dennett and Terrace emphasize that animal behavior is not reflective of complex mental processes. Instead, they believe, animal behavior is a physical response to external stimuli.

H because Dennett and Terrace are skeptical of the notion that animals display phenomenal consciousness (line 73).

J because Dennett and Terrace are skeptical of the notion that animals display phenomenal consciousness (line 73). Self-consciousness is an even higher level of consciousness. Therefore, Dennett and Terrace would not believe that animals possess self-consciousness (the capacity to think about one's experience).

Question 153. **The best answer is D** because Dennett is skeptical of the notion that animals display phenomenal consciousness (lines 70–72). Phenomenological consciousness refers to animals experiencing the world consciously the way human beings do: experiencing emotions, pain, and sensations (lines 50–51). The evidence in lines 22–35 suggests that animals have complex mental lives and capacities.

The best answer is NOT:

A because the passage's author presents various viewpoints rather than one position on the issue of animal consciousness. To the degree the author reveals her stance, she is closer to believing that animals do have some level of consciousness. She says that the animals cited in lines 22–35 "clearly aren't automatons" (line 49). Therefore, it would not be accurate to say that the evidence of animal intelligence presented in lines 22–35 *undermines* the author's viewpoint. These lines support her viewpoint.

B because the passage states that "data have emerged that would seem to have turned the tide definitively in Dr. Griffin's favor" (lines 22–24). In other words, new research supports Dr. Griffin's belief that animal behavior is more than merely a response to a physical stimulus such as peanut butter or a toy.

C because Dr. Colin McGinn believes that animals have phenomenological consciousness. In other words, animals "experience pain, desire, and other sensations the way humans do" (line 51).

Question 154. **The best answer is H** because animal rights activists like Peter Singer "believe that most if not all animals have phenomenal consciousness" (67–68). In other words, animal activists believe that animals experience emotions and sensations rather than merely reacting automatically to physical stimulus.

The best answer is NOT:

F because calling animals "stimulus response automata" implies that animals react to their environments in a preprogrammed, robotic manner, without consciousness.

G because the passage explains that animal enrichment programs "are intended to stimulate the bears' minds as well as their appetites" (lines 8–9). The passage does not introduce animal activists' position on animal enrichment programs.

J because the behaviorist doctrine holds that animals are "little more than 'stimulus response automata,' robots with a central nervous system" (lines 17–19). Behaviorism is a branch of psychology that focuses on observable behaviors in response to stimuli.

Question 155. The best answer is **B** because the passage indicates that when Dr. Griffin published a book on animals' thoughts and feelings in 1976, "other scientists were appalled. . . The idea that an ant or an elephant might have thoughts, images, experiences or beliefs was not just laughable; it was seditious" (lines 16–21).

The best answer is NOT:

A because the passage mentions early scientific work on primate gestures and facial expressions to provide an example of data that was initially "grossly misinterpreted" (lines 39–40). These studies are not characterized as prompting today's controversy over whether or not animals think.

C because the story of a parrot that can identify colors is offered as a demonstration of animal intelligence (lines 24–26). It is not what initially prompted controversy over whether or not animals think.

D because the animal enrichment programs at the Central Park Zoo did not initially prompt controversy over whether animals think. These programs are described in the first paragraph as a way to introduce Dr. Griffin whose book prompted debate over whether animals have thoughts and feelings (lines 12–21).

Question 156. The best answer is **H** because Daniel Dennett's main idea is that human beings can easily infer attributes of consciousness when observing non-conscious entities like robots. Dennett states, "It is in fact ridiculously easy to induce powerful intuitions of not just sentience [awareness] but full-blown consciousness (ripe with malevolence [hatred] or curiosity or friendship) by exposing people to quite simple robots made to move in familiar mammalian ways" (lines 77–81).

The best answer is NOT:

F because Dennett's main point is not to emphasize how humanoid robots can be. Instead, he is pointing out how human beings tend to see human attributes (like the capacity for thoughts and emotions) in robots even if the robots are simple and just "made to move in familiar mammalian ways" (line 81).

G because this quotation focuses on human beings perceiving human thoughts and feelings where, according to Dennett, they likely do not exist.

J because the quotation does not address the phenomenal consciousness of insects.

Question 157. The best answer is **A** because Dr. Griffin expresses his disagreement with Daniel Dennett who believes that proof of animal consciousness is "a wild goose chase" (line 87). Dennett believes no definitive answer will ever be found. Griffin responds to Dennett's skepticism, saying, "But there are no neurons or synapses in the human brain that aren't also in animals. It's as difficult to disprove animal consciousness as it is to prove it" (lines 88–90).

The best answer is NOT:

B because this concluding paragraph does not focus on providing specific evidence to support Donald Griffin's theory that animals demonstrate thoughts and feelings.

C because Dr. Griffin has a lighthearted attitude about the debate his work prompted. He is "mildly amused by the debate his work has helped unleash" (lines 83–84).

D because the last paragraph does not imply that Donald Griffin is prepared to provide new evidence countering Daniel Dennett's statements. Both Griffin and Dennett seem to accept that their debate may never be definitively resolved.

Question 158. The best answer is **G** because animals are described as being thought of as "'stimulus response automata,' robots with a central nervous system" (lines 17–19).

The best answer is NOT:

F because puzzles disguised as toys are examples of animal enrichment (lines 31–32).

H because Alex, the parrot that can identify colors, is offered as an example of an animal that demonstrates consciousness rather than mere automatic response to physical stimulus (lines 25–26).

J because Daniel Dennett explains that when robots are "made to move in familiar mammalian ways," people attribute human capacities like consciousness to these robots. The term "stimulus response automata" is used earlier in the passage to describe one interpretation of animal behavior as a simplistic and automatic response to physical stimuli (lines 17–19).

READING • EXPLANATORY ANSWERS

Question 159. The best answer is B because early scientific work on primate gestures and facial expressions is noted in order to provide an example of data that was initially "grossly misinterpreted" (lines 39–40). The word *misconstrued* is a synonym for *misinterpreted*.

The best answer is NOT:

A because Dr. Griffin states that "Scientists, including me, have come to be very cautious. Early work on primate gestures and facial expressions was grossly misinterpreted" (lines 37–40). Here, Griffin explains that he maintains a measured outlook about the rightness of his theory that animals display consciousness. He acknowledges that scientists often misinterpret data and that they often only discover this years later. He does not think that early studies were "overly cautious."

C because Dr. Griffin does not believe that scientists' early work on primate gestures and facial expression was laughable. However, earlier in the passage, the author indicates that Dr. Griffin's initial introduction of the concept of animal consciousness was deemed "laughable" by the scientific community (lines 20–21).

D because Dr. Griffin regards early scientific work on primate gestures and facial expressions was initially "grossly misinterpreted" (lines 39–40). This does not suggest that Dr. Griffin would characterize this early scientific work as "largely satisfactory."

Question 160. The best answer is F because phenomenal consciousness is defined in lines 50–52: "Do they [animals] experience pain, desire, and other sensations the way humans do? (Philosophers call this *phenomenal consciousness*.)"

The best answer is NOT:

G because stimulus response refers to an automatic behavior in response to a physical stimulus.

H because Dr. Griffin notes that "early work on primate gestures and facial expressions was grossly misinterpreted" (lines 37–40). Griffin indicates this in order to remind scientists to avoid jumping to conclusions when interpreting data. The word *primate* refers to a mammal group that includes human beings and apes. This portion of the passage does not address primates' experiences of pain or desire.

J because, in the ninth paragraph (lines 73–82), the word *sentience* is defined as a cognitive capacity that falls slightly below consciousness.

Passage XVII

Question 161. The best answer is **D** because the author, Margaret Atwood, describes the art of telling and listening to stories. Much of the passage focuses on the ideal role of the storyteller in relation to the listener.

> The best answer is NOT:

A because this passage also addresses the role of the writer, who must connect with the listener through strong storytelling. For example, Atwood states, "A writer with nothing but a formal sense will produce dead work, but so will one whose only excuse for what is on the page is that it really happened" (lines 31–33).

B because Atwood only briefly mentions nonstop talking and how it relates to the art of storytelling.

C because Atwood briefly refers to the oral tradition of storytelling when she says, "the story comes closest to resembling two of its oral predecessors, the riddle and the joke," but she is not attempting to persuade readers to only engage in oral storytelling (lines 61–62).

Question 162. The best answer is **F** because the first paragraph (lines 1–2) introduces a thesis that the rest of the passage explores in greater detail.

> The best answer is NOT:

G because the opinion introduced in the first paragraph is supported by the author's personal experience. Atwood's use of the word *we* reinforces this point.

H because the image of stories coming to us through the air is not difficult to imagine, and this image clearly relates to the content of the passage.

J because the main point of this passage is not that writing is easy. In fact, the passage highlights that writing is a hard-earned skill.

Question 163. The best answer is **A** because a "sense of propriety" means an awareness of what is considered appropriate. The passage suggests that this sensibility develops overtime as we mature from childhood into adulthood, gaining experience in a variety of social situations.

The best answer is NOT:

B because the word *law* is too extreme for what is discussed in this passage. Atwood refers to social norms, not codified laws. "The adult rules of censorship" (line 19) are tacit, or unspoken.

C because Atwood portrays writers as individuals who do not strictly abide by the societal norms regarding which subjects are appropriate and which are taboo. She explains, perhaps writers "remained talebearers. We learned to keep our eyes open, but not to keep our mouths shut" (lines 19–21).

D because Atwood describes the "rules of censorship" as *adult* (line 19). She suggests that children often inadvertently violate these rules, blurting out stories that were meant to remain private (lines 18–19).

Question 164. The best answer is **G** because this is a NOT question, which means you should eliminate answers that are reflected in the content of the passage: the elements of good storytelling. Atwood explains, "A writer with nothing but a formal sense will produce dead work, but so will one whose only excuse for what is on the page is that it really happened" (lines 31–32).

The best answer is NOT:

F because Atwood emphasizes that good stories require narrative skill. She describes how awful it is to be trapped on a bus with a "nonstop talker graced with no narrative skill" (lines 34–35).

H because Atwood emphasizes the importance of proper pacing when telling a story. She describes how awful it is to be trapped on a bus with a "nonstop talker graced with no narrative skill or sense of timing" (lines 34–35).

J because Atwood believes that perhaps "original and living writing is generated" from "the collisions between two kinds of stories [real and imaginary]" (lines 30–33).

Question 165. The best answer is B because Atwood writes the following: "perhaps it's from the collision between these two kinds of stories—what is often called 'real life' (and which writers greedily think of as their 'material') and what is sometimes dismissed as 'mere literature' or 'the kinds of things that happen only in stories'—that original and living writing is generated" (lines 25–31).

The best answer is NOT:

A because when Atwood references fiction as "mere literature," she is not highlighting the difference between adult readers and younger readers. Instead, she highlights the two types of stories many of us encounter in childhood that then inform our concept of what constitutes good storytelling.

C because Atwood describes real life (and not literature) as what "writers greedily think of as their 'material'" (lines 27–28).

D because Atwood does not claim that real life produces formal, dead work. Instead, she states that a writer "whose only excuse for what is on the page is that it really happened" will produce what she calls "dead work" (lines 32–33).

Question 166. The best answer is J because lines 38–84 describe the similarities between what child and adult readers hope to find in worthwhile stories.

The best answer is NOT:

F because Atwood explains that successful stories written for adults and successful tales told to children share several traits. These stories hold our attention (line 40), have a solid structure (lines 41–49), and effectively build and resolve tension through an effective plot (lines 57–61).

G because Atwood suggests that strong storytelling requires a wide range of skills, including proper pacing (line 35), a sense of urgency (line 76), and the right balance of fiction and realism (lines 25–31). Writing is never portrayed as an easy task regardless of the intended audience.

H because Atwood explains that "original and living writing" is perhaps best generated "from the collision between these two kinds of stories" [realistic and fictional] (lines 25–30).

Question 167. The best answer is C because this is an EXCEPT question, which means you should eliminate answers that describe similarities between jokes, riddles, and good stories. Atwood states that the ending to a good story "must be at one and the same time completely unexpected and inevitable" (lines 59–60).

The best answer is NOT:

A because Atwood says that jokes, riddles, and stories all "require the same mystifying buildup" (lines 62–63).

B because Atwood says that jokes, riddles, and stories all "require the same mystifying buildup, the same surprising twist" (lines 62–64).

D because Atwood says that jokes, riddles, and stories all require "the same impeccable sense of timing" (lines 62–64).

Question 168. The best answer is H because Atwood explains how children learn what is considered appropriate by listening in on or being excluded from adult conversation (lines 15–22). In this way, children "create meaning" about definitions of what constitutes appropriate storytelling.

The best answer is NOT:

F because Atwood is not suggesting that children struggle to distinguish reality from fantasy. Atwood explains that eavesdropping on and being excluded from the adult world of storytelling shape a child's sense of what is appropriate (lines 15–22).

G because Atwood explains that writers essentially dismiss the notion of "adult rules of censorship" when she writes "perhaps this is what writers are: those who never kicked the habit. We remained talebearers. We learned to keep our eyes open, but not to keep our mouths shut" (lines 19–22).

J because Atwood is not describing children "tuning out the voices of the adult word." On the contrary, Atwood emphasizes how children are eager to listen to adult stories, stating, "we have all been little pitchers with big ears, shooed out of the kitchen when the unspoken is being spoken" (lines 15–17).

Question 169. The best answer is **A** because Atwood explains "I always read to the end, out of some adult sense of duty owed" (lines 40–42). As an adult reader, she feels obligated to finish a story once she has begun reading it.

The best answer is NOT:

B because Atwood explains that, "out of some adult sense of duty owed" she continues reading a story to the end even if she starts to "fidget and skip pages" (lines 41–42).

C because she does feel guilty if she skips pages. She says when she "fidget[s] and skip[s] pages," she begins to "wonder if conscience demands" that she reread earlier parts of the story" lines 42–43).

D because Atwood's descriptions of her expectations about the end of a story do not concern whether the ending is happy or tragic.

Question 170. The best answer is **F** because Atwood addresses prospective writers' relationships with readers, saying, "They [readers] are longing to hear a story, but only if you [the writer] are longing to tell one…If you [writers] want their [readers'] full attention, you must give them yours. You need a sense of urgency" (lines 75–76). Here, Atwood equates *urgency* with full attention.

The best answer is NOT:

G because Atwood's description of the term *urgency* does not emphasize the story's pace or level of excitement. This is clear when Atwood writes "Urgency does not mean frenzy" (line 77)."

H because Atwood describes the importance of proper pacing in writing. She does not indicate that the plot should be revealed immediately.

J because Atwood focuses on a reader's sense of duty, or lack thereof, rather than on a writer's sense of duty.

Passage XVIII

Question 171. The best answer is **D** because this passage is descriptive rather than persuasive and focuses on the life cycle of stars.

The best answer is NOT:

A because the passage focuses primarily on one star: the Sun. Astrophysicists draw conclusions about the future of the sun based on observations of "other stars *like* the Sun that are at different stages in their evolution" (lines 37–38).

B because the passage suggests that scientists cannot directly observe the Sun's core.

C because this passage does not attempt to persuade the reader, and it focuses on the Sun, not on the origin of Earth and its inhabitants.

Question 172. **The best answer is J** because this is an EXCEPT question, which means you should eliminate answers that include calculations noted in the passage. The passage does indicate that the Sun will eventually emit a "dull blue glow," but it does not specify *how long* this glow will last (lines 27–28).

The best answer is NOT:

F because Rees writes "Astrophysicists have computed what the inside of the Sun should be like, and have achieved gratifying fit with its observed radius, brightness, temperature and so forth. They can tell us confidently what conditions prevail in its deep interior" (lines 30–32).

G because Rees writes that astrophysicists "can also calculate how it [the Sun] will evolve over the next few billion years" (lines 34–35).

H because Rees writes that "Even among the nearby stars, we can discern some that are still youngsters, no more than a million years old, and others in a near-terminal state, which may already have swallowed up any retinue of planets that they once possessed. Such inferences are based on the assumption that atoms and their nuclei are the same everywhere" (lines 44–50).

Question 173. **The best answer is C** because this is an EXCEPT question, which means you should eliminate answers that describe requirements of controlled fusion. Controlled fusion mimics the Sun but does not directly use "the Sun as a fuel source" in the way solar panels could, for example.

The best answer is NOT:

A because transformation of atomic nuclei is described in the passage's explanation of controlled fusion.

B because the passage explains that controlled fusion requires "temperatures of many millions of degrees" (line 7).

D because the passage explains that the ultra-hot gas involved in fusion must be "trapped by magnetic forces" (lines 8–11). One can infer that one of the gases involved in fusion is helium given that the passage opens by describing how "the Sun is fueled by conversion of hydrogen into helium" (lines 1–3).

Question 174. The best answer is G because the passage describes the anticipated life path of the Sun in lines 18–29. In the Sun's final stages, "some of its outer layers will be blown off, but the core will then settle down as a white dwarf" (lines 26–27).

The best answer is NOT:

F because the passage does not state this. The description of the Sun's last event in its life cycle emphasizes that the Sun will shine with "a dull blue glow, no brighter than a full moon today" (lines 27–28).

H because the passage does not state this. In the Sun's final stages "some of its outer layers will be blown off, but the core will then settle down as a white dwarf" (lines 26–27), but there is no indication that these layers will be blown off so explosively that they will leave the solar system entirely.

J because the passage does not state this. It explains that stars "ten times as heavy as the sun" follow a different life cycle that ends in exploding as supernovae (lines 54–55). These heavier stars "shine thousands of times more brightly, and consume their fuel more quickly. Their lifetimes are much shorter than the Sun's, and they expire in a more violent way, by exploding as supernovae" (lines 56–60).

Question 175. The best answer is C because these lines emphasize how astrophysicists use data taken at a single point in time to compare stars at various stages of their life cycle. Rees writes "Having a single 'snapshot' of each star's life is not a fatal handicap if we have a large sample, born at different times, available for study" (lines 38–41).

The best answer is NOT:

A because these lines do not emphasize astrophysicist's ability to locate stars that have the same features and birth date as the Sun. On the contrary, these lines emphasize that one must have data about stars at various ages and stages of their life cycles to infer accurate calculations about any particular star like the Sun.

B because these lines are not emphasizing the difficulty of getting clear photographs of the Sun as it undergoes changes in its structure. While it is true that it would be difficult to get pictures of the Sun that could capture its evolution over its nearly five-billion-year life cycle, that is not the point of emphasis in these lines.

D because the use of the word *fatal* in these lines is figurative. Rees writes, "Having a single 'snapshot' of each star's life is not a fatal handicap if we have a large sample, born at different times, available for study" (lines 38–41). Here, Rees is explaining that research into the Sun's life cycle doesn't grind to a halt, or die, simply because astrophysicists can only gather current data about stars as they exist today.

Question 176. The best answer is **H** because this is a NOT question, which means you should eliminate answer choices that *are* answered by information given in the passage. The passage does not answer *why* the Sun is so massive in comparison to the Earth. The passage does not even mention *that* the Sun is more massive than the Earth.

The best answer is NOT:

F because the passage explains that a white dwarf results when a star like the Sun will "brighten up and expand into the kind of star known as a 'red giant', engulfing the inner planets and vaporizing any life that remains on Earth…Some of it will settle down as a white dwarf, shining with a dull blue glow, no brighter than a full moon today" (lines 23–28).

G because the passage explains that astrophysicists draw inferences about the Sun "based on the assumption that atoms and their nuclei are the same everywhere" (lines 49–50).

J because the passage explains that astronomers are fascinated by supernovae because they "represent cataclysmic events in the life of the stars, involving some 'extreme' physical processes" (lines 65–66).

Question 177. The best answer is **A** because this paragraph aims to clarify the connection between our everyday lives and the phenomenon studied by astrophysicists. Rees explains that without supernovae, "we would never have existed" (line 74).

The best answer is NOT:

B because this answer choice describes the content of the last paragraph but does not adequately highlight the purpose of this content. This is a classic wrong answer type for a "purpose of detail" question because it highlights the content (the *what*) of the paragraph rather than the purpose (the *why*) of the paragraph.

C because the author mentions Darwin to remind readers of how evolution links us to other organisms: "the rest of the biosphere" (lines 77–79).

D because this paragraph does not attempt to persuade readers to become amateur astronomers. Instead, it encourages a level of respect for the relevance of the work done by astrophysicists and astronomers.

Question 178. **The best answer is J** because the author describes these people as those "whose business lies purely on or near the Earth's surface." The implication is that *all the others* refers to everyone who is not an astronomer, which would be most people on Earth.

The best answer is NOT:

F because "all the others" is set up as contrasting with astronomers, not with a phenomenon (like a stellar explosion) in a solar system.

G because "all the others" is set up as contrasting with astronomers, not with an object (like a planet) in a solar system.

H because astrophysicists and astronomers are cited by the author as examples of individuals who are fascinated by supernovae because these are cataclysmic events of major importance in their fields (lines 65–68).

Question 179. **The best answer is D** because Rees writes that "supernovae have created the 'mix' of atoms that the Earth is made of and that are the building blocks for the intricate chemistry of life" (lines 74–76).

The best answer is NOT:

A because the passage describes the challenges of harnessing the power of fusion. It does not mention industrial leaders opposing the pursuit of this technology (lines 1–17).

B because the passage does not describe *proximity* to the Sun as a factor that determines the age of a star.

C because the passage explains that the Trapezium stars in the constellation Orion are examples of heavier stars that have *shorter* life spans than that of the sun (lines 54–60). This is a common wrong answer because it is the opposite of what is stated in the passage.

Question 180. The best answer is **G** because the introductory paragraph emphasizes the numerous challenges that stand in the way of harnessing "fusion as a power source ('controlled fusion')" (lines 4–5).

The best answer is NOT:

F because attempts to harness fusion as a power source have not been remarkably successful. Instead, these attempts have been limited by various obstacles (lines 1–17).

H because the practical impossibilities rather than the financial limitations are emphasized in the opening paragraph (lines 1–17).

J because attempts to harness fusion as a power source are described as consistently unsuccessful rather than inconsistent across trials.

Passage XIX

Question 181. The best answer is **D** because the narrator explains that "Martha looks at you for a long time before she decides to speak" (lines 16–17) but does not indicate that the same is true for Ola. When Ola speaks in the passage, she does not seem to pause before speaking (lines 74–86).

The best answer is NOT:

A because evidence in the passage suggests that Ola and Martha have a similar sense of humor. For example, when Ola says, "if she had enough energy to yell from the road at a perfect stranger, she probably had enough strength to pick up a brush" (lines 82–85), Martha responds by tilting her head back and laughing (line 86).

B because evidence in the passage suggests that both Ola and Martha have a capacity for brutal honesty. For example, when Martha first met Ola, Martha yelled across the street to tell Ola that the "shade of yellow didn't look good from where [she] stood" (lines 74–75). Similarly, Martha tells the narrator she thought Ola "had the worst accent of anybody that I'd ever heard" (lines 68–69).

C because the passage depicts both Martha and Ola as relatively lively and vivacious. Ola has the idea for making the movie (lines 9–10) and was not afraid to invite a stranger (Martha) to "pick up a brush" (lines 84–85). Martha is not afraid to yell across the street to a new neighbor (lines 74–75) and shows interest in the narrator's project to make a film for Ola (lines 28–30).

Question 182. The best answer is F because the narrator refers to "Ola's idea about making a movie" (lines 9–10). Later, Martha shows enthusiasm for making the movie, stating that "the camera becomes a part of you" (line 20). Meanwhile, the narrator states that she wants to make the movie as a gift for Ola (lines 90–97).

The best answer is NOT:

G because the narrator refers to "Ola's idea about making a movie" (lines 9–10), which makes it clear that the movie was Ola's idea.

H because the narrator calls Martha on the phone to "tell her Ola's idea about making a movie" (lines 9–10). This suggests that the narrator knew about Ola's idea for a movie before Martha did.

J because the narrator refers to "Ola's idea about making a movie" (lines 9–10), which suggests that the movie was Ola's idea.

Question 183. The best answer is C because the narrator states that she "*can* remember to take off the lens cap sometimes" (lines 26–27), which suggests that she sometimes *forgets* to take off the lens cap. Later, after taping a crow, she says that she hopes "the lens cap hasn't been on the whole time" (lines 42–43). Both of these statements indicate that the narrator is concerned that she is not using the camera correctly.

The best answer is NOT:

A because the narrator's references to the lens cap do not indicate that her knowledge of camera technology is expanding. Rather, both references indicate that the narrator is worried about using the camera incorrectly.

B because there is no evidence to suggest that the narrator's references to the lens cap pertain to her desire to uncover her artistic vision.

D because there is no evidence to suggest that the narrator's references to the lens cap illustrate her growing eagerness to use a camera to tell stories.

Question 184. The best answer is J because Martha smirks after observing the narrator record a crow. She then says, "I guess you'll do okay by yourself now" (lines 38–39). These details indicate that Martha is enjoying watching the narrator use the camera successfully.

The best answer is NOT:

F because there is no evidence to suggest that Martha is weary with the project. In fact, the passage indicates that Martha was eager to begin filming (lines 40–41).

G because there is no evidence to suggest that Martha feels condescension towards the narrator. Instead, Martha tells the narrator, "I guess you'll do okay by yourself now" (lines 38–39), which suggests that Martha believes the narrator is capable of making the film.

H because there is no evidence to suggest that Martha is relieved. Instead, the passage indicates that she is enjoying watching the narrator use the camera (lines 37–39) and is eager to begin filming the movie (lines 37–40).

Question 185. The best answer is B because the passage indicates that the initial meeting between Martha and Ola began with a confrontational statement by Martha about Ola's yellow paint (lines 74–75). Instead of responding with anger, Ola responded by asking Martha to come over and help her paint (lines 84–85), and Martha agreed (line 86).

The best answer is NOT:

A because the passage indicates that the interaction between Martha and Ola did not result in the two agreeing to keep their distance from each other. Rather, the interaction resulted in Ola coming over to help Martha paint (lines 84–86).

C because the passage indicates that the initial meeting between Martha and Ola occurred when Martha shouted across the street to Ola, who was painting her house (lines 73–85).

D because the passage does not suggest that the encounter between Ola and Martha was accidental. Rather, the passage indicates that Martha deliberately called across the street to Ola and that both women decided to finish painting Ola's house together (lines 73–85).

Question 186. The best answer is **H** because Martha offers the narrator advice about the film, stating "No magic, no special training. Turn the camera on and shoot" (lines 29–30). Martha suggests that the narrator should let the camera become a part of her (lines 19–20). Both statements indicate that Martha believes that using a camera is a natural and intuitive process.

The best answer is NOT:

F because there is no evidence to suggest that Martha recommended that the narrator use the camera scientifically.

G because there is no evidence to suggest that Martha recommended that the narrator use the camera cautiously.

J because there is no evidence to suggest that Martha recommended that the narrator use the camera secretly.

Question 187. The best answer is **B** because Martha indicates that Ola and Diane both moved into the house on the same day they painted it yellow (line 72). Later, Ola tells the narrator, "Your mama was so embarrassed, Emmie, she begged me to stop painting it yellow" (lines 77–78). Because Martha only mentions Ola and Diane as having moved into the house on the day it was painted, and Ola's comment that the narrator's mother was embarrassed indicates that the narrator's mother was present for the house painting, one can infer that Diane was the name of the narrator's mother.

The best answer is NOT:

A because Ola directly addresses the narrator, calling her Emmie (line 77).

C because Martha indicates that Diane moved in with Ola and was not one of her neighbors (line 72).

D because there is not enough evidence to suggest that Martha and Diane were close friends. In fact, Martha only mentions Diane once when she recalls her moving in with Ola (line 72).

Question 188. The best answer is **F** because, in the last paragraph, the narrator states, "I want to make this movie on my own" (line 90) and explains that she wants to give her grandmother the movie as a gift because she believes it will be better than the other gifts she has given her (lines 94–97). These statements offer insight into the narrator's motivation for making the movie.

The best answer is NOT:

G because, while the last passage states that the narrator had previously given her grandmother gifts that "she could put on the wall or wear" (lines 94–95), it does not provide any additional background information and primarily focuses on the narrator's motivation for making the movie.

H because the last paragraph does not focus on the narrator's relationship with Martha. While the narrator does state that "Martha makes me want to know all of Ola's friends" (lines 90–91), this statement primarily serves to indicate that the narrator wants to know more of Ola's friends in order to make a movie for her grandmother.

J because the last paragraph does not contain evidence that the narrator's account is unreliable.

Question 189. The best answer is **D** because the narrator states that "if Ola loves these people, then they must be a part of me too" and that "it must be true about all of us being a part of one another like Daddy says" (lines 4–5). These statements indicate that the narrator believes her father's statement that everybody is a part of one another, and that the people that Ola loves are connected to her by Ola's love.

The best answer is NOT:

A because this paragraph only focuses on one principle that the narrator's father taught her: that "all of us [are] part of one another" (lines 5–6). The narrator does not discuss other things that her father has been right about, so there is not enough evidence to suggest whether her father is usually right in his assessments.

B because this paragraph does not reference Ola's storytelling ability or any of Ola's stories. Rather, it states that everybody Ola knows has a story (lines 1–2).

C because the paragraph does not discuss Ola's relationship with any of her neighbors. Rather, it states that everybody Ola knows has a story (lines 1–2), and that stories connect people to one another (lines 4–5).

Question 190. **The best answer is H** because the narrator states that "Ola's short and delicate—like she'd break if you held her arm too tight" (lines 59–60), before stating that "She wouldn't break, though" (line 60). This suggests that, although Ola appears delicate and breakable, she is not in fact as breakable as she looks.

The best answer is NOT:

F because the narrator is referencing her previous statement that Ola "[looks] like she'd break if you held her arm too tight" (lines 59–60). In this context, there is no evidence to suggest that the narrator is referring to her grandma's stubbornness.

G because the narrator is referencing her previous statement that Ola "[looks] like she'd break if you held her arm too tight" (lines 59–60). In this context, there is no evidence to suggest that she is implying that the narrator is discussing whether her grandma is guarded with her feelings.

J because there is no evidence to suggest that the narrator is referring to whether her grandmother is active. Instead, she is discussing whether or not her grandma would physically break if held too tight (lines 59–60).

Passage XX

Question 191. **The best answer is B** because the author indicates that the scientists were enthusiastic about the AU Lean Burger, stating that "It didn't take the Auburn scientists long to realize that they had created something special" (lines 24–25) and that they conducted multiple double-blind taste tests to show that their burger tasted good (lines 24–36).

The best answer is NOT:

A because the passage does not reference any criticisms of the fast-food industry's practices on the part of the Auburn scientists. Rather, the passage suggests that the Auburn scientists worked with McDonalds and other fast-food chains to make a hamburger out of their product (lines 63–69).

C because the passage indicates that the Auburn scientists were interested in practical work, as they conducted multiple double-blind taste tests to show that their burgers tasted good (lines 24–36).

D because the passage states that the Auburn scientists "wanted to create a leaner beef that tasted as good as regular ground beef" (lines 8–10), and that they conducted regular double-blind taste tests to show that their burgers tasted good (lines 24–36).

Question 192. The best answer is **H** because the passage indicates that "People liked AU Lean in blind taste tests because they didn't know it was AU Lean" (lines 76–77) and that "sometimes nothing is more deadly for our taste buds than the knowledge that what we are eating is good for us" (lines 89–91). This suggests that consumers knowing that they were eating AU Lean affected their perception of whether or not it tasted good.

The best answer is NOT:

F because there is no evidence in the passage to suggest that altering the order in which the families received the beef would have affected the results of the experiment.

G because there is no evidence in the passage to suggest that using more families would have affected the results of the experiment.

J because there is no evidence in the passage to suggest that lengthening the time the families used each type of ground beef would have impacted the results of the experiment.

Question 193. The best answer is **D** because it can be inferred that fast-food company executives who know about the failure of the McLean Deluxe may believe that there is a good reason to use twenty-per-cent-fat ground beef in a fast-food burger. Using less than twenty-per-cent-fat ground beef (as in the case of the McLean) previously resulted in a burger that was less profitable (lines 65–81).

The best answer is NOT:

A because there is no evidence to suggest that the McDonalds' officials who introduced the McLean Deluxe to the public in 1990 would have disagreed with this statement at the time when the burger was introduced. Rather, the fact that they introduced the McLean Deluxe to the market suggests that they believed that a burger made with less fat could be financially successful.

B because the passage indicates that the Auburn scientists completed a double-blind scientific study of a hundred families that demonstrated that consumers preferred the AU Lean beef to twenty-per-cent-fat ground beef (lines 25–36).

C because the passage states that nutritionists were delighted about the introduction of the McLean Deluxe (line 68), a burger that has only five-percent-fat ground beef (lines 21–22).

Question 194. The best answer is **G** because the passage states that the scientists "needed to find something to add to the beef that would hold an equivalent amount of water—and continue to retain that water even as the beef was being grilled" (lines 14–17). The passage indicates that they chose "Seaweed, or, more precisely, carrageenan" (lines 17–18) to serve this purpose.

The best answer is NOT:

F because the passage indicates that carrageenan was used because it operated as a substitute for fat (lines 12–18), not because it enhanced the flavor of the burger.

H because the passage indicates that carrageenan was used because it operated as a substitute for fat (lines 12–18), not because it was a source of protein.

J because the passage indicates that carrageenan is a type of seaweed (lines 17–18).

Question 195. The best answer is **A** because the passage states that "people appear more sensitive to the volume of food they consume than to its calorie content" (lines 46–47). This suggests that volume is an important factor that affects how satisfying a meal is.

The best answer is NOT:

B because the passage states that "people appear more sensitive to the volume of food they consume than to its calorie content" (lines 46–47). In other words, volume seems to have a larger effect than calories on whether people felt satisfied by a meal.

C because the passage states that "Between the relatively broad range of between five and twenty-five percent, you can add water and some flavoring and most people can't tell the difference" (lines 43–46). While the passage does indicate that people no longer liked the AU Lean when the fat went below five percent (lines 41–43), it nonetheless suggests that most people could not tell the difference if the percentage of fat was lowered to five percent.

D because the passage does not indicate that the method of cooking affects perception of how satisfying the hamburger is. Rather, it suggests that volume seems to have a significant effect on whether people felt satisfied by a meal (lines 47–49).

Question 196. The best answer is **J** because the passage states that "People liked AU Lean in blind taste tests because they didn't know it was AU Lean" (lines 76–77), and that "sometimes nothing is more deadly for our taste buds than the knowledge that what we are eating is good for us" (lines 89–91). This suggests that when consumers knew that AU Lean was supposed to be healthy, this made them less likely to purchase it (lines 80–81).

The best answer is NOT:

F because the passage does not indicate that McDonald's failed to market the McLean Deluxe. In fact, the passage states that other fast-food houses were aware of the McLean and were "scrambling" to make similar burgers of their own (lines 66–67).

G because although the passage does indicate that the McLean was rushed to market, it also states that what was "more important" was the "psychological handicap the burger faced" (lines 74–76).

H because the passage does not indicate that people believed the McLean Deluxe came from "market" hamburger.

Question 197. The best answer is **A** because the question serves to point out that people who come to McDonald's do not come there to eat healthy food (lines 78–81) as illustrated by the failure of the McLean Deluxe (line 70).

The best answer is NOT:

B because the passage indicates that people who came to McDonald's were generally not interested in buying healthy food, as evidenced by the failure of the McLean Deluxe (line 70).

C because the author does not express uncertainty about whether people enjoy healthy fast food. Rather the author states that "People liked AU Lean in blind taste tests because they didn't know it was AU Lean" (lines 76–78). The passage indicates that the knowledge that we are eating something healthy can negatively affect our opinion of the food's taste (lines 88–91).

D because, although the author discusses the reasons behind the failure of the McLean Deluxe (lines 70–91), there is no evidence to suggest that he objects to fast food restaurants selling it.

Question 198. The best answer is **G** because the author states that "transparency can backfire, because sometimes nothing is more deadly for our taste buds than the knowledge that what we are eating is good for us" (lines 88–91), suggesting that the food industry might need to reevaluate the extent to which transparency has a positive effect on health.

The best answer is NOT:

F because the author states that "transparency can backfire, because sometimes nothing is more deadly for our taste buds than the knowledge that what we are eating is good for us" (lines 88–91). This suggests that transparency doesn't necessarily lead to healthier eating.

H because the passage states that "For years, the nutrition movement in this country… has assumed that the best way to help people improve their diets is…to label certain foods good and certain foods bad. But transparency can backfire" (lines 87–89). In other words, labeling certain foods as good and bad does not seem to have improved the American diet.

J because the author states that "For years, the nutrition movement in this country… has assumed that the best way to help people improve their diets is to tell them precisely what's in their food…But transparency can backfire" (lines 87–89). The passage suggests that, in many cases, such as the case of the McLean (line 70), people will choose food with unhealthy ingredients over food with healthy ingredients (lines 88–91).

Question 199. The best answer is **C** because the passage states that the AU Lean burger is made up of "three-quarters water" (lines 21–22).

The best answer is NOT:

A because the passage states that the AU Lean burger is only five percent or so fat (lines 21–22).

B because the passage states that the AU Lean burger only contains a quarter of a percent seaweed (line 22).

D because the passage states that the AU Lean burger contains only twenty percent protein (line 21).

Question 200. The best answer is J because the passage indicates that, within the "range of between five and twenty-five percent, you can add water and some flavoring and most people can't tell the difference" (lines 43–46). Therefore, a 20-percent-fat hamburger would taste the same as an 8-percent-fat hamburger.

The best answer is NOT:

F because the passage indicates that most people cannot taste the difference between a burger with five percent fat and a burger with twenty-five percent fat (lines 43–46).

G because the passage indicates that most people cannot taste the difference between a burger with five percent fat and a burger with twenty-five percent fat (lines 43–46).

H because the passage indicates that most people cannot taste the difference between a burger with five percent fat and a burger with twenty-five percent fat (lines 43–46).

Passage XXI

Question 201. The best answer is D because the second paragraph explains how the piano was the "essential breakthrough" (line 23) that was "as large and robust as the big harpsichords" (lines 17–18) and also allowed "the dynamic range that before had only been available on the flimsy clavichords" (lines 18–20).

The best answer is NOT:

A because the first paragraph discusses why clavichords and harpsichords were "unsatisfactory for different reasons" (line 7), while the second paragraph primarily discusses how the piano was the "essential breakthrough" (line 23) that addressed the limitations of the harpsichord and clavichord.

B because the second paragraph does not discuss how the general public responded to the invention of the piano.

C because the second paragraph does not argue against what is presented in the first paragraph. Rather, the second paragraph explains how the piano was the "essential breakthrough" (line 23) that offered a solution to the limitations of the harpsichord and the clavichord (lines 8–15).

Question 202. The best answer is **H** because although the passage mentions the classical era (line 65), it does not indicate when the era began and ended.

The best answer is NOT:

F because the passage states that there is "little doubt" that Bartolomeo Cristofori invented the piano (lines 3–5).

G because the first paragraph provides a description of the clavichord and the harpsichord (lines 6–15), two popular keyboard instruments that pre-date the piano's invention in 1700 (line 2).

J because the passage states that the action is "the intricate mechanism that activates the hammers to strike the strings" (lines 56–58).

Question 203. The best answer is **A** because the passage describes Cristofori's invention of the piano as an "essential breakthrough" (line 23) and explains how the piano offered a solution to the limitations of the clavichord and the harpsichord (lines 17–21). Likewise, the passage describes Beethoven as imagining "music unlike any of his contemporaries" (line 85) and states that Beethoven's style of playing "had a strong influence on the direction of piano manufacture" (lines 72–73).

The best answer is NOT:

B because the passage states that Cristofori was an "instrument maker in Florence" (lines 2–4). The passage does not indicate whether Cristofori was a musician.

C because the passage provides evidence that Beethoven's contributions were appreciated when Beethoven was alive, claiming that, "Beethoven had a strong influence on the direction of piano manufacture" (lines 72–73). The passage also states that Beethoven was given a piano by "Broadwood, the pre-eminent English manufacturer of the day" (lines 77–78), suggesting that Beethoven's contemporaries saw him as an important figure in the music community. The passage also indicates that musicians were aware of Cristofori's invention as early as 1711 (line 21), suggesting that Cristofori was appreciated by his contemporaries as well.

D because the passage does not claim that Cristofori was a musician, instead describing him as an "instrument maker in Florence" (lines 2–4). The passage also does not indicate that Beethoven was more famous outside of his native country.

Question 204. The best answer is **G** because the passage explains that the "seed" of the piano found fertile ground "not in Italy but in eighteenth-century Germany" (lines 23–25). The passage states that, "German instrument makers incorporated Cristofori's breakthrough into a series of increasingly powerful keyboard instruments that were true pianos" (lines 26–28).

The best answer is NOT:

F because the passage indicates that Cristofori invented the piano while he was living in Florence, Italy, not in Germany (lines 3–5).

H because the passage does not discuss harpsichords or clavichords in relation to eighteenth century Germany specifically. Rather, the passage states that German instrument makers made improvements to Cristofori's piano (lines 26–28).

J because the passage does not describe a major split occurring among piano makers within eighteen-century Germany. Instead, the passage indicates that two distinct schools of piano building emerged in London, England and Vienna, Austria (lines 54–58).

Question 205. The best answer is **D** because the passage states that Cristofori's invention of an instrument "as large and robust as the big harpsichords that would also allow the dynamic range that before had only been available on the flimsy clavichords" (lines 16–20) was "the essential breakthrough" that eventually led to the invention of the modern piano (lines 22–25).

The best answer is NOT:

A because the passage does not directly discuss Cristofori's decision to let other musicians change the piano's design, nor does it indicate whether Cristofori decided to let others work on the pianos' design at all.

B because the passage states that Cristofori developed "a way of making a struck string resound loudly" (lines 5–6). The passage also indicates that piano strings are struck by hammers (lines 57–58), not plucked.

C because, while the passage does state that the piano's unique volume "freed it from the confines of the drawing room to which the harpsichord had almost always been consigned" (lines 40–42), the passage discusses Cristofori's "essential breakthrough" (line 23) in terms of his invention of the piano as a solution to the limitations of harpsichords and clavichords (lines 16–20). The passage also suggests that the piano was freed from the drawing room after it rose to prominence as a solo instrument beginning in 1786 (lines 35–42), long after Cristofori's invention.

Question 206. **The best answer is F** because the passage states that "Broadwood, the pre-eminent English manufacturer of the day, offered him [Beethoven] a grand piano that incorporated the latest features" (lines 77–79). Details in the passage suggest that Broadwood built this piano to suit Beethoven's style of playing (lines 79–80), showing that the manufacturer had a great deal of respect for Beethoven's artistry.

The best answer is NOT:

G because the passage clearly states that Beethoven was a composer "of the classical era" (lines 65–66), and does not indicate that Beethoven had any influence on the manufacture of Viennese pianos before the classical era. In fact, the passage states that Beethoven was frustrated by the design of Viennese pianos (lines 67–68).

H because the passage does not discuss Beethoven's influence on Haydn or Mozart. It simply states that all three were pianists of the classical era (lines 65–66).

J because the passage does not suggest that Beethoven played a role in the establishment of the schools in London and Vienna.

Question 207. **The best answer is B** because the passage indicates that the piano allowed musicians such as Beethoven to have "increasing dynamic contrasts" in their music, and that Beethoven was able to compose "music unlike anything his contemporaries were writing" (lines 85–86). In other words, the piano allowed Beethoven a greater range of expression.

The best answer is NOT:

A because the passage states that Beethoven imagined "music unlike anything his contemporaries were writing" (lines 85–86), suggesting that the piano allowed Beethoven to defy established rules and norms with his music.

C because the passage indicates that the piano allowed musicians such as Beethoven to have "increasing dynamic contrasts" (lines 69–70). The passage does not indicate that the piano allowed Beethoven access to higher notes.

D because the passage states that Beethoven imagined "music unlike anything his contemporaries were writing" (lines 85–86), suggesting that the piano allowed Beethoven to surpass the limitations and shortcomings that might have come with earlier instruments.

Question 208. The best answer is **H** because the passage states that Johann Sebastian Bach "was impressed by the first piano he tried, but he pointed out limitations that still needed to be worked on" (lines 29–32).

The best answer is NOT:

F because the passage does not indicate that Bach disapproved of the piano's loudness. Instead, the passage claims that Bach felt that the treble "was not loud enough" (line 32).

G because the passage does indicate that Bach felt irritation over the singing quality of the notes.

J because the passage does not indicate that Bach damaged the pianos by playing them. Instead, the passage claims that Beethoven's playing damaged the strings of both Viennese pianos (lines 71–72) and English pianos (lines 80–83).

Question 209. The best answer is **A** because the passage states that "the role of the keyboard as a solo instrument came to the fore musically" during the mid-to-late eighteenth century (lines 38–39) and that solo concerts became "the norm rather than the exception" as the piano grew in popularity (lines 49–50).

The best answer is NOT:

B because the passage states that the piano's unique volume "freed it from the confines of the drawing room to which the harpsichord had almost always been consigned" (lines 40–41).

C because, while the passage briefly notes that the Viennese pianos had delicate cabinetry (line 61), it does not compare the cabinetry of pianos to that of harpsichords.

D because the passage does not discuss whether the harpsichord or the piano was better suited to church music.

Question 210. The best answer is G because the passage states that Beethoven's *Hammerklavier* sonata strikes "many as a revelation of the piano's extreme limits of power and expressiveness" (lines 87–88), suggesting that Beethoven used the piano's full capacity when he composed the piece.

The best answer is NOT:

F because the passage indicates that Beethoven wrote the *Hammerklavier* sonata for the piano, not for the clavichord (lines 85–88). The passage also describes clavichords as having a low volume that "made them suitable only for small gatherings" (lines 9–10).

H because the passage does not indicate that the *Hammerklavier* sonata gained more favor in England than in Vienna.

J because the passage does not indicate that Mozart was inspired by Beethoven's *Hammerklavier* sonata.

Passage XXII

Question 211. The best answer is D because the passage states that bluefin and swordfish are "exquisitely adapted to the vastness of the sea" (lines 8–9) and describes how the swordfish's internal organs (lines 22–32) and the bluefin tuna's red muscles (lines 33–50) and unique swimming style (lines 51–69) allow both fish to thrive in both hot and cold waters.

The best answer is NOT:

A because the passage only discusses how swordfish and bluefin navigate the Atlantic in the last paragraph (lines 70–89). Though the passage poses questions about the fishes' migration patterns, it does not propose that additional research should be conducted.

B because the passage does not argue that swordfish are superior to bluefin. Instead, it argues that both fish are "exquisitely adapted to live in the vastness of the sea" (lines 8–9).

C because, while the passage does indicate that the specialized traits of the swordfish and bluefin are useful (lines 8–10), it does not speculate about the reasons why the fish developed these traits.

Question 212. **The best answer is F** because the author describes bluefin and swordfish as "some of the sea's most highly developed fishes" (lines 2–3) and states that both fish are "exquisitely adapted to live in the vastness of the sea" (lines 8–9), which suggests that the author feels admiration for the fishes' unique abilities.

The best answer is NOT:

G because the author does not discuss how the adaptations of bluefin and tuna may affect other fish. Instead, she simply states that other fish, such as cod, haddock, flounder, and plaice, have a limited geographic range because they are cold-blooded (lines 3–10).

H because, while the author does state that bluefin and swordfish are "relative newcomers to the marine world" (line 1), she does not express confusion about how the fish evolved. Instead, she describes the characteristics that make bluefin and swordfish "some of the sea's most highly developed fishes" (lines 2–3).

J because the author compares bluefin and tuna to other species of fish, stating that "While the cod, haddock, flounder and plaice…are cold-blooded…thus limiting their geographic range, swordfish and bluefin, exquisitely adapted to live in the vastness of the sea, are free from the boundaries imposed by temperature" (lines 3–10). In doing so, the author suggests that the other species of fish are not as "exquisitely adapted" to the sea as bluefin and tuna.

Question 213. **The best answer is D** because the passage states that the body temperatures of cold-blooded fish rise and fall "in synchrony with the surrounding water" (lines 6–7).

The best answer is NOT:

A because the passage states that being cold-blooded limits a fish's geographic range (lines 5–8), not that the fish's geographical range influences the fish's body temperature. Instead, the passage states that the body temperatures of cold-blooded fish rise and fall "in synchrony with the surrounding water" (lines 6–7).

B because the passage does not indicate that the body temperature of a cold-blooded fish is related to the speed at which it swims. Instead, the passage indicates that most bony fish (aside from the bluefin tuna) "quickly lose their heat" as they swim (lines 37–38).

C because the passage does not indicate that the body temperature of a cold-blooded fish is related to the prey it consumes.

Question 214. The best answer is F because the passage explains that swordfish generate heat via "a dark mass of tissue surrounded by insulated fat, heavy with blood, and loaded with energy-producing mitochondria" (lines 23–25). The passage also states that bluefin tuna "retain the heat they generate swimming" (lines 36–37) due to the fact that their muscles are housed deep in their body.

The best answer is NOT:

G because the passage states that bluefin tuna "do not possess organs whose chief function is to produce heat" (lines 35–36). Instead, the passage states that bluefin tuna "retain the heat they generate swimming" (lines 36–37).

H because the passage does not state that bluefin retain heat generated by ocean currents. Instead, the passage states that bluefin "retain the heat they generate swimming" (lines 36–37).

J because the passage does not state that bluefin lose most of the heat they generate. Instead, the passage states that bluefin "retain 98 percent of their body heat" (lines 43–44).

Question 215. The best answer is D because the passage states "Coincident with the relocation of its red muscle, bluefin developed the unique style of swimming for which they are so aptly named (lines 51–53), suggesting that the relocation of the red muscle occurred around the same time that bluefin began to swim in a relatively rigid manner. Because of this, it can be inferred that the location of the bluefin's muscles is related to its style of swimming.

The best answer is NOT:

A because the passage states that "warm venous blood flowing away from muscles heats cold blood coming in through the arteries" (lines 41–43), which indicates that the movement of the muscles produces heat. For this reason, it wouldn't make sense for the bluefin to avoid moving its muscles in order to retain heat.

B because the passage states that the bluefin "retain 98 percent of their body heat, giving them free reign to forage in cold waters" (lines 44–45), suggesting that the muscles of the bluefin are warm, not frozen.

C because, while the passage does describe the bluefin's skin as "taut" (line 49), it does not indicate that the tautness of the bluefin's skin is related to the rigidness of its movement.

Question 216. The best answer is **G** because the passage states that, in waters in and near the Gulf Stream, "temperatures plummet as much as 27 degrees Fahrenheit across one nautical mile" (lines 46–47). The passage also indicates that many cold-blooded fish are limited in geographic range because their body temperatures rise and fall in synchrony with the surrounding water (lines 6–7). Therefore, it is reasonable to assume that the wide range of temperatures within the Gulf Stream would pose a challenge to most species of fish.

The best answer is NOT:

F because the passage does not indicate that the Gulf Stream is home to a large number and variety of predators.

H because the passage does not indicate the Gulf Stream contains strong and swirling currents.

J because the passage does not indicate that the Gulf Stream forces fish into unfamiliar ocean regions.

Question 217. The best answer is **C** because the passage states that "bluefin developed the unique style of swimming for which they are so aptly named (*Thunnus thynuss*, from the Greek meaning to dart or lunge forward)" (lines 52–54). This suggests that the bluefin's name refers to their swimming style.

The best answer is NOT:

A because the passage does not indicate that the bluefin's name is related to its internal temperature.

B because the passage does not indicate that the bluefin's name is related to its tail shape.

D because the passage does not indicate that the bluefin's name is related to the sounds they make.

Question 218. The best answer is G because the last paragraph claims that the migration patterns of bluefin and swordfish are "not well charted" (lines 72–73) and states that "no one really knows" (lines 83–84) how the fish navigate their surroundings.

The best answer is NOT:

F because the last paragraph does not indicate that charting the Gulf Stream would help accurately predict the migration patterns of swordfish and bluefin.

H because, while the paragraph does indicate that the swordfish and bluefin travel throughout the Atlantic Ocean (lines 70–71), it primarily explores the complexity of the migration patterns of bluefin (lines 73–83) and speculates about how the fish navigate their surroundings (lines 83–89).

J because, while the paragraph does indicate that swordfish and bluefin travel throughout the Atlantic "with tremendous speed" (line 71), it primarily explores the complexity of the migration patterns of bluefin (lines 73–83) and speculates about how the fish navigate their surroundings (lines 83–89).

Question 219. The best answer is D because the passage emphasizes that "While the cod, haddock, flounder, and plaice...dwell year-round in the North Sea and the Gulf of Mexico... swordfish and bluefin...are free from the boundaries imposed by temperature" (lines 3–10). The passage also indicates that bluefin have complex migration patterns that allow them to travel throughout the Atlantic Ocean (lines 70–89).

The best answer is NOT:

A because the passage states that "cod, haddock, flounder, and plaice...dwell year-round in the North Sea and the Gulf of Mexico" (lines 3–5).

B because the passage states that "cod, haddock, flounder, and plaice...dwell year-round in the North Sea and the Gulf of Mexico" (lines 3–5).

C because the passage states that "cod, haddock, flounder, and plaice...dwell year-round in the North Sea and the Gulf of Mexico" (lines 3–5).

Question 220. The best answer is G because the passage states that, "with their warm brain and eyes, swordfish can chase their food in waters deep and shallow, near and distant" (lines 25–27), suggesting a swordfish's warm brain and eyes allow it to hunt for food in many different waters.

The best answer is NOT:

F because the passage does not indicate that the heat a swordfish generates is intended to attract cold-blooded prey seeking warmth.

H because the passage does not indicate that the heat the swordfish generates is intended to increase its speed.

J because the passage does not indicate that the heat the swordfish generates is intended to strengthen its sword.

Passage XXIII

Question 221. The best answer is C because the story primarily focuses on building tension as Sunday (in paragraphs 1–4) and Delta (in paragraphs 5–12) anticipate reuniting after years of distanced communication prompted by harsh words uttered impulsively following Nana's funeral (lines 49–54).

The best answer is NOT:

A because Sunday is not returning home to attend her Nana's funeral. The story explains that Sunday and Delta had an argument "after Nana's death" (line 51). Additionally, the passage indicates that Nana's funeral was at least five years ago.

B because the passage focuses on building tension prior to the reunion of sisters Sunday and Delta. The story does not convey what occurs once the sisters are reunited.

D because the passage mentions Sunday visiting Wake County, not moving back there. While the passage describes an argument Sunday and Delta had in the past, the story does not convey what happens when the sisters are reunited.

Question 222. The best answer is H because the main conflict in the passage involves the tension between two sisters, Delta and Sunday, who have differing views of the world (lines 66–74). It is clear that the sisters see Wake County differently (lines 63–65).

The best answer is NOT:

F because Sunday is the one who paints (lines 14–20). Additionally, Sunday believes she does effectively communicate through her paintings, which are described as the source from which "she had learned to speak her life" (lines 19–20).

G because Sunday has clearly decided to return to her hometown. Sunday rides a train "through the part of town where she grew up" (lines 21–22).

J because tensions have cooled following the fight that erupted between Sunday and Delta. This is evident because the sisters have exchanged letters and paintings (lines 32–33) for at least five years. Additionally, Sunday is taking a train to visit her sister in their hometown.

Question 223. The best answer is A because the narrator reveals Sunday's thoughts about Wake County primarily through dialogue. Sunday tells Delta that living in Wake County makes her feel like she's "in a little box" (line 56).

The best answer is NOT:

B because the reader gains the most information regarding how Sunday feels about Wake County from Sunday's words rather than her thoughts (lines 55–74). Sunday's thoughts only convey that she paints her past and that, as she travels through town, memories return.

C because Delta's words to Sunday do not provide much direct information about Sunday's view of Wake County. Delta tells Sunday that she is "a misfit who thought she was better than the folks she had left behind," but it is unclear if Delta's words accurately convey Sunday's view of Wake County (lines 78–79).

D because Delta does not describe Sunday's artwork. The passage explains that Delta "hadn't known what, specifically, to make of" Sunday's artwork (lines 46–47).

Question 224. **The best answer is G** because at line 30, the point of view shifts from Sunday's perspective to Delta's perspective.

The best answer is NOT:

F because at this point in the story, the narration consistently focuses on Sunday's perspective as she rides the train through the part of town where she grew up.

H because by line 55, the passage has been told from Delta's perspective for two paragraphs.

J because by line 66, the passage has been told from Delta's perspective for four paragraphs.

Question 225. **The best answer is C** because Sunday does not fit in while Delta feels a sense of belonging in Wake County (lines 57–59). Delta notes that "Sunday was the one she was different from" (lines 61–62).

The best answer is NOT:

A because the passage does not focus on Delta defining herself as a homemaker, caregiver, or skilled writer. In fact, Delta relies on greeting cards rather than her own writing to express her feelings (lines 35–38).

B because Delta identifies Sunday as being different from the other residents of Wake County. Delta notes that "Sunday was the one she was different from," underscoring that Delta differs from her sister rather than from the other residents of Wake County (lines 61–62).

D because Sunday seems to be concerned with becoming more worldly and breaking free from the constraints of her hometown, which makes her feel like she is "in a little box" (line 56).

Question 226. **The best answer is F** because the passage never reveals *who* suggested that Sunday should choose her own name.

The best answer is NOT:

G because the first paragraph indicates that "Girl Owens" was "on the stamped paper that certified her birth" (lines 2–3).

H because the first paragraph describes what the name Sunday represented to Sunday herself: "the time of voices, lifted in praise" (lines 5–6).

J because "Sister" acquired the name Sunday at age six when she was asked to decide what she would be called" (lines 5–6).

Question 227. **The best answer is** D because the passage is referring to Sunday as "native and exile, woman and child… she was headed home" (lines 26–29). Sunday grew up in Wake County (lines 67–68) and then moved to Chicago (line 40). She is an exile in the sense that she has not been home in several years.

The best answer is NOT:

A because the words *native* and *exile* only describe Sunday who happens to be a painter. Neither of these words refers to Sunday's sister, Delta, within the context of the passage.

B because the words *native* and *exile* are used at a point in the passage that describes Sunday's relationship with Wake County, rather than the relationship between Sunday and her sister.

C because the words *native* and *exile* refer to Sunday's change in home rather than Sunday's name change.

Question 228. **The best answer is** G because the passage explains that although Delta didn't know what to do with the paintings or what to make of them, she knew their appearance "said something about the habit of love" (lines 46–48).

The best answer is NOT:

F because Delta never suggests that her own confusion about Sunday's art stems from Sunday's lack of skill (lines 44–45).

H because while Sunday mails the paintings in order to remain in touch with Delta, the paintings are not symbolic of Delta staying in Wake County.

J because there is no connection between Delta calling Sunday a misfit and the nature of Sunday's artwork.

Question 229. **The best answer is** B because Delta calls Sunday "a misfit who thought she was better than the folks she had left behind" (lines 78–79).

The best answer is NOT:

A because Sunday accused Delta of not understanding her paintings (lines 72–73).

C because Delta does not indicate that Sunday disgraces the family when she moves away. Delta herself feels "disgraced by the recognition of her own rancor [anger]" (lines 80–82).

D because there is no indication that Delta has criticized Sunday's paintings.

Question 230. The best answer is F because Delta lashes out after Sunday accuses Delta of not even seeing her paintings (lines 82–85). Delta replies, calling Sunday a misfit who thinks she is "better than the folks she left behind" (lines 77–78). Delta realizes that this retort was petty and regrets it.

The best answer is NOT:

G because Delta realizes that she called Sunday a misfit, even though she doesn't believe it to be true. She was just being petty, or small. She wasn't being willful; this was the first time she had this argument with Sunday.

H because in this context, *smallness* refers to a motivation behind an action, not a physical size.

J because, in this context, *smallness* describes Delta's retort about Sunday's personality, not a judgement about art. Art is not mentioned in this paragraph.

Passage XXIV

Question 231. The best answer is B because Sandel writes that republican theory is based upon "the idea that liberty depends on sharing in self-government" (lines 45–46). Liberty, according to Sandel, requires a "sense of community and civic engagement" (lines 78–79).

The best answer is NOT:

A because the passage states that "republican politics cannot be neutral toward the values and ends its citizens espouse" (lines 62–63).

C because the passage describes how a political system following the republican theory would ideally include citizens who were involved in "deliberating with fellow citizens about the common good" (lines 51–53).

D because the passage presents two main positions: liberal and conservative. Sandel states that "both sides assume that freedom consists in the capacity of people to choose their own ends" (lines 35–37).

Question 232. The best answer is G because the passage does *not* indicate that citizens must have a neutral framework of rights to engage in civic discourse.

The best answer is NOT:

F because the passage states that to deliberate well about the common good, citizens must possess knowledge of public affairs (lines 56–57).

H because the passage states that to deliberate well about the common good, citizens must possess a concern for fellow citizens (lines 58–59).

J because the passage states that to deliberate well about the common good, citizens must possess "certain civic virtues" (line 61). Sandel describes how citizens wishing to deliberate must feel a sense of duty to work together with other citizens to pursue the greatest good for the greatest number of people.

Question 233. The best answer is B because the second paragraph offers examples of situations when both liberals and conservatives "invoke the ideal of neutrality" (line 16). This concept of neutrality is found "across the political spectrum" (line 15).

The best answer is NOT:

A because the examples given show that liberals and conservatives do *not* have essentially the same value system (lines 10–23).

C because the passage does not state or imply that conservatives are more interested in the nation's economy than are liberals. Each party holds different beliefs about the economy. The passage explains that Democrats believe that "those who are crushed by economic necessities are not truly free to exercise choice in other domains" (lines 32–34). Conservatives believe that the economic market should not be constrained by moral considerations imposed by the government (lines 18–23).

D because the paragraph does state that "the aspiration to neutrality" "derives from the liberal tradition of public thought" (lines 10–12). The majority of the paragraph (thus, the paragraph's main idea) explains ways in which both liberals and conservatives use neutrality to promote their ideals.

Question 234. The best answer is **J** because the fifth paragraph explains that one basic element of republican theory is that citizens should ideally deliberate "with fellow citizens about the common good" and "shape the destiny of the political community" (lines 52–53).

The best answer is NOT:

F because this paragraph does not emphasize that liberal and republican theories each demand that citizens take part in politics. The passage explains that under republican theory, merely participating in politics is not enough. Citizens should engage in deliberation to find the common good.

G because this paragraph does not mention bad points of either theory. The paragraph emphasizes the strengths of the republican theory of government with its emphasis on encouraging citizens to deliberate "with fellow citizens about the common good" (lines 51–52).

H because the fifth paragraph focuses on political theory, not the politicians themselves.

Question 235. The best answer is **A** because *formative politics* promotes important civic virtues. Sandel writes, "the republican concept of freedom" requires "a formative politics, a politics that cultivates in citizens the qualities of character that self-government requires" (lines 63–66).

The best answer is NOT:

B because *formative politics* is defined as being part of the republican theory of government, distinct from liberal concepts of government (lines 63–66).

C because the term "procedural republic" is used to describe the current state of affairs, which has led to "discontent," according to Sandel (lines 71–76). A procedural republic is "less concerned with cultivating virtue than with enabling persons to choose their own values" (lines 71–73).

D because *formative politics* is defined as being part of the republican theory of government, which emphasizes self-rule and promotes civic discourse dedicated to the common good (lines 45–54).

Question 236. The best answer is **H** because the concluding paragraph highlights the weaknesses of our current procedural republic, which Sandel believes "cannot inspire the sense of community and civic engagement that liberty requires" (lines 78–79).

The best answer is NOT:

F because the author does not distinguish *procedural* from *liberal* republics in the final paragraph. He criticizes how both parties place too great a value on "enabling persons to choose their own values" and less value on "cultivating virtue" (lines 72–73).

G because the author highlights what he views as the centerpiece of republican political theory in the fifth paragraph, not the last paragraph.

J because when the author criticizes procedural republics, he does not emphasize the differences between liberal and republican political theories. Those differences are highlighted in paragraphs 2–5.

Question 237. The best answer is **A** because Sandel writes, "Both the liberal and the republican understandings of freedom have been present throughout our *political experience*" (lines 67–70). In the sentence that follows, Sandel talks about our "recent history" as a point of contrast, which underscores that the phrase *political experience* refers to our country's past.

The best answer is NOT:

B because the passage does not address voting patterns.

C because the passage does not address presidential campaigns.

D because *political experience* describes a longer span of time than the span of an elective term; it describes our country's shared political history (lines 67–70).

Question 238. The best answer is **F** because the main point of lines 10–15 is that both liberals and conservatives invoke the ideal of neutrality in order to support citizens' rights to choose their own values.

The best answer is NOT:

G because Sandel is not making the point that liberals and conservatives themselves can be found across the political spectrum (line 15). Their "aspiration to neutrality" is found across the political spectrum.

H because the passage does not indicate that the "aspiration to neutrality" is guaranteed by the Constitution. In fact, the Constitution is never directly mentioned in the passage.

J because the liberal tradition of "invoking the ideal of neutrality" has a thorough rather than a *limited* theoretical background. The framework of neutrality forms much of the basis of the current "central idea of the public philosophy by which we live," including the liberal tradition (line 1).

Question 239. The best answer is **D** because the last paragraph defines a procedural republic as "concerned less with cultivating virtues than with enabling persons to choose their own values" (lines 71–73).

The best answer is NOT:

A because the concluding paragraph highlights the limitations of a procedural republic by emphasizing that it lacks a sense of "community and civic engagement" (line 79).

B because Sandel positions a procedural republic as the opposite of formative politics. He writes, "In recent decades, the civic, or formative, aspect of our politics has given way to a procedural republic" (lines 70–71). Here, Sandel equates the words *civic* and *formative*, underscoring how these types of political systems differ from a procedural republic.

C because Sandel emphasizes that a procedural republic is primarily concerned with "enabling persons to choose their own values" (lines 72–73). This value placed on individual freedom suggests that a procedural republic would not be highly concerned with rules and regulations.

Question 240. The best answer is G because Sandel establishes that the liberal vision of freedom draws upon the current public philosophy, which prioritizes the freedoms of citizens over cultivating certain virtues, community, or civic engagement (lines 70–73). Sandel suggests that in an ideal system, citizens would deliberate to find the common good (lines 51–52), prioritizing community over each citizen's individual freedom.

The best answer is NOT:

F because Sandel is not critical of the wide range of choices available to citizens in our current political system.

H because the passage does not describe the ideal of neutrality—the notion that citizens should have the freedom to choose their own values—as anti-government (line 16). In fact, the passage describes how liberals and conservatives both invoke the ideal of neutrality to support their stances on certain laws (lines 10–22).

J because the liberal vision does not depend too heavily on the concept of legislating morality. The passage indicates that the central idea of the current vision of freedom (among both liberals and conservatives) is that "politics should not try to form the character or cultivate the virtues of its citizens, for to do so would be to 'legislate morality'" (lines 3–5).

Passage XXV

Question 241. The best answer is B because the passage is told from the perspective of an adult reflecting on his childhood and the lessons his grandfather taught him about their family connection to the land. The narrator describes the enduring lessons he has learned: "I knew that as long as my hands had the strength to hold a hoe, I would work that garden where corn had been cared for by my grandparents and by my great grandparents before them" (lines 82–85).

The best answer is NOT:

A because the passage does not indicate that the narrator once had difficulty understanding his grandfather. Line 16 indicates that, in his youth, the narrator "didn't quite understand" when he was called "Jess's Shadow," but this does not describe an instance of the author having difficulty understanding his grandfather (line 16). The passage makes clear that the narrator was always close with his grandfather.

C because the garden clearly still exists. Bruchac writes, "I knew that as long as my hands had the strength to hold a hoe, I would work that garden where corn had been cared for by my grandparents and by my great grandparents before them" (lines 82–85).

D because the narrator does not describe unpleasant memories or emotions.

Question 242. The best answer is **J** because the narrative jumps forward thirty years beginning at line 74. At this point in the passage, the narrator applies greater meaning to the memories he relates earlier in the passage.

The best answer is NOT:

F because line 16 is a continuation of the narrator's recollection of being called his grandfather's shadow as a young child.

G because line 21 is an elaboration on the narrator's vivid childhood memory of helping his grandfather in his garden.

H because line 57 continues to focus on recollections from the narrator's childhood. The author describes a different day, but these events still took place in his childhood.

Question 243. The best answer is **D** because the passage does not indicate that the narrator feels protected from other people by his grandfather. In fact, the passage does not indicate that the narrator ever feels the need to be protected.

The best answer is NOT:

A because the nickname "Jess's Shadow" conveys how the author has a strong bond with his grandfather. He follows and mimics him (lines 59–60).

B because the nickname "Jess's Shadow" conveys that, as a child, the narrator followed his grandfather around. Lawrence Older says to Jesse Bowman, the narrator's grandfather, "that grandson of yours stays so close to you he don't hardly leave room enough for your shadow" (lines 14–15).

C because the nickname "Jess's Shadow" conveys how the narrator consciously imitated his grandfather. The author writes, "I'd watched really carefully, so I knew what to do" (lines 31–32). Later, when he gets his own hoe, the author explains, "I was, as always, trying to do exactly what he did" (lines 59–60).

Question 244. The best answer is **H** because the narrator explains that, "I'd watched really carefully, so I knew what to do. I did it so well that my grandfather allowed that I was already better at it than he was" (lines 31–33).

The best answer is NOT:

F because the narrator is not reluctant to participate in planting the corn with his grandfather. He is eager to help and pays careful attention to his grandfather (lines 31–33).

G because the narrator is not careless in his work. The narrator explains that he planted the corn so "well that my grandfather allowed that I was already better at it than he was" (lines 32–33).

J because there is no indication that the narrator's genuine interest faded as the work became more difficult.

Question 245. The best answer is **A** because the narrator's grandfather explains to his grandson that he used to find Indian arrowheads when he plowed the fields with a team of horses (lines 43–47). Later, the grandfather finds an axhead in the soil and gives it to his grandson (lines 66–73). Arrowheads are symbols of their common heritage, which the last paragraph explains further (lines 74–91).

The best answer is NOT:

B because the grandfather briefly notes that he has identified an Oriole's call, but this is not the main point of emphasis in lines 57–73. There is no indication that the narrator has any interest in birds.

C because the main point is that turning over the soil revealed the axhead. While the hoe is mentioned in this part of the passage, these paragraphs do not emphasize the value the narrator places on the hoe.

D because this answer flips the relationship between grandfather and grandson. Holding the axhead later, as an adult, prompts the narrator to remember his grandfather and his connection to the land (lines 74–79). When the tenth through fourteenth paragraphs describe the narrator's grandfather showing the axhead to his grandson, the grandfather already has an appreciation of his past.

Question 246. **The best answer is G** because the narrator describes his grandfather seeming "taller than the biggest tree" as he held the author's hand (lines 6–7). Furthermore, the author says, "He wouldn't let me fall," which underscores that the narrator felt watched over by his awe-inspiring grandfather (line 8).

The best answer is NOT:

F because the narrator does not feel overly controlled by his grandfather. Rather, the narrator is comforted by his grandfather's presence. The narrator describes his grandfather as protective and larger than life.

H because the narrator was not puzzled by his grandfather's height; he doesn't seek to understand it. The comparison between his grandfather's height and the height of a tree indicates that the narrator was in awe of his grandfather.

J because the narrator describes how impressed he is by his grandfather's height, not his garden.

Question 247. **The best answer is A** because the narrator explains that Lawrence Older (also known as Larry) "said, with a twinkle in his eye, 'that grandson of yours stays so close to you he don't hardly leave room enough for your shadow'" (lines 14–15). The twinkle in his eye implies that Larry thinks it is amusing how closely the narrator follows his grandfather.

The best answer is NOT:

B because Larry is not concerned about the narrator following his grandfather around. His eyes would not be twinkling if he were concerned.

C because Larry is not dismayed about the narrator following his grandfather around. The word *dismayed* implies worry.

D because Larry is not elated about the narrator following his grandfather around. The word *elated* implies overwhelming joy.

Question 248. The best answer is **J** because the narrator states that Sonny is the only name his grandparents called him, so he was confused when Larry referred to him as "Jess's Shadow" (lines 16–20).

The best answer is NOT:

F because the narrator's parents are not mentioned in the passage. In addition, while it is true that his grandparents call him Sonny, we know from the introduction to the passage that the author's given name is Joseph Bruchac. Sonny, then, is a nickname.

G because the narrator seems quite certain that his name is Sonny. He says, "My name was Sonny. I knew that for sure" (line 17).

H because it is clear the narrator believes that Larry is referring to him. There is no indication that the narrator wonders if Larry is referring to someone else.

Question 249. The best answer is **C** because the narrator says that the term "fitting the ground to plant" has been passed down through multiple generations in his family. "This is what Grandpa called it. This is what Jack called it. This is what their father, Lewis Bowman, had called it" (lines 54–55).

The best answer is NOT:

A because the passage does not indicate that people in the grandfather's community use this term. Until he had heard his uncle Jack use the term, he had only heard his grandfather use it (lines 50–54).

B because the grandfather inherited the word from his father (lines 54–55).

D because the phrase "fitting the ground to plant" is discussed in a part of the passage (paragraphs 5–9) that describes the narrator's young childhood. It can be inferred, then, that when the narrator was a child, he had heard his grandfather use the phrase.

Question 250. The best answer is **J** because the narrator compares the treatment of the arrowhead to "the same care that my grandmother used when she was gathering eggs in the henhouse and putting them into the basket hung over her arm" (lines 70–72).

The best answer is NOT:

F because introducing the grandmother is not the main point of this paragraph. Her actions are only used as a point of comparison.

G because describing the narrator's grandparents' work is not the main point of the paragraph. Rather, the main point is about the exchange of a meaningful object.

H because the passage does not describe an exchange of gifts. The passage describes the grandfather giving the arrowhead to the narrator, but the narrator does not give his grandfather a gift in exchange.

Passage XXVI

Question 251. The best answer is **B** because this passage includes a great deal of technical discussion about bird eggs' size, shape, and composition.

The best answer is NOT:

A because this passage does not focus much on reptile eggs. It briefly mentions them in lines 8–11: "In both reptile and bird eggs, there is a large yolk which not only supplies the needs of the embryo but will also sustain the newly hatched animal until it can feed." The third paragraph explains that twisted cords called chalazae are not present in reptilian eggs, which, unlike bird eggs, are never turned by the parent (lines 29–32). The majority of the passage, though, focuses on bird eggs without using comparisons or contrasts.

C because, as the introduction states, recent studies of birds' eggs have shown how birds are extremely similar to reptiles. In fact, the passage describes birds as "reptiles with feathers" (lines 2–3). Furthermore, no specific studies are mentioned in the passage.

D because while this passage indicates that birds' eggs have adapted to suit their species' needs within certain environments (lines 81–86), it does not suggest that birds' eggs have become *more* adapted than reptiles' eggs.

Question 252. The best answer is **J** because the passage states that "the amount of calcium needed for each egg is about 2 grams" (lines 36–37).

The best answer is NOT:

F because the passage indicates that the eggshell of a domestic hen is "peppered with 10,000 tiny pores, just visible to the naked eye as small depressions in the shell" (lines 59–61).

G because the passage indicates that the shell of a domestic hen takes 15 to 16 hours to form (line 33).

H because the passage indicates that a domestic hen's shell "consists of crystals and calcite" (line 34).

Question 253. The best answer is **C** because the final paragraph focuses on egg shape as an example of how different species' eggs have adapted. Wading birds' eggs, for example, are "shaped like spinning tops, blunt at one end and tapering sharply at the other" (lines 81–84). The eggs have adapted so that parent birds can fit these relatively large eggs under their bodies (lines 83–86).

The best answer is NOT:

A because the primary purpose of the last paragraph is to provide a clear example of how birds' eggs are shaped because of adaptation. This is the only paragraph that discusses egg shape.

B because the comparison between reptile eggs and bird eggs is introduced in the opening paragraph (lines 1–7).

D because while the paragraph mentions that scientist do not know why swifts and swallows have elliptical eggs, it does state that it is well understood (not puzzling) why wading birds have tapered eggs: this shape allows the eggs to fit safely under a parents' body (lines 81–86).

Question 254. The best answer is J because the passage provides no clear explanation for this behavior. The passage only notes that parent birds turn eggs over in the nest (lines 27–29). The passage does not indicate why this behavior could be advantageous.

The best answer is NOT:

F because the passage does not provide this explanation for why a parent bird turns the eggs in the nest. This answer sounds plausible, but there is no textual evidence to support it. The fifth paragraph describes a hen's eggs' pores, but this paragraph does not mention a relationship between these pores and a parent bird rotating eggs in the nest (lines 59–75).

G because the passage does not provide an explanation for why a parent bird turns the eggs in the nest. This answer sounds plausible, but there is no textual evidence to support this answer.

H because the passage does not provide this explanation for why a parent bird turns the eggs in the nest. This answer sounds plausible, but there is no textual evidence to support it.

Question 255. The best answer is A because the second paragraph describes an egg's makeup from the inside out. The correct order is as follows: yolk (line 12), chalazae-containing albumen (line 13 for the discussion of the albumen, lines 26–28 for the discussion of the chalazae), two shell membranes (lines 17–18), and shell (line 21).

The best answer is NOT:

B because an egg does not contain an inner shell. Instead, it contains two shell membranes (lines 17–18). Additionally, the egg cell is described as "consisting mainly of a ball of yolk" so it is not accurate to list the egg cell as coming after the yolk (lines 11–12).

C because an egg does not contain an inner shell. Instead, it contains two shell membranes (lines 17–18). Additionally, the chalazae are described as existing within the albumen, so it does not make sense to list chalazae after albumen (lines 24–26). Furthermore, the parchment-like membranes exist between the albumen and the shell (lines 17–19).

D because the chalazae are described as existing within the albumen. Therefore, it does not make sense to list the parchment membranes in between the chalazae and the albumen (lines 24–26). Furthermore, the parchment-like membranes exist between the albumen and the shell (lines 17–19).

Question 256. The best answer is **H** because the passage describes plumping as the process whereby "water and salts fill out the albumen until the membranes are taut" (lines 20–21).

The best answer is NOT:

F because this word does not refer to an adult bird increasing her nutrient intake in preparation for egg-laying. The passage describes how some birds increase their calcium, but the term *plumping* is not used to describe this process (lines 48–58).

G because the word *plumping* does not refer to the formation of two parchment-like membranes around the fertilized egg cell (lines 17–23). *Plumping*, instead, refers to the stage that follows the formation of these membranes.

J because the passage makes no mention of adjustments a nesting bird makes in its plumage to maximize its ability to warm a clutch of eggs.

Question 257. The best answer is **B** because the chalazae are described as "two twisted cords, which act as bearings to allow the yolk and embryo to rotate freely when the egg is turned by the parent bird in the nest" (lines 26–28).

The best answer is NOT:

A because the word hammock describes the part of the albumen, not the chalazae (lines 24–26).

C because the passage does not describe the chalazae as two small vessels that allow the exchange of nutrients and waste between the yolk and the embryo in a bird's egg. The passage does explain that eggs exchange gases through pores (lines 61–62).

D because the chalazae are not described as two thin layers of protein. The passage does not describe what the chalazae are made of.

Question 258. The best answer is **H** because the passage explains that protein fibers attach the shell to the underlying membrane (lines 33–36).

The best answer is NOT:

F because the passage does not state that the protein fibers in an egg shell *deliver* crystals of calcite to the bones of the developing embryo (lines 33–36). There is no mention of calcite helping form the bones of the embryo. Calcite is used to create the shell.

G because the protein fibers in the egg shell do not facilitate the movement of life-sustaining gases to the embryo (lines 33–36). The pores serve this function (lines 59–71).

J because it is a layer of the albumen that suspends the yolk in place (lines 24–25).

Question 259. **The best answer is D** because the passage explains that "birds have developed a special kind of bone, called medullary bone, which females lay down in the marrow cavity of existing bones during the weeks before laying commences and use as a source of calcium when eggshells are being formed" (lines 42–46).

The best answer is NOT:

A because the passage does not specifically describe the leg bones of any bird species.

B because medullary bone is defined as specialized bird bone. It is not bone found in small Arctic mammals.

C because the passage does not mention a pliable bone that temporarily encases the spinal cord in developing bird and reptile embryos.

Question 260. **The best answer is G** because the shape of the wading birds' eggs enables a parent to fit four eggs in a clutch "under its body better when packed points inward in the nest" (lines 85–86).

The best answer is NOT:

F because the passage does not describe how predators view the oddly shaped eggs.

H because the passage does not indicate that wading birds attempt to open their wings within their eggshells.

J because the passage does indicate that one advantage of the eggs' unique shape is that it enables the parent to sit on a clutch of four eggs (lines 81–86).

Passage XXVII

Question 261. **The best answer is B** because the narrator uses phrases like "when I was growing up" (line 1) to signal that this story is being told from the perspective of an adult remembering her childhood in China.

The best answer is NOT:

A because the story is not told from the perspective of a child. The story is told in the past tense from the perspective of an adult remembering her childhood in China.

C because the story is not told from the perspective of an inkmaker describing the process she still uses. Lines such as "I can still smell the ingredients of our ink" (line 53) indicate that the narrator no longer makes ink.

D because while the narrator mentions her great-grandmother, she does not mention having any great grandchildren of her own.

Question 262. The best answer is H because the narrator indicates that "Peking is where more of the big money was," and that this is why her father, uncles, and cousins went to this district where they sold ink from the "back room of a shop in the old Pottery-Glazing District" (lines 28–32).

The best answer is NOT:

F because the men in the narrator's family did not want to write important documents in the capital. They reasoned that "in Peking, more people wrote important documents" (lines 26–27). They moved there to sell their ink (line 30).

G because the passage explains that the narrator's family sold ink from "the back room of a shop in the old Pottery-Glazing district" (lines 31–32). They did not make pottery.

J because they did not produce the ink in the Pottery-Glazing district. They sold it there. The women in the family made the ink in a studio next to the family courtyard house (lines 33–40).

Question 263. The best answer is A because the passage explains that "the studio began as a grain *shed* that sat along the front wall of the courtyard house. Over the years, one generation of sons added brick walls and a tile roof. Another strengthened the beams and lengthened it by two pillars. The next tiled floors and dug *pits* for storing the ingredients. Then other descendants made a *cellar* for keeping the inksticks away from the heat and cold" (lines 38–45).

The best answer is NOT:

B because the house and courtyard were not part of the studio. The house and courtyard are not included in the description of the ink studio.

C because the courtyard was not part of the studio. The house and courtyard are not included in the description of the ink studio.

D because the house was not part of the ink studio. The house was near the studio. The studio was a refurbished "grain shed that sat *along* the front wall of the courtyard house" (lines 39–40).

Question 264. The best answer is **J** because the narrator explains "I can still smell the ingredients of our ink. There were several kinds of fragrant soot: pine, cassia, camphor, and the wood of the chopped-down Immortal Tree" (lines 53–56).

The best answer is NOT:

F because dried millet is what the family ate for breakfast (lines 35–37). It was not an ingredient in the inksticks.

G because the passage does not indicate that roots from the cellar were used to make the inksticks. The narrator notes that her family "made a cellar for keeping the inksticks away from the heat and cold" (lines 44–45).

H because the passage does not indicate that the wooden beams from the compound were used to make the inksticks. The passage indicates that the studio's wooden beams were strengthened at one point (line 42).

Question 265. The best answer is **C** because the last paragraph indicates that "an inkstick of ours could last ten years or more…They could last from one great period of history into another" (lines 79–83). The main point of the final paragraph is that the family was proud of the quality of their inksticks.

The best answer is NOT:

A because the main point of emphasis is that the family was proud that their inksticks last so long, creating writing that was "black and strong" even after years of storage (line 86). The paragraph notes that "if the sticks were stored in the coolness of a root cellar, as ours were, they could last from one great period of history into another" (lines 82–83). The narrator uses this as evidence to support her claim that the inksticks were of high quality.

B because although the paragraph briefly notes that the family kept its inksticks recipe a secret, this is not the purpose of the last paragraph (lines 77–78). The paragraph's focus is on the quality of the inksticks, rather than on the recipe for them.

D because the paragraph briefly notes that the ink sticks "could last from one great period of history into another" (lines 82–83). There is no discussion within the paragraph about what the "great periods" are or how they are divided.

Question 266. The best answer is **J** because the narrator describes various goods that peddlers sold, including "fresh bean curd and steamed buns, twisted dough and colorful candies" (lines 8–10). The narrator then says, "A few coppers, that was all you needed to make your stomach as happy as a rich man's" (lines 9–11). The word *coppers* refers to coins that can be used to purchase the goods sold by the peddlers.

The best answer is NOT:

F because in the context of the passage, the word *coppers* does not mean ink-storage containers. When the word *coppers* is used, the narrator has not yet introduced her family's ink business.

G because in the context of the passage, the word *coppers* does not mean metal cooking pots. The *coppers* are something that can be used to acquire the goods sold by the peddlers.

H because in the context of the passage, the word *coppers* does not mean police officers. The coppers are something that can be used to acquire the goods sold by the peddlers.

Question 267. The best answer is **B** because the passage explains that the Liu Clan "had lived in the same courtyard house that had added rooms, and later wings, when one mother four hundred years ago gave birth to eight sons" (lines 15–17).

The best answer is NOT:

A because the family built an inkmaking studio "along the front wall of the courtyard house" (lines 39–40) to support the family business.

C because the inkmaking ingredients were stored in pits in the studio built "along the front wall of the courtyard house" (lines 39–40), not rooms.

D because the passage does not say directly that *every* member of the family was involved in inkmaking. The passage states that "in our family, the women made the ink" (line 33). The narrator's father, uncles, and their sons sold the ink (lines 29–30). They were not involved in *making* it.

Question 268. **The best answer is H** because the third paragraph explains that the narrator's family viewed itself as successful because "we ate meat or bean curd at every meal. We had new padded jackets every winter, no holes. We had money to give for the temple, the opera, the fair" (lines 20–24).

The best answer is NOT:

F because the narrator indicates that the family ate dried millet for breakfast (lines 36–37), but this detail is not part of a list of reasons that the narrator's family viewed itself as successful.

G because the passage indicates that the family used sheep hides over the doorways to keep out the snow (line 52). This detail illustrates how the family protected the ink sticks from being contaminated. It does not indicate one mark of success for her family.

J because the passage indicates that "one mother four hundred years ago gave birth to eight sons, one a year" (lines 16–17). This detail illustrates why the family added rooms and wings to the courthouse. This detail is not part of a list of reasons that the narrator's family viewed itself as successful (lines 36–37).

Question 269. **The best answer is B** because the passage indicates that a fire broke out "a couple of hundred years before" (lines 60–61).

The best answer is NOT:

A because the narrator describes the Liu clan as living in "Immortal Heart for six centuries. For that amount of time, the sons had been inkstick makers" (lines 12–13). The family's secret recipe was passed down through generations. The sixth paragraph explains the various fragrances that were part of the secret recipe (lines 53–59).

C because the passage describes the family's ink as black, not yellow (line 86). The adjective *yellow* appears in the passage when the narrator describes how the family strove to keep the ink protected from "the dusty yellow winds from the Gobi Desert" (line 48).

D because the passage does not indicate that there had been an invasion of pests that had ruined the ink. The narrator describes how one season she "had to use very fine tweezers to pluck bugs that had fallen onto the sticks" (lines 69–70), but the problem of bugs in the inksticks seems routine, rather than an "invasion."

Question 270. The best answer is **G** because the passage says that Precious Auntie's "calligraphy was even better than Father's" (lines 72–76).

The best answer is NOT:

F because the passage says that Precious Auntie's "calligraphy was even better than Father's" (lines 72–76). The narrator's calligraphy is not mentioned in the passage.

H because the passage says that Precious Auntie's "calligraphy was even better than Father's" (lines 72–76). Neither Great-Granny's calligraphy nor the narrator's calligraphy is mentioned in the passage.

J because the passage says that Precious Auntie's "calligraphy was even better than Father's" (lines 72–76).

Passage XXVIII

Question 271. The best answer is **A** because the writer corrects many misconceptions about early flight throughout the passage by providing accurate historical data. For example, the passage begins by summarizing a common misconception about the Wright brothers, stating, "we regard the boys from Dayton, Ohio, as American heroes who flew the first airplane and ushered in the age of air travel" (lines 2–4). The passage clarifies that the Wright brothers' success "was a vital step in a long progression toward controlled flight" but that aviation pioneers before them had already achieved flight (lines 60–61).

The best answer is NOT:

B because the writer does not indicate that he is a relative of the Wright brothers. Additionally, the passage does not mention honoring the Wright brothers with a monument.

C because the writer does not indicate that he is an inventor.

D because the passage is not written from the perspective of someone who observed the initial Kitty Hawk flight. The writer uses the personal pronoun *we* when he writes, "We regard the boys from Dayton, Ohio as American heroes who flew the first airplane and ushered in the age of air travel" (lines 2–4). Here, the author is referring to the dominant impression held by the general public, but this does not mean that the author was an observer of the initial Kitty Hawk flight. If that were the case, then paragraph 11 would include personal pronouns such as *I, me, my, us,* or *we.*

Question 272. The best answer is **J** because the Wright brothers prevented the rolling of a plane "using flexible wing tips with wire controls so that the pilot can bring the right wing into the wind at a different inclination from the left one, creating lift" (lines 55–57).

The best answer is NOT:

F because other inventors succeeded in flying. Balloonists had been rising above the Earth for more than a century (lines 16–17). Other inventions, including a winged glider and a balloon powered by a car engine, achieved flight prior to the Wright brothers' first flight (lines 21–33).

G because the passage indicates that "The Wright brothers were also not the first to pilot a heavier-than-air craft. In 1849, Sir George Cayley, a British physicist, constructed a three-winged glider that lifted a 10-year-old child a few feet" (lines 21–24).

H because the passage states that "many early aviation pioneers employed horizontal and vertical rudders to keep their experimental aircraft from veering right or left or unintentionally diving or rising" (lines 48–51). The Wright brothers also used "flexible wing tips with wire controls" to balance the wings (line 55).

Question 273. The best answer is **C** because "before Kitty Hawk, a crowd of official witnesses and Washington bigwigs had gathered to watch what was supposed to be the maiden flight of the giant Aerodrome designed by Samuel Langley, the head of the Smithsonian Institution" (lines 73–77). That flight was unsuccessful. It "plunged into the frigid waters" of the Potomac (lines 78–79).

The best answer is NOT:

A because the passage states that a "few newspapers" wrote about the Wright brothers' flight at Kitty Hawk (lines 83–84).

B because the passage states that the Wright brothers "wanted to fly in near secrecy because they weren't sure they could patent their plane, and wanted to profit from it before others knocked off the design" (lines 67–70). In addition, the passage states that "in 1903 hardly anyone heard about their flights (lines 63–64), so nothing could be widely assumed about the Wright brothers' flights.

D because balloonists had already been flying for more than a century, but newspapers were interested in heavier-than-air crafts because they attended the unsuccessful launch of an aircraft designed by Samuel Langley, the head of the Smithsonian Institution (lines 72–77).

Question 274. The best answer is J because the last paragraph explains that "the few newspapers that wrote about Kitty Hawk got everything wrong" (lines 83–84). It explains that "the first eyewitness accounts of their subsequent flights was published more than two years after Kitty Hawk" (lines 87–89).

The best answer is NOT:

F because, throughout the passage, it is clear that the Wright brothers successfully flew an aircraft. The purpose of the final paragraph is not to show that the Wright brothers were successful in their attempts to fly. This has already been clearly established at this point in the passage.

G because the Wright brothers' first flight in an aircraft was markedly different from Alberto Santos-Dumont's 14-mile trip over the city of Paris in "a cigar-shaped balloon powered by a car engine" (lines 32–33). The final paragraph indicates that a newspaper headline misleadingly described the Wright brothers' flight as emulating that of Santos-Dumont (lines 86–87).

H because the last paragraph indicates that the Dayton Daily News was one of the few newspapers to report on the Wright brothers' first flight. The main point of this paragraph is that there was minimal news coverage of the Wright brothers' flight and that most of this reporting was not accurate (lines 83–87).

Question 275. The best answer is C because the second paragraph describes the details of the Wright brothers' first successful flight. It indicates that the brothers' propeller-driven biplane became airborne for 852 feet in Kitty Hawk, N.C.

The best answer is NOT:

A because the second paragraph's tone is descriptive rather than argumentative. Additionally, the passage opens by indicating that the Wright brothers have received a great deal of credit for their contributions to aviation.

B because the second paragraph describes the basic details of the Wright brothers' first successful flight but does not mention the eyewitnesses.

D because the second paragraph does not address the weaknesses of the Wright brothers' aircraft. This paragraph describes the basic details of the Wright brothers' first successful flight, but it does not emphasize that it took many more years before the aircraft was perfected.

Question 276. The best answer is **H** because the word *revolution* is used literally to describe the movement of Alberto Santos-Dumont's cigar-shaped balloon as it circled the city of Paris (lines 29–33). This word is used to describe the balloon's flight around the Eiffel Tower.

The best answer is NOT:

F because in the context of the passage, the word *revolution* does not refer to a "political rebellion." No rebellion is mentioned in the passage.

G because in the context of the passage, the word *revolution* does not refer to "radical change." This part of the passage describes the flight of a balloon.

J because in the context of the passage, the word *revolution* does not refer to a "pivotal invention." This part of the passage describes the flight of a balloon around the Eiffel tower.

Question 277. The best answer is **B** because the passage indicates that several inventors used engines to power their aircraft. The passage states that this was "not a difficult task by the time automobile engines had come into their own" (lines 44–46). The passage indicates that in 1901, Alberto Santos-Dumont completed a 14-mile trip over the city of Paris in "a cigar-shaped balloon powered by a car engine" (lines 32–33).

The best answer is NOT:

A because the Wright brothers' main innovation was their implementation of "flexible wing tips with wire control" (line 55). Their invention was about control rather than power.

C because horizontal and vertical rudders helped pilots control the balance and direction of aircraft. These innovations did not help power the aircrafts.

D because it can be inferred that Sir George Cayley's "boy glider" was not very powerful. It could only "send a grown man through the air for several hundred feet" (lines 26–27). One can also infer that the glider is powered by the wind.

Question 278. The best answer is F because the passage explains that the Wright brothers' first flight was not *surprising*. It was "a vital step in a long progression toward controlled flight" (lines 60–61). The passage indicates that while we may think of the Wright brothers as ushering "in the age of air travel" (lines 2–4), in reality, many inventors before them made important breakthroughs in the field of aviation. Examples of these breakthroughs are given in the third through sixth paragraphs.

The best answer is NOT:

G because past achievements in the field of aviation showed that by the 1900s, engine-powered flight was possible, not *improbable*. It is true that many inventions failed to achieve sustained, controlled flight, but the passage does not indicate that these failures eroded confidence in the possibility of flight.

H because past achievements in the field of aviation showed that by the 1900s, engine-powered flight was common, not *unusual*. It is true that many inventions failed to achieve sustained, controlled flight, but the passage does not indicate that these failures eroded confidence in the possibility of flight.

J because past achievements in the field of aviation showed that engine-powered flight was common and expected, not *remarkable*. It is true that many inventions failed to achieve sustained, controlled flight, but the passage does not indicate that these failures eroded confidence in the possibility of flight.

Question 279. The best answer is D because the passage states that the Wright brothers "wanted to fly in near secrecy because they weren't sure they could patent their plane, and wanted to profit from it before others knocked off the design" (lines 67–70). They wanted to isolate their invention from potential imitators.

The best answer is NOT:

A because the passage does not indicate that the Wright brothers tested their aircraft in secrecy to avoid negative publicity if their plane failed to fly (lines 65–71). In fact, "they expected the press to hail them as the conquerors of the air" (lines 70–71)

B because the passage does not indicate that the Wright brothers tested their aircraft in secrecy to keep away anyone who couldn't help if something went wrong during the test flight. The passage does not discuss any plans the Wright brothers may have had in case something went wrong.

C because the passage does not indicate that the Wright brothers gave many interviews about their work.

READING • EXPLANATORY ANSWERS

Question 280. The best answer is **F** because the tenth paragraph emphasizes that the Wright brothers completed their test flight in secrecy because they thought they might be able to "patent their plane" and "profit from it before others knocked off the design" (lines 68–70). Because the Wright brothers tested their aircraft in secrecy, they shouldn't have expected to be praised by the press. Indeed, "few newspapers" wrote about their first flight in Kitty Hawk (line 83).

The best answer is NOT:

G because the tenth paragraph does not indicate that North Carolina was too windy for flying experimental aircraft safely. The author doesn't not give his opinion on the location.

H because the writer does not reveal his opinion about inventors working in secrecy.

J because while the passage states that "the few newspapers that wrote about Kitty Hawk got it wrong" (lines 83–84), the writer does not reveal his opinion on the accuracy of what the press reports. He makes no generalizations about the subject.

Passage XXIX

Question 281. The best answer is **C** because the passage primarily focuses on the essential features of comic art. The suggested summary has a much broader scope than the passage covers.

The best answer is NOT:

A because the passage does not focus on how comic artists have used their art to reflect the changing culture. The passage explains that in comic art, time generally "has no effect on the lives of the characters" (line 53). The passage indicates that "only in the case of politically satiric strips, such as *Doonesbury, Bloom County,* or *Pogo,* are immediately contemporary events and personalities reflected or depicted in the comics" (lines 62–65).

B because the passage does not focus on how comic artists have developed their own storytelling methods over many decades. No specific artists are mentioned in the passage.

D because the passage does not focus on the connections between comic art and film. The introductory paragraph briefly compares comic art to film, stating, "As in a motion picture, such visual devices as cutting, framing, close-ups, and montage are used by the comic artist, and the point-of-view is free to roam the world over to places known and fantastic" (lines 12–16).

Question 282. The best answer is **F** because the first paragraph compares comic art to other artistic forms, including fiction, poetry, drama, and motion pictures.

The best answer is NOT:

G because, within the context of the passage as a whole, the first paragraph demonstrates that comic art uses techniques used in fiction, poetry, drama, and motion pictures. These techniques are mentioned to emphasize the artistic features of comic art. Techniques used specifically for comic art are described later in the passage.

H because the first paragraph does not introduce the history and development of comic art as a form of artistic expression. The history and progression of comic art are not mentioned in the passage at all.

J because the first paragraph does not focus on defining the limitations of various forms of artistic expression. In fact, the description of the similarities between film and comic art emphasizes how these modes of artistic expression allow artists to "roam the world over to places known and fantastic" (lines 15–16). This emphasizes the broad capabilities rather than the narrow limitations of these artistic modes.

Question 283. The best answer is **C** because the passage indicates that comic strips and comic books "are usually printed on inexpensive paper" and that they appear in both black and white and in color (lines 33–36). The passage states this in a matter-of-fact tone and seems to view these features of comic art as irrelevant to comic art's artistic quality. The passage emphasizes that comic strips and books are a form of art just like fiction, poetry, drama, and film.

The best answer is NOT:

A because the passage indicates that comic strips and comic books "are usually printed on inexpensive paper" (lines 33–34). The passage does not indicate that high-quality paper is necessary in the publication of the best comic art.

B because the passage does not indicate that the use of color in comic art enhances the distinction between pictures and words. The passage discusses the use of color in a matter-of-fact way only.

D because the passage indicates that comic strips and comic books "are usually printed on inexpensive paper" (lines 33–34). The passage does not refer to recycled paper.

Question 284. The best answer is **G** because the passage does not indicate that readers can slow the pace of a storyline by the speed at which they read the comics. The passage states that in comic art "ideas must be developed within a very short period of reading time, a few seconds for a comic strip and fifteen minutes or less for a comic book story" (lines 5–8).

The best answer is NOT:

F because the passage indicates that "comic strips appear on a daily basis in newspapers delivered to homes, while comic books appear on a monthly basis" (lines 29–31).

H because the passage indicates that "the dramatic narrative is open-ended, and the action, whenever the reading experience begins, is always somewhere in the middle" (lines 57–59).

J because time "has no effect on the lives of the characters in the comics. They do not grow old chronologically" (lines 52–54).

Question 285. The best answer is **D** because the passage does not describe which drawing styles are most popular in comic art.

The best answer is NOT:

A because the introduction of the passage describes elements shared by comic art and literary art, including fiction, poetry, and drama (lines 1–12).

B because the passage indicates that "especially in humor, a set of stock and stereotyped players is essential to the daily comic routines, formulaic repetition being one of those techniques which most often make people laugh" (lines 46–49).

C because the passage explains that "for sounds, comic artists must resort to the poetic device of onomatopoeia, and while many traditional words such as *slam, bang, sock, smash,* or *bump* will serve the situation, new word coinages have proven necessary. Thus the comics have enriched American English by such contributions as *wow, plop, zowie, bam,* and *whap*" (lines 74–80).

Question 286. The best answer is J because the passage states that "dialogue and noise require a certain set of *conventions*. Words are usually spoken in cloud-like puffs of smoke called balloons" (lines 69–70). Additionally, the passage states that "in order to convey ideas which cannot be expressed with words, the comic artist has also developed a vocabulary of visual symbols, such as bubble balloons for silent thoughts, stars to show pain, drops of water to express labor or worry, or radiating lines to convey pride or enlightenment. It is remarkable how effective these *conventions* are in creating the impression of a loud and noisy medium" (lines 80–87). In both cases, the word *conventions* means customary practices.

The best answer is NOT:

F because, in the context of the passage, the word *conventions* does not refer to gatherings of comic artists. The passage does not describe gatherings of any type.

G because, in the context of the passage, the word *conventions* does not mean stereotypical situations. Instead, *conventions* refers to common strategies comic artists use in comics. It is possible that one *convention* might be "stereotypical situations," but in these particular points in the passage, the *conventions* described are used with dialogue, sound, and motion.

H because, in the context of the passage, the word *conventions* does not mean "common courtesies." Common courtesies are not discussed in the passage.

Question 287. The best answer is B because the passage explains that "for sounds, comic artists must resort to the poetic device of *onomatopoeia*, and while many traditional words such as *slam, bang, sock, smash,* or *bump* will serve the situation, new word coinages have proven necessary. Thus the comics have enriched American English by such contributions as *wow, plop, zowie, bam,* and *whap*" (lines 74–80).

The best answer is NOT:

A because the passage does not indicate that rhyme is used by comic artists to create linguistic effects.

C because the passage does not indicate that metaphor is used by comic artists to create linguistic effects.

D because the passage does not indicate that hyperbole is used by comic artists to create linguistic effects.

Question 288. The best answer is **F** because the passage explains how comic art depends "on a balanced combination of word and picture, one depending fully on the other for maximum effect. Thus some commentators have suggested that in comic strips, if either the picture or the text is not essential to understanding, then a proper balance is lacking" (lines 20–26).

The best answer is NOT:

G because the passage does not indicate that balance must be achieved between humor and drama. The passage offers examples taken from humorous comics and dramatic comics but does not suggest that each comic use both humor and drama.

H because the passage does not indicate that balance must be achieved between sound and silence. The passage explores at length how comic art conveys sound, but it does not focus on the effect of silence on comic art. The passage simply states that "comic characters inhabit a world of silence" (line 66).

J because the passage does not indicate that balance must be achieved between stereotyped and original characters. It notes that "especially in humor, a set of stock and stereotyped players is essential to the daily comic routines" (lines 46–47). The passage does not focus on original characters.

Question 289. The best answer is **C** because the passage explains that "most comic strips and books feature a set of recurring characters with whom the reader becomes familiar over a period of time, with an occasional retelling of their past histories in capsule form. It is the accumulated weight of familiarity over several months or years of reading experience with the characters through which the development of personality occurs, although many characters remain essentially the same throughout their lifetimes" (lines 37–45).

The best answer is NOT:

A because the passage does *not* indicate that the development of the personalities of characters in comic art occurs as a result of dialogue. This answer is plausible since dialogue is one of the main tools of expression used by comic artists, but the passage does not indicate that dialogue develops the personalities of the characters.

B because the passage does *not* indicate that the development of the personalities of characters in comic art occurs as a result of descriptive character sketches.

D because the passage does *not* indicate that the development of the personalities of characters in comic art occurs as a result of stereotypes. The passage indicates that "especially in humor, a set of stock or stereotyped players is essential to the daily comic routines" (lines 46–47). A stereotype is immediately recognizable. It does not indicate character *development*, which happens over time.

Question 290. **The best answer is F** because the passage indicates that "only in the case of politically satiric strips, such as *Doonesbury, Bloom County,* or *Pogo,* are immediately contemporary events and personalities reflected or depicted in the comics" (lines 62–65).

The best answer is NOT:

G because the passage does not indicate that direct references to current real-world events and personalities are found only in family comics. *Family* comics are not directly mentioned in the passage.

H because the passage does not indicate that direct references to current real-world events and personalities are found only in horror comics. *Horror* comics are not directly mentioned in the passage.

J because the passage does not indicate that direct references to current real-world events and personalities are found only in science fiction comics. *Science fiction* comics are not directly mentioned in the passage.

Passage XXX

Question 291. **The best answer is B** because the passage briefly notes that "both groups have developed a single long fin that runs the whole length of the body, but in the African fish, it runs along the back whereas in the South American fish it runs along the belly" (lines 80–83). The passage does not indicate the effect of the differing fin locations.

The best answer is NOT:

A because the passage indicates that the South American and African weakly electric fish use electrolocation to "calculate the pattern of obstacles" surrounding them (lines 54–55).

C because the passage presents a simplified description of how the flow of electric current generated by the weakly electric fish enters the water. The third paragraph describes how voltmeters register voltage returning to the fish. This electrical return helps the fish avoid obstacles in the water.

D because the passage indicates that the South American and African weakly electric fish "have had to give up the normal, highly efficient, fish method of swimming" (lines 67–71). The passage goes on to explain that their "progress through the water is rather slow" (lines 74–75).

Question 292. The best answer is J because the author does not give an example of a weakly electric fish in the second paragraph. The first paragraph introduces two weakly electric fish: the South American and the African weakly electric fish (lines 1–2).

The best answer is NOT:

F because the second paragraph contrasts electric fish with other types of fish. This paragraph indicates that in most fish, muscles "contract successively and throw the body into sinuous waves, which propel it forward. In electric fish, both strongly and weakly electric ones, they [the muscles] have become a battery in the electric sense. Each segment (cell) of the battery generates voltage" (lines 14–19).

G because the second paragraph compares strongly electric fish to weakly electric fish. This paragraph indicates that "in a strongly electric fish such as an electric eel, the whole battery generates as much as 1 amp at 650 volts. An electric eel is powerful enough to knock a man out. Weakly electric fish don't need high voltages or currents for their purposes, which are purely information-gathering ones" (lines 21–26).

H because the second paragraph begins to explain electrolocation, stating that "weakly electric fish don't need high voltages or currents for their purposes, which are purely information-gathering ones" (lines 21–26). This information gathering is later described as the process through which weakly electric fish "calculate the pattern of obstacles" surrounding them (lines 54–55).

Question 293. The best answer is D because the author explains that "for human visualization, it is easiest to think in terms of a family of curved lines leaving the fish through a series of portholes spaced along the front half of the body, all curving round in the water and diving into the fish again at the tip of its tail" (lines 37–41).

The best answer is NOT:

A because the electric current is reabsorbed into the tip of the tail rather than being generated by the tail (lines 37–41)

B because the electric current is generated by the portholes only. It is reabsorbed into the tail, not the portholes (lines 37–41).

C because the electric current is reabsorbed into the tip of the tail, not the portholes (lines 37–41).

Question 294. The best answer is **J** because the passage indicates that "if some obstacle appears in the vicinity [of the fish], say a rock or an item of food, the lines of current that happen to hit the obstacle will be changed. This will change the voltage at any porthole whose current line is affected, and the appropriate voltmeter will register the fact" (lines 47–52).

The best answer is NOT:

F because the lines of current the fish generates will only be in a smooth curve around the fish "if the fish is suspended in open water with no obstacles around" (lines 43–45).

G because the passage does not indicate that weakly electric fish can be shocked by their own electric currents bouncing off objects like rocks (lines 37–52). The passage indicates that "if some obstacle appears in the vicinity [of the fish], say a rock or an item of food, the lines of current that happen to hit the obstacle will be changed. This will change the voltage at any porthole whose current line is affected, and the appropriate voltmeter will register the fact" (lines 47–55).

H because the passage does not indicate that the current that a weakly electric fish generates would create a sound when it contacts objects such as rocks.

Question 295. The best answer is **B** because the last paragraph focuses on how weakly electric fish differ from other fish in terms of how they swim. This paragraph indicates that South American and African weakly electric fish "have had to give up the normal, highly efficient, fish method of swimming" (lines 67–71). The passage goes on to explain that their "progress through the water is rather slow" (lines 74–75).

The best answer is NOT:

A because this paragraph does not focus on how weakly electric fish differ from other fish in terms of the length of their bodies. The paragraph explains that weakly electric fish have a fin running the length of their bodies, but there is no comparison about full body lengths.

C because this paragraph does not focus on how weakly electric fish differ from other fish in terms of how they use sight. While the passage describes the habitats of the South American weakly electric fish and the African weekly fish as "too muddy for vision to be effective" (line 4), the last paragraph focuses on swimming, not sight (or lack thereof).

D because this paragraph does not focus on how weakly electric fish differ from other fish in terms of the complexity of their brains. This paragraph indicates that the weakly electric fish's brain "couldn't cope with the extra distortions that would be introduced if the fish's body were bending and twisting like an ordinary fish" (lines 63–65). There are other references to weakly electric fish brains in the passage, but there is no comparison made between the weakly electric fish brains and the brains of other fish.

Question 296. The best answer is **J** because the passage indicates that the South American and African weakly electric fish "both live in the same kinds of waters in their respective continents, waters that are too muddy for vision to be effective" (lines 2–5).

The best answer is NOT:

F because the passage does not discuss the predators of weakly electric fish.

G because the passage does not discuss the migration of weakly electric fish.

H because the passage does not indicate that weakly electric fish are nocturnal.

Question 297. The best answer is **A** because the passage states that "the muscles down each side of any fish are arranged as a row of segments, a *battery* of muscle units. In most fish they contract successively to throw the body into sinuous waves, which propel it forward" (lines 12–16).

The best answer is NOT:

B because in the context of the passage, in line 14, the word *battery* does not mean "electric field produced by fish muscles." Lines 12–14 describe the physical location of muscles in fish. Later in the passage, the word *battery* is used to signify an "electric field produced by fish muscles." The portion of the passage reads, "in electric fish, both strongly and weakly electric ones, they [muscle units] have become a battery in the electric sense. Each segment (cell) of the battery generates a voltage" (lines 16–18).

C because in the context of the passage, in line 14, the word *battery* does not mean "energy that propels fish forward." Lines 12–14 describe the physical location of muscles in fish.

D because in the context of the passage, in line 14, the word *battery* does not mean "different kinds of muscles contained in fish." Lines 12–14 describe the physical location of muscles in fish, not the types of muscles in fish.

Question 298. The best answer is **H** because the electric eel is given as an example of a "strongly electric fish" (line 21).

The best answer is NOT:

F because the electric eel is not described as being South American or *weakly* electric.

G because the electric eel is not described as being African or *weakly* electric.

J because the electric eel is described as a type of fish, not as a type of snake.

Question 299. The best answer is **B** because the passage indicates that "for human visualization, it is easiest to think in terms of a family of curved lines leaving the fish through a series of portholes spaced along the front half of the body, all curving round in the water and diving into the fish again at the tip of its tail" (lines 37–41).

The best answer is NOT:

A because the phrase "family of curved lines" is not the precise scientific terminology for the phenomenon. The author prefaces this description by stating that the details are geared toward creating a simple understanding.

C because the phrase "family of curved lines" is used in the simplified visualization of how electrical currents emanate from a weakly electric fish. In reality, "there are not really discrete 'lines' but a continuous 'field,' an invisible cocoon of electricity. However, for human visualization it is easiest to think in terms of a family of curved lines" (lines 35–38).

D because the word *family* is used to convey that, in this visualization, a series of curved lines signifies the various electrical currents emanating from the fish's body (lines 32–43). The word *family* is not being used here to describe how the lines support each other.

Question 300. The best answer is **H** because the passage indicates that successful navigation for weakly electric fish requires a rigid body. The passage states that "it is very important that the fish's own body is kept absolutely rigid. The computer in the head couldn't cope with the extra distortions that would be introduced if the fish's body were bending and twisting like an ordinary fish" (lines 61–65).

The best answer is NOT:

F because the passage does not describe any breaks weakly electric fish take when in motion.

G because the passage indicates that weakly electric fish can use electrolocation to "calculate the pattern of obstacles around" them (lines 54–55).

J because the passage does not discuss the effects water current speeds have on weakly electric fish navigation.

NOTES

NOTES